Tort
Casebook

7th edition

Edited by E D Pitchfork

BSc, PhD, Barrister

HLT Publications

HLT PUBLICATIONS
200 Greyhound Road, London W14 9RY

First published 1988
7th edition 1996

© The HLT Group Ltd 1996

ISBN 0 7510 0656 4

British Library Cataloguing-in-Publication.
A CIP Catalogue record for this book is available from the British Library.

Acknowledgement
The publishers and author would like to thank the Incorporated Council of Law Reporting for England and Wales for kind permission to reproduce extracts from the Weekly Law Reports, and Butterworths for their kind permission to reproduce extracts from the All England Law Reports.

Printed and bound in Great Britain

Contents

Preface

This HLT casebook can be used as a companion volume to the *HLT Tort Textbook* but also comprises an invaluable reference tool in itself. Its aim is to supplement and enhance students' understanding and interpretation of this particular area of the law, and to provide essential background reading. For ease of reference cases are arranged alphabetically within each chapter.

Since the last edition there have been a number of important and interesting developments in the law of tort. In particular, the House of Lords has on three occasions examined the scope of *Hedley Byrne* in *Henderson* v *Merrett Syndicates Ltd* [1994] 3 WLR 761, *Spring* v *Guardian Assurance plc* [1994] 3 WLR 354 and *White* v *Jones* [1995] NLJ 251, and it now seems clear that the scope of *Hedley Byrne* is not limited to negligent misstatements but covers negligent acts and omissions. As *Hedley Byrne* is the one secure cause of action in which pure economic loss can be recovered, it seems certain that more litigation will emerge in this area. The High Court has also held that an employer's duty to provide a safe system of work includes a duty not to cause foreseeable psychiatric damage to an employee due to the stress and pressures of his workload: *Walker* v *Northumberland County Council* [1994] NLJ 1659. This, too, could prove to be a rich vein for further working.

The House of Lords has reviewed and stated the law on breach of statutory duty, negligence in the exercise of a statutory power and the co-existence of a common law duty of care in *X* v *Bedfordshire County Council* [1995] 3 WLR 152. Although the House did not add to the law as regards the first cause of action, the speech of Lord Browne-Wilkinson on the latter two areas, and the relationship between private and public law, will repay much study.

The Court of Appeal in *Hunter* v *Canary Wharf* [1995] NLJ 1645 has continued to hold that the classic interest in land described in *Malone* v *Laskey* [1907] 2 KB 141 is no longer a prerequisite to suing in nuisance, and has made another attempt to tackle the thorny issue of damages in defamation. In *John* v *Mirror Group Newspapers Ltd* (1995) The Times 14 December the court decided that some further guidance should be provided for juries in assessing such damages.

The law is stated on the basis of materials available as of 1 January 1996.

Table of Cases

1 Introduction

Bradford Corporation* v *Pickles [1895] AC 587 House of Lords (Lord Halsbury LC, Lord Watson, Lord Ashbourne and Lord Macnaghten)

Lawful act, improper motive

Facts
The defendant prevented water percolating under his land from flowing to the plaintiffs' adjoining land from which it drew its supply.

Held
His lawful act was not rendered unlawful even if he had done it with the sole object of compelling the plaintiffs to acquire rights in the water at his own price.

Lord Halsbury LC:

'If it was a lawful act, however ill the motive might be, he had a right to do it.'

2 Parties to an Action in Tort

Anderson v *Gorrie* [1895] 1 QB 668 Court of Appeal (Lord Esher MR, Kay and A L Smith LJJ)

Judicial immunity

Facts

A judge of the Supreme Court of Trinidad and Tobago acted oppressively and maliciously, to the prejudice of the plaintiff and to the perversion of justice, in so far as he committed the plaintiff for contempt of court and held him to excessive bail.

Held

The plaintiff was not entitled to damages as the defendant judge, a judge of a court of record, had acted in his judicial capacity.

Lord Esher MR:

'The ground alleged from the earliest times as that on which this rule [that no action will lie for a judicial act] rests is that if such an action would lie the judges would lose their independence, and that the absolute freedom and independence of the judges is necessary for the administration of justice ... To my mind there is no doubt that the proposition is true to its fullest extent, that no action lies for acts done or words spoken by a judge in the exercise of his judicial office, although his motive is malicious and the acts or words are not done or spoken in the honest exercise of his office ... If a judge goes beyond his jurisdiction a different set of considerations arise. The only difference between judges of the Superior Courts and other judges consists in the extent of their respective jurisdiction.'

Commentary

Considered in *Sirros* v *Moore* [1974] 3 WLR 459.

Arenson v *Casson Beckman Rutley & Co* [1975] 3 WLR 815 House of Lords (Lord Simon of Glaisdale, Lord Wheatley, Lord Kilbrandon, Lord Salmon and Lord Fraser of Tullybelton)

Valuer – immunity from suit

Facts

Under the terms of an agreement between them, the plaintiff was obliged to sell shares back to his uncle at a 'fair value', ie, the value determined by the company's auditors 'whose valuation acting as experts and not as arbitrators shall be final and binding on all parties'. The plaintiff maintained that the auditors had undervalued the shares and he sued them for damages for negligence. Could he do so?

Held

Yes, because (it seemed) the defendants had not been called upon to exercise a judicial function.

Lord Salmon:

'A valuer enjoys the immunity of a judge or arbitrator only if what he does assumes the character of a judicial enquiry, eg by the parties submitting their dispute to the valuer for adjudication and the valuer listening to or reading the contentions made by or on behalf of the parties and to any evidence which they may put before him and then publishing a decision which is final and binding save for any appeal which the law allows.'

Commentary
Applied: *Sutcliffe* v *Thackrah* [1974] 2 WLR 295.

Evans v *London Hospital Medical College* [1981] 1 WLR 184 High Court (Drake J)

Witness – immunity from civil action

Facts
At the request of the police the defendants carried out a post-mortem on the plaintiff's infant son: they reported that they had found morphine in the organs examined by them and the plaintiff was subsequently charged with her son's murder. A pathologist engaged by the plaintiff found no traces of morphine in other organs examined by him. At the plaintiff's trial the prosecution offered no evidence against her and she was acquitted: she claimed damages for negligence or malicious prosecution.

Held
Her action would fail, as to malicious prosecution because the law had not been set in motion by the defendants and, as to both grounds, because the defendants were covered by the absolute immunity from any civil action conferred on a witness in criminal proceedings in respect of his evidence.

Drake J:

'I think it essential that the immunity given to a witness should also extend to cover statements he makes prior to the issue of a writ or commencement of a prosecution, provided that the statement is made for the purpose of a possible action or prosecution and at a time when a possible action or prosecution is being considered. In a large number of criminal cases the police have collected statements from witnesses before anyone is charged with an offence; indeed sometimes before it is known whether or not *any* criminal offence has been committed.'

Commentary
Distinguished: *Saif Ali* v *Sydney Mitchell & Co* [1978] 3 WLR 849.

Jones v *Northampton Borough Council* (1990) The Times 21 May Court of Appeal (Purchas, Ralph Gibson and Farquharson LJJ)

Club officer – liability

Facts
The plaintiff was a member and Mr Owen (the second defendant) was chairman of the Northampton branch of the Shepherd Social Club which was formed among the employees of the Shepherd group of companies. The members on the committee, which included the plaintiff, decided to play five-a-side football and a sports centre, owned and operated by the council, was hired for that purpose. The hiring form was signed by Mr Owen. The plaintiff was injured when another player slipped on a pool of water

on the floor which had come from a hole in the roof and collided heavily with him. He sued the council (the first defendants) and Mr Owen for damages. The council settled the action for £3,000 and claimed a full indemnity from Mr Owen under the Civil Liability (Contribution) Act 1978. The judge found that the leak in the roof and the risk of slipping caused by the wetness of the floor were known to the council before both the booking of the hall by the second defendant and the plaintiff's accident; that the second defendant was told about it and given the choice of cancelling the competition or waiting for the rain to stop; and that the second defendant had decided to carry on with the competition.

Held
The council's claim would be successful. Ralph Gibson LJ said that the first question was whether the second defendant owed any duty of care to the plaintiff with reference to the safety of the pitch on which those men were playing football. It was submitted that, as a matter of law, no duty of care of a relevant nature was owed by one club member to another. Reliance was placed on *Prole* v *Allen* [1950] All ER 476 and *Robertson* v *Ridley* [1989] 1 WLR 474. In his Lordship's judgment there was nothing in either of those cases upon which could be founded a form of immunity available in law to one member of a club against a claim by another member of the club, being an immunity based merely on their joint membership, if the claimant could demonstrate that, according to ordinary principles of law, the defendant member of the club was under a duty of care in respect of the circumstances which caused the claimant's injury and that the defendant was guilty of negligence. The judge's findings supported his conclusion that the second defendant owed a duty of care to the plaintiff and that he was in breach of it. That was a conclusion which the judge had been entitled to reach on the evidence and it was impossible for the court to disturb it.

Morriss v *Marsden* [1952] 1 All ER 925 High Court (Stable J)
Liability of person of unsound mind

Facts
The defendant violently attacked the plaintiff, a hotel manager. On a charge of criminal assault, the defendant was found unfit to plead and was directed to be detained to await His Majesty's pleasure. The plaintiff claimed damages for assault and battery and it was found that, although the defendant knew the nature and quality of his act, his mental illness was such that he did not know that what he was doing was wrong.

Held
The plaintiff was entitled to damages.

Stable J:

> 'I have come to the conclusion that knowledge of wrongdoing is an immaterial averment, and that, where there is the capacity to know the nature and quality of the act, that is sufficient although the mind directing the hand that did the wrong was diseased.'

Commentary
Applied: *National Coal Board* v *J E Evans & Co (Cardiff) Ltd* [1951] 2 KB 861.

Newton v *Edgerley* [1959] 1 WLR 1031 High Court (Lord Parker CJ)
Parent's liability

Facts
The defendant allowed his son, aged 12, to buy himself a .410 gun and showed him how to use it, but he told him that he must not take the gun off the farm where they lived and that he was not to use the gun when other children were present. The defendant did not instruct the boy how to handle the gun in the presence of others. The boy disobeyed his father and another boy, the plaintiff, was shot in the head when the gun went off.

Held
The defendant was liable in negligence. He could not possibly have ensured that his orders would be obeyed and he had failed to teach his son how to handle the gun when others were present.

Lord Parker CJ:

'I hold that there was a failure on the part of the defendant to use reasonable care to prevent his son using a gun at all, or alternatively, if the son was to be allowed to use a gun, not to instruct him as to its use if the boy succumbed to temptation and went out with others.'

Palacath Ltd v *Flanagan* [1985] 2 All ER 161 High Court (Mars-Jones J)

Surveyor – immunity from suit

Facts
The plaintiff landlord alleged that the defendant surveyor had been negligent in determining the rent under a rent review clause in a lease. The lease provided that the surveyor would 'act as an expert and not as an arbitrator ...'

Held
The defendant was not immune from suit.

Mars-Jones J:

'In the instant case the defendant was specifically enjoined in cl 8 of the second schedule to act as an expert, and was not to be limited or fettered in any way by the statement of reasons or valuations submitted by the parties, but was entitled to rely on his own judgment and opinion. In the light of those express provisions it is impossible for me to hold that the parties intended that the defendant should act as an arbitrator or quasi-arbitrator in determining the revised rent. I am satisfied that the provisions of clause 8 were not intended to set up a judicial or quasi-judicial machinery for the resolution of this dispute or difference about the amount of the revised rent. Its object was to enable the defendant to inform himself of the matters which the parties considered were relevant to the issue. He was not obliged to make any finding or findings accepting or rejecting the opposing contentions. Nor, indeed, as I see it was he obliged to accept as valid and binding on him matters on which the parties were agreed. He was not appointed to adjudicate on the cases put forward on behalf of the landlord and the tenant. He was appointed to give his own independent judgment as an expert, after reading the representations and valuations of the parties (if any) and giving them such weight as he thought proper (if any). That being so, there can be no basis for conferring immunity on the defendant in respect of a claim for damages for negligence in and about giving that independent expert view.'

Commentary
See also *Arenson* v *Carson Beckman Rutley & Co* [1975] 3 WLR 815 and *Sutcliffe* v *Thackrah* [1974] 2 WLR 295.

R v *Manchester City Justices, ex parte Davies* [1989] QB 631 Court of Appeal (O'Connor, Neill LJJ and Sir Roger Ormrod)

Magistrates acting in excess of jurisdiction

Facts

Mr Davies was committed to prison for failing to pay the balance of his rates. By statute, before taking this step, the magistrates were required to consider whether Mr Davies' default had been caused by his wilful refusal or culpable neglect: on the facts, the magistrates had not conducted such an inquiry. Mr Davies claimed damages for unlawful imprisonment.

Held

He was entitled to succeed as the magistrates had acted outside or in excess of their jurisdiction.

Neill LJ:

> '[The trial judge] concluded that it was established by the decision of the House of Lords in *McC* v *Mullan* [1985] AC 528 that there were three categories of case in which justices would be regarded as either not having jurisdiction or having exceeded their jurisdiction. I do not find it necessary to decide in the present case whether these three categories are all-embracing, but I am content for the purposes of the present case gratefully to adopt the judge's analysis.
>
> In the first category are cases where the justices do not have "jurisdiction of the cause" to use the phrase of Coke CJ in *Marshalsea Case* (1612) 10 Co Rep 68b at 76a.
>
> A simple example of a case in this category is provided by *Houlden* v *Smith* (1850) 14 QB 841 where the plaintiff recovered damages because he had been imprisoned by the order of a county court judge whose jurisdiction was limited to a geographical area which did not include the town where the plaintiff lived and carried on his business.
>
> In the second category are cases where the justices have properly entered on a summary trial of a matter within their jurisdiction but where "something quite exceptional" has occurred in the course of the proceedings so as to oust their jurisdiction. Lord Bridge gave as an example of such an exceptional event a case where a justice absented himself for part of the hearing and then relied on another justice to tell him what had happened during his absence (see [1985] AC 528 at 546-547). Lord Bridge expressed the opinion that in such a case, because of the gross and obvious irregularity of the procedure, the justices would have acted without jurisdiction or in excess of jurisdiction.
>
> As will appear when I come to consider the relevant legislation and the facts, the third category of cases is the one which has particular relevance in the present appeal. In this third category are cases where, though the justices have "jurisdiction of the cause" and may have conducted the trial impeccably, they may nevertheless be liable in damages on the ground of acting in excess of jurisdiction if their conviction of the defendant or other determination does not provide a proper foundation in law for the sentence or order made against him.'

Commentary

See also *McC* v *Mullan* [1984] 3 WLR 1227.

Sirros v *Moore* [1974] 3 WLR 459 Court of Appeal (Lord Denning MR, Buckley and Ormrod LJJ)

Judicial immunity

Facts

The plaintiff, a citizen of Turkey, was brought before a magistrate for breach of the Aliens Order 1953. He was fined £50 and the magistrate recommended that he be deported, adding that he should not be detained pending the Home Secretary's final decision as to deportation. The plaintiff's appeal to the Crown Court against the deportation recommendation was dismissed, but the circuit judge ordered police officers to detain the plaintiff and he was taken away in custody. The plaintiff sued the defendants, the circuit judge and the police officers, for damages for assault and false imprisonment.

Held

Although the plaintiff's detention had been unlawful (the appeal against the magistrate's order having merely been dismissed), the plaintiff had no cause of action against the circuit judge as he had acted judicially and under the honest (though mistaken) belief that his act was within his jurisdiction. No action lay against the police officers as they had acted at the judge's direction, not knowing it was wrong.

Lord Denning MR:

'Today we are concerned with judges of a new kind. The judges of the Crown Court. It is, by definition, a superior court of record: see s4(1) of the 1971 Act. The judges of it should, in principle, have the same immunity as all other judges, high or low. The Crown Court is manned by judges of every rank. Judges of the High Court, circuit judges, recorders, justices of the peace, all sit there. No distinction can or should be drawn between them. Each one shares responsibility for the decisions given by the court. If the High Court judge is not liable to an action, it should be the same with the circuit judge, the recorder or the justice of the peace. No distinction can be taken on the seriousness of the case. Any one of them may sit on one day on a case of trifling importance, on the next on a case of the utmost gravity. No distinction can be taken as to the nature of the case. It may be a matter triable only on indictment, or it may be a man up for sentence, or an appeal from magistrates. If they are not liable in trials on indictment, they should not be liable on other matters. But, whatever it is, the immunity of the judges – and each of them – should rest on the same principle. Not liable for acts done by them in a judicial capacity. Only liable for acting in bad faith, knowing they have no jurisdiction to do it.'

Commentary

Considered: *Anderson* v *Gorrie* [1895] 1 QB 668.

Sutcliffe v *Thackrah* [1974] 2 WLR 295 House of Lords (Lord Reid, Lord Morris of Borth-y-Gest, Lord Hodson, Viscount Dilhorne and Lord Salmon)

Arbitrator – immunity from liability

Facts

The plaintiff employed the defendant architects to design and supervise the construction of a house. Things did not work out well and the plaintiff claimed damages for breach of duty and negligence.

Held

The plaintiff would succeed as the defendants were not, on the facts, immune from liability.

Lord Morris of Borth-y-Gest:

'In summarising my conclusions I must preface them by the observation that each case will depend on its own facts and circumstances and on the particular provisions of the relevant contract. But in general any architect or surveyor or valuer will be liable to the person who employs him if he causes loss by reason of his negligence. There will be an exception to this and judicial immunity will be accorded if the architect or surveyor or valuer has by agreement been appointed to act as an arbitrator. There may be circumstances in which what is in effect an arbitration is not one that is within the provisions of Arbitration Act. The expression quasi-arbitrator should only be used in that connection. A person will only be an arbitrator or quasi-arbitrator if there is a submission to him either of a specific dispute or of present points of difference or of defined differences that may in future arise and if there is agreement that his decision will be binding. The circumstance that an architect in valuing work must act fairly and impartially does not constitute him either an arbitrator or a quasi-arbitrator. The circumstance that a building owner and contractor agree between themselves that a certificate of an architect showing a balance due is to be conclusive evidence of the works having been duly completed and that the contractor is entitled to receive payment does not of itself involve that the architect is an arbitrator or quasi-arbitrator in giving his certificate.'

Commentary

Applied in *Arenson* v *Casson Beckman Rutley & Co* [1975] 3 WLR 815.

3   Joint and Several Tortfeasors

Brooke v *Bool* [1928] 2 KB 578 High Court (Salter and Talbot JJ)

Joint tortfeasors

Facts
The plaintiff tenant of a lock-up shop had asked her landlord, who lived in adjoining premises, to visit the shop occasionally at night to see that everything was secure. When the defendant landlord's lodger complained of a smell of gas from the shop, both went to investigate. Both used naked lights, but the lodger's caused an explosion and the plaintiff sought damages from the defendant in respect of damage to her goods.

Held
The plaintiff's action should succeed. The lodger was the defendant's agent, the defendant had been in control of the proceedings and they had been engaged in a joint tortious enterprise.

Commentary
Applied: *The Koursk* [1924] P 140.
    Approved and applied in *Honeywill & Stein Ltd* v *Larkin Bros (London's Commercial Photographers) Ltd* [1934] 1 KB 191.

Koursk, The [1924] P 140 Court of Appeal (Bankes, Scrutton and Sargant LJJ)

Joint tortfeasors?

Facts
Some ships, including the Itria, the Clan Chisholm and the Koursk, were in convoy. Due to K's negligent navigation, it threatened to run into the C and, although C took avoiding action, a collision took place. As a result of attempting to avoid the collision, C ran into the I. C's navigation had also been negligent. I sued C, but the amount recovered was insufficient to cover I's loss. I then sued K.

Held
I's second action was not barred as the two negligences had been separate and independent and not committed in concert or as part of a common plan.

Bankes LJ:

'It is easy to put instances the mere mention of which indicates that the law must require something more than the single damnum to convert two quite separate and distinct torts into a joint tort. For instance, A, who wishes to approach B's house in order to commit a burglary trespass on his land and crosses a brook by an already damaged bridge, which he seriously weakens by his weight. Next day, C, wishing to approach the same house, mistaking it for that of a friend, trespasses on B's land, and in crossing the same bridge, breaks it completely down by his weight. Can it possibly be said that the damage to the

9

bridge was caused by a joint tort, or that A and C are joint tortfeasors? I think not, and if this view is correct it follows that in order to constitute a joint tort there must be some connection between the act of the one alleged tortfeasor and that of the other. It would be unwise to attempt to define the necessary amount of connection. Each case must depend upon its own circumstances.'

Commentary
Applied in *Brooke* v *Bool* [1928] 2 KB 578.

4 Vicarious Liability

Bayley v ***Manchester, Sheffield and Lincolnshire Rail Co*** (1873) LR 8 CP 148 Court of Exchequer Chamber (Kelly CB, Martin, Cleasby and Pigott BB, Blackburn, Mellor and Lush JJ)

Scope of porter's authority

Facts
The plaintiff was violently pulled from one of the defendants' carriages by one of the defendants' porters, just after the train had started: the porter had erroneously believed that the plaintiff was travelling in the wrong train. The plaintiff fell and suffered injuries. While it was part of porters' duties to prevent passengers going by wrong trains so far as they were able to do so, the defendants' byelaws expressly provided that they (passengers) were not to be removed.

Held
The defendants were liable as the porter had acted within the scope of his authority.

Kelly CB:

'When we look for the principle which governs all the cases, the result is that, where a servant, acting within the scope of his authority, does even that which he is told not to do, his master, who gave him the general authority, is responsible. The defendants had given a general authority to their servants to prevent passengers from travelling in wrong carriages as far as possible; and it was the duty of each servant to act on this general authority and to prevent travellers from so travelling accordingly. It could not be said that a servant was not acting within the scope of his authority when, in order to prevent this, he pulled a passenger out of a carriage by force; for there might be circumstances – where a carriage is too full for instance – in which a porter might really think it is his duty to use force. The cases in which the servant has been held not to have acted within the scope of his authority are cases where the act complained of was an isolated act, done in disobedience of an express or implied injunction, and are on that ground distinguishable from the present case. There is, indeed, here a statement in byelaw 6 that it is not the duty of the porters to remove passengers from wrong trains or carriages; but where a porter finds inconsistent directions, such as this and the other to do his best to prevent persons from travelling in wrong carriages, he may well follow one and disregard the other. This porter was interfering in a state of things in which, acting on the discretion which the defendants had given him, it was his duty to interfere. Consequently, the defendants are responsible for what he did.'

Bhoomidas v ***Port of Singapore Authority*** [1978] 1 All ER 956 Privy Council (Lord Simon of Glaisdale, Lord Salmon, Lord Keith of Kinkel, Sir Garfield Barwick and Sir Richard Wild)

Vicarious liability – loan of employee

11

Facts

A gang of stevedores was employed by the respondents who engaged them, paid them, prescribed the jobs they were to undertake and alone had power to dismiss them. While loading a cargo of timber, due to the negligence of a member, or members, of the gang, another member was fatally injured. Harbour by-laws provided that 'labourers employed in ... loading vessels should be under the superintendence of the ship's officers; the [respondents] undertake no responsibility as stevedores'.

Held

The by-law did not exclude the respondents' liability.

Lord Salmon:

'Their Lordships consider that this byelaw falls far short of putting the servants of the respondent under the entire and absolute control of the ship. It does not seem to their Lordships in the least inconsistent with their being the servants of the respondent, and not the servants of the shipowners. It throws no light on the extent of the superintendence of the ship's officers. Superintendence is a somewhat loose and ambiguous word. For example a building owner's architect superintends on behalf of the building owner the work of the building contractor's workmen, but this does not make them the building owner's servants. The ship's officers no doubt have the right to superintend the loading by directing into which holds the cargo is to be loaded and the order in which it is to be loaded but this in no way puts the servants of the respondent so completely and entirely under the control and at the disposition of the ship's officers as to make them the servants of the shipowners, who neither pay them, nor select them, nor could discharge them.'

Commentary

Applied: *Mersey Docks and Harbour Board* v *Coggins & Griffiths (Liverpool) Ltd* [1947] AC 1.

Century Insurance Co Ltd v *Northern Ireland Road Transport Board* [1942] AC 509 House of Lords (Viscount Simon LC, Lord Wright, Lord Romer, Lord Porter)

Vicarious liability – course of employment

Facts

The defendants' employee, a petrol tanker driver, was waiting by his tanker whilst the tanks of a petrol station were being filled. He lit a cigarette and threw the match on the ground, causing an explosion and fire. The plaintiffs, the defendants' insurers, argued that the negligent act of the driver was not done in the course of his employment so as to make the defendants vicariously liable for him.

Held

The driver's act in lighting a cigarette was not done for his employers' benefit but for his own convenience. That does not matter: it was one and indivisible from the carrying out of his work and was within the scope of his employment.

General Engineering Services Ltd v *Kingston and Saint Andrew Corp* [1989] 1 WLR 69 Privy Council (Lord Bridge of Harwick, Lord Templeman, Lord Ackner, Lord Oliver of Aylmerton and Sir John Stephenson)

Intentional wrongful acts

Facts

The plaintiffs' property was completely destroyed by fire and the damage was increased by the fact that the firemen who answered the plaintiffs' emergency call were involved in a 'go-slow' in support of a pay claim and took 17 minutes rather than three and a half minutes to reach the plaintiffs' property. The plaintiffs alleged that the defendants, who were the employers of the firemen, were vicariously liable for the acts of the firemen.

Held

This was not the case.

Lord Ackner:

'It is, of course, common ground that a master is not responsible for a wrongful act done by his servant unless it is done in the course of his employment. Further, it is well established that the act is deemed to be so done if it is either (1) a wrongful act authorised by the master, or (2) a wrongful and unauthorised mode of doing some act authorised by the master ...

Their Lordships have no hesitation in agreeing ... that the members of the fire brigade were not acting in the course of their employment when they, by their conduct ..., permitted the destruction of the building and its contents. Their unauthorised and wrongful act was so to prolong the time taken by the journey to the scene of the fire, as to ensure that they did not arrive in time to extinguish it, before the building and its contents were destroyed. Their mode and manner of driving, the slow progression of stopping and starting, was not so connected with the authorised act, that is driving to the scene of the fire as expeditiously as reasonably possible, as to be a mode of performing that act ...

Here the unauthorised and wrongful act by the firemen was a wrongful repudiation of an essential obligation of their contract of employment, namely the decision and its implementation not to arrive at the scene of the fire in time to save the building and its contents. This decision was not in furtherance of their employers' business. It was in furtherance of their industrial dispute, designed to bring pressure on their employers to satisfy their demands, by not extinguishing fires until it was too late to save the property.

Such conduct was the very negation of carrying out some act authorised by the employer, albeit in a wrongful and unauthorised mode. Indeed in preventing the provision of an essential service, members of the fire brigade were ... guilty of a criminal offence.'

Heasmans v *Clarity Cleaning Co Ltd* [1987] ICR 949 Court of Appeal (Purchas and Nourse LJJ)

Vicarious liability – conversion

Facts

An office cleaning contractor company employed a cleaning lady whose task it was to go into offices after hours and clean the offices. Whilst in the office she used the telephone to make personal calls (adding up to £1,500 in total). The plaintiffs, the owner of the office, sued the defendant, the contractor, as being vicariously liable for the conversion of the cleaning lady.

Held

The defendants were not vicariously liable for the cleaning lady's phone calls. They were not made in the course of employment, as phoning was not part of her duties, though cleaning the phone was.

Limpus* v *London General Omnibus Co (1892) 1 H & C 526 Court of Exchequer Chamber (Wightman, Williams, Crompton, Willes, Byles and Blackburn JJ)

Vicarious liability – course of employment

Facts
The defendant's drivers were expressly forbidden to obstruct or race with other buses. S did so and caused damage to P.

Held
S's act was done for defendants' purposes not his own and defendants were vicariously liable.

Commentary
Distinguished in *Conway* v *George Wimpey & Co Ltd* [1951] 2 KB 266.

Lister* v *Romford Ice & Cold Storage Co Ltd [1957] 2 WLR 158 House of Lords (Viscount Simonds, Lord Morton of Henryton, Lord Ratcliffe, Lord Tucker and Lord Somervell of Harrow)

Vicarious liability – injury to fellow workman

Facts
The appellant, a lorry driver employed by the respondents, was backing his lorry and negligently ran into and injured his father, another of the respondents' employees. The respondents being vicariously liable, the father obtained judgment against them. The respondents sought to recover this amount from the appellant.

Held
They should succeed as the appellant had been in breach of his duty to them to take due care.

Lloyd* v *Grace, Smith & Co [1912] AC 716 House of Lords (Lord Loreburn LC, Earl of Halsbury, Lord Macnaghten, Lord Atkinson, Lord Shaw and Lord Robson)

Vicarious liability – employee's fraud

Facts
Authorised to undertake conveyancing matters on the firm's behalf, a managing clerk defrauded a client in the course of a conveyancing transaction. The client sued the solicitors , the clerk's employers.

Held
Although the solicitors were innocent of the fraud and it was committed for the clerk's, not their, benefit, they were liable as it had been committed in the course of the clerk's employment.

Commentary
Applied in *Morris* v *C W Martin & Sons Ltd* [1965] 3 WLR 276

Mersey Docks & Harbour Board v *Coggins & Griffith (Liverpool) Ltd* [1947] AC 1
House of Lords (Viscount Simon, Lord Macmillan, Lord Porter, Lord Simonds and Lord Uthwatt)

Vicarious liability – employee on loan

Facts
M1 hired to M2 a crane and driver. Whilst on hire, M1 was responsible for paying the driver and could dismiss him, but the hire agreement declared the driver to be M2's employee. Due to the driver's negligence in operating the crane, one of M2's employees was injured. Was M1 or M2 vicariously liable?

Held
M1, being the permanent employer, retained control over the driver and was vicariously liable.

Lord Porter:

> 'Many factors are relevant, but in such a case as the present, particular importance may be attached to who may give orders as to how the work was to be done. If this power to control the method of performing the work is transferred from the general employer (M1) to the temporary employer (M2) then the latter may be liable. But, this is not so here.'

Viscount Simon:

> 'The permanent employer carries the burden of proving responsibility for the servant has shifted to the temporary employer ... I see the test as being – who had the authority to direct or delegate to the workman the manner in which the vehicle was driven? Here, in operating the crane the driver was using his own discretion which had been delegated to him by his regular employers. If he made a mistake in operating the crane, this was nothing to do with the hirers.'

Commentary
Applied in *Bhoomidas v Port of Singapore Authority* [1978] 1 All ER 956.

Morgans v *Launchbury* [1972] 2 WLR 1217 House of Lords (Lord Wilberforce, Viscount Dilhorne, Lord Pearson, Lord Cross of Chelsea and Lord Salmon)

Vicarious liability – negligent driving of agent

Facts
The respondents were passengers in a car owned by the appellant and driven by C. They were injured in an accident in which C and the appellant's husband, who was also in the car, were killed, due to C's negligent driving. The car was used jointly by the appellant and her husband. On the day of the accident, the appellant's husband went drinking with friends and, finding himself unfit to drive, he asked C to drive, having on several occasions previously promised his wife that if he drank too much, he would ask someone else to drive. At the time of the accident, C was not driving the appellant's husband straight back home, but was on the way to a restaurant. The respondents alleged that the appellant was vicariously liable for C, who at the time was acting as her agent.

Held
The appellant was not liable. When the husband asked C to drive that did not suffice to make C the appellant's agent.

Lord Wilberforce:

'I regard it as clear that in order to fix vicarious liability on the owner of a car in such a case as the present, it must be shown that the driver was using it for the owner's purposes, under delegation of a task or duty. The substitution for this clear conception of a vague test based on "interest" or "concern" has nothing in reason or authority to commend it. Every man who gives permission for the use of his chattel may be said to have an interest or concern in its being carefully used, and, in most cases if it is a car, to have an interest or concern in the safety of the driver, but it has never been held that mere permission is enough to establish vicarious liability.'

Commentary
Distinguished: *Ormrod* v *Crosville Motor Services Ltd* [1953] 1 WLR 1120.

Morris v *CW Martin & Sons Ltd* [1965] 3 WLR 276 Court of Appeal (Lord Denning MR, Diplock and Salmon LJJ)

Vicarious liability for criminal act

Facts
The plaintiff gave her fur coat to be cleaned by the defendants and it was stolen by one of their employees. The plaintiff sought to hold the defendants vicariously liable.

Held
The plaintiff's claim would succeed.

Lord Denning MR:

'When can a servant's fraud or dishonesty done for his own benefit, be said to be in the course of his employment? ... The essential point in the present case is that the defendants were bailees of the coat and thus they owed the plaintiff a duty of care with regard to its safekeeping. If they entrust this duty to their servant, they remain under a duty – they cannot delegate it.'

Diplock LJ:

'The defendants were bailees for reward and the servant who had stolen it was acting as their agent, entrusted with the duty of cleaning it. This act was therefore done within the course of his employment and the defendants were vicariously liable. Had the coat been stolen by some other employee, the result might be different.'

Salmon LJ:

'A bailee for reward is not answerable for the theft by any of his servants: only of the person to whom he has delegated the duty because that person alone can be said to act within the scope of his employment.'

Commentary
Overruled: *Cheshire* v *Bailey* [1905] 1 KB 237.
 Applied: *Lloyd* v *Grace, Smith & Co* [1912] AC 716.
 Approved in *Port Swettenham Authority* v *T W Wu & Co (M) Sdn Bhd* [1978] 3 WLR 530.

O'Kelly v *Trusthouse Forte plc* [1984] QB 90 Court of Appeal (Sir John Donaldson MR, Ackner and Fox LJJ)

Distinction between contract of service and contract for services

Facts

The applicants were 'regular casual' banqueting staff at the employers' hotel, ie, they were engaged on a regular basis to such an extent that some regular casuals had no other regular work. After seeking recognition as permanent employees working under contracts of employment, the applicants were dismissed. Were they working under contracts of employment and therefore entitled to complain of unfair dismissal?

Held

No. There was no overall contract between the parties and the applicants were in business on their own account as independent contractors supplying services.

Ackner LJ:

'The following factors were considered by the industrial tribunal to be *inconsistent* with a contract of employment: (n) the engagement was terminable without notice on either side. (o) The respondents had the right to decide whether or not to accept work, although whether or not it would be in their interest to exercise the right to refuse work is another matter. (p) The employers had no obligation to provide any work. (q) During the subsistence of the relationship it was the parties' view that casual workers were independent contractors engaged under successive contracts for services. (r) It is the recognised custom and practice of the industry that casual workers are engaged under a contract for services.'

Commentary

Considered: *Young & Woods Ltd* v *West* [1980] IRLR 201.

Ormrod v *Crosville Motor Services Ltd* [1953] 1 WLR 1120 Court of Appeal (Singleton, Denning and Morris LJJ)

Vicarious liability – car driven by friend

Facts

A friend agreed to drive the owner's car from Birkenhead to Monte Carlo. He was to take a suitcase for the owner and, after meeting up in Monte Carlo, they were to go on holiday together, with the car, in Switzerland. While driving through France the car was in collision with a coach.

Held

In so far as the friend was guilty of negligence, the owner was vicariously liable.

Denning LJ:

'The law puts an especial responsibility on the owner of a vehicle who allows it to go on the road in charge of someone else, no matter whether it is his servant, his friend, or anyone else. If it is being used wholly or partly on the owner's business or for the owner's purposes, the owner is liable for any negligence on the part of the driver. The owner only escapes liability when he lends it or hires it to a third person to be used for purposes in which the owner has no interest or concern ... That is not this case.'

Commentary

Distinguished in *Morgans* v *Launchbury* [1972] 2 WLR 1217.

Poland v *John Parr and Sons* [1927] 1 KB 236 Court of Appeal (Bankes, Scrutton and Atkins LJJ)

Vicarious liability – defence of employer's property

Facts

A carter, the defendant's employee, honestly and reasonably thought that the plaintiff, a boy aged 12, was pilfering, or about to pilfer, some sugar. He struck the boy on the back of the neck. The boy fell forward, one of the wagon's wheels went over his foot and the boy's leg had to be amputated in consequence.

Held

The defendants were liable. The carter had implied authority to make reasonable efforts to protect their property and the force used was not so excessive as to take his act – the striking of the boy – outside the scope of that authority.

Commentary

Considered in *Warren* v *Henlys Ltd* [1948] 2 All ER 935.

Racz v *Home Office* [1993] 2 WLR 23 House of Lords (Lord Templeman, Lord Goff, Lord Jauncey, Lord Browne-Wilkinson and Lord Mustill)

Misfeasance in public office – whether Home Office vicariously liable

Facts

The plaintiff, a remand prisoner, alleged that he had been ill-treated by prison officers and brought an action against the Home Office for damages in assault, misfeasance in public office and false imprisonment. The defendants sought to strike out the plaintiff's claim relating to misfeasance in public office: this application was granted by Ebsworth J and upheld by the Court of Appeal. The plaintiff appealed to the House of Lords.

Held

The House of Lords allowed the plaintiff's appeal and held that the Home Office could be vicariously liable for acts of prison officers that amounted to misfeasance in public office. The plaintiff's allegations of misfeasance in public office could only be struck out where it inevitably followed that if the allegations were true, that the unauthorised act of the prison officers had been so unconnected with their authorised duties as to be independent of and outside them, which was a question of fact and degree that should go to trial.

Commentary

Distinguished: *R* v *Deputy Governor of Parkhurst Prison, ex parte Hague* [1992] 1 AC 58.

Ready Mixed Concrete (South East) Ltd v *Minister of Pensions and National Insurance* [1968] 2 WLR 775 High Court (MacKenna J)

Employee or independent contractor?

Facts

The plaintiff company devised a scheme whereby concrete was to be delivered to its customers ready-mixed. L entered into a contract with the company to deliver such concrete on a daily basis. L was to buy, run, maintain, repair, insure and drive his own lorry. He was paid by the company on a mileage plus bonus basis. He was subject to all the rules and regulations of the company which had a high degree of control over him and his work. Was L an employee or an independent contractor?

Held

He was an independent contractor as the provisions of his contract were inconsistent with its being a contract of service.

MacKenna J:

A contract of service exists if the following three conditions are fulfilled:

'(i) The servant agrees that in consideration of a wage or other remuneration he will provide his own work and skill in the performance of some service for his master. (ii) He agrees, expressly or impliedly, that in the performance of that service he will be subject to the other's control in a sufficient degree to make that other master. (ii) The other provisions of the contract are consistent with its being a contract of service.'

Rose v *Plenty* [1976] 1 WLR 141 Court of Appeal (Lord Denning MR, Lawton and Scarman LJJ)

Vicarious liability – prohibited act

Facts

Contrary to his employers' orders, the first defendant, a milkman, took with him on his milk-round the plaintiff, a boy aged thirteen, to help with the work. Due to the milkman's negligent driving of the float, the boy was injured. Were the milkman's employers vicariously liable?

Held

Yes, as the milkman's employment of the boy was within the scope of his own employment and had been for the purpose of his employers' business.

Lord Denning MR:

'An employer's prohibition of the doing of an act is not necessarily such as to exempt the employer from liability, provided the act is done not for the employee's own purposes, but in the course of his service and for his employer's benefit.'

Commentary

Applied: *Limpus* v *London General Omnibus Co* (1862) 1 H & C 526.

Distinguished: *Twine* v *Bean's Express Ltd* (1946) 175 LT 131 and *Conway* v *George Wimpey & Co Ltd* [1951] 2 KB 266.

Smith v *Stages* [1989] 2 WLR 529 House of Lords (Lord Keith of Kinkel, Lord Brandon of Oakbrook, Lord Griffiths, Lord Goff of Chieveley and Lord Lowry)

Different place of work

Facts

Two peripatetic laggers were working on a power station in the Midlands when they were sent to carry out urgent work in Wales. No stipulation was made as to the mode of travel, but they were paid for the travelling time and the equivalent of the rail fare. They travelled in the car of one of the laggers, the first defendant, and the other lagger was injured on the return journey when, as a result of the first defendant's negligence, his car crashed through a brick wall. The first defendant was uninsured: were the employers, the second defendants, also liable?

Held
They were as the laggers had been travelling in their (the employers') time.

Lord Lowry:

'The paramount rule is that an employee travelling on the highway will be acting in the course of his employment if, and only if, he is at the material time going about his employer's business. One must not confuse the duty to turn up for one's work with the concept of already being "on duty" while travelling to it.

It is impossible to provide for every eventuality and foolish, without the benefit of argument, to make the attempt, but some prima facie propositions may be stated with reasonable confidence. (1) An employee travelling from his ordinary residence to his regular place of work, whatever the means of transport and even if it is provided by the employer, is not on duty and is not acting in the course of his employment, but, if he is obliged by his contract of service to use the employer's transport, he will normally, in the absence of an express condition to the contrary, be regarded as acting in the course of his employment while doing so. (2) Travelling in the employer's time between workplaces (one of which may be the regular workplace) or in the course of a peripatetic occupation, whether accompanied by goods or tools or simply in order to reach a succession of workplaces (as an inspector of gas meters might do), will be in the course of the employment. (3) Receipt of wages (though not receipt of a travelling allowance) will indicate that the employee is travelling in the employer's time and for his benefit and is acting in the course of his employment, and in such a case the fact that the employee may have discretion as to the mode and time of travelling will not take the journey out of the course of his employment. (4) An employee travelling in the employer's time from his ordinary residence to a workplace other than this regular workplace or in the course of a peripatetic occupation or to the scene of an emergency (such as a fire, an accident or a mechanical breakdown of plant) will be acting in the course of his employment. (5) A deviation from or interruption of a journey undertaken in the course of employment (unless the deviation or interruption is merely incidental to the journey) will for the time being (which may include an overnight interruption) take the employee out of the course of his employment. (6) Return journeys are to be treated on the same footing as outward journeys.

All the foregoing propositions are subject to any express arrangements between the employer and the employee or those representing his interests. They are not, I would add, intended to define the position of salaried employees, with regard to whom the touchstone of payment made in the employer's time is not generally significant.'

Commentary
Applied: *Canadian Pacific Railway Co v Lockhart* [1942] AC 591.
    Approved: *Vandyke v Fender* [1970] 2 WLR 929.

Twine v Bean's Express Ltd (1946) 175 LT 131 Court of Appeal (Lord Greene MR, Morton and Tucker LJJ)

Vicarious liability – unauthorised passenger

Facts
The plaintiff's husband was killed when the van in which he was being carried was involved in an accident due to the negligence of the driver, the defendants' servant. The deceased and the driver knew that the giving of lifts to unauthorised persons was forbidden.

Held

The plaintiff's claim would fail as the driver was acting outside the scope of his employment.

Lord Greene MR:

'The deceased had no right to be in the van and the driver had no right to give him a lift: the deceased was therefore a trespasser and was owed no duty of care by the employers of the driver ... The driver, in giving a lift to the deceased, was clearly acting outside the scope of his employment. He had no right whatsoever to do such a thing and in this respect, he was on a frolic of his own.'

Commentary

Applied in *Conway* v *George Wimpey & Co Ltd* [1951] 2 KB 266.

Warren v *Henlys Ltd* [1948] 2 All ER 935 High Court (Hilbery J)

Vicarious liability – assault on customer

Facts

Mistakenly believing that the plaintiff had tried to drive away without paying for his petrol, the pump attendant had used violent language when calling on him to stop. The plaintiff told the attendant that he would report him to his employers (the defendants) and the attendant 'gave him one on the chin to get on with'.

Held

The defendants were not liable as the act – the assault – was one of personal vengeance and not in the course of the attendant's employment.

Commentary

Considered: *Poland* v *John Parr & Sons* [1927] 1 KB 243.

5 Liability for Independent Contractors

Alcock v *Wraith* (1991) The Times 23 December Court of Appeal (Neill LJ and Cazalet J)

Liability for independent contractor

Facts
Mr and Mrs Swinhoe engaged Mr Wraith to re-roof their terraced house. Some months later the plaintiff noticed damp in his adjoining property and, Mr Wraith having been adjudged bankrupt, the county court judge upheld the plaintiff's claim for damages and held that Mr and Mrs Swinhoe were liable to him in trespass, in nuisance and in negligence. Mr and Mrs Swinhoe appealed.

Held
Their appeal would be dismissed. Neill LJ affirmed that where someone employs an independent contractor to do work on his behalf he is not in the ordinary way responsible for any tort committed by the contractor in the course of the execution of the work. However, there are exceptions to that general rule which include cases which involve the withdrawal of support from neighbouring land and cases which involve extra-hazardous acts. Both the general rule and the exceptions apply whether an action has been framed in negligence or nuisance and no different approach is adopted in an action for trespass. It is not possible to provide a list of activities which would be regarded as 'extra-hazardous' so as to fall within the exception of liability where a contractor was employed to carry out a task which was extra-hazardous, but it is clear that the activity has to involve some special risk of damage or that it has to be work which from its very nature is likely to cause danger or, more appropriately, damage.

His Lordship said that the crucial questions were:

i)   Did the work involve some special risk or was it from its very nature likely to cause damage?
ii) Could one apply by analogy the exception to the general rule which could be relied upon in cases which involved party walls?

The fact that the work necessarily, because they were terraced properties, involved the creation of a fresh joint between the adjoining roofs made the case similar to a party-wall case. The true basis for the exception in the party-wall cases was that where the law conferred a right to carry out work on a wall or other division between two properties, and that work involved a risk of damage to the adjoining property, the law also imposed a duty on the party carrying out the work to ensure that it was carried out carefully. Mr and Mrs Swinhoe had the right to interfere with the joint between the two roofs but if they exercised that right, they were under a duty to see that reasonable skill and care was used in the operation. That duty could not be delegated to an independent contractor.

Balfour v *Barty-King* [1957] 2 WLR 84 Court of Appeal (Lord Goddard CJ, Morris LJ, Vaisey J)

Escape of fire – negligence of independent contractor

Facts

The defendant and plaintiff owned adjacent properties. The defendant employed an independent contractor to thaw frozen pipes in a loft which contained large amounts of combustible material. He used a blowlamp which ignited the lagging, the loft and eventually P's premises.

Held

D was liable for such an escape of fire when it resulted from a dangerous object being brought onto his premises at his invitation.

Commentary

Applied: *Musgrove* v *Pandelis* [1919] 2 KB 43.

Applied in *Emanuel (H & N) Ltd* v *Greater London Council* [1971] 2 All ER 835.

Holliday v *National Telephone Co* [1899] 2 QB 392 Court of Appeal (Earl of Halsbury LC, A L Smith and Vaughan Williams LJJ)

Negligence – independent contractor

Facts

When laying telephone wires in trenches under a highway, the defendants engaged a plumber – an independent contractor – to carry out some aspects of the work. Due to the negligence of the plumber's employee, there was an explosion and molten solder flew out and injured the plaintiff who was passing along the footway.

Held

The defendants were liable.

A L Smith LJ:

'Where a person is executing work upon a public highway, he cannot escape liability by employing an independent contractor, because there is a duty cast upon him to see that the work upon the highway is so carried out as not to injure persons who are using the highway.'

Honeywill & Stein Ltd v *Larkin Bros (London's Commercial Photographers) Ltd* [1934] 1 KB 191 Court of Appeal (Lord Hewart CJ, Lord Wright and Slessor LJ)

Independent contractor – negligence

Facts

After they had installed sound reproduction apparatus in a cinema, the plaintiffs employed the defendants to take photographs of the cinema's interior. The defendants negligently set light to the cinema's curtains and the plaintiffs sought to recover from the defendants the compensation which they (the plaintiffs) had paid to the cinema's owners.

Held

They should succeed as they were themselves liable to the cinema owners for the defendants' negligence.

Slessor LJ:

'To take a photograph in the cinema with a flashlight was, on the evidence stated above, a dangerous operation in its intrinsic nature, involving the creation of fire and explosion on another person's premises, that is, in the cinema, the property of the cinema company. The plaintiffs, in procuring this work to be performed by their contractors, the defendants, assumed an obligation to the cinema company which was, as we think, absolute, but which was at least an obligation to use reasonable precautions to see that no damage resulted to the cinema company from those dangerous operations. That obligation they could not delegate by employing the defendants as independent contractors, but they were liable in this regard for the defendants' acts. For the damage actually caused the plaintiffs were, accordingly, liable in law to the cinema company, and are entitled to claim and recover from the defendants damages for their breach of contract or negligence in performing their contract to take photographs.'

Commentary

Approved and applied: *Brooke* v *Bool* [1928] 2 KB 578.

Morgan v *Incorporated Central Council of the Girls' Friendly Society* [1936] 1 All ER 404 High Court (Horridge J)

Negligence – independent contractor

Facts

On his way to an office in the defendants' building, seeing the lift door partially open the plaintiff stepped through it. The lift was not there: the plaintiff fell down the shaft and was injured. The defendants had contracted with the Express Lift Co for the lift's maintenance and they – the independent contractors – had been guilty of negligence.

Held

The defendants were not liable for the plaintiff's injuries.

Horridge J:

'I am satisfied that the Express Lift Co were independent contractors, and that it was their duty to have discovered this defect. If they were independent contractors, the relationship of master and servant does not exist between defendants and themselves, and therefore the defendants are not liable for the acts of the contractors unless they can bring themselves within any known exceptions ... This case is an ordinary case of an independent contractor. The negligence was that of the independent contractor. Notwithstanding that, the defendants may be liable on other grounds. First it is said that they ought to have found the defect out. I do not agree. They employed people who knew better than they about lifts. I do not think the defendants were guilty of any default.'

Salsbury v *Woodland* [1970] 1 QB 324 Court of Appeal (Harman, Sachs and Widgery LJJ)

Independent contractor – negligence

Facts

Defendant one, the occupier of a house, employed defendant two, an apparently competent tree-feller, to cut down a large tree in the front garden. D2 did so negligently so that the tree brought down some telephone wires which fell onto the road. P, who lived opposite, went to remove the wires from the road and was struck by a car driven negligently by D3. All three defendants were held liable. D1 appealed on the grounds that he was not vicariously liable for the negligence of his independent contractor, D2.

Held

The appeal would be allowed. as the work involved was not inherently dangerous. An employer is only liable for the torts of an independent contractor in limited circumstances where the employer himself is under a direct duty to see that care is taken throughout the operation.

6   Negligence: the Duty of Care

Afzal v *Ford Motor Co Ltd* [1994] 4 All ER 720 Court of Appeal (Neill, Beldam and Steyn LJJ)

Small personal injury claims – whether arbitration or trial in court

Facts
In a number of actions the plaintiff employees brought claims against their employers for damages in respect of minor personal injuries sustained in the workplace. Mostly the claims did not exceed £1,000 and under CCR O.19 r.3 such claims would be automatically referred for arbitration by a district judge, unless he was satisfied that he should order a court trial on the grounds, inter alia, that a difficult question of law and a question of fact of exceptional complexity was involved (r.3(2)(a)) or that it would be unreasonable for the claim to proceed to arbitration having regard to its subject matter, the size of any counterclaim, the circumstances of the parties or the interests of any other person likely to be affected by the award (r.3(2)(2)). The plaintiffs applied for the reference to arbitration to be rescinded, contending that compulsory arbitration was unsuitable for personal injury claims, particularly in cases involving employers' liability, since the issues involved were too complex for summary judgment. In addition, the costs recoverable in arbitrated claims were limited so trade unions would be deterred from assisting claimants, who would then be at a serious disadvantage. The judge granted the employees' applications on the basis of O.19 r.3(2)(d) and ordered that all the claims should be tried in court in view of the subject matter and the circumstances of the parties and, in particular, the fact that the employees could not be expected to present their own cases where breaches of statutory duty, medical evidence and discovery might play a large part without legal representation. The defendant appealed, on the grounds that the judge had applied the wrong test as he had not shown, pursuant to r.3(2(d) that it was unreasonable for the claims as a class to be referred to arbitration and that, while a reference to arbitration could be rescinded after r.3(2)(a) if the case raised difficult problems of law or fact, no such considerations arose in the instant cases.

Held
The appeals were allowed. The court should not rescind an automatic reference to arbitration under O.19 r.3(1) merely because a question of law was involved or the facts were complex, since r.3(2)(a) made it clear that a question of law had to be difficult or a question of fact exceptionally complex for a claim to be tried in court. The law applicable to employers' liability claims was often straightforward, and although the facts could be complex, in most instances the question was whether the employer had taken reasonable care and the medical issues were unlikely to be complex where the amount involved was less than £1,000. Further, the hardship of an employee representing himself against a legally represented employer was one faced in all cases where the financial resources of the parties were unequal. Thus it was wrong to approach employers' liability claims involving amounts below £1,000 as a class of case which was, in general, unsuited to arbitration.

The court also held that the intentional overstatement of a claim to avoid automatic reference to arbitration was a clear misuse of process.

Commentary

As a result of this decision the Lord Chancellor announced that he did not intend to take any further action on his proposals regarding small personal injury claims.

Al-Kandari v *J R Brown & Co* [1988] 2 WLR 671 Court of Appeal (Lord Donaldson of Lymington MR, Dillon and Bingham LJJ)

Negligence – solicitor's duty of care

Facts

The plaintiff was married to a Kuwaiti national and their two children were included on his passport. In 1981 the couple separated and the husband abducted the children to Kuwait. He was persuaded to return with them: the wife was given custody, care and control of the children and the husband undertook to deposit his passport with his solicitors, the defendants. Wishing to return to Kuwait, the husband wanted to have the children's names removed from it. To this end, the defendants forwarded the passport to London agents with instructions to take it to the Kuwait embassy. While it was there, the husband persuaded the embassy to release it to him. He then arranged for the plaintiff to be kidnapped and he used the passport to take the children to Kuwait. The plaintiff claimed damages for, inter alia, negligence.

Held

She was entitled to succeed. The defendants owed the plaintiff a duty to take reasonable care to keep the passport in their possession and they had been in breach of that duty. The damage suffered by the plaintiff had been a natural and probable consequence of the breach of duty.

Bingham LJ:

'The judge found against the plaintiff on the ground that it was not reasonably foreseeable that Mr Al-Kandari would be given any opportunity to abduct the children. The correct approach is to consider the breach of duty which has been proved and to ask whether an ordinarily competent solicitor in the defendants' position would have foreseen damage of the kind which actually occurred as a not unlikely result of that breach ... In my judgment such a solicitor would have foreseen the damage which the plaintiff has in fact suffered as a possible and by no means fanciful consequence of the breach of duty established. I would not, therefore, agree with the judge that this damage was too remote to be recoverable in law.'

Alcock v *Chief Constable of the South Yorkshire Police* [1991] 3 WLR 1057 House of Lords (Lord Keith of Kinkel, Lord Ackner, Lord Oliver of Aylmerton, Lord Jauncey of Tullichettle and Lord Lowry)

Persons entitled to damages for nervous shock

Facts

The defendant admitted liability in negligence in respect of the 95 deaths and over 400 physical injuries in the Hillsborough Stadium disaster. Scenes from the ground were broadcast live on television from time to time and later on television news. News of the disaster was also broadcast over the radio. None of the television broadcasts depicted the suffering or dying of recognisable individuals. Sixteen persons, some of whom were at the match but not in the area where the disaster occurred, and all of whom were relatives, or in one case the fiance, of persons who were in that area, brought actions against the defendant claiming damages for nervous shock resulting in psychiatric illness alleged to have been caused by seeing or hearing news of the disaster. The question of law having been tried as a preliminary issue and the Court of Appeal having decided against them, ten of the plaintiffs made a final appeal.

Held

Their appeals would be dismissed, either because the plaintiffs had not been at the match or their relationship to a victim had not been sufficiently close.

Lord Keith of Kinkel:

'The question of liability in negligence for what is commonly, if inaccurately, described as "nervous shock" has only twice been considered by this House, in *Hay (or Bourhill)* v *Young* [1943] AC 92 and in *McLoughlin* v *O'Brian* [1983] 1 AC 410. In the latter case ... Lord Wilberforce ... expressed the opinion that foreseeability did not of itself and automatically give rise to a duty of care owed to a person or class of persons and that considerations of policy entered into the conclusion that such a duty existed. He then considered the arguments on policy which had led the Court of Appeal to reject the plaintiff's claim, and concluded that they were not of great force. ...

Lord Bridge of Harwich, with whom Lord Scarman agreed ... appears to have rested his finding of liability simply on the test of reasonable foreseeability of psychiatric illness affecting the plaintiff as a result of the consequences of the road accident ... Lord Edmund-Davies and Lord Russell of Killowen both considered the policy arguments which had led the Court of Appeal to dismiss the plaintiff's claim to be unsound ... Neither speech contained anything inconsistent with that of Lord Wilberforce.

It was argued for the appellants in the present case that reasonable foreseeability of the risk of injury to them in the particular form of psychiatric illness was all that was required to bring home liability to the respondent. In the ordinary case of direct physical injury suffered in an accident at work or elsewhere, reasonable foreseeability of the risk is indeed the only test that need be applied to determine liability. But injury by psychiatric illness is more subtle, as Lord Macmillan observed in *Bourhill* v *Young*. In the present type of case it is a secondary sort of injury brought about by the infliction of physical injury, or the risk of physical injury, upon another person. That can affect those closely connected with that person in various ways. One way is by subjecting a close relative to the stress and strain of caring for the injured person over a prolonged period, but psychiatric illness due to such stress and strain has not so far been treated as founding a claim in damages. So I am of the opinion that in addition to reasonable foreseeability liability for injury in the particular form of psychiatric illness must depend in addition upon a requisite relationship of proximity between the claimant and the party said to owe the duty. Lord Atkin in *M'Alister (or Donoghue)* v *Stevenson* [1932] AC 562 at 580, described those to whom a duty of care is owed as being –

"persons who are so closely and directly affected by my act that I ought reasonably to have them in contemplation as being so affected when I am directing my mind to the acts or omissions which are called in question."

The concept of a person being closely and directly affected has been conveniently labelled "proximity", and this concept has been applied in certain categories of cases, particularly those concerned with pure economic loss, to limit and control the consequences as regards liability which would follow if reasonable foreseeability were the sole criterion.

As regards the class of persons to whom a duty may be owed to take reasonable care to avoid inflicting psychiatric illness through nervous shock sustained by reason of physical injury or peril to another, I think it sufficient that reasonable foreseeability should be the guide. I would not seek to limit the class by reference to particular relationships such as husband and wife or parent and child. The kinds of relationship which may involve close ties of love and affection are numerous, and it is the existence of such ties which leads to mental disturbance when the loved one suffers a catastrophe. They may be present in family relationships or those of close friendship, and may be stronger in the case of engaged couples than in that of persons who have been married to each other for many years. It is common knowledge that such ties exist, and reasonably foreseeable that those bound by them may in certain circumstances be at real risk of psychiatric illness if the loved one is injured or put in peril. The closeness of the tie would, however, require to be proved by a plaintiff, though no doubt being capable of being presumed in appropriate cases. The case of a bystander unconnected with the victims of an accident is difficult. Psychiatric injury to him would not ordinarily, in my view, be within the range of reasonable foreseeability but could not perhaps be entirely excluded from it if the circumstances of a catastrophe occurring very close to him were particularly horrific.

In the case of those within the sphere of reasonable foreseeability the proximity factors mentioned by Lord Wilberforce in *McLoughlin* v *O'Brian* must, however, be taken into account in judging whether a duty of care exists. The first of these is proximity of the plaintiff to the accident in time and space. For this purpose the accident is to be taken to include its immediate aftermath, which in *McLoughlin*'s case was held to cover the scene at the hospital which was experienced by the plaintiff some two hours after the accident. In *Jaensch* v *Coffey* (1984) 54 ALR 417 the plaintiff saw her injured husband at the hospital to which he had been taken in severe pain before and between his undergoing a series of emergency operations, and the next day stayed with him in the intensive care unit and thought he was going to die. She was held entitled to recover damages for the psychiatric illness she suffered as a result. Deane J said:

"... the aftermath of the accident extended to the hospital to which the injured person was taken and persisted for so long as he remained in the state produced by the accident up to and including immediate post-accident treatment ... Her psychiatric injuries were the result of the impact upon her of the facts of the accident itself and its aftermath while she was present at the aftermath of the accident at the hospital."

As regards the means by which the shock is suffered, Lord Wilberforce said in *McLoughlin*'s case that it must come through sight or hearing of the event or of its immediate aftermath. He also said that it was surely right that the law should not compensate shock brought about by communication by a third party. On that basis it is open to serious doubt whether *Hevican* v *Ruane* [1991] 3 All ER 65 and *Ravenscroft* v *Rederiaktiebolaget Transatlantic* [1991] 3 All ER 73 were correctly decided, since in both of these cases the effective cause of the psychiatric illness would appear to have been the fact of a son's death and the news of it.

Of the present appellants two, Brian Harrison and Robert Alcock, were present at the Hillsborough ground, both of them in the West Stand, from which they witnessed the scenes in pens 3 and 4. Brian Harrison lost two brothers, while Robert Alcock lost a brother-in-law and identified the body at the mortuary at midnight. In neither of these cases was there any evidence of particularly close ties of love or affection with the brothers or brother-in-law. In my opinion the mere fact of the particular relationship was insufficient to place the plaintiff within the class of persons to whom a duty of care could be owed by the defendant as being foreseeably at risk of psychiatric illness by reason of injury or peril to the individuals concerned. The same is true of other plaintiffs who were not present at the ground and who lost brothers, or in one case a grandson. I would, however, place in the category of members to which risk of psychiatric illness was reasonable foreseeable Mr and Mrs Copoc, whose son was killed, and Alexandra Penk, who lost her fiance. In each of these cases the closest ties of love and affection fall to be presumed from the fact of the particular relationship, and there is no suggestion of anything which might tend to rebut that presumption. These three all watched scenes from Hillsborough on television, but none of these depicted suffering of recognisable individuals, such being excluded by the broadcasting code of ethics, a position known to the defendant. In my opinion the viewing of these scenes cannot be equiparated with the viewer being within "sight or hearing of the event or of its immediate aftermath", to use the words of Lord Wilberforce in *McLoughlin* v *O'Brian*, nor can the scenes reasonably be regarded as giving rise to shock, in the sense of a sudden assault on the nervous system. They were capable of giving rise to anxiety for the safety of relatives known or believed to be present in the area affected by the crush, and undoubtedly did so, but that is very different from seeing the fate of the relative or his condition shortly after the event. The viewing of the television scenes did not create the necessary degree of proximity.'

Commentary
See also *Ravenscroft* v *Rederiaktiebolaget Transatlantic* [1992] 2 All ER 470n.

Alexandrou v *Oxford* [1993] 4 All ER 328 Court of Appeal (Slade, Parker and Glidewell LJJ)

Duty of care owed by police to victim of a crime

Facts

The plaintiff's shop was burgled, and an alarm was activated at both the shop and the local police station. Two police officers checked the premises but failed to inspect the rear of the shop where the burglars had forced entry. Some hours later a substantial amount of goods was removed from the shop. The plaintiff sued the chief constable alleging that the police had been negligent in failing to take adequate precautions to discover why the alarm had been activated and in assuming that it was a false alarm. The trial judge found as a fact that the theft would have been prevented had the police officers properly inspected the rear of the building and were thus in breach of the duty of care they owed to the plaintiff. The chief constable appealed.

Held

A plaintiff who alleged that a defendant owed him a duty to take reasonable care to prevent loss caused by the actions of a third party had to prove not only that loss was foreseeable if the defendant did not exercise reasonable care, but also that he stood in a special relationship to the defendant from which the duty of care arose. In the present case there was no such special relationship between the plaintiff and the police because the call to the police was an emergency call which did not differ from an emergency call by a member of the public. If a duty of care was owed to the plaintiff that duty would be owed to all members of the public, and on the principle in *Hill* v *Chief Constable of West Yorkshire* [1988] 2 All ER 238 such a duty did not exist.

Further, it would not be in the public interest to impose such a duty of care on the police as it would not promote a higher standard of care but would result in a significant diversion of resources from the suppression of crime.

Allen v *Bloomsbury Health Authority* [1993] 1 All ER 651 High Court (Brooke J)

Unwanted pregnancy – assessment of damages

Facts

After divorcing her husband, the plaintiff mother of two children aged 10 and 11 underwent a sterilisation operation at the defendants' hospital. The defendants failed to notice that she was four weeks pregnant by her then partner, whom she had no wish to marry, and by the time that the pregnancy was diagnosed the plaintiff felt that it was too late to have a termination. Had the pregnancy been diagnosed at the time of the operation the plaintiff would have had an abortion. She feared that the foetus would have been damaged by the operation, but she gave birth to a healthy daughter (Faye). The defendants admitted liability and the only issue was as to the quantum of damages.

Held

The plaintiff would be awarded damages totalling £96,631.

Brooke J:

'Although a claim of this type has not yet been considered by the House of Lords, the principles on which damages are to be awarded have been considered a number of times by the Court of Appeal, and I was referred to all the leading cases which have been decided in the last seven years. I derive from these cases the following principles which should guide me when I consider Mrs Allen's claim.

(1) If a doctor fails to act towards his patient with the standard of care reasonably to be expected of him, and as a foreseeable result of the doctor's breach of duty a child is born whose potential for life would have been lawfully terminated but for the doctor's negligence, the law entitles the mother to recover damages for the foreseeable loss and damage she suffers in consequence of the doctor's negligence (see *Emeh* v *Kensington and Chelsea and Westminster Area Health Authority* [1984] 3 All ER 1044).

(2) A plaintiff mother is entitled to recover general damages (and any associated financial special damage) for the discomfort and pain associated with the continuation of her pregnancy and the delivery of her child, although she must set off against this claim a sum in respect of the benefit of avoiding the pain and suffering and associated financial loss which would have resulted from the termination of her pregnancy under general anaesthetic, since in the events which have happened she has not had to undergo that operation (see *Emeh's* case [1984] 3 All ER 1044 at 1056 per Purchas LJ, *Thake* v *Maurice* [1986] 1 All ER 497 at 508 per Kerr LJ, *Gardiner* v *Mountfield* (1989) 5 BMLR 1 at 5–6 per Scott Baker J).

(3) She is also entitled to damages for economic loss quite unassociated with her own physical injury which falls into two main categories: (i) the financial loss she suffers because when the unwanted baby is born she has a growing child to feed, clothe, house, educate and care for until the child becomes an adult; (ii) the financial loss she suffers because she has lost or may lose earnings or incur other expense because of her obligations towards her child which she would have sought to avoid (see *Emeh's* case [1984] 3 All ER 1044 at 1053, 1056 per Slade and Purchas LJJ respectively; adopted and applied by the Court of Appeal in *Thake* v *Maurice* [1986] 1 All ER 497.

(4) Although the law recognises that it is foreseeable that if an unwanted child is born following a doctor's negligence a mother may suffer wear and tear and tiredness in bringing up a healthy child, the claim for general damages she might otherwise have had on this account is generally set off against and extinguished by the benefit of bringing a healthy child into the world and seeing one's child grow up to maturity (see *Thake* v *Maurice* [1986] 1 All ER 497 at 508 per Kerr LJ).

(5) However, the law is willing to recognise a claim for general damages in respect of the foreseeable additional anxiety, stress and burden involved in bringing up a handicapped child, which is not treated as being extinguished by any countervailing benefit, although this head of damages is different in kind from the typical claim for anxiety and stress associated with and flowing from an injured plaintiff's own personal injuries (see *Emeh's* case [1984] 3 All ER 1044 at 1052 per Waller LJ) ...

For my purpose I am content to assume that the Court of Appeal has recognised that in the unique circumstances surrounding the breach of a doctor's duty to a pregnant woman (or a woman who may become pregnant against her wishes) she should be entitled to recover damages for the two quite distinct foreseeable heads of loss which I identified when I was analysing the principles which should guide me in this case. The first, a claim for damages for personal injuries during the period leading up to the delivery of the child, is a claim which is comparable to, though different from, a claim for damages for personal injuries resulting from the infliction of a traumatic injury to a plaintiff by a negligent defendant. The second, a claim for the economic loss involved in the expense of losing paid employment and the obligation of having to pay for the upkeep and care of an unwanted child, is a totally different type of claim, although it may in turn be associated with a different type of claim for damages for the loss of amenity associated with bringing up a handicapped child ...

One important issue does, however, arise for my decision. This relates to the principles by which the financial cost of bringing up the unwanted child is to be measured. By definition the mother has decided in this class of case that she did not want to have another baby, and in many cases she could not afford to have another baby without considerable hardship to herself and/or the other members of her family. The baby, for its part, did not choose to be born and has no claim itself for the cost of being reared (see *McKay* v *Essex Area Health Authority* [1982] 2 All ER 771).

Should the tortfeasor whose negligence has "caused" the baby's "wrongful birth" be compelled to pay the "reasonable" costs of its upkeep? If so, how should those costs be measured, given that it is of the essence of the tortfeasor's negligence that the cost of upkeep is being borne by a mother who looked to him to exercise reasonable care in preventing her from incurring it? Alternatively, should the tortfeasor merely have to pay what is "necessary", whatever that word means in this context? Is it "necessary" for a child to have extra music lessons or to go on school trips or to go away for holidays or to be able to buy books and equipment for his interests and hobbies like his school contemporaries? If the test is necessity, how does a judge measure necessity without descending to the criteria adopted by the old poor law guardians or the modern curators of the social fund? ...

It will be evident that there is not yet any clear guidance from the Court of Appeal about the basis on which the future cost of maintaining the unplanned child should be assessed ...

In my judgment in this type of case defendants are liable to pay for all such expenses as may be reasonably incurred for the education and upkeep for the unplanned child, having regard to all the circumstances of the case and, in particular, to his condition in life and his reasonable requirements at the time the expenditure is incurred.

Before I leave this consideration of the legal principles which I should apply when qualifying Mrs Allen's claim, I remind myself that the Court of Appeal has made it clear that I should exclude all the considerations which moral philosophers or theologians might regard as relevant when I compute the figure which I consider appropriate for the cost of Faye's care ...

If an unplanned child is borne after a failure by a hospital doctor to exercise the standard of care reasonably to be expected of him and the child's parents have sent all their other children to expensive private boarding schools for the whole of their education then it appears to me that as the law now stands a very substantial claim for the cost of private education of a healthy child of a reasonably wealthy family might have to be met from the funds of the health authority responsible for the doctor's negligence. However, if this is regarded as inappropriate on policy grounds it is, as Waller LJ pointed out in *Emeh's* case, for Parliament, not the courts to determine policy questions: judges at first instance, at any rate, can do no more than try to identify and apply principles approved by the higher courts unless and until Parliament intervenes.

Having stated the legal principles which I should apply I turn finally to the itemised heads of damage which Mrs Allen claims ...

In these circumstances, I make the following award of general damages:

Mrs Allen's future loss of earnings till Faye is 11	£29,715.84
Child-minding costs when Faye is 11 to 14	2,850.00
Cost of maintaining Faye till she is 18	27,152.00
Mrs Allen's claim for pain and suffering and loss of amenity	2,500.00
Interest on £2,500 at agreed rate of 5%	125.00
	£62,342.84

The award
Subject to any further adjustment for interest, to take into account the short period between trial and judgment, the total award, therefore is:

Special damages	£25,232.77
Interest on special damages	9,055.68
General damages (including interest)	62,342.84
	£96,631.29'

Ancell v McDermott [1993] 4 All ER 355 Court of Appeal (Norse and Beldam LJJ, Sir John Megaw)

Duty of care owed by police to road users

Facts
The first defendant drove over an obstruction in the road, rupturing his fuel tank. He continued to drive without stopping to see whether his car had suffered any damage, leaving a trail of diesel fuel on the road.

Some officers of Hertfordshire police noticed the diesel fuel and notified Bedfordshire police of the spillage. Some 20 minutes after the spillage commenced an officer of Bedfordshire police noticed the spillage and reported it to Bedfordshire highways department. Ten minutes later a car skidded on the diesel fuel and was involved in a collision. The passengers and husband of the driver who was killed as a result sued (inter alia) the Hertfordshire and Bedfordshire chief constables. The chief constables applied to strike out the claims against them, but this was refused by the judge on the grounds that whether a duty of care existed depended on the precise circumstances, including the nature of the hazard, the extent of the danger created and the likelihood of injury, and that those matters could only be determined at trial. The chief constables appealed.

Held
The police were under no duty of care to protect road users from, or to warn them of, hazards discovered by the police on the highway. There was no special relationship between the plaintiffs and the police giving rise to an exceptional duty to prevent harm from dangers created by another. The extreme width and scope of such a duty would impose on the police a potential liability of almost unlimited scope, which would be against public policy because it would divert extensive police resources and manpower from, and hamper the performance of, ordinary police duties. Hence the police did not owe a duty of care in the circumstances.

Anns v *Merton London Borough Council* [1978] AC 728 House of Lords (Lord Wilberforce, Lord Diplock, Lord Simon of Glaisdale, Lord Salmon and Lord Russell of Killowen)

Duty of care

Facts
The plaintiffs were lessees and occupiers of flats in a block built in 1962 by a private builder and developer. Some of the plaintiffs had taken their leases in 1962, others had acquired them subsequently by assignment from original lessees. In 1970, the building began to suffer damage, eg cracks in the walls, due to the movement of the foundations. Under by-laws made pursuant to the Public Health Act 1936, the local authority – the defendants – had a power (but no duty) to inspect the foundations of new buildings. The most likely cause of the movement was inadequate (too shallow) foundations. Assuming this to be so, and assuming that the local authority had carried out an inspection pursuant to its powers, but had done so negligently, it owed a duty of care to subsequent occupiers.

Held
Both a statutory power and a statutory duty could give rise to a duty of care and if there had been a negligent exercise by the council of their power to inspect the foundations, they would be liable to the plaintiffs.

Obiter: the builder may also be liable, either under *Donoghue* v *Stevenson* or for breach of his statutory duty to comply with the relevant bye-laws.

Lord Wilberforce:

'Through the trilogy of cases in this House, *Donoghue* v *Stevenson*, *Hedley Byrne & Co Ltd* v *Heller & Partners* and *Home Office* v *Dorset Yacht*, the position has now been reached that in order to establish that a duty of care arises in a particular situation, it is not necessary to bring the facts of that situation within those of previous situations in which a duty of care has been held to exist. Rather, the question has to be approached in two stages. First, one has to ask whether, as between the alleged wrongdoer and the person who has suffered damage there is a sufficient relationship of proximity or neighbourhood such that, in the reasonable contemplation of the former, carelessness on his part may be likely to cause damage to the latter, in which case a prima facie duty of care arises. Secondly, if the first question is answered affirmatively, it is necessary to consider whether there are any considerations which ought to negate, or to reduce or limit the scope of the duty of the class of person to whom it is owed, or the damages to which a breach of it may give rise ... Examples of this are *Hedley Byrne* ... where the class of potential plaintiffs was reduced to those shown to have relied on the correctness of statements made and *Weller & Co v Foot & Mouth Disease Research Institute* ... and cases about 'economic loss' where a duty having been held to exist, the nature of the recoverable damages was limited (see *SCM v Whittall, Spartan Steel v Martin*).'

It was also contended on behalf of the council that the plaintiffs do not even allege that they relied on the inspection of the foundations by the council. Nor they did, and I daresay they never even knew about it. This, however, is irrelevant. I think that the noble Lords who decided *Hedley Byrne & Co Ltd v Heller & Partners Ltd* would have been very surprised that what they said about reliance in that case would one day be cited as relevant to a case such as the present. There are a wide variety of instances in which a statement is negligently made by a professional man which he knows will be relied on by many people besides his client, eg a well-known firm of accountants certifies in a prospectus the annual profits of the company issuing it and unfortunately due to negligence on the part of the accountants, the profits are seriously overstated. Those persons who invested in the company in reliance on the accuracy of the accountants' certificate would have a claim for damages against the accountants for any money they might have lost as a result of the accountants' negligence: see the *Hedley Byrne* case.

In the present case, however, the loss is caused not by any reliance placed by the plaintiffs on the council or the building inspector, but by the fact that if the inspection had been carefully made, the defects in the foundations would have been rectified before the erection of the building was begun. The categories of negligence, as Lord Macmillan said, are never closed and there are now a great many of them. In a few, reliance is of importance. In the present case, reliance is not even remotely relevant.'

If there was at one time a supposed rule that the doctrine of *Donoghue v Stevenson* did not apply to realty, there is no doubt under modern authority that a builder of defective premises may be liable in negligence to persons who thereby suffer injury. (The authorities) expressly leave open the question whether the immunity against action of builder-owners, established by older authorities *Bottomley v Bannister*) still survives ... I am unable to understand why this principle or proposition should prevent recovery in a suitable case, by a person who has subsequently acquired the house, on the principle of *Donoghue v Stevenson* the same rules should apply to all careless acts of a builder: whether he happens to own the land or not ...'

Commentary

Applied: *Home Office v Dorset Yacht Co Ltd* [1970] 2 WLR 1140.

Distinguished: *East Suffolk Rivers Catchment Board v Kent* [1941] AC 74.

Disapproved: *Bottomley v Bannister* [1932] 1 KB 458.

Explained in *Peabody Donation Fund (Governors) v Sir Lindsay Parkinson & Co Ltd* [1984] 3 WLR 953.

In *Murphy v Brentwood District Council* [1990] 3 WLR 414, the House of Lords said that *Anns* had been wrongly decided as regards the scope of any private law duty of care resting on local authorities in relation to their function of taking steps to secure compliance with building bye-laws or regulations.

Antonelli v *Wade Gery Farr* (1992) The Times 29 December High Court (Turner J)

Liability of counsel regarding conduct of trial

Facts

Counsel had wasted the court's time in that her submissions had been rambling with many embarrassing pauses and she had failed to prepare written submissions when requested by the judge.

Held

That where time had been wasted by counsel during the conduct of proceedings, and the court was satisfied that counsel had acted negligently, unreasonably or improperly, the court could make an order for wasted costs against counsel. Section 51(6) of the Supreme Court Act 1981 (as modified by s4 Courts and Legal Services Act 1990) removed the immunity of counsel from liability for the conduct of proceedings in that it allowed an order for wasted costs to be made against counsel.

Attia v *British Gas plc* [1987] 3 WLR 1101 Court of Appeal (Dillon, Woolf and Bingham LJJ)

Negligence – nervous shock

Facts

While installing central heating in the plaintiff's house, the defendants negligently caused it to catch fire. The plaintiff was out at the time and she returned home to see smoke pouring from the loft. She claimed damages, inter alia, for nervous shock and psychological reaction caused by seeing her house on fire.

Held

Whether the plaintiff's psychiatric damage was a reasonably foreseeable consequence of the defendants' negligence was a question of fact to be decided at the trial.

Bingham LJ:

'Since the defendants were working in the house where the plaintiff lived, it must have been obvious to them that she would be so closely and directly affected by their performance of their work that they ought reasonably to have had her in contemplation as being so affected when they carried out the work. It is not, I think, contested that the defendants owed her a duty to take reasonable care to carry out the work so as to avoid damaging her home and property. But it is said that the defendants owed her no duty to take reasonable care to carry out the work so as to avoid causing her psychiatric damage. This analytical approach cannot, I think, be said to be wrong, but it seems to me to be preferable, where a duty of care undeniably exists, to treat the question as one of remoteness and ask whether the plaintiff's psychiatric damage is too remote to be recoverable because it was not reasonably foreseeable as a consequence of the defendants' careless conduct. The test of reasonable foreseeability is, as I understand it, the same in both contexts, and the result should be the same on either approach. So the question in any case such as this, applying the ordinary test of remoteness in tort, is whether the defendant should reasonably have contemplated psychiatric damage to the plaintiff as a real, even if unlikely, result of careless conduct on his part.'

Commentary

Considered: *Hay (or Bourhill)* v *Young* [1943] AC 92 and *McLoughlin* v *O'Brian* [1982] 2 WLR 982.

Bourhill (or Hay) v *Young* [1943] AC 92 House of Lords (Lord Thankerton, Lord Russell of Killowen, Lord Macmillan, Lord Wright and Lord Porter)

Negligence – shock

Facts

The appellant claimed damages against the estate of the respondent, now deceased, who due to his negligent riding of a motor-cycle was involved in a collision with a motor car. The appellant was getting off a tram when she heard the sound of the collision some fifty feet away. Shortly after she saw blood on the road. She sustained nervous shock and had a miscarriage. At no time was there any danger of physical injury to the appellant herself, who brought an action in negligence.

Held

The cyclist owed no duty of care to the appellant as he could not have reasonably foreseen the likelihood that the appellant, placed as she was, could be affected by his negligent act.

Lord Thankerton:

'Clearly (the duty of the motor-cyclist) is to drive the cycle with such reasonable care as will avoid the risk of injury to such persons as he can reasonably foresee might be injured by failure to exercise such reasonable care. It is now settled that such injury includes injury by shock although no direct physical impact or lesion occurs. If then the test of proximity or remoteness is to be applied, I am of the opinion that such a test involves that injury must be within that which the cyclist ought reasonably to have contemplated as the area of potential danger which would arise as the result of his negligence and the question in the present case is whether the appellant was within that area. I am clearly of the opinion that she was not ...'

Lord Wright:

'The general concept of reasonable foresight as the criterion of negligence or breach of duty ... may be criticised as too vague; but negligence is a fluid principle, which has to be applied to the most diverse conditions and problems of human life. It is a concrete, not an abstract idea. It has to be fitted to the facts of the particular case ... It is also always relative to the individual affected. This raises a serious additional difficulty in the cases where it has to be determined not merely whether the act itself is negligent against someone, but whether it is negligent vis-a-vis the plaintiff. This is a crucial point in cases of nervous shock. Thus, in the present case, John Young was certainly negligent in an issue between himself and the owner of the car which he ran into, but it is another question whether he was negligent vis-a-vis the appellant ...

I cannot accept that Young could reasonably have foreseen, or more correctly the reasonable hypothetical observer could reasonably have foreseen, the likelihood that anyone placed as the appellant was, could be affected in the manner in which she was.'

Lord Porter:

'The duty (of care) is not owed to the world at large ... In order to establish a duty towards herself, the pursuer must show that the cyclist should reasonably have foreseen emotional injury to her as a result of his negligent driving and I do not think she has done so ... The driver of a car or vehicle, even though careless, is entitled to assume that the ordinary frequenter of the streets has sufficient fortitude to endure such incidents as may from time to time occur in them, including the noise of a collision and the sight of injury to others and is not to be considered negligent towards one who does not possess the customary phlegm...'

Commentary

Applied in *King* v *Phillips* [1953] 2 WLR 526.

Burton v *Islington Health Authority* [1992] 3 WLR 637 Court of Appeal (Dillon, Balcombe and Leggatt LJJ)

Foetus – duty of care

Facts

The plaintiff's mother was admitted to hospital for a D and C but, unknown to the hospital, her mother was pregnant with the plaintiff, to whom she subsequently gave birth. The plaintiff was born with a number of abnormalities and she alleged that the defendants had been negligent. The defendants argued that, at the time of the D and C, the plaintiff was an embryo which had no legal status and therefore no right to sue. The damage was occasioned to the plaintiff prior to the coming into force of the Congenital Disabilities (Civil Liability) Act 1976.

Held

The decision was to be made in the light of the law in force prior to the 1976 Act, ie, the common law, and giving due weight to United States and Commonwealth cases it followed that children with disabilities caused by alleged negligent medical treatment before they were born had a cause of action against the health authorities.

Calveley v *Chief Constable of Merseyside* [1989] 2 WLR 624 House of Lords (Lord Bridge of Harwich, Lord Ackner, Lord Oliver of Aylmerton, Lord Goff of Chieveley and Lord Lowry)

Police disciplinary proceedings

Facts

Following complaints, the plaintiff police officers had been suspended on full pay and allowances pending the outcome of investigations. In disciplinary proceedings the complaints had either been dismissed, quashed on appeal or discontinued, but the plaintiffs now sought general damages for anxiety, vexation and loss of reputation and special damages for loss of overtime pay, alleging, inter alia, that the investigating officer had been in breach of duty at common law in failing to proceed expeditiously.

Held

Their claims could not succeed.

Lord Bridge of Harwich:

'Leading counsel for the plaintiffs submitted that a police officer investigating any crime suspected to have been committed, whether by a civilian or by a member of a police force, owes to the suspect a duty of care at common law. It follows, he submits, that the like duty is owed by an officer investigating a suspected offence against discipline by a fellow officer. It seems to me that this startling proposition founders on the rocks of elementary principle. The first question that arises is: what injury to the suspect ought reasonably to be foreseen by the investigator as likely to be suffered by the suspect if the investigation is not conducted with due care which is sufficient to establish the relationship of legal neighbourhood or proximity in the sense explained by Lord Atkin in *Donoghue (or M'Alister)* v *Stevenson* [1932] AC 562 at 580-582 as the essential foundation of the tort of negligence? The submission that anxiety, vexation and injury to reputation may constitute such an injury needs only to be stated to be seen to be unsustainable. Likewise, it is not reasonably foreseeable that the negligent conduct of a criminal investigation would cause injury to the health of the suspect, whether in the form of depressive illness or otherwise. If the allegedly negligent investigation is followed by the suspect's conviction, it is obvious that an indirect challenge to that conviction by an action for damages for negligent conduct of the investigation cannot be permitted. One must therefore ask the question whether foreseeable injury to the suspect may be caused on the hypothesis either that he has never been charged or, if charged, that he has been acquitted at trial or on appeal, or that his conviction has been quashed on an application for judicial review. It is, I accept, foreseeable that in these situations the suspect may be put to expense, or may conceivably suffer some other economic loss, which might have been avoided had a more careful investigation established his innocence at some earlier stage. However, any suggestion that there should be liability in negligence in such circumstances runs up against the formidable obstacles in the way of liability in negligence for purely economic loss. Where no action for malicious prosecution would lie, it would be strange indeed if an acquitted defendant could recover damages for negligent investigation. Finally, all other considerations apart, it would plainly be contrary to public policy, in my opinion, to prejudice the fearless and efficient discharge by police officers of their vitally important public duty of investigating crime by requiring them to act under the shadow of a potential action for damages for negligence by the suspect.

If no duty of care is owed by a police officer investigating a suspected crime to a civilian suspect, it is difficult to see any conceivable reason why a police officer who is subject to investigation ... should be in any better position. Junior counsel for the plaintiffs, following, put the case in negligence on a very much narrower basis. He submitted that in the case of a police officer subject to investigation a specific duty of care is owed to him to avoid any unnecessary delay in the investigation precisely because the officer is, or is liable to be, suspended from duty until the investigation is concluded. The short answer to this submission is that suspension from duty is not in itself and does not involve any foreseeable injury of a kind capable of sustaining a cause of action in negligence ... In the light of the provision made by the relevant regulations suspension is not a foreseeable cause of even economic loss.'

Candlewood Navigation Corp Ltd v *Mitsui Osk Lines Ltd, The Mineral Transporter* [1985] 3 WLR 381 Privy Council (Lord Fraser of Tullybelton, Lord Roskill, Lord Brandon of Oakbrook, Lord Templeman and Lord Griffiths)

Negligence – title to sue

Facts
The first plaintiff was the owner of vessel IM, which he hired to the second plaintiff (the bareboat charterer) so that the latter took complete control over her and effectively became her owner during the period of hire. The second plaintiff then rehired the vessel to the first plaintiff for a set period of time (time charter). This gave the first plaintiff the exclusive right to use the vessel during this period. The vessel MT collided with the vessel IM whilst the latter was still at anchor, thereby causing damage under the bareboat charter; the second plaintiff had agreed to pay the cost of any repairs resulting from collision. Under the time charter the first plaintiff was liable for a reduced rate of hire whilst the necessary repairs were being carried out. The plaintiffs claimed damages against the defendant.

Held
The first plaintiff was not entitled to recover damages. He was suing only in his capacity as time charterer. As such he did not have a proprietary or a possessory right in the chartered vessel (even though he was, in another capacity, the owner of that vessel). The time charterer had only a contractual interest in the vessel which had been damaged by the defendants. His contractual use of the vessel was made less profitable as a result of their negligence. This was not recoverable from the defendants but simply irrecoverable pure economic loss. However, the losses incurred by the bareboat charterer (the second plaintiff) would be recoverable. These included the amount by which the hire had been reduced in consequence of the negligence including delays occasioned by a union ban, requiring final repair to be carried out in Japan. There was no ground to distinguish between industrial strikes and strikes which are essentially political in nature as submitted by the defendants. Such a distinction would be unrealistic especially since many strikes have both political and industrial objectives.

Commentary
Applied: *Cattle* v *Stockton Waterworks Co* (1875) LR 10 QB 453.

Caparo Industries plc v *Dickman* [1990] 2 WLR 358 House of Lords (Lord Bridge of Harwich, Lord Roskill, Lord Ackner, Lord Oliver of Aylmerton and Lord Jauncey of Tullichettle)

Auditor – duty of care

Facts

The plaintiff shareholder in Fidelity plc received the accounts audited by the defendants and at first purchased more shares and then made a successful takeover bid. The plaintiffs alleged that the accounts had been inaccurate and misleading: instead of showing a pre-tax profit for the year of some £1.2m, they should have revealed a loss of over £400,000. Had the defendants owed the plaintiffs a duty of care?

Held

They had not, either as shareholders or potential investors.

Lord Jauncey of Tullichettle:

'... the purpose of annual accounts, so far as members are concerned, is to enable them to question the past management of the company, to exercise their voting rights, if so advised, and to influence future policy and management. Advice to individual shareholders in relation to present or future investment in the company is not part of the statutory purpose of the preparation and distribution of the accounts ...

If the statutory accounts are prepared and distributed for certain limited purposes, can there nevertheless be imposed on auditors an additional common law duty to individual shareholders who choose to use them for another purpose without the prior knowledge of the auditors? The answer must be No. Use for that other purpose would no longer be ... use for the "very transaction" which Denning LJ in *Candler* v *Crane Christmas & Co* [1951] 2 KB 164 at 183 regarded as determinative of the scope of any duty of care. Only where the auditor was aware that the individual shareholder was likely to rely on the accounts for a particular purpose such as his present or future investment in or lending to the company would a duty of care arise. Such a situation does not obtain in the present case.

... it was argued that the relationship of the unwelcome bidder in a potential takeover situation was nearly as proximate to the auditor as was the relationship of a shareholder to whom the report was directed. Since I have concluded that the auditor owed no duty to an individual shareholder, it follows that this argument must also fail. The fact that a company may at a time when the auditor is preparing his report be vulnerable to a takeover bid cannot per se create a relationship of proximity between the auditor and the ultimate successful bidder. Not only is the auditor under no statutory duty to such a bidder but he will have reason at the material time to know neither of his identity nor of the terms of his bid. In this context the recent case of *Al Saudi Banque* v *Clark Pixley* [1990] 2 WLR 344 is in point. There Millett J held that the auditors of a company owed no duty of care to a bank which lent money to the company, regardless of whether the bank was an existing creditor or a potential one, because no sufficient proximity of relationship existed in either case between the auditor and the bank. I have no doubt that this case was correctly decided ...'

Commentary

See also *Mariola Marine Corporation* v *Lloyd's Register of Shipping, The Morning Watch* [1990] 1 Lloyd's Rep 547 and *Punjab National Bank* v *de Boinville* [1992] 1 WLR 1138.

CBS Songs Ltd v *Amstrad Consumer Electronics plc* [1988] AC 1013 House of Lords (Lord Keith of Kinkel, Lord Templeman, Lord Griffiths, Lord Oliver of Aylmerton and Lord Jauncey of Tullichettle)

Infringement of copyright – negligence

Facts
(See chapter 12 – Breach of Statutory Duty)

Held
The plaintiffs' appeal would be dismissed.

Lord Templeman:

'Finally, [the plaintiffs] submit that Amstrad committed the tort of negligence, that Amstrad owes to all owners of copyright a duty to take care not to cause or permit purchasers to infringe copyright or, alternatively, that Amstrad owes a duty to take care not to facilitate by the sale of their models or by their advertisement the infringement of copyright. My Lords, it is always easy to draft a proposition which is tailor-made to produce the desired result. Since *Anns* v *Merton London Borough Council* [1978] AC 728 put the floodgates on the jar, a fashionable plaintiff alleges negligence. The pleading assumes that we are all neighbours now, Pharisees and Samaritans alike, that foreseeability is a reflection of hindsight and that for every mischance in an accident-prone world someone solvent must be liable in damages. In *Governors of the Peabody Donation Fund* v *Sir Lindsay Parkinson & Co Ltd* [1985] AC 210 the plaintiffs were the authors of their own misfortune but sought to make the local authority liable for the consequences. In *Yuen Kun-yeu* v *A-G of Hong Kong* [1988] AC 175 the plaintiff chose to invest in a deposit-taking company which went into liquidation; the plaintiff sought to recover his deposit from the commissioner charged with the public duty of registering deposit-taking companies. In *Rowling* v *Takaro Properties Ltd* [1988] 2 WLR 418 a claim for damages in negligence was made against a minister of the Crown for declining in good faith to exercise in favour of the plaintiff a statutory discretion vested in the minister in the public interest. In *Hill* v *Chief Constable of West Yorkshire* [1988] 2 WLR 1049 damages against a police force were sought on behalf of the victim of a criminal. In the present proceedings damages and an injunction for negligence are sought against Amstrad for a breach of statutory duty which Amstrad did not commit and in which Amstrad did not participate. The rights of [the plaintiffs] are to be found in the 1956 Act and nowhere else. Under and by virtue of that Act Amstrad owed a duty not to infringe copyright and not to authorise an infringement of copyright. They did not owe a duty to prevent or discourage or warn against infringement.'

Chadwick v *British Transport Commission* [1967] 1 WLR 912 High Court (Waller J)

Negligence – nervous shock

Facts
Due to the horrific scenes which he witnessed while giving assistance to the victims of the Lewisham rail disaster, the plaintiff's husband (now deceased) suffered severe nervous shock. The disaster had occurred as a result of negligence for which the defendants were legally responsible.

Held
The test of liability is whether injury by nervous shock was reasonably foreseeable. The defendants having been negligent vis-a-vis the dead and injured passengers, they should have foreseen the likelihood of someone trying to rescue them. In the circumstances, it was clearly foreseeable that such a rescuer might be shocked by what he saw and the plaintiff should succeed.

Curran v *Northern Ireland Co-ownership Housing Association Ltd* [1987] AC 718 House of Lords (Lord Bridge of Harwich, Lord Fraser of Tullybelton, Lord Griffiths, Lord Ackner and Lord Oliver of Aylmerton)

Duty of care

Facts

The plaintiffs' predecessor in title built a house extension with the aid of an improvement grant provided by the Northern Ireland Housing Executive. The Housing (Northern Ireland) Order 1976 required the executive to be satisfied that a dwelling for which a grant was given met certain standards and, in particular, that the improvement work should be 'executed to the satisfaction of the Executive'. After the plaintiffs had purchased the house they discovered that the extension's construction was seriously defective.

Held

The executive owed no duty of care to the recipients of improvement grants (or to their successors in title) to ensure that grant-aided works had been properly executed.

Lord Bridge:

'... the order which must be considered in the instant case not only confers on the executive no powers of control of building operations analogous to those on which the decision in *Anns* v *Merton London Borough* depended, it confers no powers of such control at all. Once approval has been given to an application for an improvement grant, the executive has no powers under the order to control the building owner, still less the builder whom he chooses to employ, in the execution of the works. Its only power is to withhold payment of the grant, or of an instalment of the grant, if the works or the relevant part of the works have not been executed to its satisfaction ... to hold that the executive owes a duty of care to a building owner which it can only perform by refusing to pay him the grant it has approved seems to me an almost bizarre conclusion. In so far as the 1976 order imposes any duty on the executive to satisfy itself that the grant-aided works have been properly executed, as opposed to conferring a power to withhold payment if not so satisfied, it seems to me clear that the purpose of imposing any such duty is for the protection of the public revenue, not of the recipients of the grant or their successors in title. I can conceive of no reason why the legislature should be thought in this single provision to have intended to duplicate the kind of control of building operations which is entrusted in Northern Ireland, as in England, to local authorities so that persons interested in dwellings improved with the aid of a grant should enjoy a double protection.'

Commentary

Distinguished: *Anns* v *Merton London Borough Council* [1978] AC 728.

D & F Estates Ltd v *Church Commissioners for England* [1988] 3 WLR 368 House of Lords (Lord Bridge of Harwich, Lord Templeman, Lord Ackner, Lord Oliver of Aylmerton and Lord Jauncey of Tullichettle)

Negligence – extent of duty – economic loss

Facts

The third defendants (Wates) were the main contractors for the construction of a block of flats (Chelwood House) owned by the first defendants: they engaged a sub-contractor, whom they reasonably believed to be skilled and competent, to carry out the plastering, but he did the work negligently. Some 15 years after construction, and again some three years later, the plaintiffs, lessees and occupiers of one of the flats, found that the plaster in their flat was loose: they sued, inter alia, Wates, claiming the cost of remedial work already carried out and the estimated cost of future remedial work.

Held

Their claim could not succeed as (a) it was for pure economic loss and (b) Wates' only duty was to engage a competent contractor which they had done.

Lord Bridge of Harwich:

'In relation to both issues, it is instructive and, I think, necessary to consider two developments of the law in relation to a builder's liability in tort for defective premises which have been effected on the one hand by statute and on the other by judicial development of the law by the adaptation and application of common law principles to situations to which they had not previously been applied. Both these developments have taken place since 1970. Both have effected far-reaching changes in the law, at all events as it had been supposed to be before 1970. But the two developments have been markedly different in their scope and effect. The statutory development enacted by the Defective Premises Act 1972 effected clear and precise changes in the law imposing certain specific statutory duties subject to carefully defined limitations and exceptions. This change did not, of course, operate retrospectively. The common law developments have effected changes in the law which inevitably lack the kind of precision attainable by statute though limits have had to be and are still being worked out by decisions of the courts in a spate of ensuing litigation, including the instant case, and since our jurisprudence knows nothing of the American doctrine of "prospective overruling" and the law once pronounced authoratively by the courts here is deemed always to have been the law, the changes have full retrospective operation ...

In the instant case the only hidden defect was in the plaster. The only item pleaded as damage to other property was "cost of cleaning carpets and other possessions damaged or dirtied by falling plaster; £50". Once it appeared that the plaster was loose, any danger of personal injury or of further injury to other property could have been simply avoided by the timely removal of the defective plaster.

It seems to me clear that the cost of replacing the defective plaster itself, either as carried out ... or as intended to be carried out in future, was not an item of damage for which the builder of Chelwood House could possibly be made liable in negligence under the principle of *Donoghue* v *Stevenson* [1932] AC 562 or any legitimate development of that principle To make him so liable would be to impose on him for the benefit of those with whom he had no contractual relationship the obligation of one who warranted the quality of the plaster as regards materials, workmanship and fitness for purpose. I am glad to reach the conclusion that this is not the law, if only for the reason that a conclusion to the opposite effect would mean that the courts, in developing the common law, had gone much farther than the legislature were prepared to go in 1972 ... in making builders liable for defects in the quality of their work to all who subsequently acquire interests in buildings they have erected. The statutory duty imposed by the 1972 Act was confined to dwelling houses and limited to defects appearing within six years. The common law duty, if it existed, could not be so confined or so limited. I cannot help feeling that consumer protection is an area of law where legislation is much better left to the legislators ...

The submission in support of the appeal was put in three ways which amount, as it seems to me, to three alternative formulations of what is, in essence, the same proposition of law. Expressed in summary form the three formulations are (i) that Wates were vicariously liable for the negligence of their sub-contractor; (ii) that Wates as main contractors responsible for building Chelwood House owed a duty to future lessees and occupiers of flats to take reasonable care that the building should contain no hidden defects of the kind which might cause injury to persons or property and that this duty could not be delegated; (iii) that Wates as main contractors owed a duty of care to future lessees and occupiers of flats to supervise their sub-contractors to ensure that the sub-contracted work was not negligently performed so as to cause such defects.

It is trite law that the employer of an independent contractor is, in general, not liable for the negligence or other torts committed by the contractor in the course of the execution of the work. To this general rule there are certain well-established exceptions or apparent exceptions. Without enumerating them it is sufficient to say that it was accepted by counsel for the plaintiffs that the instant case could not be accommodated within any of the recognised and established categories by which the exceptions are classified ... If Wates are to be held liable for the negligent workmanship of their sub-contractors (assumed for this purpose to result in dangerously defective work) it must first be shown that in the circumstances that they had assumed a personal duty to all the world to ensure that Chelwood House should be free of dangerous defects. This was the assumption on which the judge proceeded when he said:

'The duty of care itself is of course not delegable.' Whence does this non-delegable duty arise? Counsel for the plaintiffs submits that it is a duty undertaken by any main contractor in the building industry who contracts to erect an entire building. I cannot agree because I cannot recognise any legal principle to which an assumption of duty can be related. Just as I may employ a building contractor to build me a house, so may the building contractor, subject to the terms of my contract with him, in turn employ another to undertake part of the work. If the mere fact of employing a contractor to undertake building work automatically involved the assumption by the employer of a duty of care to any person who may be injured by a dangerous defect in the work caused by the negligence of the contractor, this would obviously lead to absurd results. If the fact of employing a contractor does not involve the assumption of any such duty by the employer, then one who has himself contracted to erect a building assumes no such liability when he employs an apparently competent independent sub-contractor to carry out part of the work for him. The main contractor may, in the interests of the proper discharge for his own contractual obligations, exercise a greater or lesser degree of supervision over the work done by the sub-contractor. If in the course of supervision the main contractor in fact comes to know that the sub-contractor's work is being done in a defective and foreseeably dangerous way and if he condones that negligence on the part of the sub-contractor, he will no doubt make himself potentially liable for the consequences as a joint tortfeasor. But the judge made no finding against Wates of actual knowledge ...

The conclusion I reach is that Wates were under no liability to the plaintiffs for damage attributable to the negligence of their plastering sub-contractor in failing to follow the instructions of the manufacturer of the plaster they were using, but that in any event such damage could not have included the cost of renewing the plaster.'

Commentary

Not followed: *Anns* v *Merton London Borough Council* [1978] AC 728 and *Junior Books Ltd* v *Veitchi Co Ltd* [1983] AC 520.

Doubted: *Batty* v *Metropolitan Property Realizations Ltd* [1978] QB 554.

Followed in *Department of the Environment* v *Thomas Bates & Son* [1990] 3 WLR 457 and *Nitrigin Eireann Teoranta* v *Inco Alloys Ltd* [1992] 2 WLR 407.

Davis v *Radcliffe* [1990] 1 WLR 821 Privy Council (Lord Keith of Kinkel, Lord Brandon of Oakbrook, Lord Templeman, Lord Goff of Chieveley and Lord Lowry)

Licensing of banks – duty of care

Facts

By statute, and subject to the directions of the Isle of Man Finance Board, the Treasurer had power to issue, revoke and suspend banking licences: he issued such a licence to Savings and Investment Bank Ltd (SIB) with which the plaintiffs deposited money. SIB was wound up and it appeared that the plaintiffs would receive no more than a small dividend from the liquidator. The plaintiffs sued the Treasurer and the Board alleging negligence and/or breach of statutory duty: their claim was struck out: they appealed.

Held

Their appeal would be dismissed as the defendants had not owed them a duty of care.

Lord Goff of Chieveley:

'Their Lordships feel great sympathy for those who, like the [plaintiffs], have deposited substantial sums of money with a bank in the confident expectation that a bank is a safe place for their money, only to find that the bank has become insolvent and that the most they can expect to receive is a small dividend payable in its winding up. But, when it is sought to make some third person responsible in negligence for the loss suffered through the bank's default, the question whether that third person owes a duty of care to the depositor has to be decided in accordance with the established principles of the law of negligence. In the present case the [judge], having reviewed the authorities with care, concluded that neither the members of the Finance Board nor the Treasurer owed any such duty to the [plaintiffs], and so struck out their statement of case as disclosing no reasonable cause of action. Their Lordships are in no doubt that [he] was right to reach that conclusion, substantially for the reasons given by him. Indeed they are in agreement with him that the present case is, for all practical purposes, indistinguishable from the decision of their Lordships' Board in *Yuen Kun-yeu* v *A-G of Hong Kong* [1987] 3 WLR 776 ... The [judge] also dismissed, in a terse paragraph, an alternative plea based on breach of statutory duty, on the principle set out in *Cutler* v *Wandsworth Stadium Ltd* [1949] AC 398. Their Lordships entirely agree with [his] conclusion on this point, which was plainly right.'

Department of the Environment v *Thomas Bates & Son Ltd* [1990] 3 WLR 457
House of Lords (Lord Keith of Kinkel, Lord Brandon of Oakbrook, Lord Ackner, Lord Oliver of Aylmerton and Lord Jauncey of Tullichettle)

Negligence – economic loss

Facts
The plaintiffs were underlessees of the upper storeys of an office block built by the defendants in 1970 and 1971. In 1981 and 1982 it was discovered that low-strength concrete had been used in the pillars which, although they could support the existing load, could not support the design load safely. The plaintiffs strengthened the pillars and sought to recover the cost from the defendants; the trial judge found, inter alia, that there had been no imminent danger to the health or safety of the plaintiffs' employees or the public.

Held
The plaintiffs could not succeed as the cost of the remedial work was purely economic loss.

Lord Keith of Kinkel:

'The foundation of the plaintiffs' case is *Anns* v *Merton London Borough* [1977] 2 WLR 1024 ... It has been held by this House in *Murphy* v *Brentwood DC* [1990] 3 WLR 414 that *Anns* was wrongly decided and should be departed from, by reason of the erroneous views there expressed as to the scope of any duty of care owed to purchasers of houses by local authorities when exercising the powers conferred on them for the purpose of securing compliance with building regulations. The process of reasoning by which the House reached its conclusion necessarily included close examination of the position of the builder who was primarily responsible, through lack of care in the construction process, for the presence of defects in the building. It was the unanimous view that, while the builder would be liable under the principle of *Donoghue* v *Stevenson* [1932] AC 562 in the event of the defect, before it had been discovered, causing physical injury to persons or damage to property other than the building itself, there was no sound basis in principle for holding him liable for the pure economic loss suffered by a purchaser who discovered the defect, however such discovery might come about, and who was required to expend money in order to make the building safe and suitable for its intended purpose.

In the present case it is clear that the loss suffered by the plaintiffs is pure economic loss. At the time the plaintiffs carried out the remedial work on the concrete pilars the building was not unsafe by reason of the defective construction of these pillars. It did, however, suffer from a defect of quality which made the plaintiffs' lease less valuable than it would otherwise have been, in respect the the building could not be loaded up to its design capacity unless any occupier who wished so to load it had incurred the expenditure necessary for the strengthening of the pillars. It was wholly uncertain whether during the currency of their lease the plaintiffs themselves would ever be likely to require to load the building up to its design capacity, but a purchaser from them might well have wanted to do so. Such a purchaser, faced with the need to strengthen the pillars, would obviously have paid less for the lease than if they had been sound. This underlines the purely economic character of the plaintiffs' loss. To hold in favour of the plaintiffs would involve a very significant extension of the doctrine of *Anns* so as to cover the situation where there existed no damage to the building and no imminent danger to personal safety or health. If *Anns* was correctly decided, such an extension could reasonably be regarded as entirely logical. The undesirability of such an extension, for the reasons stated in in *Murphy*, formed an important part of the grounds which led to the conclusion that *Anns* was not correctly decided. That conclusion must lead inevitably to the result that the plaintiffs' claim fails.'

Donoghue (or McAlister) v *Stevenson* [1932] AC 562 House of Lords (Lord Buckmaster, Lord Atkin, Lord Tomlin, Lord Thankerton and Lord Macmillan)

Negligence – duty of care

Facts

The appellant went, together with her friend, to a cafe, where the friend purchased a bottle of ginger beer which was sealed and in opaque glass. Both drank from the ginger beer before realising that it contained a dead snail. The appellant suffered gastro-enteritis and shock as a result and sued the manufacturer of the ginger beer for damages on the ground that he had been negligent in the production of the product. The only question before the House of Lords was whether the respondent (manufacturer) owed a duty of care to the appellant.

Held (Lord Buckmaster and Lord Tomlin dissenting)

The respondent owed the appellant a duty of care, although he did not know the product to be dangerous and no contractual relationship existed between the parties. On proof of the facts the appellant would be entitled to damages.

Lord Atkin:

'You must take reasonable care to avoid acts or omissions which you can reasonably foresee would be likely to injure your neighbour. Who then, in law, is my neighbour? The answer seems to be – persons who are so closely and directly affected by my act that I ought reasonably to have them in contemplation as being so affected when I am directing my mind to the acts or omissions which are called in question.'

Lord Macmillan:

'In the daily contacts of social and business life, human beings are thrown into, or place themselves in, an infinite variety of relations with their fellows; and the law can refer only to the standards of the reasonable man in order to determine whether any particular relation gives rise to a duty to take care, as between those who stand in that relation to each other. The grounds of action may be as various and manifold as human errancy; and the conception of legal responsibility may develop in adaptation to altering social conditions and standards. The criterion of judgment must adjust and adapt itself to the changing circumstances of life. The categories of negligence are never closed.'

Dulieu v *White & Sons* [1901] 2 KB 669 High Court (Kennedy and Phillimore JJ)

Negligence – nervous shock

Facts

The plaintiff was standing behind the bar of her husband's public house when the defendant's employee negligently drove his van through the wall. The plaintiff suffered nervous shock with a resultant miscarriage.

Held

The plaintiff had a good cause of action as a plaintiff is entitled to recover if the nervous shock is caused by being put in fear of immediate physical injury to himself, due to the negligence of the defendant.

Commentary

Applied in *Janvier* v *Sweeney* [1919] 2 KB 316.

East Suffolk Rivers Catchment Board v *Kent* [1941] AC 74 House of Lords (Viscount Simon LC, Lord Atkin, Lord Thankerton, Lord Romer and Lord Porter)

Negligence – repair of sea-wall

Facts

The respondent's low-lying land was flooded when high tides caused breaches of a sea-wall which the appellant Board had power to repair under statute, but no duty to do so. The Board did attempt repairs, but so inefficiently that it took far longer than it should have done had they acted with reasonable efficiency.

Held (Lord Atkin dissenting)

The respondent's claim was ill-founded.

Lord Romer:

> 'Where a statutory authority is entrusted with a mere power, it cannot be made liable for any damage sustained by a member of the public by reason of a failure to exercise that power. If, in the exercise of that discretion, they embark upon an execution of that power, the only duty they owe to any member of the public is not thereby to add to the damages which he would have suffered if they had done nothing.'

Commentary

Distinguished in *Dutton* v *Bognor Regis Urban District Council* [1972] 2 WLR 299.

Emeh v *Kensington and Chelsea and Westminster Area Health Authority* [1985] 2 WLR 233 Court of Appeal (Waller, Slade and Purchas LJJ)

Negligence – unwanted pregnancy

Facts

At the same time as she was having an abortion, the plaintiff, a mother of three normal children, was sterilised to prevent further pregnancies. The sterilisation was performed negligently and she became pregnant again, a fact that she did not discover until she was some 20 weeks into the pregnancy. As she did not want any more operations she decided against another abortion and she gave birth to a child which was congenitally abnormal. The appeal concerned the damages to which the plaintiff was entitled.

Held

The plaintiff's entitlement extended to any reasonably foreseeable financial loss directly caused by her unexpected pregnancy. Accordingly, she was entitled to damages for loss of future earnings, maintenance of the child up to trial, maintenance of the child in the future, the plaintiff's pain and suffering up to the time of the trial and future loss of amenity and pain and suffering, including the extra care that the child would require. The plaintiff's decision not to have an abortion was not a novus actus interveniens or a failure to mitigate damage, because the health authority, by the negligence for which it was itself responsible, had confronted the plaintiff with the very dilemma of whether to have the child or an abortion which she had sought to avoid by having herself sterilised. Furthermore, there was no rule of public policy which prevented the plaintiff from recovering in full the financial damage sustained by her as the result of the negligent failure to perform the sterilisation operation properly, regardless of whether the child was healthy or abnormal.

Commentary
Doubted: *Udale* v *Bloomsbury Area Health Authority* [1983] 1 WLR 1098.
　　Applied in *Allen* v *Bloomsbury Health Authority* [1993] 1 All ER 651, above.

Esso Petroleum Co Ltd v *Mardon* [1976] 2 WLR 583 Court of Appeal (Lord Denning MR, Ormrod and Shaw LJJ)

Negligence – pre-contract negotiations

Facts
The defendant took a lease of a petrol filling-station from the plaintiffs, relying on the plaintiffs' representations as to the expected turnover. These representations turned out to be grossly inaccurate and the defendant suffered loss.

Held
The plaintiffs' statements were, inter alia, a negligent misrepresentation for which the defendant could recover damages in tort. The plaintiffs, though not in the business of giving advice, were possessed of the special knowledge or expertise necessary to give the information requested.

Ormrod LJ:

'There is no magic in the phrase "special relationship". It means no more than a relationship, the nature of which is such that one party, for a variety of reasons, will be regarded by the law as under a duty of care to another.'

Commentary
Applied: *Hedley Byrne & Co Ltd* v *Heller and Partners Ltd* [1963] 3 WLR 101.
　　Applied in *Batty* v *Metropolitan Property Realizations Ltd* [1978] 2 WLR 500.

Gran Gelato Ltd v *Richcliff (Group) Ltd* [1992] 1 All ER 865 High Court Sir Donald Nicholls V-C

Whether solicitor acting for seller owes a duty of care when answering preliminary inquiries

Facts
The plaintiffs acquired an underlease from Richcliff which was expressed to be for 10 years. The plaintiffs sent pre-contract enquiries to Richcliff's solicitors, the second defendants, which, inter alia, asked whether there were any 'rights affecting the ... superior leasehold titles which would ... in any way inhibit the enjoyment of the property by the tenant in accordance with the terms of the present draft

lease'. The second defendants replied 'Not to the lessor's knowledge'. In fact the head leases contained redevelopment break clauses which, when exercised, had the effect of reducing the term of the underlease to five years. The head lessors later exercised the break clause and the plaintiffs brought a claim for damages for misrepresentation against Richcliff and their solicitors.

Held

The plaintiffs had established a good cause of action for damages against Richcliff under s2(1) of the Misrepresentation Act 1967 but the claim against the solicitors would be dismissed. Sir Donald Nicholls V-C said that the foreseeability requirement was satisfied and that there was a close and direct relationship between the plaintiffs and the second defendants. But a vital factor in persuading his Lordship to conclude that the second defendants did not owe a duty of care to the plaintiffs was that in making the representations the second defendants were acting as agents for Richcliff. This was not, however, enough in itself to displace the existence of a duty of care because the fact that the person making the representation was acting for a known principal does not necessarily negative the existence of a duty of care. A further vital factor which persuaded him to conclude that no duty of care was owed was that the second defendants were solicitors. He held that in 'normal conveyancing transactions solicitors who are acting for a seller do not in general owe to the would-be buyer a duty of care when answering enquiries before contract or the like'. His Lordship identified three factors to support his conclusion. The first was the context in which the representations were made (a contract for the sale of an interest in land). The second was that the buyer has a remedy against the seller in respect of any misrepresentations in the answers given by his solicitors. The third was that to impose a duty of care upon the solicitors would be to expose them to conflicting duties: one owed to their client and the other to his contracting party. His Lordship did not accept this argument in its entirety but concluded that 'in general, in a case where the principal himself owes a duty of care to the third party, the existence of a further duty of care, owed by the agent to the third party, is not necessary for the reasonable protection of the latter'. It was true that this conclusion might lead to a buyer being left without a remedy in the situation where the seller becomes insolvent but the risk of insolvency is 'an ordinary risk of everyday living'.

Sir Donald Nicholls V-C added two caveats to his judgment. The first was that there will be special cases where the general rule does not apply and a duty of care will be owed by a solicitor to a buyer, for example where the solicitor steps outside his normal role and assumes a responsibility towards the buyer (see *Al-Kandari* v *JR Brown* [1988] QB 655). The second was that a solicitor does owe a duty to his own client when answering enquiries before contract and, if the client is exposed to a claim for damages as a result of his carelessness, the solicitor will be liable to indemnify his client on well-established principles.

Harris v *Wyre Forest District Council* see *Smith* v *Eric S Bush*

Hedley Byrne & Co Ltd v *Heller & Partners* [1963] 3 WLR 101 House of Lords (Lord Reid, Lord Morris of Borth-y-Gest, Lord Hodson, Lord Devlin and Lord Pearce)

Negligence – duty of care in relation to information or advice

Facts

The appellants, an advertising agency, wished to make enquiries about the financial reliability of one of their customers, Easipower Ltd. Their bankers made enquiries of the respondents, Easipower's bankers. The respondents replied, first orally then in writing, stating that Easipower Ltd was financially sound, although this information was given 'without responsibility'. The appellants relied on this advice which proved to be inaccurate and they suffered considerable losses when Easipower went into liquidation.

Held

A duty of care in making statements may arise when the parties are in a 'special relationship'. But the appeal was dismissed because the respondents had excluded their responsibility.

Lord Hodson:

'... if in a sphere where a person is so placed that others could reasonably rely on his judgment or on his skill or on his ability to make careful enquiry, such person takes it on himself to give information or advice to, or allows his information or advice to be passed on to, another person who, as he knows or should know, will place reliance on it, then a duty of care will arise.'

Lord Devlin:

'A defendant who is given a car to overhaul and repair if necessary is liable to the injured driver if (a) he overhauls and repairs it negligently and tells the driver that it is safe when it is not; (b) he overhauls it and negligently finds it not to be in need of repair and tells the driver that it is safe when it is not; (c) he negligently omits to overhaul it at all and tells the driver that it is safe when it is not. It would be absurd in any of these cases to argue that the proximate cause of the driver's injury was not what the defendant did or failed to do, but his negligent statement on the faith of which the driver drove the car and for which he could not recover.'

Lord Pearce:

'The reason for some divergence between the law of negligence in word and that of negligence in act is clear. Negligence in word creates problems different from those of negligence in act. Words are more volatile than deeds. They travel fast and far afield. They are used without being expended and take effect in combination with innumerable facts and other words ... Damage by negligent acts to persons or property on the other hand is more visible and obvious, its limits are more easily defined ...'

Commentary

Distinguished in *Dutton* v *Bognor Regis Urban District Council* [1972] 2 WLR 299.

Hemmens v *Wilson Browne* [1993] 4 All ER 826 High Court (Judge Moseley QC)

Applicability of *Ross* v *Caunters* where testator or donor still alive

Facts

P instructed a solicitor to draft a document giving the plaintiff the right to call on P at any time in the future to pay her £110,000. The document as drafted did not confer any enforceable rights on the plaintiff. Some weeks later the plaintiff called upon P to fulfil his promise and he refused. The plaintiff sued the solicitor claiming (inter alia) that he owed her a duty of care and was in breach of that duty.

Held

Although the solicitor's carelessness had resulted in a document being drafted which gave the plaintiff no enforceable rights, and it was reasonably foreseeable that the plaintiff would suffer damage from such carelessness and there was a sufficient degree of proximity between the solicitor and the plaintiff, it would not be fair, just or reasonable for a duty of care to be imposed because P was still alive and could rectify the situation and could also sue the solicitor. Hence it was not necessary for the law to give the plaintiff a remedy as it was in *Ross* v *Caunters*.

Henderson* v *Merrett Syndicates Ltd [1994] 3 WLR 761 House of Lords (Lords Keith, Goff, Browne-Wilkinson, Mustill and Nolan)

Liability for pure economic loss – co-existence of tort and contract

Facts

The plaintiffs, who were underwriting members ('Names') at Lloyds, brought proceedings against the defendant underwriting agents, alleging that the defendants had been negligent in their conduct of the Names' business and were also in breach of contract. In fact, the House in *Henderson* decided some five appeals with slightly differing factual situations, but made several clear statements of the law.

Held

The House of Lords held that a duty of care was owed by the underwriting agents to the Names, and that the existence of such a duty was not excluded by the existence of a contractual relationship.

Lord Goff:

'From … *Hedley Byrne*, we can derive some understanding of the breadth of the principle underlying the case. We can see that it rests upon a relationship between the parties, which may be general or specific to the particular transaction, and which may or may not be contractual in nature. All of their Lordships spoke in terms of one party having assumed or undertaken a responsibility towards the other. …

In subsequent cases concerned with liability under the *Hedley Byrne* principle in respect of negligent misstatements, the question has frequently arisen whether the plaintiff falls within the category of persons to whom the maker of the statement owes a duty of care. In seeking to contain that category of persons within reasonable bounds, there has been some tendency on the part of the courts to criticise the concept of "assumption of responsibility" as being "unlikely to be a helpful or realistic test in most cases" (see *Smith* v *Eric S Bush* [1990] 1 AC 831, 864, 865, per Lord Griffiths; and see also *Caparo Industries plc* v *Dickman* [1990] 2 AC 605, 628, per Lord Roskill). However, at least in cases such as the present, in which the same problem does not arise, there seems to be no reason why recourse should not be had to the concept, which appears after all to have been adopted, in one form or another, by all of their Lordships in *Hedley Byrne* [1964] AC 465 …

Approached as a matter of principle, therefore, it is right to attribute to that assumption of responsibility, together with its concomitant reliance, a tortious liability, and then to inquire whether or not that liability is excluded by the contract because the latter is inconsistent with it. This is the reasoning which Oliver J, as I understand it, found implicit, where not explicit, in the speeches in *Hedley Byrne*. With his conclusion I respectfully agree. But even if I am wrong in this, I am of the opinion that this House should now, if necessary, develop the principle of assumption of responsibility as stated in *Hedley Byrne* to its logical conclusion so as to make it clear that a tortious duty of care may arise not only in cases where the relevant services are rendered gratuitously, but also where they are rendered under a contract.'

Hill* v *Chief Constable of West Yorkshire [1989] AC 53 House of Lords (Lord Keith of Kinkel, Lord Brandon of Oakbrook, Lord Templeman, Lord Oliver of Aylmerton and Lord Goff of Chieveley)

Negligence – duty of care

Facts

A claim brought on behalf of the estate of Jacqueline Hill for damages under the Law Reform (Miscellaneous Provisions) Act 1934, against the Chief Constable of an area where the 'Yorkshire Ripper' had murdered many women, Jacqueline Hill being his last victim. The Chief Constable sought to strike out the claim on the ground that the statement of claim did not disclose a cause of action and the trial judge decided in his favour.

Held

The proceedings had been properly struck out.

Lord Keith of Kinkel:

'It has been said almost too frequently to require repetition that foreseeability of likely harm is not in itself a sufficient test of liability in negligence. Some further ingredient is invariably needed to establish the requisite proximity of relationship between the plaintiff and defendant, and all the circumstances of the case must be carefully considered and analysed in order to ascertain whether such an ingredient is present. The nature of the ingredient will be found to vary in a number of different categories of decided cases ...

It is plain that vital characteristics which were present in the *Dorset Yacht* case and which led to the imposition of liability are here lacking. Sutcliffe was never in the custody of the police force. Miss Hill was one of a vast number of the female general public who might be at risk from his activities but was at no special distinctive risk in relation to them, unlike the owners of yachts moored off Brownsea Island in relation to the foreseeable conduct of the borstal boys. It appears from the ... speech of Lord Diplock in the *Dorset Yacht* case that in his view no liability would rest on a prison authority, which carelessly allowed the escape of an habitual criminal, for damage which he subsequently caused, not in the course of attempting to make good his getaway, to persons at special risk, but in further pursuance of his general criminal career to the person or property of members of the general public. The same rule must apply as regards failure to recapture the criminal before he had time to resume his career. In the case of an escaped criminal his identity and description are known. In the instant case the identity of the wanted criminal was at the material time unknown and it is not averred that any full or clear description of him was ever available. The alleged negligence of the police consists in a failure to discover his identity. But, if there is no general duty of care owed to individual members of the public by the responsible authorities to prevent the escape of a known criminal or to recapture him, there cannot reasonably be imposed on any police force a duty of care similarly owed to identify and apprehend an unknown one. Miss Hill cannot for this purpose be regarded as a person at special risk simply because she was young and female. Where the class of potential victims of a particular habitual criminal is a large one the precise size of it cannot in principle affect the issue. All householders are potential victims of a habitual burglar, and all females those of a habitual rapist. The conclusion must be that although there existed reasonable foreseeability of likely harm to such as Miss Hill if Sutcliffe were not identified and apprehended, there is absent from the case any such ingredient or characteristic as led to the liability of the Home Office in the *Dorset Yacht* case. Nor is there present any additional characteristic such as might make up the deficiency. The circumstances of the case are therefore not capable of establishing a duty of care owed towards Miss Hill by the West Yorkshire police.

That is sufficient for the disposal of the appeal. But in my opinion there is another reason why an action for damages in negligence should not lie against the police in circumstances such as those of the present case, and that is public policy ... I consider that ... the police were immune from an action of this kind on grounds similar to those which in *Rondel* v *Worsley* were held to render a barrister immune from actions for negligence in his conduct of proceedings in court.'

Commentary

Applied: *Rondel* v *Worlsey* [1969] 1 AC 191.

Applied in *Clough* v *Bussan* [1990] 1 All ER 431, *Hughes* v *National Union of Mineworkers* [1991] 4 All ER 278 and *Alexandrou* v *Oxford* [1993] 4 All ER 328.

Distinguished: *Home Office* v *Dorset Yacht Co Ltd* [1970] 2 WLR 1140.

Holt v *Payne Skillington* (1995) The Times 22 December Court of Appeal (Hirst and Peter Gibson LJJ, Forbes J)

Duty of care arising between parties to a contract – wider obligations possible in tortious duty

Facts
The plaintiffs purchased a property, and the first defendants acted as solicitors and the second defendants as estate agents in respect of the purchase. The plaintiffs alleged that both defendants were in breach of duty in both contract and tort. At first instance the judge held (inter alia) that the plaintiffs could not succeed against the second defendants in contract but could succeed in tort. The second defendants appealed.

Held
That where a duty of care in tort arose between parties to a contract, wider obligations could be imposed by the duty of care in tort than those arising under the contract. There was no reason in principle why a *Hedley Byrne* type of duty could not arise where the same parties entered into a contractual relationship involving more limited obligations that those imposed by the tortious duty of care.

Commentary
In *Aiken* v *Stewart Wrightson Members Agency Ltd* [1995] 1 WLR 1281 it was held that a concurrent duty of care in tort could fall short of a duty imposed by the express terms of a contract.

Home Office v *Dorset Yacht Co Ltd* [1970] 2 WLR 1140 House of Lords (Lord Reid, Lord Morris of Borth-y-Gest, Viscount Dilhorne, Lord Pearson and Lord Diplock)

Negligence – escape of trainees

Facts
The appellants were responsible for the operation and running of a Borstal institution. Several inmates were on a training exercise under the supervision of three Borstal officers when they escaped one night and damaged the respondents' yacht which was moored nearby. Did the appellants owe any duty of care to the yacht owners?

Held (Viscount Dilhorne dissenting)
Yes. The appellants should reasonably have foreseen that if they failed to exercise reasonable care in controlling and supervising the boys in their charge, damage of the kind which occurred was likely to be caused. There was no ground in public policy for granting the appellants immunity from liability in negligence.

Commentary
Applied in *Anns* v *Merton London Brough Council* [1978] AC 728.
    See also *Peabody Donation Fund (Governors)* v *Sir Lindsay Parkinson & Co Ltd* [1984] 3 WLR 953.

Hughes v *National Union of Mineworkers* [1991] 4 All ER 278 High Court (May J)

Negligence – duty of care

Facts

On duty at a colliery during a strike, the plaintiff police officer sustained injuries when the police were attacked by some 4,000 mineworkers. The plaintiff alleged that the officer in charge had been negligent in the deployment of the police, but the chief constable sought to have his action struck out on the ground that he had not owed the plaintiff a duty of care.

Held

The plaintiff's claim was bound to fail and it would be struck out.

May J:

'The plaintiff was one of a number of police officers deployed to control serious public disorder by a vast number of picketing miners. He was injured by some of those disorderly miners. Having considered *Hill* v *Chief Constable of West Yorkshire* [1988] 2 All ER 238 on the one hand and *Knightley* v *Johns* [1982] 1 All ER 851 and *Rigby* v *Chief Constable of Northamptonshire* [1985] 2 All ER 985 on the other, in my judgment, as a matter of public policy, if senior police officers charged with the task of deploying what may or may not be an adequate force of officers to control serious public disorder are to be potentially liable to individual officers under their command if those individuals are injured by attacks from rioters, that would be significantly detrimental to the control of public order.

It will no doubt often happen that in such circumstances critical decisions have to be made with little or no time for considered thought and where many individual officers may be in some danger of physical injury of one kind or another. It is not, I consider, in the public interest that those decisions should generally be the potential target of a negligence claim if rioters do injure an individual officer, since the fear of such a claim would be likely to affect the decisions to the prejudice of the very task which the decisions are intended to advance. Accordingly, in my judgment, public policy requires that senior police officers should not generally be liable to their subordinates who may be injured by rioters or the like for on the spot operational decisions taken in the course of attempts to control serious public disorder. That, in my judgment, should be the general rule in cases of policing serious public disorders. There may be exceptions where the plaintiff's injuries arise, as in *Knightley* v *Johns*, from specifically identified antecedent negligence or specific breach of identified regulations, orders or instructions by a particular senior officer. There is no such specific allegation in the statement of claim in this case and none has been suggested in argument. It follows that the plaintiff's claim against the [chief constable] taken at its pleaded highest is bound to fail and that the claim should be struck out.'

James McNaughton Papers Group Ltd v *Hicks Anderson & Co* [1991] 2 WLR 641
Court of Appeal (Neill, Nourse and Balcombe LJJ)

Negligence – accountants' duty of care

Facts

The plaintiffs were negotiating an agreed takeover of a rival company which was in financial difficulty. The chairman of the target company had asked the defendants, the target company's accountants, to prepare draft accounts as quickly as possible so that they could be used in the negotiations for the takeover. After the takeover had been completed, the plaintiffs alleged that they had relied on the draft accounts (which, they said, contained certain discrepancies) and also upon a statement made by a representative of the defendants at a meeting with the plaintiffs to the effect that, as a result of rationalisation, the target company was breaking even or doing a little worse.

Held

The plaintiffs' action for damages for negligence could not succeed. On the facts no duty of care was owed by the defendants because: (i) the accounts were produced only for the vendor; (ii) the accounts were in draft form; (ii) the defendants were not participants in the negotiating process; (iv) the target company was, to the knowledge of the plaintiffs, in poor financial health; (v) the parties were experienced businessmen and, in particular, the plaintiffs had their own independent advisers; and (vi) the statement of the representative of the defendants at the meeting with the plaintiffs was a very general one and the defendants could not have known that the plaintiffs would rely on the statement without making further inquiry or seeking further advice.

In deciding whether or not a duty of care arose in a case in which a plaintiff has suffered economic loss as a result of reliance upon a negligent statement Neill LJ identified the following relevant factors: (i) the precise purpose for which the statement was made; (ii) the purpose for which the statement was communicated; (iii) the relationship between the adviser, advisee and any relevant third party; (iv) the size of any class to which the advisee belongs; (v) the state of knowledge of the adviser; and (vi) the reliance by the advisee (including whether the advisee was entitled to rely on the statement, whether he did so rely, whether he should have relied upon his own judgment and whether he should have sought and obtained independent advice). Two further points are worthy of note. The first is that this case underlines the unwillingness of the courts to extend the scope of liability beyond the person directly intended by the maker of the statement to act upon it. The second is that Neill LJ stated that *Caparo Industries plc* v *Dickman*, above, had not been affected by anything said by their Lordships in *Murphy* v *Brentwood District Council*, below.

Jones v *Department of Employment* [1988] 2 WLR 493 Court of Appeal (Slade, Glidewell LJJ and Caulfield J)

Adjudication officer's alleged negligence

Facts
The plaintiff's claim for unemployment benefit was disallowed by the adjudication officer but allowed by the appeal tribunal. The plaintiff sought damages alleging negligence on the part of the adjudication officer.

Held
His action could not succeed as, inter alia, the adjudication officer had not owed the plaintiff a duty of care.

Glidewell LJ:

> 'The question ... is whether, taking all [the] circumstances into account, it is just and reasonable that the adjudication officer should be under a duty of care at common law to the claimant to benefit. Having regard to the non-judicial nature of the adjudication officer's responsibilities, and in particular to the fact that the statutory framework provides a right of appeal which, if a point of law arises, can eventually bring the matter to this court, it is my view that the adjudication officer is not under any common law duty of care. In other words ... his decision is not susceptible of challenge at common law unless it be shown that he is guilty of misfeasance.
>
> Indeed, in my view, it is a general principle that, if a government department or officer, charged with the making of decisions whether certain payments should be made, is subject to a statutory right of appeal against his decisions, he owed no duty of care in private law. Misfeasance apart, he is only susceptible in public law to judicial review or to the right of appeal provided by the statute under which he makes his decision.'

Junior Books Ltd v *Veitchi Co Ltd* [1982] 3 WLR 477 House of Lords (Lord Fraser of Tullybelton, Lord Russell of Killowen, Lord Keith of Kinkel, Lord Roskill and Lord Brandon of Oakbrook)

Duty of care: proximity

Facts

The plaintiff engaged building contractors to build a factory at Grangemouth. The defendant was a specialist company engaged by the main contractors to lay composition flooring in the factory. P claimed that D was negligent in laying the floor with the result that it was defective and had to be replaced. There was no contractual relationship between P and D and P claimed damages in negligence against D, the damages consisting mainly of the direct and indirect cost of replacing the floor. Assuming D had been negligent in laying a defective floor, was D liable for economic loss caused to P which was not related to any injury to P's person or property?

Held

The economic loss would be recoverable, notwithstanding that it was 'pure' economic loss, unrelated to injury to the person or to property.

Lord Roskill:

'I therefore ask first whether there was the requisite degree of proximity so as to give rise to the relevant duty of care ... I regard the following facts as of crucial importance in requiring an affirmative answer to that question (1) the appellants were nominated sub-contractors; (2) the appellants were specialists in flooring; (3) the appellants knew what products were required by the respondents and their main contractors and specialised in the production of those products; (4) the appellants alone were responsible for the composition and construction of the flooring; (5) the respondents relied on the appellants' skill and experience; (6) the appellants as nominated sub-contractors must have known that the respondents relied on their skill and experience; (7) the relationship between the parties was as close as it could be short of actual privity of contract; (8) the appellants must be taken to have known that if they did the work negligently (as it must be assumed that they did) the resulting defects would at some time require remedying by the respondents expending money on the remedial measures as a consequence of which the respondents would suffer financial or economic loss ... On the facts I have just stated, I see nothing whatever to restrict the duty of care arising from the proximity of which I have spoken ... I see no reason why what was called during the argument "damage to the pocket" simpliciter should be disallowed when "damage to the pocket" coupled with physical damage has hitherto always been allowed. I do not think that this development, if development it may be, will lead to untoward consequences.'

Commentary

Applied: *Anns* v *Merton London Borough Council* [1977] 2 WLR 1024; *Home Office* v *Dorset Yacht Co Ltd* [1970] 2 WLR 1140.

   Distinguished in *Nitrigin Eireann Teoranta* v *Inco Alloys Ltd* [1992] 2 WLR 407.

King v *Liverpool City Council* [1986] 1 WLR 890 Court of Appeal (Purchas and Nicholls LJJ and Caulfield J)

Negligence – act of third party

Facts

Liverpool City Council were the owners of a flat occupied by the plaintiff. She informed the council of the fact that the flat immediately above her own was vacant and requested it be secured against trespassers. Trespassers entered the flat and damaged the pipes causing the plaintiff's property to be flooded. The plaintiff claimed damages in nuisance and negligence against the council.

Held

The duty of care which was owed to the plaintiff had to be assessed by reference to the individual circumstances of the case. Even if the flat had been secured it would not have been possible to prevent damage by flooding. The water supply could not be cut off without affecting the other flats. Therefore there was no effective measure which the council could have taken to prevent damage of this kind. The council did not therefore owe a duty to prevent trespassers from entering the premises and doing this kind of damage.

Commentary

Followed: *P Perl (Exporters) Ltd* v *Camden London Borough Council* [1983] 3 WLR 769.

Kirkham v *Chief Constable of the Greater Manchester Police* [1990] 2 WLR 987 Court of Appeal (Lloyd, Farquharson LJJ and Sir Denys Buckley)

Prisoner's suicide – duty of care

Facts

When a man was arrested, his wife, the plaintiff, told the police that he had recently attempted to commit suicide. At the police station, appropriate precautions were taken but, when the man was remanded, the police failed to inform the prison authorities of his suicidal tendencies. At the remand centre he was treated like a normal prisoner: he hanged himself in his cell: the plaintiff claimed damages.

Held

She was entitled to succeed as the police, by failing to pass on the relevant information, had been in breach of their duty of care. The maxims volenti non fit injuria and ex turpi causa non oritur actio did not afford the police a good defence.

Lamb v *Camden London Borough Council* [1981] 2 WLR 1038 Court of Appeal (Lord Denning MR, Oliver and Watkins LJJ)

Damage – foreseeability

Facts

In 1972, the plaintiff let her house while she spent some time abroad. In 1973 an employee of the defendants negligently fractured a water main outside her house which flooded the foundations and caused the house to subside. The tenants consequently moved out and squatters moved in during 1974, though they were subsequently evicted. In 1975, there was a second 'invasion' by squatters who ripped out fixtures in the house and the central heating. The plaintiff brought an action against the defendant council for negligence, including a claim for the damage which had been caused to the house by the squatters.

Held

The plaintiff could not recover damages for the actions of the squatters, since they were not reasonably foreseeable.

Oliver LJ:

'Few things are less certainly predictable than human behaviour, and if one is asked whether in any given situation a human being may behave idiotically, irrationally or even criminally the answer must always be that that is a possibility, for every society has its proportion of idiots and criminals. It cannot be said that you cannot foresee the possibility that people will do stupid or criminal acts, because people are constantly doing stupid or criminal acts. But the question is not what is foreseeable merely as a possibility but what would the reasonable man actually foresee if he thought about it ... If the instant case is approached as a case of negligence and one asks the question, did the defendants owe a duty not to break a water pipe so as to cause the plaintiff's house to be invaded by squatters a year later, the tenuousness of the linkage between act and result becomes apparent. I confess that I find it inconceivable that the reasonable man, wielding his pick in the road in 1973, could be said reasonably to foresee that his puncturing of a water main would fill the plaintiff's house with uninvited guests in 1974.'

Lancashire & Cheshire Association of Baptist Churches v *Howard & Seddon Partnership* [1993] 3 All ER 467 High Court (Judge Michael Kershaw QC)

Co-existence of tort and contract – pure economic loss

Facts

The plaintiffs wished to build a new sanctuary for their church and contracted with the defendant firm of architects to design the sanctuary and supervise its building. The plaintiffs alleged that the completed sanctuary contained defects in design as regards ventilation and condensation, and claimed damages for breach of contract and negligence. At the date of issue of the writ the plaintiffs' claim in contract was statute-barred, but the plaintiffs claimed that the damage had occurred within the limitation period for tort. The defendants contended that where there was a contract between the parties, or at least where there was a contract for professional services, there could not, as a matter of law, be a duty in tort.

Held

The High Court held that a duty of care could exist where the parties were in a contractual professional relationship, as it was illogical that a contracting party could not sue in respect of a negligent act, whereas a non-contracting party could. The principle that the law of tort could not alter the contractual rights existing between parties applied only to rights created by the terms of the contract and not to rights in respect of the limitation period. Thus a duty in tort did exist and the extent of this duty was regulated by the express and implied terms of the contract.

Unfortunately for the plaintiffs, however, the Court went on to hold that when the defendants submitted designs for the sanctuary they made no express statement as to its technical qualities. Thus in the absence of actual damage to the person or to property the cost of putting right the defects was pure economic loss and the defendants owed no duty of care to prevent such loss.

The defendants relied on *Tai Hing Cotton Mill* v *Liu Chong Hing Bank* [1985] 2 All ER 947, a Privy Council decision, where Lord Scarman said at p957: 'Their Lordships do not believe that there is anything to the advantage of the law's development in searching for a liability in tort where the parties are in a contractual relationship. This is particularly so in a commercial relationship.' The plaintiffs relied, of course, on the decision of Oliver J in *Midland Bank Trust* v *Hett Stubbs & Kemp* [1978] 3 All ER 571 where the duty of care was held to co-exist with the contractual duty.

The High Court decided to follow the *Midland Bank* decision rather than the obiter dictum in *Tai Hing*, encouraged by the speech of Lord Bridge in *Caparo* v *Dickman* [1990] 1 All ER 568 where he expressly recognised the co-existence of duties in tort and contract.

Lonrho plc v *Tebbit* [1992] 4 All ER 280 Court of Appeal (Dillon and Stocker LJJ and Sir Michael Kerr)

Duty of care – minister's delay in releasing plaintiffs from their undertaking to him

Facts

The plaintiffs gave an undertaking to the defendants that they would not acquire more than 30 per cent of the share capital of House of Fraser pending a reference to the Monopolies and Mergers Commission (MMC). In November 1984 the plaintiffs sold the vast majority of their 29.9 per cent shareholding to a company controlled by the Al-Fayed brothers. On 14 February 1985 the MMC reported that the proposed merger between the plaintiffs and House of Fraser would not be contrary to the public interest. On 4 March the company controlled by the Al-Fayed brothers made a public offer for the remainder of the shares in House of Fraser which enabled them to acquire more than 50 per cent of the shares. When the defendants released the plaintiffs from their undertaking on 14 March it was too late for them to make a successful bid for House of Fraser. The plaintiffs sought to recover damages from the defendants on the ground that the Secretary of State had been negligent in the exercise of his statutory power because of his delay in releasing the plaintiffs from their undertaking. The defendants sought to strike out the plaintiffs' claim but Sir Nicolas Browne-Wilkinson V-C refused their application. The defendants appealed to the Court of Appeal.

Held

The appeal would be dismissed.

Dillon LJ:

'... there is, as I have said, no allegation of bad faith against the defendants, but it is alleged that they acted ultra vires, that is to say beyond their powers, in deferring the release of the undertaking until 14 March 1985 when the MMC report had become available on or about 14 February. If that is so, the likely conclusion is that the defendants acted as they did in good faith, believing that they were entitled to time for consideration and to look at the matter in the round and consider at the same time whether the undertaking given by Lonrho should be released, and whether the bid by Holdings for House of Fraser should be referred to the MMC. Reference was made to an apparently unlimited dictum of Nourse LJ in *Bourgoin SA* v *Ministry of Agriculture Fisheries and Food* [1985] 3 All ER 585 at 633:

"In this country the law has never allowed that a private individual should recover damages against the Crown for an injury caused to him by an ultra vires order made in good faith."

But the fields of law with which we are concerned in this case are difficult and developing. [Counsel for the defendants] gave us an admirable summary of the principal authorities. In the law of negligence he referred us to the two-stage test suggested by Lord Wilberforce in *Anns* v *Merton London Borough* [1977] 2 All ER 492 at 500, and showed how that had been rejected in later authorities and particularly in *Murphy* v *Brentwood DC* [1990] 2 All ER 908. The preferred approach is now what is called "the incremental approach" as stated by Brennan J in *Sutherland Shire Council* v *Heyman* (1985) 60 ALR 1 at 43–44 ...

[Counsel] referred us also to authorities which show that a civil action for damages cannot be brought as a result of a "policy decision" of a public authority and to judgments where a distinction is suggested between "policy decisions" which cannot be justiciable and "operational decisions" which may be justiciable. But in *Rowling* v *Takaro Properties Ltd* [1988] 1 All ER 163 ... some of the difficulties of that approach are explored in the opinion of Lord Keith and the conclusion of their Lordships seems to be that the question whether a duty of care should be imposed is a question of an intensely pragmatic character, well-suited for gradual development but requiring most careful analysis (see [1988] 1 All ER 163 at 172). That is in line with the incremental approach to the development of the tort of negligence.

The imposition of the undertaking on Lonrho in 1981 was of course a matter of public law in the public interest when the MMC had considered that the acquisition by Lonrho of the share capital of House of Fraser might be expected to operate against the public interest. The public interest in having the undertaking released when the acquisition by Lonrho of the share capital of House of Fraser was no longer expected to operate against the public interest is considerably more remote and sophisticated. But the private interest of Lonrho in having the undertaking released as soon as it was no longer needed in the public interest is obvious. It does not therefore appal me that it should be suggested that, if the Secretary of State imposes the restrictions of the undertaking on Lonrho in the public interest, the Secretary of State should thereby assume a private law duty to Lonrho to release the undertaking when it is no longer needed and that the restriction on Lonrho's freedom to conduct its business no longer has a rationale. There is an arguable case for Lonrho, therefore, against which may have to be set the sort of considerations militating against the imposition of liability which Lord Keith rehearses in *Rowling* v *Takaro Properties Ltd*. These raise questions which the court in *Rowling* v *Takaro* did not have to resolve. Moreover, the nature of any private law duty would have to be carefully defined. Is it, for instance, an absolute duty to release the undertaking when no longer required in the public interest, or is it only a duty of care, within the field of the tort of negligence – with the result in the latter case that there would be no liability on the defendants if delay in releasing the undertaking was due to an error of law which was not negligent?

In these circumstances, I agree with Browne-Wilkinson V-C that Lonrho's claim should not be struck out as disclosing no reasonable cause of action. Lonrho faces considerable difficulties, and others may arise on the facts as the evidence emerges at a trial, but I cannot say that Lonrho has no arguable case, or … that the claim is obviously foredoomed to fail.

I turn to the final question whether, if Lonrho's claim is not struck out on the ground that it discloses no reasonable cause of action, it ought none the less to be struck out as an abuse of the process of the court on the ground that Lonrho ought to be required to get a ruling by way of judicial review before it starts any proceedings by way of writ and civil action against the defendants.

[Counsel for the defendants] founds this submission on *Cocks* v *Thanet DC* [1982] 3 All ER 1135. He says in effect that it is a matter of public law for the plaintiff to establish the necessary public law basis on which it can ground a private right, as in *Cocks's* case. Therefore the plaintiff must obtain a declaration in proceedings for judicial review on which to found a claim to a private right or for breach of a private law duty.

I see the matter differently. The plaintiff is asserting a private law right, albeit arising out of a background of public law. That can be asserted in an action by writ as in *Roy* v *Kensington and Chelsea and Westminster Family Practitioner Committee* [1992] 1 All ER 705. If the plaintiff fails to establish the private law right claimed, the action will fail. But it is not necessary to apply for judicial review before bringing the action.'

McFarlane v *EE Caledonia Ltd* [1994] 2 All ER 1 Court of Appeal (Ralph Gibson, Stuart-Smith and McCowan LJJ)

Duty owed to bystander at a horrific event

Facts

The plaintiff was employed on the Piper Alpha oil rig in the North Sea. He was off duty on a support vessel some 550 metres from the rig when a series of massive explosions and a fire engulfed the rig. For an hour and three quarters the plaintiff witnessed the explosions and destruction of the rig which caused the death of 164 men, and he came within 100 metres of the fire. The plaintiff suffered psychiatric illness as a result of witnessing these events and sued the defendants, the owners and operators of the rig. In the High Court it was held that the plaintiff succeeded as he was reasonably in fear of his life and safety and the fear had caused the shock which led to his injury and he was therefore a participant in the event. The judge found that the plaintiff was not a rescuer, and expressed no opinion on the submission that the plaintiff could recover even if he was only a bystander at an event if it was so horrendous that it was reasonably foreseeable that it would cause psychiatric injury to a bystander. The defendants appealed.

Held

The Court of Appeal found as a fact that the plaintiff was not genuinely in fear for his safety, and agreed with the trial judge's finding that the plaintiff was not a rescuer.

In *Alcock* v *Chief Constable of South Yorkshire* [1991] 4 All ER 907 three Law Lords (Keith, Ackner and Oliver) thought that a mere bystander could recover if the circumstances of an accident occurring close to him were particularly horrific. Despite these dicta the Court of Appeal held that as the whole basis of the decision in *Alcock* is that reasonable foreseeability is not enough, there must additionally be a sufficiently close tie of love and affection between the plaintiff and the victim.

Stuart-Smith LJ:

'The whole basis of the decision in Alcock's case is that where the shock is caused by fear of injury to others as opposed to fear of injury to the participant, the test of proximity is not simply reasonable foreseability. There must be a sufficiently close tie of love and affection between the plaintiff and the victim. To extend the duty to those who have no such connection, is to base the test purely on reasonable foreseeability.'

McLoughlin v *O'Brian* [1982] 2 WLR 982 House of Lords (Lord Wilberforce, Lord Edmund-Davies, Lord Russell of Killowen, Lord Scarman and Lord Bridge of Harwich)

Negligence – foreseeable harm

Facts

The plaintiff's husband and three young children were involved in a serious road accident caused by the negligence of the defendant. The plaintiff's husband and two of her children were very badly injured. The other child was killed. At the time that the accident occurred, the plaintiff was at home two miles away. She was informed of the accident by a neighbour and was taken to the hospital where she saw the extent of the injuries of her family and was told of her daughter's death. In consequence of seeing and hearing the results of the accident, the plaintiff suffered severe and persistent nervous shock. The plaintiff claimed damages against the defendant for nervous shock, distress and injury to health caused by the negligence of the defendant.

Held

The test of liability for damages for nervous shock was simply reasonable foreseeability of the plaintiff being injured by the defendant's negligent act or omission. Applying this test, the plaintiff was entitled to recover damages because even though the plaintiff was not at or near the scene of the accident, either at the time or shortly afterwards, the nervous shock suffered by the plaintiff was a reasonably foreseeable consequence of the defendant's negligence.

Lord Wilberforce:

' ... Although we continue to use the hallowed expression "nervous shock", English law, and common understanding, have moved some distance since recognition was given to this symptom as a basis for liability. Whatever is unknown about the mind-body relationship (and the area of ignorance seems to expand with that of knowledge), it is now accepted by medical science that recognisable and severe physical damage to the human body and system may be caused by the impact, through the senses, of external events on the mind. There may thus be produced what is as identifiable an illness as any that may be caused by direct physical impact. It is safe to say that this, in general terms, is understood by the ordinary man or woman who is hypothesised by the courts in situations where claims for negligence are made. Although in the only case which has reached this House (*Hay (or Bourhill)* v *Young* [1943] AC 92), a claim for damages in respect of "nervous shock" was rejected on its facts, the House gave clear recognition to the legitimacy, in principle, of claims of that character. As the result of that and other cases, assuming that they are accepted as correct, the following position has been reached:

1. While damages cannot, at common law, be awarded for grief and sorrow, a claim for damages for "nervous shock" caused by negligence can be made without the necessity of showing direct impact or fear of immediate personal injuries for oneself ...

2. A plaintiff may recover damages for "nervous shock" brought on by injury caused not to him or herself but to a near relative, or by the fear of such injury ...

3. Subject to the next paragraph, there is no English case in which a plaintiff has been able to recover nervous shock damages where the injury to the near relative occurred out of sight and earshot of the plaintiff. In *Hambrook* v *Stokes Bros* an express distinction was made between shock caused by what the mother saw with her own eyes and what she might have been told by bystanders, liability being excluded in the latter case.

4. An exception from, or I would prefer to call it an extension of, the latter case has been made where the plaintiff does not see or hear the incident but comes on its immediate aftermath ...

5. A remedy on account of nervous shock has been given to a man who came on a serious accident involving people immediately thereafter and acted as a rescuer of those involved (*Chadwick* v *British Transport Commission* [1967] 1 WLR 912). 'Shock' was caused neither by fear for himself nor by fear or horror on account of a near relative. The principle of 'rescuer' cases was not challenged by the respondents and ought, in my opinion, to be accepted. But we have to consider whether, and how far, it can be applied to such cases as the present.

If one continues to follow the process of logical progression it is hard to see why the present plaintiff also should not succeed. She was not present at the accident, but she came very soon after on its aftermath. If, from a distance of some 100 yards she had found her family by the roadside, she would have come within principle 4 above. Can it make any difference that she comes on them in an ambulance, or, as here, in a nearby hospital, when as the evidence shows, they were in the same condition, covered with oil and mud, and distraught with pain? If Mr Chadwick can recover when, acting in accordance with normal and irresistible human instinct, and indeed moral compulsion, he goes to the scene of an accident, may not a mother recover if, acting under the same motives, she goes to where her family can be found? ... To argue from one factual situation to another and to decide by analogy is a natural tendency of the human and legal mind. But the lawyer still has to inquire whether, in so doing, he has crossed some critical line behind which he ought to stop ... Foreseeability which involves a hypothetical person, looking with hindsight at an event which has occurred, is a formula.adopted by English law, not merely for defining, but also for limiting the persons to whom duty may be owed, and the consequences for which an actor may be held responsible. It is not merely an issue of fact to be left to be found as such. When it is said to result in a duty of care being owed to a person or a class, the statement that there is a "duty of care" denotes a conclusion into the forming of which considerations of policy have entered. That foreseeability does not of itself and automatically lead to a duty of care is, I think, clear ... cases of "nervous shock" and the possibility of claiming damages for it are not necessarily confined to those arising out of accidents in public roads. To state, therefore, a rule that recoverable damages must be confined to persons on or near the highway is to state not a principle in itself but only an example of a more general rule that recoverable damages must be confined to those within sight and sound of an event caused by negligence or, at least, to those in close, or very close, proximity to such a situation.

The policy arguments against a wider extension can be stated under four heads. First, it may be said that such extension may lead to a proliferation of claims, and possibily fraudulent claims, to the establishment of an industry of lawyers and psychiatrists who will formulate a claim for nervous shock damages, including what in America is called the customary miscarriage, for all, or many road accidents and industrial accidents. Second, it may be claimed that an extension of liability would be unfair to defendants, as imposing damages out of proportion to the negligent conduct complained of. In so far as such defendants are insured, a large additional burden will be placed on insurers, and ultimately on the class of persons insured: road users or employers. Third, to extend liability beyond the most direct and plain cases would greatly increase evidentiary difficulties and tend to lengthen litigation. Fourth, it may be said (and the Court of Appeal agreed with this) that an extension of the scope of liability ought only to be made by the legislature, after careful research. This is the course which has been taken in New South Wales and the Australian Capital Territory ... In *Hambrook* v *Stokes Bros* [1924] All ER 110, indeed it was said that liability would not arise in such a case, and this is surely right. It was so decided in *Abramzik* v *Brenner* (1967) 65 DLR (2d) 651. The shock must come through sight or hearing of the event or of its immediate aftermath. Whether some equivalent of sight or hearing, eg through simultaneous television, would suffice may have to be considered.

My Lords, I believe that these indications, imperfectly sketched, and certainly to be applied with common sense to individual situations in their entirety, represent either the existing law, or the existing law with only such circumstantial extension as the common law process may legitimately make. They do not introduce a new principle. Nor do I see any reason why the law should retreat behind the lines already drawn. I find on this appeal that the appellant's case falls within the boundaries of the law so drawn. I would allow her appeal.'

Commentary
Applied: *Alcock* v *Chief Constable of the South Yorkshire Police* [1991] 3 WLR 1057.

Mariola Marine Corporation v *Lloyd's Register of Shipping, The Morning Watch* [1990] 1 Lloyd's Rep 547 High Court (Phillips J)

Purchaser of vessel – duty of care

Facts
Shortly after *The Morning Watch* had been examined by a Lloyd's surveyor and given a clean bill of health, the plaintiffs purchased it. The plaintiffs now alleged that the vessel had serious defects and was in fact unseaworthy: in their action for damages for negligence they maintained that the alleged defects should have been detected had the survey been properly conducted.

Held
The plaintiffs' claim would be dismissed. Phillips J said that the plaintiffs had established that it was reasonably foreseeable to Lloyd's that Mariola might rely on the survey result. But that was not in itself enough to establish a duty of care in a case of economic loss. There must also be a sufficient degree of proximity between plaintiff and defendant and it must be just and reasonable to impose on the defendant a duty of care to the plaintiff. There was no universal test to determine whether the necessary proximity existed. After referring to the decision of the Court of Appeal in *Caparo Industries plc* v *Dickman* [1989] 2 WLR 316, he said that in the present case there was no statutory scheme and no relationship akin to contract. There was no more a voluntary assumption by Lloyd's of responsibility to purchasers, than there was a voluntary assumption by auditors of responsibility to potential purchasers of shares. Nor was the case analogous with *Smith* v *Eric S Bush* [1989] 2 WLR 790 where the court had found a relationship akin to contract and the valuer had assumed responsibility to the purchaser. The House of Lords had since reversed the decision of the Court of Appeal in *Caparo Industries plc* v *Dickman* [1990] 2 WLR 358 and nothing in their Lordships' speeches had altered his view of the present case.

Morgan Crucible Co plc v *Hill Samuel Bank Ltd* [1991] 2 WLR 655 Court of Appeal (Slade, Mustill and Nicholls LJJ)

Negligence – duty of care to takeover bidder

Facts
This case arose out of a contested takeover bid and the plaintiffs' action was brought against the directors, bank and accountants of the target company. The directors responded to the plaintiffs' bid by issuing circulars to the shareholders advising them to reject the offer and stating, inter alia, that the profits of the company were forecast to increase by 38 per cent. The latter circular was accompanied by a statement by the company's accountants that the forecast had been prepared in accordance with the company's accounting procedures and a statement by their bank stating that, in their opinion, the forecast had been made after due and careful inquiry. As a result of such circulars the plaintiffs increased their bid for the company and it was accepted. The plaintiffs subsequently alleged that the pre-bid financial statements and the profit forecast were negligently misleading and that, had they known the true situation, they would never have bid for the company. All three defendants alleged that the plaintiffs' statement of claim, as amended, disclosed no cause of action.

Held
The plaintiffs had an arguable case and their claim would not be struck out. The point of distinction between this case and *Caparo* was that the statements relied upon were made *after* the plaintiffs had made their bid and not before (it was conceded that no duty was owed before the initial bid was made). Slade LJ noted the six factors identified by Neill LJ in *McNaughton* (above) and stated that they were neither 'conclusive or exhaustive'. In the present case the directors were aware that the plaintiffs would rely upon the circulars and *they intended that they should rely upon them*. It was also arguable that, for the same reasons, the bank and the accountants owed a duty of care to the plaintiffs.

Commentary
Distinguished: *Caparo Industries plc* v *Dickman* [1990] 2 WLR 358.

Morrell v *Owen* (1993) The Times 14 December High Court (Mitchell J)

Duty of care owed by organiser and coaches of a disabled persons' sporting event to the disabled participant

Facts
The plaintiff, who was disabled, was taking part in an archery contest for disabled persons when she was injured by a participant in another disabled sporting event, a discus-throwing contest taking place in the same arena. The plaintiff sued, inter alia, the archery coach and the discus coach of the event in question.

Held
The court found that these defendants were in breach of their duty by failing to provide safety instructions and precautions. Mitchell J held that the misthrow which caused the plaintiff's injuries was entirely foreseeable as was the actual accident. The judge added that organisers and coaches of a disabled persons' sporting event owed a greater duty of care to participants than would have been owed had the participants been able-bodied.

Commentary

While a final evaluation of the judgment in *Morrell* must await a full report of the case, the statement as reported must be regarded as inaccurate. English law has never accepted the concept of a variable duty of care in these circumstances: see for example *Ogwo* v *Taylor* [1987] 3 All ER 961 (House of Lords) for a rejection of this concept. The *duty* of care owed to disabled and able-bodied athletes by the organisers of a sporting event is identical, namely to take reasonable steps to ensure that the participants do not suffer any reasonably foreseeable injury. However, the actions that might constitute a *breach* of this duty will differ in the case of disabled and able-bodied athletes – precautions that are sufficient for the latter may well be insufficient for the former. The fact that different actions may constitute a breach of duty does not mean that a different duty is owed in each case.

Muirhead v *Industrial Tank Specialities Ltd* [1985] 3 WLR 993 Court of Appeal (O'Connor, Robert Goff and Nourse LJJ)

Negligence – economic loss

Facts

The plaintiff was a wholesale fish merchant. The first defendant was required to install a tank to store lobsters. The second defendants supplied the pumps for the tank. The third defendants manufactured and supplied the motors for the pumps. The plaintiff's entire lobster stock died when the motors cut out as they were unsuited to UK voltage. The plaintiff claimed inter alia, and in particular, against the third defendant, damages for the loss of the lobsters and consequential economic loss thereupon, including loss of profit which the plaintiff could have made by keeping the lobsters and selling them at Christmas.

Held

The third defendant was liable for the physical damage suffered to the plaintiff's lobster stock and loss of profit in consequence of the physical damage as such damage was of the type reasonably foreseeable by the third defendant. However, the plaintiff could not recover his whole economic loss.

Nourse LJ:

'In his analysis of *Junior Books Ltd* v *Veitchi Co Ltd* Robert Goff LJ has identified the three features of that case on which the decision that the nominated sub-contractor had voluntarily assumed a direct responsibility to the building owner was founded. The first two of these were very close proximity between the sub-contractor and the building owner and reliance by the building owner on the sub-contractor. Having been so decided, that case cannot, in my respectful opinion, be taken to be authority for the proposition that where those features are absent a defendant is liable in tort in respect of economic loss which is not consequent on physical damage to the person or property of the plaintiff. Where those features are absent, I agree with O'Connor LJ that we remain bound by the decision of this court in *Spartan Steel and Alloys Ltd* v *Martin & Co (Contractors) Ltd*. I too regard the recent observations of the Privy Council in *Candlewood Navigation Corp Ltd* v *Mitsui Osk Lines Ltd, The Mineral Transporter, The Ibaraki Mar* was being significant in this respect.

In the present case there was no very close proximity between the manufacturers and the plaintiff. Contractually they were several stages removed from each other. More important, there was no reliance by the plaintiff on the manufacturers in the sense in which that concept was applied in *Junior Book*. The people on whom the plaintiff relied to install the system and to get the right equipment, including pumps with electric motors which worked, were ITS. They were the people who stood in the same factual relationship with the plaintiff as the sub-contractor did with the building owner in *Junior Books*. The two features of very close proximity and reliance having been absent, it is unnecessary to look further in the present case. The plaintiff's claim in respect of pure economic loss must fail. I therefore agree that the appeal should be allowed to that extent.'

Commentary

Applied: *Spartan Steel and Alloys Ltd* v *Martin & Co (Contractors) Ltd* [1972] 2 WLR 649.

Murphy v *Brentwood District Council* [1990] 3 WLR 414 House of Lords (Lord Mackay of Clashfern LC, Lord Keith of Kinkel, Lord Bridge of Harwich, Lord Brandon of Oakbrook, Lord Ackner, Lord Oliver of Aylmerton and Lord Jauncey of Tullichettle)

Negligence – economic loss

Facts

The plaintiff purchased a house in 1970 from builders who had constructed it in 1969. The house was built upon a single concrete raft foundation because the site had been filled and levelled. The foundation raft was designed by a firm of civil engineers but its design was inadequate and differential settlement of the ground beneath the raft caused it to distort and caused cracks to appear in the building. When the plaintiff discovered the extent of the damage to the house he decided that it was impractical to have the necessary remedial work performed himself and so he sold it, at a price considerably below the market price of a house which was sound, to a builder who knew the cause of the damage. The plaintiff then brought an action against the local authority alleging that they had been negligent in passing plans which were inadequate. The defendants had in fact referred the plans to an independent firm of consulting engineers and, in reliance upon their report, had passed the plans. The Court of Appeal ([1990] 2 WLR 944) concluded, being bound by the decision of the House of Lords in *Anns* v *Merton London Borough Council* [1978] AC 728, that the local authority did owe a duty of care to the plaintiff as an innocent purchaser who had bought the house from the builder who was in breach of the building regulations. It was further held that the duty owed by the council was a non-delegable one so that they could not discharge their duty simply by entrusting the work to an apparently competent form of consultant engineers. The court held that, on the facts, the plaintiff was entitled to recover damages measured by the diminution in value on resale caused by the defects up to an amount which did not exceed the cost of eliminating the danger. On appeal to the House of Lords:

Held

The appeal would be allowed.

Lord Bridge of Harwich:

'... these considerations lead inevitably to the conclusion that a building owner can only recover the cost of repairing a defective building on the ground of the authority's negligence in performing its statutory function of approving plans or inspecting buildings in the course of construction if the scope of the authority's duty of care is wide enough to embrace purely economic loss. The House has already held in *D & F Estates* that a builder, in the absence of any contractual duty or of a special relationship of proximity introducing the *Hedley Byrne* principle of reliance, owes no duty of care in tort in respect of the quality of his work. As I pointed out in *D & F Estates*, to hold that the builder owed such a duty of care to any person acquiring an interest in the product of the builder's work would be to impose on him the obligations of an indefinitely transmissible warranty of quality.

By s1 of the Defective Premises Act 1972 Parliament has in fact imposed on builders and others undertaking work in the provision of dwellings the obligations of a transmissible warranty of the quality of their work and of the fitness for habitation of the completed dwelling. But, besides being limited to dwellings, liability under that Act is subject to a limitation period of six years from the completion of the work and to the exclusion provided for by s2. It would be remarkable to find that similar obligations in the nature of a transmissible warranty of quality, applicable to buildings of every kind and subject to no such limitations or exclusions as are imposed by the 1972 Act, could be derived from the builder's common law duty of care or from the duty imposed by building byelaws or regulations. In *Anns* Lord Wilberforce expressed the opinion that a builder could be held liable for a breach of statutory duty in respect of buildings which do not comply with the byelaws. But he cannot, I think, have meant that the statutory obligation to build in conformity with the byelaws by itself gives rise to obligations in the nature of transmissible warranties of quality. If he did meant that, I must respectfully disagree. I find it impossible to suppose that anything less than clear express language such as is used in s1 of the 1972 Act would suffice to impose such a statutory obligation.

As I have already said, since the function of a local authority in approving plans or inspecting buildings in the course of construction is directed to ensuring that the builder complies with building byelaws or regulations, I cannot see how, in principle, the scope of the liability of the authority for a negligent failure to ensure compliance can exceed that of the liability of the builder for his negligent failure to comply.

There may, of course, be situations where, even in the absence of contract, there is a special relationship of proximity between builder and building owner which is sufficiently akin to contract to introduce the element of reliance so that the scope of the duty of care owed by the builder to the owner is wide enough to embrace purely economic loss. The decision in *Junior Books Ltd* v *Veitchi Co Ltd* [1983] 1 AC 520 can, I believe, only be understood on this basis.

In *Sutherland Shire Council* v *Heyman* (1985) 60 ALR 1 the critical role of the reliance principle as an element in the cause of action which the plaintiff sought to establish is the subject of close examination, particularly in the judgment of Mason J. The central theme of his judgment, and a subordinate theme in the judgments of Brennan and Dean JJ, who together with Mason J formed the majority rejecting the *Anns* doctrine, is that a duty of care of a scope sufficient to make the authority liable for damage of the kind suffered can only be based on the principle of reliance and that there is nothing in the ordinary relationship of a local authority, as statutory supervisor of building operations, and the purchaser of a defective building capable of giving rise to such a duty. I agree with these judgments. It cannot, I think, be suggested, nor do I understand *Anns* or the cases which have followed *Anns* in Canada and New Zealand to be in fact suggesting, that the approval of plans or the inspection of a building in the course of construction by the local authority in performance of their statutory function and a subsequent purchase of the building by the plaintiff are circumstances in themselves sufficient to introduce the principle of reliance which is the foundation of a duty of care of the kind identified in *Hedley Byrne*.'

Commentary
Applied in *Department of the Environment* v *Thomas Bates & Son Ltd* [1990] 3 WLR 457.

Mutual Life & Citizens' Assurance Co Ltd v *Evatt* [1971] 2 WLR 23 (Privy Council) Lord Reid, Lord Morris of Borth-y-Gest, Lord Hodson, Lord Guest and Lord Diplock)

Negligence – advice

Facts
The plaintiff was a policyholder in the defendant company. Wishing to make some investments in P Ltd, with whom the defendants had close connections, the plaintiff asked for the defendants' advice. The advice was negligently given and the plaintiff, who had relied upon it, lost his investments.

Held (Lord Reid and Lord Morris of Borth-y-Gest dissenting)
The defendants were neither in the business of giving advice, nor held themselves out as having the skill to do so, and thus owed no duty to the plaintiff.

Lord Diplock:

'The carrying on of a business or profession which involves the giving of advice of a kind which calls for special skill and competence is the normal way in which a person lets it be known to the recipient of the advice that he claims to possess that degree of skill and competence and is willing to exercise that degree of diligence which is generally possessed and exercised by persons who carry on the business or profession of giving advice of the kind sought ...'

Commentary
Distinguished: *Hedley Byrne & Co Ltd* v *Heller & Partners Ltd* [1963] 3 WLR 101.

Nitrigin Eireann Teoranta v *Inco Alloys Ltd* [1992] 1 WLR 498 High Court (May J)

Negligence – economic loss and physical damage

Facts
The defendants had supplied steel alloy tubing for the plaintiffs' chemical plant. An allegedly defective pipe was supplied in summer 1981. In 1983 the plaintiffs discovered that it was damaged by cracking. They were unable to find the cause but repaired the pipe. On 27 June 1984 the pipe burst and there was an explosion which caused damage to the structure of the plant around the pipe. A writ alleging negligent manufacture was issued on 21 June 1990 and the plaintiffs alleged it was issued within six years of the accrual of their cause of action in negligence. Did the plaintiffs have a cause of action in negligence and, if they did, was it statute-barred?

Held
They did have a cause of action which was not statute-barred.

May J accepted the plaintiffs' argument, on the basis of *D & F Estates* v *Church Commissioners* [1989] AC 177, that cracking in the pipe in 1983 was a defect in the quality of the pipe itself which did not cause personal injury or damage to other property, so they had no cause of action in 1983 for that pure economic loss. By contrast, the 1984 explosion did cause damage to other property and a cause of action then arose which was not statute-barred. His Lordship declined to apply *Junior Books Ltd* v *Veitchi Co Ltd* [1983] 1 AC 520, which was a unique case depending on there being a special relationship between plaintiff and defendant amounting to reliance. There was no such relationship in the present case.

Nocton v *Lord Ashburton* [1914] AC 932 House of Lords (Viscount Haldane LC, Lord Dunedin, Lord Atkinson, Lord Shaw and Lord Parmoor)

Misrepresentation – liability of adviser

Facts
The respondent alleged that his solicitor, the appellant, had improperly advised and induced him to advance £65,000 upon a mortgage by other clients of the solicitor, a transaction out of which the solicitor was said to have gained advantage for himself. Charges of fraud were not made out.

Held
The solicitor had been in a fiduciary position towards the respondent and he was therefore under a duty to make a full, and not a misleading, disclosure of facts known to him when advising the respondent. For any loss caused by a breach of this duty the respondent was entitled to compensation.

Lord Shaw:

'The principle to be found running through this branch of the law is, in my opinion, this. Once the relations of parties have been ascertained to be those in which a duty is laid upon one person of giving information or advice to another upon which that other is entitled to rely as the basis of a transaction, responsibility for error amounting to misrepresentation in any statement made will attach to the adviser or informer, although the information and advice have been given, not fraudulently, but in good faith. It is admitted in the present case that misrepresentations were made; that they were material; that they were the cause of loss; that they were made by a solicitor to his client in a situation in which the client was entitled to rely, and did rely, upon the information received. I, accordingly, think that the situation is plainly open for the application of the principle of liability to which I have referred – namely, liability for the consequences of a failure of duty in circumstances in which it was a matter equivalent to contract between the parties that that duty should be fulfilled.'

Osman v *Ferguson* [1993] 4 All ER 344 Court of Appeal (McCowan, Beldam and Simon Brown LJJ)

Duty of care owed by police to victim of crime

Facts

P, a schoolteacher, formed an unhealthy attachment to a 15-year-old male pupil and harassed him. In May 1987 he damaged property belonging to the boy's father. In mid-1987 P was dismissed from the school but continued the harassment. The police were aware of these facts and in late 1987 P told a police officer that the loss of his job was distressing and he feared he would do something criminally insane. In December 1987 P deliberately rammed a vehicle in which the boy was a passenger. The police laid an information against P in January 1988 alleging driving without due care and attention but it was not served. In March 1988 P shot and severely injured the boy and killed his father. The mother, as administratix of the father's estate, and the boy sued the police alleging negligence in that although the police had been aware of P's activities since May 1987 they had failed to apprehend or interview him, search his home or charge him with a more serious offence before March 1988. The police's action to strike out the statement of claim was dismissed and the police appealed.

Held

As the boy and his family had been exposed to a risk over and above that suffered by members of the public, there was an arguable case that there was a very close degree of proximity amounting to a special relationship between the plaintiff's family and the investigating police officers. However, the general duty of the police to suppress crime did not carry with it liability to individuals for damage caused to them by criminals the police had failed to apprehend when it was possible to do so. Applying *Hill* and *Alexandrou* the Court held it would be against public policy to impose such a duty for the reasons stated in *Alexandrou*.

Page v *Smith* [1995] 2 WLR 644 House of Lords (Lords Keith, Ackner, Jauncey, Browne-Wilkinson and Lloyd)

Nervous shock – no personal injury caused to primary victim

Facts

The plaintiff's car was involved in a collision with the defendant's car in which the plaintiff suffered no physical injury. For 20 years prior to the accident the plaintiff had suffered from ME (myalgic encephalomyelitis) which had manifested itself from time to time with different degrees of severity. The plaintiff claimed damages for personal injuries, alleging that as a result of the accident his condition had become chronic and permanent. At first instance the High Court found for the plaintiff, and an appeal to the Court of Appeal allowed the defendant's appeal on the grounds that the plaintiff's injury was not foreseeable. The plaintiff appealed to the House of Lords.

Held

(Lords Keith and Jauncey dissenting) the appeal would be allowed. Once it was established that the defendant was under a duty of care to avoid causing personal injury to the plaintiff, it was immaterial whether the injury sustained was physical, psychiatric or both. Thus the question is whether the defendant should have reasonably foreseen that the plaintiff might suffer personal injury as a result of his negligence. It was unnecessary to ask whether the defendant should have reasonably foreseen injury by shock. It was also irrelevant that the plaintiff did not sustain external physical injury.

The House also stated that in cases of nervous shock it was essential to distinguish between primary victims and secondary victims. In the case of secondary victims, the law insists on certain control mechanisms to limit the number of potential claimants. Where the plaintiff is the primary victim, these control mechanisms have no place.

Partington v *Wandsworth London Borough Council* (1989) The Independent 8 November High Court (Schiemann J)

Handicapped person – duty of care

Facts

The plaintiff suffered injury when she was pushed to the ground by a mentally handicapped 17 year old girl who was, at the time of the incident, in the care of the defendants and was being accompanied by a supervisor.

Held

The plaintiff's claim could not succeed. Although the defendants had been under a duty to take reasonable care to prevent the girl from inflicting injury upon others, the difficulty lay in whether or not that duty had been breached. Schiemann J said that the court must seek to balance what was best for the handicapped person against what was best for the rest of the world. There was no need to keep an autistic girl locked up, nor was it necessary to keep a physical hold of her while out on walks. In the light of these considerations, it had not been proved that the defendants had breached their duty of care because, although the autistic girl had acted in an anti-social manner from time to time, no one knew when she would so act and, in particular, it was not known that she would attack the plaintiff.

Peabody Donation Fund (Governors) v *Sir Lindsay Parkinson & Co Ltd* [1984] 3 WLR 953 House of Lords (Lord Keith of Kinkel, Lord Scarman, Lord Bridge of Harwich, Lord Brandon of Oakbrook and Lord Templeman)

Negligence – duty of care

Facts

The plaintiffs were developers of a housing estate. The local authority (Lambeth LBC) was statutorily required to ensure that the proposed housing estate had a suitable drainage system. The plaintiffs' architects submitted plans of the drainage system which were approved by the local authority, but a drainage inspector without authority agreed that a different system should be installed which was in reality drainage which was unsatisfactory and in breach of public health legislation. A number of the drains failed in due course and the plaintiffs sought damages for the cost of reconstruction.

Held

The local authority did not owe a duty of care to the plaintiff developers, even though loss may have been foreseeable. The purpose of the statutory powers was to protect the public, not developers.

Lord Keith of Kinkel:

'The true question in each case is whether the particular defendant owed to the particular plaintiff a duty of care having the scope which is contended for, and whether he was in breach of that duty with consequent loss to the plaintiff. A relationship of proximity in Lord Atkin's sense must exist before any duty of care can arise, but the scope of the duty must depend on all the circumstances of the case. In *Home Office* v *Dorset Yacht Co Ltd* [1970] AC 1004 at 1038-1039 Lord Morris, after observing that at the conclusion of his speech in *Donoghue* v *Stevenson* [1932] AC 562 at 599 Lord Atkin said that it was advantageous if the law "is in accordance with sound common sense" and expressing the view that a special relation existed between the prison officers and the yacht company which gave rise to a duty on the former to control their charges so as to prevent them doing damage, continued:

"Apart from this I would conclude that in the situation stipulated in the present case it would not only be fair and reasonable that a duty of care should exist but that it would be contrary to the fitness of things were it not so. I doubt whether it is necessary to say, in cases where the court is asked whether in a particular situation a duty existed, that the court is called on to make a decision as to policy. Policy need not be invoked where reasons and good sense will at once point the way. If the test whether in some particular situation a duty of care arises may in some cases have to be whether it is fair and reasonable that it should so arise the court must not shrink from being the arbiter. As Lord Radcliffe said in his speech in *Davis Contractors Ltd* v *Fareham Urban District Council* [1956] AC 696 at 728, the court is 'the spokesman of the fair and reasonable man'."

So in determining whether or not a duty of care of particular scope was incumbent on a defendant it is material to take into consideration whether it is just and reasonable that it should be so.

In the instant case Peabody, the owners of the building site and the undertakers of the development thereon, bore responsibility, under ... the Act, for securing that the drains conformed to the design approved by Lambeth ... Peabody no doubt had no personal knowledge or understanding of what was going on. They relied on the advice of their architects, engineers and contractors, and in the event they were sadly let down, particularly by the architects. But it would be neither reasonable nor just, in these circumstances, to impose on Lambeth a liability to indemnify Peabody against loss resulting from such disastrous reliance.

The purpose for which the powers contained in [the Act] have been conferred on Lambeth is not to safeguard building developers against economic loss resulting from their failure to comply with approved plans. It is in my opinion to safeguard the occupiers of houses built in the local authority's area, and also members of the public generally, against dangers to their health which may arise from defective drainage installation. The provisions are public health measures. In *Anns* v *Merton London Borough* [1978] AC 728 at 758, a case concerned with defective foundations, Lord Wilberforce said, under the heading *To whom the duty is owed*:

"There is, in my opinion, no difficulty about this. A reasonable man in the position of the inspector must realise that if the foundations are covered in without adequate depth or strength as required by the byelaws, injury to safety or health may be suffered by owners or occupiers of the house. The duty is owed to them, not of course to a negligent building owner, the source of his own loss."

The plaintiffs in that case were lessees under long leases which they had acquired from a building developer, either directly or at a certain remove. The damages which they were held entitled to recover consisted in such sums as each of them required to expend in order to put his house in such a state that it was no longer a danger to safety or health... It is important to notice that these sums were not recoverable as economic loss pure and simple, but as representing expenditure necessary to avert injury to safety or health. ... Lord Wilberforce would appear to be saying that the duty is owed separately to owners and to occupiers. In fact, the plaintiffs, as long lessees, were in substance both owners and occupiers, and in my opinion the decision should be treated as restricted to that situation. Further, the reference to "a negligent building owner, the source of his own loss" to some extent begs the question whether a duty is owed to the owner since negligence on the part of a claimant does not necessarily, since the Law Reform (Contributory Negligence) Act 1945, preclude recovery of damages against a negligent defendant, though it may reduce them. The question whether a building owner's negligence is the sole cause of his loss raises a question of causation, not liability. It is also to be observed that the basis on which the measure of damages was arrived at would present difficulties in the case of a claim by one occupying on terms which did not permit of his carrying out any alterations to the structure of the house. The solution of these difficulties is not, however, necessary to the determination of the instant appeal. It is sufficient to hold that Lambeth owed no duty to Peabody to activate their [statutory] powers, notwithstanding that they might reasonably have foreseen that failure to do so would result in economic loss to Peabody, because the purpose of avoiding such loss was not one of the purposes for which these powers were vested in them.'

Commentary
Explained: *Anns* v *Merton London Borough Council* [1978] AC 728.

Perl (P) (Exporters) Ltd v *Camden London Borough Council* [1983] 3 WLR 769
Court of Appeal (Waller, Oliver and Robert Goff LJJ)

Negligence – duty to adjacent occupier

Facts
The appellant local authority owned a block of flats which included an unoccupied basement flat, which shared a common wall with the basement of the respondent company's neighbouring flat. The appellants' flat was not secured against admission by intruders and they did nothing to improve security despite the fact that there had been burglaries in other flats in the block and there had been complaints. Thieves entered the unoccupied flat and knocked a hole in the common wall, thereby gaining access to the respondents' flat, and stole a large amount of their property. At the trial, the judge held that Camden LBC should have foreseen that damage to property would ensure from their failure to keep their property secure; there had been an absence of reasonable care and he therefore awarded damages to the respondent company.

Held
The appeal would be allowed. In the absence of any special relationship of control existing between the occupier of premises and a third party, the occupier did not owe a duty of care to an occupier of neighbouring premises to protect his own premises so as to prevent a third party gaining access to them and from there gaining access to the adjoining premises and damaging the neighbour's property.

Oliver LJ:

'What gave rise to the duty in the *Dorset Yacht* case was the special relationship which existed between the defendant and the third person who inflicted the damage, in as much as the defendants had both the statutory right and the statutory duty to exercise control over those persons.'

Waller LJ:

'... no case has been cited to us where a party has been held liable for the acts of a third party when there was no element of control over the third party. While I do not take the view that there can never be such a case I do take the view that the absence of control must make the court approach the suggestion that there is liability for a third party who was not under the control of the defendant with caution.'

Commentary

Followed in *King* v *Liverpool City Council* [1986] 1 WLR 890.

Distinguished in *Topp* v *London Country Bus (South West) Ltd* (1993) The Times 15 February.

Petch v *Commissioners of Customs and Excise* (1993) The Times 4 March Court of Appeal (Dillon, Beldam and Roch LJJ)

Duty of care owed to subject of statement

Facts

The plaintiff, who was employed by the defendants, was retired from the Civil Service on medical grounds. The plaintiff claimed injury benefit under the Civil Service pension scheme which was administered by the Treasury, and the Treasury requested certain information from the defendants. The plaintiff alleged that the defendants had negligently furnished inaccurate written information to the Treasury as regards the plaintiff's work record, and at first instance the High Court held that a duty of care was imposed on the defendants in respect of this information. The defendants appealed.

Held

The Court of Appeal upheld the appeal and held that an employer answering queries from pension scheme trustees regarding a former employee's work record owed no duty of care to the employee. The majority of the Court (Dillon and Beldam LJJ) could see no difference between the present case and *Spring* (below), while Roch LJ concurring in the decision left open the question whether an employer or former employer owed an employee or former employee a duty to take care in providing factual information at the request of a third party that the information provided was correct where the employer or former employer knew that the third party would use such information to determine the employee's or former employee's entitlement to financial payments from the third party.

Reid v *Rush & Tompkins Group plc* [1990] 1 WLR 212 Court of Appeal (May, Neill and Ralph Gibson LJJ)

Employer – duty of care to employee

Facts

The plaintiff was seriously injured in a road accident in Ethiopia while working for the defendants. The other driver's negligence was the sole cause of the accident, but his identity was unknown: there was no compulsory third party insurance or scheme to cover uninsured third parties. The plaintiff alleged that the defendants had been in breach of their duty of care as employers in failing either to insure him against such accidents or to advise him to effect such cover himself.

Held

No reasonable cause of action had been disclosed and the plaintiff's claim had therefore been properly struck out.

May LJ:

' ... the ordinary duty of care owed by a master to his servant arises both in contract and in tort. I agree that it is impossible to imply any term into the plaintiff's contract of service with the defendants in the instant case of which, on the facts alleged in the statement of claim, a breach would entitle the plaintiff to recover by way of damages compensation for the loss he has sustained. This being so, then I also agree that it is not open to us to extend the duty of care owed by the defendants to the plaintiff by imposing a duty in tort which is not contained in any express or implied term of the contract.'

Rondel v *Worsley* [1967] 3 WLR 1666 House of Lords (Lord Reid, Lord Morris of Borth-y-Gest, Lord Pearce, Lord Upjohn and Lord Pearson)

Negligence – barrister's immunity

Facts

Facing a charge of causing grievous bodily harm, the appellant obtained the services of the respondent as counsel to defend him on a dock brief. The appellant was convicted and, nearly six years later, he issued a writ alleging, in effect, negligence on the part of the respondent in the conduct of his defence.

Held

Even if the respondent had been guilty of negligence, an action did not lie at the suit of the appellant.

Lord Morris of Borth-y-Gest:

'Though in most cases, by reason of the special and distinctive features of the work of advocates in which personal discretion is so much involved, assertions of negligence could readily be repelled, a cause of action alleging professional negligence could nevertheless always be framed. Is it, then, desirable in the public interest, while rejecting the wide immunity which has hitherto been proclaimed, to retain an immunity relating only to the limited field of the conduct and management of a case in court? Is it, as a matter of public policy, expedient that actions which involve a searching review almost amounting to a re-trial in different actions of previous actions or cases already concluded should not be allowed? Is the administration of justice (which is so much the concern of the community) better promoted if such actions are not countenanced? If it is recognised that there could be some cases where negligence (as opposed to errors of judgment) could be established, is it nevertheless on a balance of desirabilities wise to disallow the bringing of such cases? In my view, the answer to these questions is that it is in the public interest that such actions should not be brought.'

Commentary

Applied in *Hill* v *Chief Constable of West Yorkshire* [1989] AC 53

Ross v *Caunters* [1979] 3 WLR 605 High Court (Sir Robert Megarry V-C)

Duty of care – solicitors

Facts

A testator instructed the defendant solicitors to draw up his will under which the plaintiff was a beneficiary. Due to the defendants' negligence, the will was invalid and the gift to the plaintiff failed and she brought an action to recover her loss.

Held

The plaintiff was entitled to succeed. The defendants owed her a duty of care because she was within their direct contemplation as a person so closely and directly affected by their acts and omissions that they could reasonably foresee she would be injured by those acts or omissions.

Sir Robert Megarry V-C:

'*Hedley Byrne* is important, of course, as opening the door to the recovery of damages for negligence to at least some cases where the negligence has caused purely financial loss, without any injury to person or property; to that I shall come under the second main head of counsel for the defendants. But, for present purposes, its importance is that the House of Lords rejected pure *Donoghue* v *Stevenson* principles as forming the basis of liability for negligent misstatements and instead based liability on the plaintiff having trusted the defendant to exercise due care in giving information on a matter in which the defendant had a special skill and knew, or ought to have known, of the plaintiff's reliance on his skill and judgment. In this type of case, reliance forms part of the test of liability, as well as part of the chain of causation: and the effect of such a test of liability is to confine the extent of liability far more closely than would an application of pure *Donoghue* v *Stevenson* principles. If liability for negligently putting into circulation some innocent misrepresentation were to be imposed on the same basis as negligently putting into circulation some dangerous chattel, the resulting liability might be for enormous sums to a great multiplicity of plaintiffs. One way of preventing any such liability being imposed is to make the test of liability more strict: and that was the way adopted in *Hedley Byrne*. But, that does not affect those cases in which the principles of *Donoghue* v *Stevenson* apply. If I am right in thinking that the case before me falls within those principles, then there is no need to consider questions of reliance.

There are at least two ways in which *Hedley Byrne* may be regarded. First, it may be regarded as establishing a special category of case in which alone, by way of exception from the general rule, purely financial loss may be recovered in an action for negligence. Second, it may alternatively be regarded as establishing that there is no longer any general rule (if there ever was one) that purely financial loss is irrecoverable in negligence. Instead, such loss may be recovered in those classes of case in which there are no sufficient grounds for denying recovery and, in particular, no danger of exposing the defendant to a degree of liability that is unreasonable in its extent.'

Commentary
See *White* v *Jones* [1995] 2 WLR 187.

Rowling v *Takaro Properties Ltd* [1988] 2 WLR 418 Privy Council (Lord Mackay of Clashfern LC, Lord Keith of Kinkel, Lord Brandon of Oakbrook, Lord Templeman and Lord Goff of Chieveley)

Negligence – minister's duty of care

Facts
Rush, a United States' citizen, established a high class travel lodge in New Zealand, but it incurred heavy losses. A rescue package needed the approval of the Minister of Finance: he refused his consent, the rescue collapsed and a receiver was appointed for Rush's company. Both Rush and the company sought damages against the minister, alleging that he had been negligent in the exercise of his statutory powers arising out of his negligent construction of the regulations under which he had refused to approve the rescue scheme.

Held
Even if the minister had owed a duty of care to construe the relevant legislation correctly, he had not been in breach of that duty as, inter alia, his view had been tenable and he had not been unreasonable or negligent in holding it.

Lord Keith of Kinkel:

'Their Lordships wish to refer in particular to certain matters which they consider to be of importance. The first is that the only effect of a negligent decision, such as is here alleged to have been made, is delay. This is because the processes of judicial review are available to the aggrieved party; and, assuming that the alleged error of law is so serious that it can properly be described as negligent, the decision will assuredly be quashed by a process which, in New Zealand as in the United Kingdom, will normally be carried out with promptitude.

The second is that, in the nature of things, it is likely to be very rare indeed that an error of law of this kind by a minister or other public authority can properly be categorised as negligent. As is well known, anybody, even a judge, can be capable of misconstruing a statute; and such misconstruction, when it occurs, can be severely criticised without attracting the epithet 'negligent'. Obviously, this simple fact points rather to the extreme unlikelihood of a breach of duty being established in these cases ... but it is nevertheless a relevant factor to be taken into account when considering whether liability in negligence should properly be imposed.

The third is the danger of overkill. It is to be hoped that, as a general rule, imposition of liability in negligence will lead to a higher standard of care in the performance of the relevant type of act; but sometimes not only may this not be so, but the imposition of liability may even lead to harmful consequences. In other words, the cure may be worse than the disease. There are reasons for believing that this may be so in cases where liability is imposed on local authorities whose building inspectors have been negligent in relation to the inspection of foundations, as in [*Anns* v *Merton London Borough Council*], because there is a danger that the building inspectors of some local authorities may react to that decision by simply increasing, unnecessarily, the requisite depth of foundations, thereby imposing a very substantial and unnecessary financial burden on members of the community. A comparable danger may exist in cases such as the present, because, once it became known that liability in negligence may be imposed on the ground that a minister has misconstrued a statute and so acted ultra vires, the cautious civil servant may go to extreme lengths in ensuring that legal advice, or even the opinion of the court, is obtained before decisions are taken, thereby leading to unnecessary delay in a considerable number of cases.

Fourth, it is very difficult to identify any particular case in which it can properly be said that a minister is under a duty to seek legal advice. It cannot, their Lordships consider, reasonably be said that a minister is under a duty to seek legal advice in every case in which he is called on to exercise a discretionary power conferred on him by legislation; and their Lordships find it difficult to see how cases in which a duty to seek legal advice should be imposed should be segregated from those in which it should not. In any event, the officers of the relevant department will be involved; the matter will be processed and presented to the minister for decision in the usual way, and by this means his mind will be focused on the relevant issue. Again, it is not to be forgotten that the minister, in exercising his statutory discretion, is acting essentially as a guardian of the public interest; in the present case, for example, he was acting under legislation enacted not for the benefit of applicants for consent to share issues but for the protection of the community as a whole. Furthermore, he is, so far as their Lordships are aware, normally under no duty to exercise his discretion within any particular time; and if, through a mistaken construction of the statute, he acts ultra vires and delay thereby occurs before he makes an intra vires decision, he will have in any event to exercise his discretion anew and, if his discretion is then exercised in the plaintiff's favour, the effect of the delay will only be to postpone the receipt by the plaintiff of a benefit which he had no absolute right to receive.

No doubt there may be possible answers to some of these points, taken individually. But, if the matter is looked at as a whole, it cannot be said to be free from difficulty ... In all the circumstances, it must be a serious question for consideration whether it would be appropriate to impose liability in negligence in these cases, or whether it would not rather be in the public interest that citizens should be confined to their remedy, as at present, in those cases where the minister or public authority has acted in bad faith.'

Commentary

See also *Lonrho plc* v *Tebbit* [1992] 4 All ER 280.

Saif Ali v *Sydney Mitchell & Co* [1978] 3 WLR 849 House of Lords (Lord Wilberforce, Lord Diplock, Lord Salmon, Lord Russell of Killowen and Lord Keith of Kinkel)

Negligence – barrister's immunity

Facts

The plaintiff was injured in a car accident and was advised to institute proceedings against the owner of the vehicle involved. Counsel negligently failed to advise suing the driver of the vehicle so that the plaintiff was eventually left without remedy. Was counsel immune from proceedings for professional negligence?

Held (Lord Russell of Killowen and Lord Keith of Kinkel dissenting)

No, because a barrister's immunity extends only to those matters of pre-trial work which are so intimately connected with the conduct of the cause in court that they could fairly be said to be preliminary decisions affecting the cause's conduct at the hearing.

Lord Salmon:

'Unless what seems to me to be an untenable proposition is accepted, namely that public policy always requires that a barrister should be immune from liability for his neglect or incompetence in respect of all paperwork, he is rightly in no better position than any other professional man who is sued for negligence. The normal rule applied by the law is that, if anyone holding himself out as possessing reasonable competence in his avocation undertakes to advise or to settle a document, he owes a duty to advise or settle the document with reasonable competence and care. This duty is owed to anyone he should foresee may suffer loss if the duty is breached.

If in breach of that duty he fails to exercise reasonable competence or care and as a result the person to whom the duty was owed suffers damage, he is liable to compensate that person for the damage he has suffered. The law requires the damage to be borne by the person whose breach of duty has caused it, rather than by the innocent person who has suffered it.

I am far from saying that if the advice or document turns out to be wrong, it necessarily follows that he who gave or drew it is liable for the loss caused by its imperfection. The barrister is under no duty to be right; he is only under a duty to exercise reasonable care and competence. Lawyers are often faced with finely balanced problems. Diametrically opposite views may and not infrequently are taken by barristers and indeed by judges, each of whom has exercised reasonable, and sometimes far more than reasonable, care and competence. The fact that one of them turns out to be wrong certainly does not mean that he has been negligent. In my opinion, however, it can only be in the rarest of cases that the law confers any immunity on a barrister against a claim for negligence in respect of any work he has done out of court; and this case is certainly not amongst them.

I ought to add that when *Rondel* v *Worsley* came to the Court of Appeal, I felt bound ... to deal with points which I considered to be wholly irrelevant to anything we had to decide. I may have put the case too high if I used words which might give the impression that counsel's immunity always extended to the drafting of pleadings and to advising on evidence. I should have said that the immunity might *sometimes* extend to drafting pleadings and advising on evidence. If in an advice on evidence counsel states that he will not call Y as a witness whom he believes his client wishes to call solely to prejudice his opponent, counsel is immune on grounds of public policy from being sued in negligence by his client for advising that Y must not be called or for refusing to call him. In such a case the advice would be so closely connected with the conduct of the case in court that it should be covered by the same immunity. It would be absurd if counsel who is immune from an action in negligence for refusing in court to call a witness could be sued in negligence for advising out of court that the witness should not be called. If he could be sued for giving such advice it would make a travesty of the general immunity from suit for anything said or done in court and it is well settled that any device to circumvent this immunity cannot succeed ... The advice given made it impossible for the plaintiff's unanswerable case to be heard in court. It was not even remotely connected with counsel's duty to the court or with public policy.'

Commentary
But see *Antonelli* v *Wade Gery Farr* (1992) The Times 29 December.

Sheppard v *Glossop Corporation* [1921] 3 KB 132 Court of Appeal (Bankes, Scrutton and Atkin LJJ)

Negligence – exercise of statutory discretion

Facts
Under the Public Health Act 1875, the defendants could light their district but they had no obligation to do so. One Christmas night the defendants turned off a particular gas lamp at 9 pm. In the dark, the plaintiff fell and injured himself. The judge found that the accident would not have happened if the lamp had remained alight.

Held
The defendants were not liable.

Atkin LJ:

'It appears to me that if a local authority having statutory powers decides to exercise those powers, then in doing that which it so decides to do it is under a duty to persons interested to take reasonable care not to cause damage so far as the avoidance of damage is consistent with the exercise of the statutory powers. On the other hand, it is under no legal duty to act reasonably in deciding whether it shall exercise its statutory powers or not, or in deciding to what extent those powers shall be exercised – for example, over what area or for what time. Thus, it appears to me that, if it decides to light any area, its lamps and appliances must be placed and maintained with reasonable care so as to avoid danger to wayfarers or owners or occupiers of adjoining property. If gas or electricity is conducted to the lamps, reasonable care must be taken that the gas or electricity do not escape so as to cause damage. There is no duty to exercise the power of lighting at all, nor, if the local authorities do light, are they obliged to light the whole of their urban district or any particular part of it. They are under no duty to light all dangerous places or any dangerous particular place, and, if they do light a dangerous place for some of the time, they are under no duty to light it for all the time. In the present case the local authority did not cause the danger. The danger was in existence, because there was a steep place adjoining a highway over which a wayfarer at night might easily fall in the dark. The real complaint of the plaintiff is not that the local authority caused the danger, but that, the danger being there, if they had lighted the place, he would have seen the danger and avoided it. As I have said, in my opinion, there was no duty upon the local authority to light that dangerous place. Putting it in another way, during the hours of 6 to 9 pm, while, in pursuance with their decision, they were lighting the entrance to Dun Lane, they were under a duty to exercise reasonable care in the way I have mentioned; but after nine o'clock, when they had decided not to light the place, they were under no duty to light it at all.'

Simaan General Contracting Co v *Pilkington Glass Ltd (No 2)* [1988] 2 WLR 761 Court of Appeal (Lord Donaldson of Lymington MR, Dillon and Bingham LJJ)

Negligence – duty of care – economic loss

Facts

The plaintiffs were the main contractors for a building to be erected in Abu Dhabi and the defendants' double glazed units of green glass were specified. A subcontractor duly ordered the glass, but the glass supplied was not of a uniform colour and the building owner withheld payment from the plaintiffs until the glass was replaced. The plaintiffs sued the defendants for the economic loss caused by the withholding of payment.

Held

In the absence of a contract between the parties or damage to property owned by the plaintiffs, the plaintiffs could not bring a direct claim against the defendants for economic loss alone.

Dillon LJ:

> 'In my judgment there are at least two reasons (there may well be more) why the submissions of counsel for Simaan cannot be accepted and Simaan's direct claim for economic loss against Pilkington must fail.
>
> (1) It is clear, as Lord Keith point out in *Yuen Kun-yeu v A-G of Hong Kong* [1987] 3 WLR 776 at 783 that foreseeability of harm or loss does not of itself and automatically lead to a duty of care. Foreseeability of harm is a necessary ingredient of a relationship in which a duty of care will arise, but not the only ingredient. Foreseeability of harm does not become enough to make the harm recoverable by the plaintiff just because what was foreseeable was harm to the plaintiff as an individual rather than as a member of a general and unascertained class ...
>
> If, however, foreseeability does not automatically lead to a duty of care, the duty in a *Hedley Byrne* type of case must depend on the voluntary assumption of responsibility towards a particular party giving rise to a special relationship, as Lord Keith held in *Yuen Kun-yeu v A-G of Hong Kong* ... that *Hedley Byrne & Co Ltd v Heller & Partners Ltd* [1963] 3 WLR 101 was concerned with the assumption of responsibility ...
>
> But in the present case I can see nothing whatever to justify a finding that Pilkington had voluntarily assumed a direct responsibility to Simaan for the colour and quality of Pilkington's glass panels. On the contrary, all the indications are the other way and show that a chain of contractual relationships was deliberately arranged the way it was without any direct relationship between Simaan and Pilkington.
>
> (2) The approach of the law to awarding damages for economic loss on the grounds of negligence where there has been no injury to the person or property has throughout been greatly affected by pragmatic considerations ...
>
> It might at first glance seem reasonable that, if Simaan have a right of action in contract against Feal [the subcontractors] and Feal have in respect of the same general factual matters a claim in contract, albeit a different contract, against Pilkington, Simaan should be allowed a direct claim against Pilkington. But in truth to allow Simaan a direct claim against Pilkington where there is no contract between them would give rise to formidable difficulties.
>
> If Simaan have a direct claim against Pilkington, so equally or a fortiori has the sheikh [the building owner]. Feal have their claim in contract also. All three claims should be raised in separate proceedings, whether by way of arbitration or litigation, and possibly in separate jurisdictions. The difficulties of awarding damages to any one claimant would be formidable, in view of the differing amounts of retentions by the sheikh against Simaan and by Simaan against Feal and other possibilities of set-off, and in view, even more, of the fact that none of the parties have yet actually incurred the major cost of replacing Pilkington's (assumedly) defective glass panels with new panels of the correct colour. It would not be practicable, in my view, for the court to award damages against Pilkingtons in a global sum for all possible claimants and for the court subsequently to apportion that fund between all claimants and administer it accordingly.
>
> Moreover, if in principle it were to be established in this case that a main contractor or an owner has a direct claim in tort against the nominated supplier to a sub-contractor for economic loss occasioned by defects in the quality of the goods supplied, the formidable question would arise, in future cases if not in this case, as to how far exempting clauses in the contract between the nominated supplier and the sub-contractor were to be imported into the supposed duty in tort owed by the supplier to those higher up the chain ...

If, by contrast, the court does not extend, and in my judgment it would be an extension, the principle of *Hedley Byrne* to cover a direct claim by Simaan against Pilkington, no party will be left without a remedy, by English law at any rate, which is the only system of law we have been asked to consider. There will be the normal chain of liability ... in that the sheikh can sue Simaan on the main building contract, Simaan can sue Feal on the sub-contract and Feal can sue Pilkington. Each liability would be determined in the light of such exemptions as applied contractually at that stage. There is thus no warrant for extending the law of negligence to impose direct liability on Pilkington in favour of Simaan.'

Commentary
Considered: *Junior Books Ltd* v *Veitchi Co Ltd* [1982] 3 WLR 477, in relation to which Dillon LJ said:

'My own view of *Junior Books* is that the speeches of their Lordships have been the subject of so much analysis and discussion with differing explanations of the basis of the case that the case cannot now be regarded as a useful pointer to any development of the law, whatever Lord Roskill may have had in mind when he delivered his speech. Indeed I find it difficult to see that future citation from *Junior Books* can ever serve any useful purpose.'

Smith v *Eric S Bush, Harris* v *Wyre Forest District Council* [1989] 2 WLR 790
House of Lords (Lord Keith of Kinkel, Lord Brandon of Oakbrook, Lord Templeman, Lord Griffiths and Lord Jauncey of Tullichettle)

Valuation – duty of care

Facts
In *Smith*, wishing to buy a terraced house at the lower end of the housing market, the plaintiff applied to the Abbey National Building Society for a mortgage. She paid an inspection fee and signed an application form which stated that she would receive a copy of the survey report and mortgage valuation; the form also contained a disclaimer of responsibility for the contents of the report and valuation. The society instructed the defendant surveyors to carry out the inspection: the plaintiff duly received a copy of their report and valuation which also included a disclaimer. On the strength of the report, which stated that no essential repairs were required, the plaintiff purchased the house, but the defendants had carried out their work negligently, overlooking a serious defect. Eighteen months later, as a result of that defect, some flues collapsed and caused substantial damage. The facts of *Harris* were essentially the same except that the inspection was carried out by their own surveyor.

Held
The defendants were liable: they had owed the plaintiff in tort a duty to exercise reasonable skill and care, they had been in breach of that duty and the disclaimer clauses were ineffective.

Lord Templeman said that in each case the valuer knew that the purchaser was providing the money for the valuation, that the purchaser would only contract to purchase the house if the valuation was satisfactory and that the purchaser might suffer injury or damage or both if the valuer did not exercise reasonable skill and care. In those circumstances his Lordship would expect the law to impose on the valuer a duty owed to the purchaser to exercise reasonable skill and care in carrying out the valuation. The considerations referred to by Denning LJ in *Candler* v *Crane, Christmas & Co* [1951] 2 KB 164, 176-181, whose dissenting judgment was subsequently approved by the House of Lords in *Hedley Byrne & Co Ltd* v *Heller & Partners Ltd* [1964] AC 465, applied to the valuers in the present appeals. The statutory duty of the council to value the house did not prevent the council coming under a contractual or tortious duty to the plaintiffs who in *Harris* were informed of the valuation and relied on it.

The contractual duty of a valuer to value a house for the Abbey National did not prevent the valuer coming under a tortious duty to Mrs Smith who was furnished with a report of the valuation and relied on it. In general, his Lordship was of the opinion that in the absence of a disclaimer of liability the valuer who valued a house for the purpose of a mortgage, knowing that the mortgagee would, and the mortgagor would probably rely on the valuation, knowing that the purchaser mortgagor had in effect paid for the valuation, was under a duty to exercise reasonable skill and care, and that duty was owed to both parties to the mortgage for which the valuation was made. Indeed, in both appeals the existence of such a dual duty was tacitly accepted and acknowledged because notices excluding liability for breach of the duty owed to the purchaser were drafted by the mortgagee and imposed on the purchaser. In those circumstances it was necessary to consider the second question which arose in the appeals, namely, whether the disclaimers of liability were notices which fell within the Unfair Contract Terms Act 1977. In his Lordship's opinion, both ss11(3) and 13(1) supported the view that the 1977 Act required that all exclusion notices which would at common law provide a defence to an action for negligence must satisfy the requirement of reasonableness. Here, they did not and the evidence and findings of Mr Justice Park in *Yianni v Edwin Evans & Sons* [1982] QB 438, supported the view that it was unfair and unreasonable for a valuer to rely on an exclusion clause directed against a purchaser in the circumstances of the present appeals.

Lord Griffiths, concurring, said that it had to be remembered that each of the appeals concerned a dwelling house of modest value in which it was widely recognised by valuers that purchasers were in fact relying on their care and skill. It would obviously be of general application in broadly similar circumstances. But his Lordship expressly reserved his position in respect of valuations of quite different types of property for mortgage purposes, such as industrial property, large blocks of flats or very expensive houses. In such cases it might well be that the general expectation of the behaviour of the purchaser was quite different. With very large sums of money at stake prudence would demand that the purchaser obtain his own structural survey to guide him in his purchase and, in such circumstances, with such large sums of money at stake, it might be reasonable for the valuers acting on behalf of the mortgagees to exclude or limit their liability to the purchaser.

Smith v *Littlewoods Organisation Ltd* [1987] 2 WLR 480 House of Lords (Lord Keith of Kinkel, Lord Brandon of Oakbrook, Lord Griffiths, Lord Mackay of Clashfern and Lord Goff of Chieveley)

Negligence – act of third party

Facts
The defendants purchased a cinema in Dunfermline with a view to demolishing it and building a supermarket on the site. From June 1976 the site was empty and unattended. Vandals broke into the old cinema and attempted to set fire to the building. On 5 July 1976 a fire was started in the building and spread to neighbouring properties, including the plaintiffs' property. The plaintiffs sued the defendants in negligence, alleging that they had failed to take reasonable steps to prevent damage.

Held
The defendants were not liable. An occupier was under a general duty to exercise reasonable care in order to ensure that the condition of his premises was not a source of danger to neighbouring properties. Although it was expressly found that the damage by fire was foreseeable, the defendants had done all that a reasonable owner of the property could do in boarding up the cinema. There was no duty to patrol the premises all the time to keep vandals away.

Lord Griffiths:

'The fire in this case was caused by the criminal activity of third parties on Littlewoods' premises. I do not say that there will never be circumstances in which the law will require an occupier of premises to take special precautions against such a contingency but they would surely have to be extreme indeed. It is common ground that only a 24-hour guard on these premises would have been likely to prevent this fire, and even that cannot be certain, such is the determination and ingenuity of young vandals.

There was nothing of an inherently dangerous nature stored in the premises, nor can I regard an empty cinema stripped of its equipment as likely to be any more alluring to vandals than any other recently vacated premises in the centre of a town. No message was received by Littlewoods from the local police, fire brigade or any neighbour that vandals were creating any danger on the premises. In short, so far as Littlewoods knew, there was nothing significantly different about these empty premises from the tens of thousands of such premises up and down the country. People do not mount 24-hour guards on empty properties and the law would impose an intolerable burden if it required them to do so save in the most exceptional circumstances. I find no such exceptional circumstances in this case ...

I doubt myself if any search will reveal a touchstone that can be applied as a universal test to decide when an occupier is to be held liable for a danger created on his property by the act of a trespasser for whom he is not responsible. I agree that mere foreseeability of damage is certainly not a sufficient basis to found liability. But with this warning I doubt that more can be done than to leave it to the good sense of the judges to apply realistic standards in conformity with generally accepted patterns of behaviour to determine whether in the particular circumstances of a given case there has been a breach of duty sounding in negligence.'

Commentary
Applied in *Topp* v *London Country Bus (South West) Ltd* [1993] 3 All ER 448.
    NB: distinguished in *Walpole* v *Partridge and Wilson* [1994] 1 All ER 385 (CA).

Somasundaram v *M Julius Melchior & Co* [1988] 1 WLR 1394 Court of Appeal (May, Stocker and Stuart-Smith LJJ)

Lawyers' immunity

Facts
Charged with offences relating to the stabbing of his wife, the appellant at first instructed his solicitors, the respondents, that he intended to plead guilty, but then changed his mind. The respondents arranged a conference with counsel who advised the appellant to plead guilty: he did, but the sentence was reduced on appeal. The appellant alleged that the respondents had overpersuaded him to change his story and now claimed damages for negligence. His action was struck out.

Held
His appeal against this decision would be dismissed as, on the facts, his action had no reasonable chance of success. Additionally, it had been an abuse of the process of the court for the appellant to bring an action which necessarily involved an attack on the conviction and sentence imposed by the Crown Court and upheld in the Court of Appeal, subject to the reduction of sentence.

May LJ:

'The remaining ground on which counsel for the respondents submits that the action should be struck out is on the ground that the respondents are immune from suit in respect of the allegations in the statement of claim and the action is therefore bound to fail. This submission was supported by counsel as amicus curiae. Both counsel submit, rightly in our judgment, that advice as to a plea is something which is so intimately connected with the conduct of the cause in court that it can fairly be said to be a preliminary decision affecting the way that the cause is to be conducted when it comes to a hearing, within the test ... approved by the House of Lords in *Saif Ali's* case [1980] AC 198. Indeed it is difficult to think of any decision more closely so connected. Counsel submitted that such immunity must therefore extend to solicitors and he relied on passages in the speeches of their Lordships in *Rondel* v *Worsley* [1969] 1 AC 191 to this effect. But to our minds it is clear that in extending the immunity to solicitors, their Lordships limited it to the occasions when they were acting as advocates, as of course they frequently do in the magistrates' courts and county courts and occasionally in those Crown Courts where they have rights of audience ...

Counsel as amicus curiae submitted that in a case where there was both solicitor and barrister, it would be anomalous if the immunity in relation to advising on plea extended to the barrister, but not to the solicitor. That may be so; but we would not be willing to extend the immunity that protects barristers and solicitors qua advocates any further than is necessary in the interests of justice and public policy. Thus we are not persuaded in this case that the action should be struck out on the grounds of immunity from suit ...

In practice of course it makes no difference, because in a criminal case advice on plea is likely to result in a decision of the court, which would first have to be upset by the proper appeal process before any action for damages could be sustained. Moreover where, as here, the advice as to plea was later confirmed by counsel, any action against the solicitor would almost certainly be bound to fail either on the ground that the solicitor has also been advised by counsel and was not negligent or, as a matter of causation, counsel's intervention broke any link between the solicitor's advice and the eventual plea.'

Spartan Steel & Alloys Ltd v *Martin & Co (Contractors) Ltd* [1972] 3 WLR 502
Court of Appeal (Lord Denning MR, Edmund-Davies and Lawton LJJ)

Negligence – remoteness of damage

Facts
Due to the negligence of the defendants' servants who were carrying out roadworks, an electricity supply cable was damaged. This caused a loss of power for about 14 hours which meant that the plaintiffs' smelting works a quarter of a mile away had to be shut down. The result was that the molten metal ('melt') which was in the furnace had to be drawn out to avoid the danger of it solidifying and causing damage to the mould. The plaintiffs claimed damages as follows:

a) Actual physical damage to furnace: £368;
b) Loss of profit on the melt which could not be properly completed: £400;
c) Loss of profit due to being unable to process further melts for 14 hours: £1,767.

Held (Edmund-Davies LJ dissenting):
The plaintiffs could recover (a). They could also recover (b) because it was truly consequential upon (a). But (c) was not recoverable as it was economic loss independent of the physical damage.

Lord Denning MR:

'At bottom I think the question of recovering economic loss is one of policy. Whenever the courts draw a line to mark out the bounds of duty, they do it as a matter of policy so as to limit the responsibility of the defendant. Wherever courts set bounds to the damages recoverable – saying that they are, or are not, too remote – they do it as a matter of policy so as to limit the liability of the defendant.'

Commentary
Applied in *Muirhead* v *Industrial Tank Specialities Ltd* [1985] 3 WLR 993.

Spring v Guardian Assurance plc [1994] 3 WLR 354 House of Lords (Lord Keith, Lord Goff, Lord Lowry, Lord Slynn and Lord Woolf)

Duty of care owed to subject of reference

Facts

The plaintiff, who was employed by the defendants, was dismissed and sought employment with a competitor of the defendants. The competitors were obliged by the LAUTRO rules to obtain a reference from the plaintiff's previous employer, and received such a bad reference from the defendants that they refused to employ the plaintiff. The plaintiff sued the defendants in negligence claiming damages for the loss caused by the reference. At first instance the judge found that the defendants owed a duty of care to the plaintiff as regards the reference, that they had been negligent in preparing the reference and that the plaintiff was entitled to damages. The defendants appealed to the Court of Appeal who allowed the appeal and held that no duty of care existed. The plaintiff appealed to the House of Lords.

Held

The appeal was allowed. An employer who gives a reference in respect of a former employee owes that employee a duty to take reasonable care in its preparation. The imposition of such a duty was not contrary to public policy on the ground that it might inhibit the giving of full and frank references, and the fact that in an action for defamation or injurious falsehood the employer would have a defence of qualified privilege did not bar an action in negligence where no such defence was available.

Lord Slynn and Lord Woolf also held that it was an implied term of the contract between the employer and employee that the employer would take reasonable care in compiling and giving a reference, and that the employers were in breach of this implied term.

Lord Goff:

'In my opinion, the source of duty of care lies in the principle derived from *Hedley Byrne & Co Ltd* v *Heller & Partners Ltd* [1964] AC 465, viz an assumption of responsibility by those companies to the plaintiff in respect of the reference, and reliance by the plaintiff upon the exercise by them of due care and skill in respect of its preparation.

The wide scope of the principle recognised in *Hedley Byrne* is reflected in the broad statements of principle which I have quoted. All the members of the Appellate Committee in this case spoke in terms of the principle resting upon an assumption or undertaking of responsibility by the defendant towards the plaintiff, coupled with reliance by the plaintiff on the exercise by the defendant of due care and skill. Lord Devlin, in particular, stressed that the principle rested upon an assumption of responsibility when he said, at p531, that "the essence of the matter in the present case and in others of the same type is the acceptance of responsibility". For the purpose of the case now before your Lordships it is, I consider, legitimate to proceed on the same basis. Furthermore, although *Hedley Byrne* itself was concerned with the provision of information and advice, it is clear that the principle in the case is not so limited and extends to include the performance of other services, as for example the professional services rendered by a solicitor to his client (see in particular, Lord Devlin, at pp529, 530). Accordingly, where the plaintiff entrusts the defendant with the conduct of his affairs, in general or in particular, the defendant may be held to have assumed responsibility to the plaintiff, and the plaintiff to have relied on the defendant to exercise due skill and care, in respect of such conduct.'

Lord Lowry:

'I also agree with my noble and learned friend Lord Goff's interpretation of *Hedley Byrne.*'

Commentary

Henderson and *Spring* are important in that in both cases the House of Lords, and Lord Goff in particular, held that *Hedley Byrne* is not limited to cases of negligent misstatement, but can cover the performance of services where there is a voluntary assumption of responsibility by the defendant or where the special relationship exists. This is particularly important since *Hedley Byrne* is the one course of action in which recovery for pure economic loss is unquestioned.

Topp v *London Country Bus (South West) Ltd* [1993] 3 All ER 448 Court of Appeal (Dillon, Rose LJJ and Peter Gibson J)

Duty of care – minibus stolen

Facts
The defendants' minibus had been stolen from outside a public house by an unknown person who had, while driving the minibus, shortly afterwards knocked down and killed the plaintiff's wife. The vehicle had been left unattended with the ignition key in the lock. May J dismissed the plaintiff's claim in negligence.

Held
The plaintiff's appeal would be dismissed.

Dillon LJ said that the plaintiff's claim was founded in negligence on the basis that the defendant, knowing that the bus might be stolen and driven dangerously, was in breach of duty in failing to collect the bus or to render it incapable of being driven away by unauthorised persons. In so far as the case was put on the basis that leaving the bus with the key in the ignition switch was to create a special risk, it was pertinent to refer to *P Perl (Exporters) Ltd* v *Camden London Borough Council* [1984] QB 342. The cases referred to in that case were far different from the present. There was no evidence in the instant case that the malefactor had been frequenting the public house, nor was there any presumption that persons frequenting the public house were likely to steal vehicles. There was no valid distinction between the present case and *Denton* v *United Counties Omnibus Co* (1986) The Times 6 May where a bus was unlawfully taken by an unknown person from a bus station and driven about and it collided with a parked motor car. The bus company owed no duty of care to the plaintiff owner of the car and his claim failed.

All such cases, continued Dillon LJ, in a sense depended on their own facts, but it was inevitable to consider what valid distinctions there could be between them. There were none between the present case and *Denton's* case. It did not matter that in the present case the bus was parked on the highway. His Lordship recalled that in *Smith* v *Littlewoods Organisation Ltd* [1987] AC 41 Lord Mackay of Clashfern LC had pointed out that the determination of the question whether there was a duty to protect against the wrongful act of a third party was a matter for the judges of fact. There was no basis for interfering with the judge's decision in the present case.

Van Oppen v *Clerk to the Bedford Charity Trustees* [1990] 1 WLR 235 Court of Appeal (O'Connor, Croom-Johnson and Balcombe LJJ)

School – duty of care

Facts
The plaintiff, when aged sixteen and a half, suffered injury at the defendant school during an inter-house rugby match. He sued for damages on two distinct bases: (1) an allegation that the school was negligent in failing to take reasonable care for his safety on the rugby field, by failing to coach or instruct him in proper tackling techniques (the rugby claim); and (2) an allegation that the school was negligent in (a) failing to inform or advise his father (i) of the inherent risk of serious injury in the game

of rugby, (ii) of the consequent need for personal accident insurance, and (iii) that the school had not arranged such insurance for him; and (b) in default of such information or advice failing itself to ensure that he was covered by personal accident insurance (the insurance claim). The trial judge dismissed both claims ([1989] 1 All ER 272); the plaintiff appealed in respect of the insurance claim.

Held

The appeal would be dismissed.

O'Connor LJ:

'There is no dispute that had a personal accident policy been in position the plaintiff would have received the appropriate payment as a result of his injury. It is the plaintiff's case that he has suffered this loss as a result of the negligence of the school and that although it is pure economic loss it is recoverable.

Counsel for the plaintiff accepts that there is no duty on parents to take out personal accident insurance policies in favour of their children. He accepts that there is no general duty on schools to take out personal accident policies in favour of their pupils and quite plainly it is no part of a school's function to advise parents or anybody else on insurance matters.

The next matter which is of importance is that it is not suggested that the school was negligent in allowing the plaintiff to play rugby knowing that there was no personal accident policy in position. I am satisfied that the plaintiff's "insurance claim" cannot be brought within the scope of the duty owed by school to pupil arising out of the relationship which existed between them.

When one considers the duty owed by a school to its pupils one finds first of all the duties which the law imposes on all schools because they are schools. These duties are of general application whether the school be provided by the state, or privately, and regardless of whether it be fee-paying or free. Next one must look at the individual school to see whether it owes some additional duty to its pupils. On analysis such may be no more than a special standard of care to discharge the general duties, for example a school for the blind. The terms on which the school accepts pupils may show that it would be fair and reasonable to impose some additional duty on the school. Personal accident insurance is a very good example of such a term. If a school decides that all pupils are to be covered by personal accident insurance under a block policy taken out by the school and the school negligently fails to renew the policy, then in my judgment an injured pupil would have a good claim against the school.

However, I can see no justification for the court to write in such a term for a period before the school has introduced it, whether by agreement with the parents or unilaterally.

It is said that knowledge reaching the school ... on the rugby injury/personal accident insurance topic put them under a duty ... to warn parents of the desirability of taking out personal accident insurance. I do not think that the facts support this contention.'

Walpole v *Partridge and Wilson* [1993] 3 WLR 1093 Court of Appeal (Ralph Gibson, Beldam and Peter Gibson LJJ)

Use of negligence as a challenge to a court decision

Facts

Solicitor acting for the plaintiff failed, in breach of duty, to advance an appeal on a point of law which would probably have been successful. At first instance the judge struck out the plaintiff's claim as an abuse of process within *Hunter* v *Chief Constable of West Midlands Police* [1982] AC 529.

Held

Allowing the appeal, that although proceedings which amounted to a collateral attack on a final decision of a court, which the plaintiff had had a full opportunity to contest, might be an abuse of the process of the court, an action in which the plaintiff alleged that his legal advisers had failed in breach of duty to advance an appeal on a point of law which might have been decided in favour of the plaintiff was not an abuse. The fresh proceedings did not amount to relitigation of an issue decided in the earlier proceedings. The point of law in question was arguable and the defendants had failed to show that the decision of the Crown Court was a final decision. It would thus be manifestly unfair to deny the plaintiff an opportunity to have his case tried on its merits.

White v *Jones* [1995] 2 WLR 481 House of Lords (Lord Keith, Lord Goff, Lord Browne-Wilkinson, Lord Mustill and Lord Nolan)

Validity of *Ross* v *Caunters*

Facts

A testator quarrelled with his two daughters and instructed his solicitor, the defendants, to prepare a will cutting his daughters out of his estate. After this was done the testator became reconciled with his daughters and instructed the defendants to prepare a fresh will leaving £9,000 to each daughter. The defendants did nothing for a month and then began preparation of the new will. They arranged to visit the testator one month later, but unfortunately the testator died three days before the meeting. The distribution of the estate was governed by the old will, and so the daughters lost their bequests of £9,000 each. They sued the defendants, alleging that they had been negligent in the preparation of the new will and claimed £9,000 each by way of damages. The trial judge held that the defendants owed no duty of care to the plaintiffs and dismissed the action.

Held

The Court of Appeal held that *Ross* v *Caunters* [1979] 3 All ER 580 was still good law and that each plaintiff was entitled to damages of £9,000. The court held that in these circumstances liability arose because:

1. it was foreseeable that the disappointed beneficiary would suffer financial loss;
2. there was a sufficient degree of proximity between the solicitor and the intended beneficiary; and
3. it was fair, just and reasonable that liability should be imposed in negligence on the solicitor to compensate the intended beneficiary where the solicitor was in breach of his professional duty, but there was no remedy in contract and no effective remedy for the client's estate. Had damages been paid to the estate they would have passed under the original will and so would not have been received by the plaintiffs. Thus if no liability had been imposed, the only person with a valid claim (the estate) had suffered no loss, and the only person who suffered a loss (the plaintiffs) would have had no valid claim.

The House of Lords dismissed the appeal by a bare majority on the ground that the assumption of responsibility by a solicitor to his client, who had given instructions for the drawing up of a will, extended to an intended beneficiary under that will where the solicitor could reasonably foresee that his negligence might result in the loss of the intended legacy without either the testator or his estate having a remedy against him.

Lord Goff:

'For the reasons I have already given, an ordinary action in tortious negligence on the lines proposed by Sir Robert Megarry V-C in *Ross* v *Caunters* [1980] Ch 297 must, with the greatest respect, be regarded as inappropriate, because it does not meet any of the conceptual problems which have been raised. Furthermore, for the reasons I have previously given, the *Hedley Byrne* [1964] AC 465 principle cannot, in the absence of special circumstances, give rise on ordinary principles to an assumption of responsibility by the testator's solicitor towards an intended beneficiary. Even so it seems to me that it is open to your Lordships' House ... to fashion a remedy to fill a lacuna in the law and so prevent the injustice which would otherwise occur on the facts of cases such as the present. ... In my opinion, therefore, your Lordships' House should in cases such as these extend to the intended beneficiary a remedy under the *Hedley Byrne* principle by holding that the assumption of responsibility by the solicitor towards his client should be held in law to extend to the intended beneficiary who (as the solicitor can reasonably foresee) may, as a result of the solicitor's negligence, be deprived of his intended legacy in circumstances in which neither the testator nor his estate will have a remedy against the solicitor. Such liability will not of course arise in cases in which the defect in the will comes to light before the death of the testator, and the testator either leaves the will as it is or otherwise continues to exclude the previously intended beneficiary from the relevant benefit. I only wish to add that, with the benefit of experience during the 15 years in which *Ross* v *Caunters* has been regularly applied, we can say with some confidence that a direct remedy by the intended beneficiary against the solicitor appears to create no problems in practice. That is therefore the solution which I would recommend to your Lordships.'

Wigg v *British Railways Board* (1986) The Times 4 February High Court (Tucker J)

Negligence – nervous shock

Facts
The plaintiff was a train driver of 20 years' standing. On the occasion in question he started the train having received a signal from the guard that it was safe to do so. In fact a person had been attempting to board the train as it pulled away and he was pulled under the train. The plaintiff attempted to comfort the victim on realising what had happened. He remained with him for ten minutes and suffered nervous shock. This was aggravated by the fact that he had encountered two previous incidents of this nature in the recent years.

Held
The guard had been negligent in failing to notice that the carriage door was open and therefore in allowing the train to start. British Rail were therefore vicariously liable for his negligence. It was a reasonably foreseeable consequence of that negligence that the plaintiff might suffer nervous shock since he was in sufficient proximity to the accident by hearing it and seeing the aftermath. The plaintiff was entitled to damages.

Yuen Kun-yeu v *Attorney-General of Hong Kong* [1987] 3 WLR 776 Privy Council (Lord Keith of Kinkel, Lord Templeman, Lord Griffiths, Lord Oliver of Aylmerton and Sir Robert Megarry)

Negligence – test for establishing whether duty of care exists

Facts
The Commissioner of Deposit-taking Companies in Hong Kong had a wide statutory discretion as to the registration of deposit-taking businesses. The appellants made substantial deposits with a registered deposit-taking company: subsequently it went into liquidation and they lost their money. The appellants alleged negligence by the commissioner in the discharge of his functions and sought an award of damages.

Held

They should not succeed as there was no special relationship between the commissioner and the company, or between the commissioner and would-be depositors, capable of giving rise to a duty of care.

Lord Keith:

'In their Lordships' opinion the circumstance that the commissioner had, on the appellants' averments, cogent reason to suspect that the company's business was being carried on fraudulently and improvidently did not create a special relationship between the commissioner and the company of the nature described in the authorities. They are also of opinion that no special relationship existed between the commissioner and those unascertained members of the public who might in future become exposed to the risk of financial loss through depositing money with the company. Accordingly, their Lordships do not consider that the commissioner owed to the appellants any duty of care on the principle which formed the ratio of the *Dorset Yacht* case. To hark back to Lord Atkin's words, there were not such close and direct relations between the commissioner and the appellants as to give rise to the duty of care desiderated.

The appellants, however, advanced an argument based on their averment of having relied on the registration of the company when they deposited their money with it. It was said that registration amounted to a seal of approval of the company, and that by registering the company and allowing the registration to stand the commissioner made a continuing representation that the company was creditworthy. In the light of the information in the commissioner's possession that representation was made negligently and led to the appellant's loss ... While the investing public might reasonably feel some confidence that the provisions of the ordinance as a whole went a long way to protect their interests, reliance on the fact of registration as a guarantee of the soundness of the particular company would be neither reasonable nor justifiable, nor should the commissioner reasonable be expected to know of such reliance, if it existed. Accordingly their Lordships are unable to accept the appellants' arguments about reliance as apt, in all the circumstances, to establish a special relationship between them and the commissioner such as to give rise to a duty of care.'

Commentary

Followed in *Davis* v *Radcliffe* [1990] 1 WLR 821 and *Clough* v *Bussan* [1990] 1 All ER 431.

7 Negligence: Breach of the Duty

Airedale NHS Trust v *Bland* [1993] 2 WLR 316 House of Lords (Lord Keith of Kinkel, Lord Goff of Chievely, Lord Lowry, Lord Browne-Wilkinson and Lord Mustill)

Withdrawal of treatment – breach of duty of care?

Facts

When aged 17½ Anthony Bland was crushed in the 1989 Hillsborough football disaster. He had since then been in a persistent vegetative state, without hope of recovery or improvement of any kind. The plaintiffs now sought a declaration that they could lawfully discontinue all life-sustaining treatment.

Held

The declaration had been properly granted.

Lord Browne-Wilkinson:

'... this House in *F* v *West Berkshire Health Authority* [1989] 2 WLR 1025 developed and laid down a principle, based on concepts of necessity, under which a doctor can lawfully treat a patient who cannot consent to such treatment if it is in the best interests of the patient to receive such treatment. In my view, the correct answer to the present case depends on the extent of the right to continue lawfully to invade the bodily integrity of Anthony Bland without his consent. If in the circumstances they have no right to continue artificial feeding, they cannot be in breach of any duty by ceasing to provide such feeding.

What then is the extent of the right to treat Anthony Bland which can be deduced from *F* v *West Berkshire Health Authority*? Both Lord Brandon of Oakbrook and Lord Goff make it clear that the right to administer invasive medical care is wholly dependent upon such care being in the best interests of the patient ... Moreover, a doctor's decision whether invasive care is in the best interests of the patient falls to be assessed by reference to the test laid down in *Bolam* v *Friern Hospital Management Committee* [1957] 1 WLR 582, viz is the decision in accordance with a practice accepted at the time by a responsible body of medical opinion? ... In my judgment it must follow from this that, if there comes a stage where the responsible doctor comes to the reasonable conclusion (which accords with the views of a responsible body of medical opinion) that further continuance of an intrusive life support system is not in the best interests of the patient, he can no longer lawfully continue that life support system: to do so would constitute the crime of battery and the tort of trespass to the person. Therefore he cannot be in breach of any duty to maintain the patient's life. Therefore he is not guilty of murder by omission ...

Finally, the conclusion I have reached will appear to some to be almost irrational. How can it be lawful to allow a patient to die slowly, though painlessly, over a period of weeks from lack of food but unlawful to produce his immediate death by a lethal injection, thereby saving his family from yet another ordeal to add to the tragedy that has already struck them? I find it difficult to find a moral answer to that question. But it is undoubtedly the law and nothing I have said casts doubt on the proposition that the doing of a positive act with the intention of ending life is and remains murder.'

Barkway v South Wales Transport Co Ltd [1950] AC 185 House of Lords (Lord Porter, Lord Normand, Lord Morton of Henryton, Lord Reid and Lord Radcliffe)

Negligence – accident due to burst tyre

Facts

The offside front tyre of the respondents' bus burst and the vehicle veered across the road and fell over an embankment. The appellant's husband, a passenger in the bus, was killed. The tyre had been defective.

Held

The appellant should succeed as the defect in the tyre might have been discovered if the respondents had exercised due diligence.

Lord Ratcliffe:

'I do not think that the appellant was entitled to judgment in the action because of any special virtue in the maxim *res ipsa loquitur*. I find nothing more in that maxim than a rule of evidence, of which the essence is that an event which in the ordinary course of things is more likely than not to have been caused by negligence is by itself evidence of negligence. In this action much more is known than the bare fact that the omnibus mounted the pavement and fell down the bank. The true question is not whether the appellant adduced some evidence of negligence, but whether on all the evidence she proved that the respondents had been guilty of negligence in a relevant particular. In my view, the important thing is that the tyre on the respondents' omnibus was defective.'

Blyth v Birmingham Waterworks Co (1856) 11 Exch 781 Court of Exchequer (Alderson, Martin and Bramwell BB)

Negligence – frost of exceptional severity

Facts

In pursuance of statutory powers, the defendants laid down water pipes. During 'one of the severest frosts on record', a plug failed to work correctly and a large quantity of water escaped into the plaintiff's house.

Held

On the facts, the defendants were not liable.

Alderson B:

'The case turns upon the question whether the facts proved show that the defendants were guilty of negligence. Negligence is the omission to do something which a reasonable man, guided upon those considerations which ordinarily regulate the conduct of human affairs, would do, or doing something which a prudent and reasonable man would not do. The defendants might have been liable for negligence, if, unintentionally, they omitted to do that which a reasonable person would have done, or did that which a person taking reasonable precautions would not have done. A reasonable man would act with reference to the average circumstances of the temperature in ordinary years. The defendants had provided against such frosts as experience would have led men, acting prudently, to provide against; and they are not guilty of negligence, because their precautions proved insufficient against the effects of the extreme severity of the frost of 1855, which penetrated to a greater depth than any which ordinarily occurs south of the polar regions. Such a state of circumstances constitutes a contingency against which no reasonable man can provide. The result was an accident, for which the defendants cannot be held liable.'

Bolam v *Friern Hospital Management Committee* [1957] 1 WLR 582 High Court (McNair J)

Negligence – two schools of thought

Facts

Suffering from mental illness, the plaintiff agreed to undergo electro-convulsive therapy. The method of treatment adopted was favoured by one body of medical opinion, but another preferred a different approach. The plaintiff suffered injury in the course of his treatment and he sought damages for negligence.

Held

His action failed.

McNair J:

'I must explain what in law we mean by "negligence". In the ordinary case which does not involve any special skill, negligence in law means this: some failure to do some act which a reasonable man in the circumstances would do, or doing some act which a reasonable man in the circumstances would not do; and if that failure or doing of that act results in injury, then there is a cause of action. How do you test whether this act or failure is negligent? In an ordinary case it is generally said, that you judge that by the action of the man in the street. He is the ordinary man. In one case it has been said that you judge it by the conduct of the man on the top of a Clapham omnibus. He is the ordinary man. But where you get a situation which involves the use of some special skill or competence, then the test whether there has been negligence or not is not the test of the man on the top of a Clapham omnibus, because he has not got this special skill. The test is the standard of the ordinary skilled man exercising and professing to have that special skill. A man need not possess the highest expert skill at the risk of being found negligent. It is well-established law that it is sufficient if he exercises the ordinary skill of an ordinary competent man exercising that particular art. I do not think that I quarrel much with any of the submissions in law which have been put before you by counsel. Counsel for the plaintiff put it in this way, that in the case of a medical man negligence means failure to act in accordance with the standards of reasonably competent medical men at the time. That is a perfectly accurate statement, as long as it is remembered that there may be one or more perfectly proper standards; and if a medical man conforms with one of those proper standards then he is not negligent. Counsel for the plaintiff was also right, in my judgment, in saying: that a mere personal belief that a particular technique is best is no defence unless that belief is based on reasonable grounds. That again is unexceptionable.'

Commentary

Applied in *Clark* v *MacLennan* [1983] 1 All ER 416 and *Airedale NHS Trust* v *Bland* [1993] 2 WLR 316.
    See also *Whitehouse* v *Jordan* [1981] 1 WLR 246 and *F* v *West Berskhire Health Authority* [1989] 2 All ER 545.

Bolton v *Stone* [1951] AC 850 House of Lords (Lord Porter, Lord Normand, Lord Oaksey, Lord Reid and Lord Radcliffe)

Negligence – injury from cricket ball

Facts

The plaintiff was standing on the highway when she was hit by a cricket ball which had been struck from the defendant's adjoining cricket ground. The evidence showed that, in the many years that cricket had been played on the ground, only very occasionally had the ball been hit so far. The ball had travelled over 100 yards after being hit and had cleared a seven foot boundary fence. The plaintiff sued in, inter alia, negligence. In the House of Lords it was conceded that, in the circumstances, nuisance could not be established unless negligence was proved.

Held

The defendants were not negligent in failing to take steps to guard against such a small risk: such an injury would not have been anticipated by a reasonable man.

Lord Oaksey:

> 'An ordinary, careful man does not take precautions against every foreseeable risk. He can, of course, foresee the possibility of many risks, but life would be almost impossible if he were to attempt to take precautions against every risk which he can foresee. He takes precautions against risks which are reasonably likely to happen.'

Lord Reid:

> 'In the crowded conditions of modern life, even the most careful person cannot avoid creating some risks and accepting others. What a man must not do ... is to create a risk which is substantial.'

Commentary

Distinguished in *Overseas Tankship (UK) Ltd* v *The Miller Steamship Co Pty Ltd (The Wagon Mound No 2)* [1966] 3 WLR 498.

Condon v *Basi* [1985] 1 WLR 866 Court of Appeal (Sir John Donaldson MR, Stephen Brown LJ and Glidewell J)

Negligence – injury during football match

Facts

The plaintiff and defendant were playing on opposite sides in a football match, and the defendant made a foul tackle on the plaintiff resulting in breaking the plaintiff's leg. The plaintiff claimed damages for negligence and assault.

Held

His claim should succeed. The duty of care between sports players is a duty to take reasonable care in the light of the circumstances in which they are playing. A player is negligent if he fails to exercise reasonable care *or* if he acts in a way to which another player cannot be expected to consent. On the facts of the case, there had been, in the words of the county court judge, 'serious and dangerous foul play which showed a reckless disregard of the plaintiff's safety'.

Glasgow Corporation v *Muir* [1943] 2 AC 448 House of Lords (Lord Thankerton, Lord Macmillan, Lord Wright, Lord Romer and Lord Clauson)

Negligence – danger reasonably foreseeable?

Facts

The defendants owned a tea-room in Glasgow run by a manageress, a Mrs Alexander. On the day in question, a party of children were in the room. The manageress gave permission for a church party to use the room to eat their sandwiches. The latter group made their tea in an urn and were carrying it along a narrow passage into the tea-room itself when it was accidentally dropped. Scalding-hot tea injured six of the children in the tea-room. An action was brought on behalf of the children alleging negligence against the manageress.

Held
The plaintiffs' claim would fail as the manageress had not acted in a way which amounted to negligence.

Lord Macmillan:

'The standard of foresight of the reasonable man is in one sense an impersonal test. It eliminates the personal equation and is independent of the idiosyncracies of the particular person whose conduct is in question. Some persons are, by nature, unduly timorous and imagine every path beset with lions; others, of more robust temperament, fail to foresee or nonchalantly disregard even the most obvious dangers. The reasonable man is presumed to be free both from over-apprehension and from over-confidence. But, there is a sense in which the standard of care of the reasonable man involves in its application a subjective element. It is still left to the judge to decide what, in the circumstances of the particular case, the reasonable man would have had in contemplation and what accordingly the party sought to be made liable ought to have foreseen. Here there is room for diversity of view, as indeed is well illustrated in the present case. What to one judge may seem far-fetched may seem to another both natural and probable.'

Lord Wright:

'In the present case, as I have stated, as the permitted operation was intrinsically innocuous, I do not think any obligation rested on Mrs Alexander to attempt to supervise how it was carried out. As a reasonable person, not having any ground for anticipating harm, she was entitled to go on with her proper work and leave the church party to do what was proper. There might, of course, be circumstances in which, because there was an obvious risk, a duty might rest on the occupier to supervise how the operation was actually conducted, if the permission was given. I do not see what Mrs Alexander could have done in that respect, unless she had seen that all the children were removed from the passage when the urn was being carried through. That might be her obligation if the operation she permitted had been intrinsically dangerous, but it was not so in the circumstances as I apprehended them. No doubt some difficult questions of fact may arise in these cases. In the present case, however, as I think that there was no reasonably foreseeable danger to the children from the use of the premises which the appellants permitted to be made, I think the respondent's claim cannot be supported.'

Commentary
Distinguished in *Hughes* v *Lord Advocate* [1963] 2 WLR 779.

Haley v *London Electricity Board* [1964] 3 WLR 479 House of Lords (Lord Reid, Lord Morton of Henryton, Lord Evershed, Lord Hodson and Lord Guest)

Negligence – street works

Facts
The Board's workmen dug a hole in the pavement and left it guarded by a wooden handle resting some nine inches above the ground. The plaintiff, a blind man accustomed to the stretch of pavement, was unable to detect the barrier with his stick and tripped over it, causing himself injuries.

Held
The Board were liable as they had been guilty of negligence. They owed a duty of care, not only to

able-bodied pedestrians, but also to the blind or infirm as it was reasonably foreseeable that the latter might use the pavement.

Lord Morton of Henryton:

'(The Board's) duty is to take reasonable care not to act in a way likely to endanger other persons who may reasonably be expected to walk along the pavement. That duty is owed to blind persons if the operators foresee or ought to have foreseen that blind persons may walk along the pavement and is in no way different from the duty owed to persons with sight, though the carrying out of the duty may involve extra precautions in the case of blind pedestrians. I think that everyone living in Greater London must have seen blind persons walking slowly along on the pavement and waving a white stick in front of them so as to touch any distraction which may be in their way and I think that the respondent's workmen ought to have foreseen that a blind person might well come along the pavement in question.'

Henderson v *Henry E Jenkins & Sons* [1969] 3 WLR 732 House of Lords (Lord Reid, Lord Guest, Viscount Dilhorne, Lord Donovan and Lord Pearson)

Negligence – burden of proof

Facts
While the respondents' five year old lorry was descending a steep hill, its brakes failed: the lorry struck and killed a van driver. A hole had developed in the brake fluid pipe, a very uncommon fault of which the lorry driver would have had no warning.

Held (Lord Guest and Viscount Dilhorne dissenting)
It was for the respondents to prove that, in all the circumstances which they knew or ought to have known, they took all proper steps to avoid danger. As they had failed to do this, the van driver's estate was entitled to damages.

Lord Pearson:

'... it seems to me clear, as a prima facie inference, that the accident must have been due to default of the respondents in respect of inspection or maintenance or both. Unless they had a satisfactory answer, sufficient to displace the inference, they should have been held liable.'

Latimer v *AEC Ltd* [1953] 2 AC 643 House of Lords (Lord Porter, Lord Oaksey, Lord Reid, Lord Tucker and Lord Asquith of Bishopstone)

Negligence – slippery factory floor

Facts
A sudden rainstorm caused flooding in the defendants' factory and resulted in the floor becoming slippery. Sawdust was spread over the floor, but they did not have sufficient quantities to cope with the extreme situation. The plaintiff, an employee, slipped on a part of the floor which had not been covered in sawdust and was injured.

Held
There was no negligence on the part of the defendants. They had acted reasonably when faced with an extreme situation and had taken prompt action to make the floor as safe as they could. The only other thing would have been to shut down the factory altogether, but the risk was not of such gravity as to compel any reasonable, prudent employer to do this.

Luxmoore-May v *Messenger May Baverstock* [1990] 1 WLR 1009 Court of Appeal (Slade, Mann LJJ and Sir David Croom-Johnson)

Auctioneer – standard of care

Facts

The plaintiffs owned two paintings of foxhounds and they asked the defendant provincial auctioneers to look at them: their representative, Mrs Zarek, thought they were worth about £30 but took them away 'for research'. The defendants offered expert advice by a Mr Thomas, an independent contractor. He valued them at £30 to £50. Shortly before the sale, Mrs Zarek took the paintings to Christie's of London but they made no favourable comment about them. The paintings were sold at auction for £840: five months later they were sold at Sotheby's for £88,000: the plaintiffs sued for the difference.

Held

Their claim could not succeed as the defendants had not been guilty of negligence.

Slade LJ:

' ... I am of the opinion that the judge ... demanded too high a standard of skill on the part of the defendants and of Mr Thomas, in concluding that no competent valuer could have missed the signs of Stubbs [a noted 18th century sporting artist] potential. In my judgment, the question whether the foxhound pictures had Stubbs potential ... was one which competent valuers, and indeed competent dealers, could have held widely differing views. It has not been argued that a valuation of £30 to £40 would have been too low if these pictures were simply to be regarded as objects to be hung on a wall *without* Stubbs potential. For these reasons, I am of the opinion that negligence on the part of Mr Thomas has not been established, and accordingly that negligence on the part of the defendants would not have been established, even if Mrs Zarek, after taking Mr Thomas's advice, had taken no further advice in relation to the pictures.'

Commentary

Applied: *Maynard* v *West Midlands Regional Health Authority* [1984] 1 WLR 634.

McHale v *Watson* [1966] ALR 513 High Court of Australia (McTiernan ACJ, Kitto, Menzies and Owen JJ)

Negligence – standard of care

Facts

The plaintiff girl was injured when a steel spike thrown by the defendant, a boy of 12, glanced off a post at which he was aiming and hit the plaintiff in the eye. The plaintiff had been standing about five feet to the left of the post.

Held

The defendant had not been negligent.

Kitto J:

'To expect a boy of that age to consider before throwing the spike whether the timber was hard or soft, to weigh the chances of being able to make the spike stick in the post and to foresee that it might glance off and hit the girl, would be, I think, to expect a degree of sense and circumspection which nature ordinarily withholds till life has become less rosy.'

Maynard v *West Midlands Regional Health Authority* [1984] 1 WLR 634 House of Lords (Lord Fraser of Tullybelton, Lord Elwyn-Jones, Lord Scarman, Lord Roskill and Lord Templeman)

Negligence – conflicting medical opinion

Facts

A consultant physician and a surgeon thought that the plaintiff in this case was probably suffering from tuberculosis when they made a diagnosis, but also thought it might be Hodgkin's disease, carcinoma or sarcoidosis. Hodgkin's disease can be fatal unless treated early so they carried out an operation which carried with it a risk of damage to a nerve of the larynx, even if carried out correctly. The operation was carefully performed, but damage was caused to the patient's nerve. The disease was eventually found to be TB and there was conflicting medical opinion at the trial to the effect that the TB was diagnosable as such at that early stage on the one hand, and that the defendants' course of action was approved on the other hand.

Held

The plaintiff's action for negligence would fail. In the medical profession, there was room for differences of opinion and practice and it was insufficient to prove negligence by showing merely that a body of competent professional opinion considered the decision in question wrong, if another body thought that what the defendant did was reasonable.

Commentary

Applied in *Luxmoore-May* v *Messenger May Baverstock* [1990] 1 All ER 1067.

Nettleship v *Weston* [1971] 3 WLR 370 Court of Appeal (Lord Denning MR, Salmon and Megaw LJJ)

Negligence – duty to passenger in car

Facts

The plaintiff took the defendant for driving lessons in a car belonging to the defendant's husband. The plaintiff had first checked to satisfy himself that he would be covered by the defendant's insurance in the event of an accident. During one of the lessons an accident occurred when the defendant, having taken a corner, failed to straighten the car up and crashed into a lamp-post despite the plaintiff's own attempts to stop the car. The plaintiff was injured and claimed damages from the defendant.

Held

The plaintiff should succeed. The standard of care which the law expects of a learner driver is the same as that of any other reasonably competent driver. There can be no such thing as a varying standard of care. However, the damages awarded were reduced by 50 per cent: if the plaintiff had acted more quickly the accident would have been avoided.

Lord Denning MR:

'In all that I have said, I have treated Mrs Weston as the driver who was herself in control of the car. On that footing, she is plainly liable for the damage done to the lamp-post. She is equally liable for the injury done to Mr Nettleship. She owed a duty of care to each. The standard of care is the same in either case. It is measured objectively by the care to be expected of an experienced skilled and careful driver.

Mr Nettleship is not defeated by the maxim volenti non fit injuria. He did not agree, expressly or impliedly, to waive any claim for damages owing to her failure to measure up to the standard. But his damages may fall to be reduced owing to his failure to correct her error quick enough. Although the judge dismissed the claim, he did (in case he was wrong) apportion responsibility. He thought it would be just and equitable to regard them equally to blame. I would accept this apportionment.'

Commentary
Applied: *Dann* v *Hamilton* [1939] 1 KB 509 and *Wooldridge* v *Sumner* [1962] 3 WLR 616.

Paris v *Stepney Borough Council* [1951] AC 367 House of Lords (Lord Simonds, Lord Normand, Lord Oaksey, Lord Morton of Henryton and Lord MacDermott)

Negligence – employers' liability

Facts
The plaintiff, who had lost the sight in one eye, was employed by the defendants who knew of his condition. One day, when he was repairing a vehicle, he hit a bolt with a hammer to release it. The impact caused a piece of metal to fly off and enter his other eye, causing total loss of sight. He alleged his employers had been negligent in failing to supply him with protective goggles.

Held (Lord Simonds and Lord Morton of Henryton dissenting)
The plaintiff's claim succeeded. In assessing what a reasonable employer would do to ensure the safety of his employees, it is necessary to take into account not only the likelihood of the accident occuring, but also the gravity of its consequences. The employer's duty is owed to each individual workman and account must be taken of the relative gravity as regards each.

Lord Oaksey:

'In the present case the question is whether an ordinarily prudent employer would supply goggles to a one-eyed workman whose job was to knock bolts out of a chassis with a steel hammer while the chassis was elevated on a ramp so that the workman's eye was close to and under the bolt. In my opinion, Lynskey J was entitled to hold that an ordinarily prudent employer would take that precaution. The question was not whether the precaution ought to have been taken with ordinary two-eyed workmen.'

Roe v *Ministry of Health* [1954] 2 WLR 915 Court of Appeal (Somervell, Denning and Morris LJJ)

Negligence – liability for staff

Facts
The plaintiff underwent a minor operation in hospital. He was given an anaesthetic injected into the spine. The anaesthetic was kept in glass ampoules which were stored in a jar containing phenol (carbolic acid) to prevent infection. Unknown to anyone, tiny cracks were present in the ampoules and some of the phenol had seeped in and contaminated the anaesthetic. This resulted in the plaintiff being permanently paralysed. He brought a claim against the Ministry (the owner of the hospital) and the anaesthetist who worked at the hospital part-time.

Held
The plaintiff's claim should fail as, having regard to the standard of knowledge at the time, the anaesthetist had not been guilty of negligence.

Denning LJ:

> 'The hospital authorities are responsible for the whole of their staff, not only for the nurses and doctors, but also for the anaesthetists and the surgeons. It does not matter whether they are permanent or temporary, resident or visiting, whole-time or part-time. The hospital authorities are responsible for all of them. The reason is because, even if they are not servants, they are the agents of the hospital to give the treatment. The only exception is the case of consultants or anaesthetists selected and employed by the patient himself ... (see) *Cassidy* v *Ministry of Health* [1951] 2 KB 343 ...'

Scott v *London & St Katherine Docks Co* (1865) 3 H & C 596 Court of Exchequer Chamber (Erle CJ, Crompton, Byles, Blackburn, Keating and Mellor JJ)

Negligence – res ipsa loquitur

Facts

The plaintiff was passing the defendants' warehouse, where bags of sugar were being lowered by a crane, when he was struck and injured by a bag which apparently had fallen off the crane. The plaintiff relied on this fact alone as establishing negligence on the part of the defendants or their servants.

Held

There should be a new trial as there was evidence of negligence by the defendants' servants.

Erle CJ:

> 'The majority of the court have come to the following conclusion. There must be reasonable evidence of negligence, but, where the thing is shown to be under the management of the defendant, or his servants, and the accident is such as, in the ordinary course of things, does not happen if those who have the management of the machinery use proper care, it affords reasonable evidence, in the absence of explanation by the defendant, that the accident arose from want of care.'

Sidaway v *Bethlem Royal Hospital Governors* [1985] AC 871 House of Lords (Lord Scarman, Lord Diplock, Lord Keith of Kinkel, Lord Bridge of Harwich and Lord Templeman)

Negligence – risk of misfortune

Facts

The plaintiff underwent an operation on the spinal cord to relieve neck pain, and was told by the surgeon of the possibility of disturbing a nerve root and the consequences of that, but not of the possibility of danger to the spinal cord. As a result of the operation, the plaintiff was severely disabled. In the plaintiff's action for damage to her spinal cord, based on an alleged breach of duty to warn her of the risks involved, it was found that there was a 1 – 2 per cent risk of damage to nerve roots and an even lower percentage of risk of damage to the spinal cord.

Held (Lord Scarman dissenting)

The plaintiff's action would fail. The test was whether the surgeon had acted in accordance with a practice accepted at the time as proper by a responsible body of medical opinion.

Lord Bridge:

> 'I can see no reasonable ground on which the judge could properly reject the conclusion to which the unchallenged medical evidence led in the application of the *Bolam* test. The trial judge's assessment of the

risk at 1 per cent or 2 per cent covered both nerve root and spinal cord damage and covered a spectrum of possible ill-effects 'ranging from the mild to the catastrophic'. In so far as it is possible and appropriate to measure such risks in percentage terms (some of the expert medical witnesses called expressed a marked and understandable reluctance to do so), the risk of damage to the spinal cord of such severity as the appellant in fact suffered was, it would appear, certainly less than 1 per cent. But there is no yardstick either in the judge's findings or in the evidence to measure what fraction of 1 per cent that risk represented. In these circumstances, the appellant's expert witness's agreement that the non-disclosure complained of accorded with a practice accepted as proper by a responsible body of neuro-surgical opinion afforded the respondents a complete defence to the appellant's claim.'

Ward v *Tesco Stores Ltd* [1976] 1 WLR 810 Court of Appeal (Megaw, Lawton and Ormrod LJJ)

Negligence – burden of proof

Facts

The plaintiff was shopping in the defendants' supermarket when she slipped on some yoghurt which had been spilt on the floor. The evidence was that the floor was swept some six times a day and in addition, staff were instructed to deal promptly with spillages, which were a common occurence. The plaintiff was unable to say how long the yoghurt had been on the floor on the day she fell, but said that on a subsequent visit she had seen a spillage remain uncleared for some time. The plaintiff alleged the defendants were negligent in their maintenance of the floor.

Held (Ormrod LJ dissenting)

The plaintiff should succeed. She had made out a prima facie case which the defendant had not rebutted.

Megaw LJ:

'It is for the plaintiff to show that there has occurred an event which is unusual and which, in the absence of explanation, is more consistent with fault on the part of the defendants than the absence of fault; and to my mind the learned judge was wholly right in taking that view of the presence of this slippery liquid on the floor of the supermarket in the circumstances of this case: that is that the defendants knew or should have known that it was a not uncommon occurrence; and that if it should happen, and should not be promptly attended to, it created a serious risk that customers would fall and injure themselves. When the plaintiff has established that, the defendants can still escape from liability. They could escape from liability if they could show that the accident must have happened, or even on balance of probability would have been likely to have happened, irrespective of the existence of a proper and adequate system, in relation to the circumstances, to provide for the safety of customers. But, if the defendants wish to put forward such a case, it is for them to show that, on balance of probability, either by evidence or by inference from the evidence that is given or is not given, this accident would have been at least equally likely to have happened despite a proper system designed to give reasonable protection to customers. That, in this case, they wholly failed to do.'

Watt v *Hertfordshire County Council* [1954] 1 WLR 835 Court of Appeal (Singleton, Denning and Morris LJJ)

Negligence – liability of fire authority

Facts

The plaintiff, a fireman, was on duty when an emergency call was received to free a woman who was trapped under a heavy vehicle. Those on duty were given instructions to load a jack onto a lorry and proceed to the scene. The jack could not be properly secured on this particular vehicle (a specially fitted vehicle was properly on duty elsewhere) and the plaintiff and two others rode on the back of the lorry to hold it. In the course of the journey, the driver was forced to brake suddenly and the jack fell over, injuring the plaintiff.

Held
The plaintiff was not entitled to damages as his employers had not been guilty of negligence.

Denning LJ:

> 'It is well settled that in measuring due care one must balance the risk against the measures necessary to eliminate the risk ... In this case the risk in sending out the lorry was not so great as to prohibit the attempt to save life ... It is always a question of balancing the risk against the end.'

Welsh v *Chief Constable of the Merseyside Police* [1993] 1 All ER 692 High Court (Tudor Evans J)

Negligence – immunity of Crown Prosecution Service

Facts
The plaintiff alleged that the Crown Prosecution Service (CPS) had negligently failed to inform a magistrates' court, from which he had been bailed on charges of theft, that those offences had subsequently been taken into consideration at the Crown Court, and that, as a result of that failure, he had been arrested and detained and thereby suffered loss, damage and distress. The registrar struck out the plaintiff's claim.

Held
The claim would be reinstated.

Tudor Evans J:

> 'It is not necessary to go further than ... *Saif Ali* v *Sydney Mitchell & Co* [1978] 3 All ER 1033 ... If ... a solicitor acting on behalf of the [CPS] failed as an advocate in court to inform the court that the offences had been taken into consideration, the [CPS] and the solicitor would be immune from any action based on that failure.
>
> I am therefore solely concerned with the question whether the [CPS] owed the plaintiff a duty of care apart from [such a failure].
>
> Counsel [for the plaintiff] formulated the following proposition as containing the criteria by which it is necessary to decide whether a duty of care is owed to a particular plaintiff: first, it is necessary to consider the principle of reasonable foreseeability of loss and damage and, in so far as different factors may be involved, the question of proximity. It is then necessary to consider whether it would be fair, just and reasonable to hold such a duty to exist and finally the question has to be answered whether there is any ground of public policy for excluding a duty.
>
> I have been referred to a large number of authorities in support of this proposition, but I need only list them since [counsel for the CPS] accepted the proposition as I have stated it. The authorities to which I referred are *Anns* v *Merton London Borough* [1977] 2 All ER 492, *Governors of the Peabody Donation Fund* v *Sir Lindsay Parkinson & Co Ltd* [1984] 3 All ER 529, *Yuen Kun-yeu* v *A-G of Hong Kong* [1987] 2 All ER 705, *Davis* v *Radcliffe* [1990] 2 All ER 536, *Caparo Industries plc* v *Dickman* [1990] 1 All ER 568, *James McNaughton Papers Group Ltd* v *Hicks Anderson & Co (a firm)* [1991] 1 All ER 134 and *Morgan Crucible Co plc* v *Hill Samuel Bank Ltd* [1991] 1 All ER 148 ...
>
> I think it appropriate ... to consider the proposition agreed between the parties as containing the test by which to decide whether a duty of care exists. First, [counsel for the CPS] accepted that it was

reasonably foreseeable by the [CPS] that the plaintiff would suffer loss if the magistrates' court were not informed that the offences had been taken into consideration but he qualified this concession by submitting that the plaintiff was represented by solicitors and that the [CPS] would therefore contemplate that the plaintiff's solicitors would inform the court. In my view that is an argument based on causation, that is that the effective cause of the damage was the failure of the plaintiff's solicitors to inform the court. Causation is not an argument available at this stage. Then [he] submitted that the parties were not proximate. He contended that they could not be neighbours bearing in mind that they were antagonists in adversarial litigation. Counsel relied on the decision of Scott J in *Business Computers International Ltd* v *Registrar of Companies* [1987] 3 All ER 465 and *Al-Kandari* v *J R Brown & Co (a firm)* [1988] 1 All ER 833 ...

Both of these cases were concerned with civil litigation. I think that it is highly arguable that the CPS, responsible for the preparation and presentation of criminal charges of many types and of varying gravity is not in the same position as a solicitor acting at arm's length in adversarial civil litigation. The traditions which govern the attitude of a prosecutor in criminal cases in this country suggest otherwise. The Code for Prosecutors issued under the powers conferred by s10 of the [Prosecution of Offences Act] 1985 ... stating, for example in para 8, the factors to be taken into consideration when deciding whether to prosecute in cases where a conviction might otherwise be secured is another example which emphasises the difference. There are many other instances: for example, the duty to make available to the defence witnesses who can give material evidence and whom the prosecution do not intend to call and also the obligation to inform the defence of any previous convictions of a prosecution witness. All these practices are alien to civil litigation.

Apart from [counsel for the plaintiff's] other submissions on proximity, the question of proximity is raised by the plaintiff as arising from [the fact that the CPS's] "solicitor for Ormskirk" approved of the offences being taken into consideration and, by reasonable inference, he agreed to note the file. The plaintiff relies in this context on *Kirkham* v *Chief Constable of the Greater Manchester Police* [1990] 3 All ER 246 at 250 where Lloyd LJ said:

> "The question depends in each case on whether, having regard to the particular relationship between the parties, the defendant has assumed a responsibility towards the plaintiff, and whether the plaintiff has relied on that assumption of responsibility."

In my view the solicitor for Ormskirk assumed responsibility towards the plaintiff ... or at least it is highly arguable that he did. Moreover, the assumed facts show that the plaintiff was relying on that responsibility. He did not expect to have to answer to his bail ...

Next, in my view it is fair, just and reasonable to hold that a duty of care exists on the assumed facts of this case. [Counsel for the CPS] submitted that it would be wrong to look at this aspect of the question of duty within the narrow confines of this case. There may be cases, he contended, in which there are a very large number of offences taken into consideration and the burden on the [CPS] would be such that it would not be fair or just or reasonable to cast a duty. I do not agree.

Finally, is there any ground of public policy for excluding a duty? To hold that a duty exists does not impugn the decision of the magistrates' court. It does not infringe any of the immunities which arise from the conduct of cases or from the evidence of witnesses. In *Business Computers International Ltd* v *Registrar of Companies* [1987] 3 All ER 465 Scott J, in rejecting the existence of a duty of care in the circumstances of that case, was influenced by the existence of safeguards against impropriety which are to be found in the rules and procedure that controlled the litigation. There are none such on the facts of the present case. I can find no reason for excluding a duty on the grounds of public policy.

It follows that in my view, by every one of the agreed tokens by which to test the existence of a duty, a duty is found to exist. [Counsel for the CPS] has not produced an authority which unambiguously states that proof of malice is an integral part in an action which touches on a judicial process. No authority has been produced to show that a duty of care cannot exist at stages anterior to litigation or resumed litigation. In these circumstances ... I would decline to strike out this action.'

Whitehouse v *Jordan* [1981] 1 WLR 246 House of Lords (Lord Wilberforce, Lord Edmund-Davies, Lord Fraser of Tullybelton, Lord Russell of Killowen and Lord Bridge of Harwich)

Negligence – error of judgment

Facts

The defendant, a senior hospital registrar, delivered the plaintiff baby. The birth was a difficult one and the defendant decided to use forceps, but after pulling five or six times, he delivered the baby by Caesarean section. The prolonged use of the forceps resulted in brain damage to the plaintiff, who sued the defendant in negligence.

Held

Even if the defendant had pulled too hard and too long (which was not shown by the evidence to be the case), this did not here amount to legal negligence.

Lord Edmund-Davies:

'To say that a surgeon committed an error of clinical judgment is wholly ambiguous, for, while some such errors may be completely consistent with the due exercise of professional skill, other acts or omissions in the course of exercising "clinical judgment" may be so glaringly below proper standards as to make a finding of negligence inevitable. Indeed, I should have regarded this as a truism were it not that, despite the exposure of the "false antithesis" by Donaldson LJ in his dissenting judgment in the Court of Appeal, counsel for the defendants adhered to it before your Lordships. But doctors and surgeons fall into no special category, and, to avoid any future disputation of a similar kind, I would have it accepted that the true doctrine was enunciated, and by no means for the first time, by McNair J in *Bolam* v *Friern Hospital Management Committee* [1957] 1 WLR 582 at 586 in the following words:

" ... where you get a situation which involves the use of some special skill or competence, then the test as to whether there has been negligence or not is not the test of the man on the top of a Clapham omnibus because he has not got this special skill. The test is the standard of the ordinary skilled man exercising and professing to have that special skill."

If a surgeon fails to measure up to that standard in any respect ("clinical judgment" or otherwise), he has been negligent and should be so adjudged.'

Commentary

Applied in *Clark* v *MacLennan* [1983] 1 All ER 416.

Wilks v *The Cheltenham Home Guard Motor Cycle and Light Car Club* [1971] 1 WLR 668 Court of Appeal (Lord Denning MR, Edmund-Davies and Phillimore LJJ)

Negligence – duty of care to spectators

Facts

Spectators at a motor cycle scramble, the plaintiffs were lined against the 'spectators' rope'. Ten feet beyond there was a 'wrecking rope'. During a race, the second defendant's machine suddenly veered to one side, crossed the ropes and landed amongst the spectators, injuring the plaintiffs. There was no explanation of how the accident had, or could have, occurred.

Held

The plaintiffs were not entitled to damages: there was no evidence of negligence and a slip or misjudgment not amounting to negligence could have accounted for the accident.

Lord Denning MR:

'This result may indicate that the club, the first defendants, ought to have been made liable. They ought to have provided safety precautions which are sufficient to protect spectators from harm owing to a motor cycle running off the course. But they gave evidence which persuaded the judge that they had done all that was reasonable. They had erected the 'wrecking rope' and the 'spectators' rope' in accordance with the requirements of the Auto-Cycle Union. They had driven the stakes in well at the correct intervals and had kept the ropes taut. There is no appeal from the judge's finding in their favour. So we must accept it as correct. On that footing there is only one conclusion possible, and that is that this was one of those rare accidents which do occur from time to time when nobody is at fault. No doubt, in consequence of it, stricter precautions will be taken in future. The world gets wiser as it gets older. But it does not mean that there was negligence on the first happening.'

Wooldridge v *Sumner* [1963] 3 WLR 616 Court of Appeal (Sellers, Danckwerts and Diplock LJJ)

Negligence – injury to spectator

Facts

The plaintiff, a photographer, was attending a horse show and was standing on the edge of the arena. One of the horses, owned by the defendant, suddenly panicked on one of the corners and began to gallop towards where the plaintiff was standing. In his attempt to move out of the way, the plaintiff was struck and injured by the horse.

Held

There was no breach of duty by the defendant and the plaintiff's claim failed.

Diplock LJ:

'A person attending a game or competition takes the risk of any damage caused to him by any act of a participant done in the course of and for the purposes of the game or competition, notwithstanding that such an act may involve an error of judgment or lapse of skill, unless the participant's conduct is such as to evince a reckless disregard of the spectator's safety.

The spectator takes the risk because such an act involves no breach of the duty of care owed by the participant to him. He does not take the risk by virtue of the doctrine expressed or obscured by the maxim volenti non fit injuria. The maxim states a principle of estoppel applicable originally to a Roman citizen who consented to being sold as a slave. Although pleaded and argued below, it was only faintly relied on by counsel for the first defendant in this court. In my view, the maxim, in the absence of express contract, has no application to negligence simpliciter where the duty of care is based solely on proximity or 'neighbourship' in the Atkinian sense. The maxim in English law presupposes a tortious act by the defendant. The consent that is relevant is not consent to the risk of injury, but consent to the lack of reasonable care that may produce that risk and requires on the part of the plaintiff at the time at which he gives his consent full knowledge of the nature and extent of the risk that he ran. In *Dann v Hamilton*, Asquith J expressed doubts whether the maxim ever could apply to license in advance a subsequent act of negligence, for if the consent precedes the act of negligence, the plaintiff cannot at that time have full knowledge of the extent as well as the nature of the risk which he will run. Asquith J, however, suggested that the maxim might, nevertheless, be applicable to cases where a dangerous physical condition had been brought about by the negligence of the defendant and the plaintiff with full knowledge of the existing danger elected to run the risk thereof. With the development of the law of negligence in the last twenty years, a more consistent explanation of this type of case is that the test of liability on the part of the person creating the dangerous physical condition is whether it was reasonably foreseeable by him that the defendant would so act in relation to it as to endanger himself. This is the principle which has been applied in the rescue cases (see *Cutler* v *United Dairies (London) Ltd* and contrast *Haynes* v *Harwood*) and the part of Asquith J's judgment in *Dann* v *Hamilton* dealing with the possible application of the maxim to the law of negligence was not approved by the Court of Appeal in *Ward* v *TE Hopkins & Son Ltd; Baker* v *Same*. In the type of case envisaged by Asquith J, if I may adapt the words of Morris LJ in *Ward* v *Hopkinn*, the plaintiff could not have agreed to run the risk that the defendant might be negligent, for the plaintiff would only play his part after the defendant had been negligent.'

Commentary

Applied in *Nettleship* v *Weston* [1971] 3 WLR 370 and *White* v *Blackmore* [1972] 3 WLR 296.

8 Negligence: Causation

Allied Maples Group Ltd v *Simmons & Simmons* [1995] 1 WLR 1602 Court of Appeal (Stuart-Smith, Hobhouse and Millett LJJ)

Causation – loss of a chance

Facts
The plaintiffs wished to purchase certain properties from G. Four of these properties could not be conveyed to the plaintiffs because there were conditions against alienation or planning consents which were personal to G's subsidiary, K Ltd, in which the properties were vested. The plaintiffs, on the advice of the defendant solicitors, acquired all the shares in K Ltd, intending to sell the unwanted properties of K and keep the four desired. However, some of the properties owned by K had liabilities which, after the acquisition, resulted in claims against K, and hence the plaintiffs. The plaintiffs sued the defendants to recover their losses. In the High Court it was held that the plaintiffs were entitled to succeed because if the defendants had given the advice on liability which they ought to have given, the plaintiffs would have taken steps to obtain a warranty from G or to protect themselves in some other way. The defendants appealed to the Court of Appeal.

Held
Where the plaintiff's loss depends on the hypothetical action of a third party, the plaintiff can succeed if he shows that he had a substantial chance rather than a speculative one. He does not have to prove on the balance of probabilities that the third party would have acted so as to confer a benefit or avoid the risk to the plaintiff. If he proves as a matter of causation that he has a real or substantial chance as opposed to a speculative one, the evaluation of the chance is part of the assessment of the quantum of damage, the range lying somewhere between something that just qualifies as real or substantial on the one hand, and near certainty on the other.

Baker v *Willoughby* [1970] 2 WLR 50 House of Lords (Lord Reid, Lord Guest, Viscount Dilhorne, Lord Donovan and Lord Pearson)

Damages – subsequent further injury

Facts
The plaintiff was knocked down by the defendant whilst crossing the road. The effect of the injuries was to reduce the movement in his left leg so that he could no longer carry on with his previous employment. Shortly afterwards, the plaintiff was shot in the leg by robbers and had to have his left leg amputated. What was the extent of the defendant's liability?

Held
The second injury was irrelevant for the purpose of assessing the damages to which the plaintiff was entitled in respect of the first injury.

Lord Reid:

> 'A man is not compensated for the physical injury; he is compensated for the loss which he suffers as a result of that injury. His loss is not in having a staff leg; it is in his inability to lead a full life, his inability to enjoy those amenities which depend on freedom of movement and his inability to earn as much as he used to earn or could have earned if there had been no accident. In this case, the second injury did not diminish any of these. So why should it be regarded as having obliterated or superseded them?'

Commentary

Doubted and not followed in *Jobling* v *Associated Dairies Ltd* [1981] 3 WLR 155.

Barnett v *Chelsea & Kensington Hospital Management Committee* [1968] 2 WLR 422 High Court (Nield J)

Negligence – cause of death

Facts

The plaintiff's husband went to the casualty department of the defendants' hospital complaining of stomach pains and vomiting after drinking tea. A doctor was contacted, but did not come to examine the husband and sent a message that he should go home to bed and call his own doctor. The plaintiff's husband died shortly after from arsenic poisoning.

Held

Although the doctor was negligent in failing to examine the deceased, the defendants were not liable because this was not the cause of his death.

Nield J:

> 'It remains to consider whether it is shown that the deceased's death was caused by this negligence or whether, as the defendants have said, the deceased must have died in any event. In his concluding submission counsel for the plaintiff submitted that Dr Banerjee should have examined the deceased and, had he done so, he would have caused tests to be made which would have indicated the treatment required and that, since the defendants were at fault in these respects, therefore the onus of proof passed to the defendants to show that the appropriate treatment would have failed, and authorities were cited to me. I find myself unable to accept this argument and I am of the view that the onus of proof remains on the plaintiff ... However, were it otherwise and the onus did pass to the defendants, then I would find that they have discharged it.'

Cork v *Kirby Maclean Ltd* [1952] 2 All ER 402 Court of Appeal (Singleton, Denning and Romer LJJ)

Negligence – cause of accident

Facts

A painter entered the defendants' employment without telling them that he was subject to epileptic fits and that his doctor had forbidden him to work at heights. While working on a platform, which did not comply with statutory requirements, he had a fit, fell to the ground, and was killed.

Held

Both the defendants and the painter had been at fault and the damages recoverable by his estate would therefore be reduced by one half.

Denning LJ:

'Subject to the question of remoteness, causation is, I think, a question of fact. If you can say that the damage would not have happened but for a particular fault, then that fault is in fact a cause of the damage; but if you can say that the damage would have happened just the same, fault or no fault, then the fault is not a cause of the damage. It often happens that each of the parties at fault can truly say to the other: "But for your fault, it would not have happened." In such a case both faults are in fact causes of the damage.

In this case, on the facts, I am clearly of opinion that both faults were causes of the damage. The man's fault (in not telling his employers he was forbidden to work at heights) was clearly one of the causes of his death. But for that fault on his part, he would never have been on this platform at all and would never have fallen. The employers' fault (in not providing a guard-rail or toe-boards) is more doubtful a cause. One cannot say that but for that fault the accident *would* not have happened. All that can be said is that it *might* not have happened. A guard-rail and toe-boards *might* have saved him from falling. If this was a very remote possibility, it could not be said to be a cause at all. But the judge did not so regard it. He thought that it probably would have saved him. On that view the employers' fault was also one of the causes of the man's death.'

Cutler v *Vauxhall Motors Ltd* [1971] 1 QB 418 Court of Appeal (Russell, Edmund-Davies and Karminski LJJ)

Negligence – operation inevitable at future date

Facts
An accident at work (for which D was liable) aggravated P's pre-existing varicose condition and necessitated an operation.

Held (Russell LJ dissenting)
The plaintiff could not recover losses due to the operation as his condition would anyway have required surgery in the near future.

Galoo Ltd v *Bright Grahame Murray* [1994] 1 WLR 1360 Court of Appeal (Glidewell, Evans and Waite LJJ)

Negligence – causation

Facts
The plaintiffs claimed that they incurred trading losses as a result of relying on the defendants' negligent auditing and thus continued to trade when they otherwise would not have done, and that these trading losses were caused by the defendants' breach of duty.

Held
In considering whether a breach of duty, whether the duty was imposed by contract or in tort in a situation analogous to contract, was the cause of the loss or merely the occasion for the loss, the court had to arrive at a decision on the basis of the application of common sense. The 'but for' test of causation was not sufficient.

Hotson v *East Berkshire Area Health Authority* [1987] 3 WLR 232 House of Lords (Lord Bridge of Harwich, Lord Brandon of Oakbrook, Lord Mackay of Clashfern, Lord Ackner and Lord Goff of Chieveley)

Negligence – causation

Facts

A boy aged 13, the plaintiff, injured his hip in a fall. He was taken to the defendants' hospital; the injury was not correctly diagnosed and he was sent home. Even if a correct diagnosis had been made, there was a 75 per cent risk that the boy's disability would have developed, but the medical staff's breach of duty had turned the risk into an inevitability.

Held

The boy was without a remedy.

Lord Ackner:

> '… the plaintiff was not entitled to any damages in respect of the deformed hip because the judge had decided that this was not caused by the admitted breach by the authority of their duty of care but was caused … when he fell some 12 feet from a rope on which he had been swinging.'

Jobling v *Associated Dairies Ltd* [1981] 3 WLR 155 House of Lords (Lord Wilberforce, Lord Edmund-Davies, Lord Russell of Killowen, Lord Keith of Kinkel and Lord Bridge of Harwich)

Injury – subsequent further injury

Facts

In 1973 P slipped and fell in the course of his employment as a result of a breach of statutory duty by his employer, D. His back was injured and in consequence his earning capacity was reduced by 50 per cent. In 1976 P was found to be suffering from spondylotic myelopathy, a spinal disease which was unrelated to the accident but which made him totally unfit to work. The trial of his claim against D took place in 1979.

Held

In a case where a supervening illness was apparent and known of before the trial, the court had to take it into account in order to prevent P from being overcompensated. However, the question was left open whether the same principle would apply where the supervening disability was the result of a tortious act by a second tortfeasor as opposed to a natural illness or purely accidental injury.

Lord Wilberforce:

> "We do not live in a world governed by the pure common law and its logical rules. We live in a mixed world where a man is protected against injury and misfortune by a whole web of rules and dispositions with a number of timid legislative interventions. To attempt to compensate him on the basis of selected rules without regard to the whole must lead either to logical inconsistencies or to over or under-compensation. As my noble and learned friend Lord Edmund-Davies has pointed out, no account was taken in *Baker* v *Willoughby* of the very real possibility that the plaintiff might obtain compensation from the Criminal Injuries Compensation Board. If he did in fact obtain this compensation he would, on the ultimate decision, be over-compensated.
>
> In the present case, and in other industrial injury cases, there seems to me no justification for

disregarding the fact that the injured man's employer is insured (indeed since 1972 compulsorily insured) against liability to his employees. The state has decided, in other words, on a spreading of risk. There seems to me no more justification for disregarding the fact that the plaintiff (presumably; we have not been told otherwise) is entitled to sickness and invalidity benefit in respect of his myelopathy, the amount of which may depend on his contribution record, which in turn may have been affected by his accident. So we have no means of knowing whether the plaintiff would be over-compensated if he were, in addition, to receive the assessed damages from his employer, or whether he would be under-compensated if left to his benefit. It is not easy to accept a solution by which a partially incapacitated man becomes worse off in terms of damages and benefit through a greater degree of incapacity. Many other ingredients, of weight in either direction, may enter into individual cases. Without any satisfaction I draw from this the conclusion that no general, logical or universally fair rules can be stated which will cover, in a manner consistent with justice, cases of supervening events, whether due to tortious, partially tortious, non-culpable or wholly accidental events.

If rationalisation is needed, I am willing to accept the "vicissitudes" argument as the best available. I should be more firmly convinced of the merits of the conclusion if the whole pattern of benefits had been considered, in however general a way. The result of the present case may be lacking in precision and rational justification, but so long as we are content to live in a mansion of so many different architectures this is inevitable.'

Commentary

Doubted and not followed: *Baker* v *Willoughby* [1970] 2 WLR 50.

Kay v *Ayrshire and Arran Health Board* [1987] 2 All ER 417 House of Lords (Lord Keith of Kinkel, Lord Brandon of Oakbrook, Lord Griffiths, Lord Mackay of Clashfern and Lord Ackner)

Negligence – causation

Facts

A boy suffering from pneumococcal meningitis was negligently given an overdose of penicillin. After recovering from the meningitis he was found to be suffering from deafness. Expert evidence on behalf of the hospital was to the effect that there was no recorded case of a penicillin overdose having caused deafness, although it was a common sequela of meningitis.

Held

Where there were two competing causes of damage, the law could not presume that the tortious cause was responsible if it was not first proved that it was an accepted fact that the tortious cause was capable of causing or aggravating such damage. Accordingly, in the light of the evidence, the deafness had to be regarded as resulting solely from the meningitis and the boy's claim therefore failed.

Lord Ackner:

'[the boy] can derive no assistance from your Lordships' decision in *McGhee* v *National Coal Board*. In *McGhee's* case the absence of washing facilities was known to be a factor which increased the risk of dermatitis arising from the circumstances in which the pursuer worked. In this case, as previously stated, there is no evidence to incriminate the overdose of intrathecal penicillin. Moreover, if, contrary to the view which I have expressed, the decision in *McGhee's* case can be used to transfer to the respondents the onus of establishing that the excessive injection of penicillin did not cause the deafness, then in my judgment they have discharged that onus.'

Commentary

Distinguished: *McGhee v National Coal Board* [1973] 1 WLR 1.

McGhee v *National Coal Board* [1973] 1 WLR 1 House of Lords (Lord Reid, Lord Wilberforce, Lord Simon of Glaisdale, Lord Kilbrandon and Lord Salmon)

Negligence – causation

Facts

The respondent employers sent the appellant to clean out brick kilns, but they negligently failed to provide him with adequate washing facilities. In consequence, he cycled home, continuing to exert himself, covered in sweat and grime. He was found to be suffering from dermatitis caused by working conditions in the brick kilns, but his journeys home had added materially to the risk that he might develop the disease.

Held

The respondents were liable.

Lord Salmon:

> 'I would suggest that the true view is that, as a rule, when it is proved, on a balance of probabilities, that an employer has been negligent and that his negligence has materially increased the risk of his employee contracting an industrial disease, then he is liable in damages to that employee if he contracts the disease notwithstanding that the employer is not responsible for other factors which have materially contributed to the disease.
>
> … In the circumstances of the present case, the possibility of a distinction existing between (a) having materially increased the risk of contracting the disease, and (b) having materially contributed to causing the disease may no doubt be a fruitful source of interesting academic discussions between students of philosophy. Such a distinction is, however, far too unreal to be recognised by the common law.'

Commentary

Distinguished in *Kay v Ayrshire and Arran Health Board* [1987] 2 All ER 417.

McWilliams (or Cummings) v *Sir William Arrol & Co Ltd* [1962] 1 WLR 295 House of Lords (Viscount Kilmuir LC, Viscount Simonds, Lord Reid, Lord Morris of Borth-y-Gest and Lord Devlin)

Negligence – causation

Facts

The plaintiff was the widow of a steel erector who was employed by the defendants. On one occasion when he was erecting a steel tower some seventy feet from the ground, he slipped and fell to his death. His widow alleged the defendants were at fault in not providing safety belts, an item which clearly would have saved the deceased. The defendants alleged that, although such belts were customary, even if they had provided one, there was a high degree of probability that the deceased would not have worn it and that, therefore, any breach of duty on their part was not the cause of the deceased's death.

Held

The plaintiff's claim failed as the defendants' breach of duty (if there was one) was not the cause of the accident since (a) on the evidence the deceased would not have worn a safety belt if it had been provided and (b) there was no duty on the defendants to instruct or exhort the deceased to wear a safety belt.

Mattocks v *Mann* (1992) The Times 19 June Court of Appeal (Nourse, Stocker and Beldam LJJ)

Negligence – plaintiff's impecuniosity

Facts
The plaintiff's car was damaged in an accident that was caused by the admitted negligence of the defendant. The only issue before the court concerned damages and (inter alia) whether the plaintiff could recover for the hire period between completion of the repairs to her car and the release of payment by the defendant's insurers of the cost of repairs. The defendant claimed that under the principle in *The Liesbosch* [1933] AC 449 that it was the plaintiff's impecuniosity that led to her inability to provide resources to pay the repair bill and that was the effective cause of the additional hire period.

Held
The plaintiff could recover the hire charges for this period.

Beldam LJ:

'... the law of damages had not stood still since 1933 and in *Perry* v *Sidney Phillips & Son* [1982] 1 WLR 1297, 1307 Lord Justice Kerr had said that the authority of what Lord Wright said in *The Liesbosch* was consistently being attenuated in more recent decisions.

In the varied web of affairs after an accident, only in exceptional circumstances was it possible or correct to isolate impecuniosity of a plaintiff as a separate cause and as terminating the consequences of a defendant's wrong.'

Performance Cars Ltd v *Abraham* [1961] 3 WLR 749 Court of Appeal (Lord Evershed MR, Harman and Donovan LJJ)

Negligence – successive torts

Facts
The plaintiffs' car was damaged in an accident and the respraying of the lower part of its body was necessary as a result. Two weeks later, and before the car had been resprayed, it was involved in a collision with the defendant's car. The defendant admitted liability and respraying of the lower part of the car was again required. Could the plaintiffs recover the cost of this respraying from the defendant?

Held
No, because that damage did not flow from the defendant's wrongful act.

Lord Evershed MR:

'In my judgment in the present case the defendant should be taken to have injured a motor car that was already injured in certain respects, that is, in respect of the need for respraying; and the result is that to the extent of that need or injury the damage claimed did not flow from the defendant's wrongdoing. It may no doubt be unfortunate for the plaintiffs that the collisions took place in the order in which they did. Had the first collision been that brought about by the defendant and had they recovered the £75 now in question from him, they could not clearly have recovered the same sum again from the other wrongdoer.

It is, however, in my view irrelevant (if unfortunate for the plaintiffs) that the judgment obtained against the other wrongdoer has turned out to be worthless.'

Topp v *London Country Bus (South West) Ltd* [1993] 3 All ER 448 Court of Appeal (Dillon and Rose LJJ and Peter Gibson J)

Causation – intervening act of the third party

Facts

The defendants' minibus was parked with the key in the ignition switch, unlocked and unattended, at a bus stop at a lay-by outside a public house. Some nine hours later, while being driven without authority on a public road by an unidentified third party, the bus was involved in an accident in which the plaintiff's wife was killed. The plaintiff sued the defendants in negligence and his claim was dismissed in the High Court. The plaintiff appealed.

Held

That even if the defendants had been at fault in leaving the bus unlocked on the highway, near a public house and with the key in the ignition, they were not responsible in law for the injury caused by a voluntary act of the third party since he was a complete stranger to them. The majority of the Court of Appeal also doubted whether there was a relationship of proximity between the defendants and the plaintiff's wife.

Wilsher v *Essex Area Health Authority* [1988] 2 WLR 557 House of Lords (Lord Bridge of Harwich, Lord Fraser of Tullybelton, Lord Lowry, Lord Griffiths and Lord Ackner)

Negligence – causation – burden of proof

Facts

The plaintiff was an infant who had been born prematurely. He was being kept on life support system and being looked after by a team of doctor and nurses. A junior doctor, whilst checking on the plaintiff, inserted a catheter into a vein, instead of an artery. The doctor asked a registrar to ensure that the catheter had been put in correctly. The registrar failed to do so, and indeed repeated the error later. The plaintiff as a result received too much oxygen and it was alleged that this had caused him brain damage. The plaintiff sued the Area Health Authority.

Held

As the plaintiff's condition could have been caused by any one of a number of different agents and it had not been proved that it was caused by excess oxygen, the plaintiff had not discharged the burden of proof as to causation. There was no presumption that the defendants' negligence had caused the injury. Accordingly, there must be a retrial.

Wright v *Lodge* [1993] 4 All ER 299 Court of Appeal (Parker, Woolf and Staughton LJJ)

Causation – negligent and reckless acts

Facts

A Mini driven by the respondent, Miss Shepherd, broke down on an unlit dual carriageway at night when visibility was very poor owing to fog. The car came to a stop in the nearside lane of the carriageway and while the respondent was attempting to start it a Scania articulated container lorry driven by the appellant, Mr Lodge, crashed into the back of it, causing a passenger in the rear seat of the Mini to be seriously injured. The lorry then veered out of control across the central reservation and came to rest on its side in the opposite westbound carriageway where it was struck by three cars and a lorry. The driver of one of the cars was killed and another driver was injured. At the time of the collision the appellant's lorry was travelling at 60mph. The injured driver and the personal representatives of the dead driver sued the appellant and the respondent while the injured passenger in the respondent's car sued the appellant who joined the respondent as a third party. The appellant admitted liability but claimed contribution from the respondent. Hobhouse J found that the appellant was driving recklessly and ordered that the respondent should contribute 10 per cent in respect of the claim by her passenger but dismissed the contribution claims relating to the injured and dead drivers. The appellant appealed contending that the judge should have ordered a 10 per cent contribution in respect of those claims.

Held

The driver of a motor vehicle could owe different duties of care to different road users since different questions of foreseeability, causation and remoteness could arise in respect of different road users affected by his negligence. Thus, if his vehicle was involved in a collision with another vehicle partly as a result of his own negligence, he was not necessarily responsible for subsequent events which occurred as the result of another driver's reckless driving which caused damage which would not have occurred if that driver had merely been driving negligently, since reckless driving was in a different category from negligent driving and an obstruction on the highway which was a danger only to a reckless driver was not necessarily a relevant danger in considering the liability of the person who negligently caused the obstruction to be present. On the facts, although the respondent had been negligent in not removing her car from the carriageway onto the verge, the sole cause of the lorry ending up on the westbound carriageway and the drivers' consequent death and injuries was the appellant's reckless driving, which was the only relevant legal cause of that event. The judge had accordingly been correct to find that the respondent was not liable to make a contribution in respect of the appellant's liability in regard to the dead and injured drivers' claims. The appeal would therefore be dismissed.

Parker LJ:

'In any event approaching the matter as if he [the trial judge] were a jury and taking a common sense view, he was, as we are, clearly entitled to conclude that the presence of the Scania in the westbound carriageway was wholly attributable to Mr Lodge's reckless driving. It was unwarranted and unreasonable. It was the violence of the swerve and braking which sent his lorry out of control. Such violence was due to the reckless manner in which he was driving and it was his reckless speed which resulted in the swerve, loss of control and headlong career onto, and overturn on, the westbound carriageway. It is true that it would not have been there had the Mini not obstructed the nearside lane of the eastbound carriageway but the passages which I have cited show clearly that this is not enough. It does not thereby necessarily become a legally operative cause. The subsequent conduct of Mr Lodge was such that any judge or jury could in my judgment exclude Miss Shepherd's conduct as being causative of the subsequent accident. The judge did exclude it and in my judgment he was right to do so.'

9 Negligence: Remoteness of Damage

Bradford v *Robinson Rentals Ltd* [1967] 1 WLR 337 High Court (Rees J)

Negligence – foreseeability of damage

Facts
The plaintiff was employed by the defendants as a service engineer which involved a considerable amount of travel by road. In the extraordinarily severe winter of 1963, the defendants ordered him to undertake a journey of some 450 miles. On the day in question, conditions were especially bad due to heavy snow and ice. Due to the poor state of the vehicle provided for him and in particular the absence of a working heater, the plaintiff sustained severe frostbite.

Held
The plaintiff was entitled to damages as the injury which he suffered was of the kind that was foreseeable. It was not necessary for the precise nature of the injury to be reasonably foreseeable before liability resulted.

Commentary
Applied: *Hughes* v *Lord Advocate* [1963] 2 WLR 779.
    Distinguished in *Tremain* v *Pike* [1969] 1 WLR 1556.

Carslogie Steamship Co Ltd v *Royal Norwegian Government, The Carslogie* [1952] AC 292 House of Lords (Viscount Jowitt, Lord Normand, Lord Morton of Henryton, Lord Tucker and Lord Asquith of Bishopstone)

Negligence – damage

Facts
The plaintiffs' ship was damaged by the defendants' negligence and had to undergo a voyage to a shipyard for repairs. En route, it was further damaged by a severe storm.

Held
The defendants were not liable for damage by the storm which was an unforeseeable novus actus unconnected with their negligence.

Doughty v *Turner Manufacturing Co Ltd* [1964] 2 WLR 240 Court of Appeal (Lord Pearce, Harman and Diplock LJJ)

Negligence – foreseeability

Facts

A fellow workman inadvertently knocked an asbestos cement cover into a cauldron of extremely hot molten liquid. The extreme heat caused the abestos cement to undergo a chemical change creating or releasing water: the water turned to steam which, a minute or two later, caused an eruption of the molten liquid from the cauldron. The plaintiff was injured by some of this liquid. Until the accident had been investigated, no one knew or suspected that heat would cause the chemical change which had taken place.

Held

The employers were not liable as the eruption had been unforeseeable by a reasonable man. Although risk by splashing was foreseeable, the accident which had occurred was of an entirely different kind.

Harman LJ:

'We ought, in my opinion, to start with the premise that the criterion in English law is foreseeability. I take it that whether *The Wagon Mound* is or is not binding on this court we ought to treat it as the law. Our inquiry must, therefore, be whether the result of this hard-board cover slipping into the cauldron, which we know now to be inevitably an explosion, was a thing reasonably foreseeable at the time when it happened. It is acknowledged by the plaintiff that no one in the employer's service knew of the likelihood of such an event, and it is clear that no one in the room at the time thought of any dangerous result. There was a striking piece of evidence of the two men who went and looked over the edge of the cauldron to see where the piece of board had gone. Neither they, nor anyone else, thought that they were doing anything risky.

The plaintiff's argument most persuasively urged by Mr James rested, as I understood it, on admissions made that, if this lid had been dropped into the cauldron with sufficient force to cause the molten material to splash over the edge, that would have been an act of negligence or carelessness for which the employers might be vicariously responsible. Reliance was put on *Hughes* v *Lord Advocate* where the exact consequences of the lamp overturning were not foreseen, but it was foreseeable that if the manhole were left unguarded boys would enter and tamper with the lamp and it was not unlikely that serious burns might ensue for the boy. Their lordships' House distinguished *The Wagon Mound* on the ground that the damage which ensued though differing in degree was the same in kind as that which was foreseeable. So it is said here that a splash causing burns was foreseeable and that this explosion was really only a magnified splash which also caused burns and that, therefore, we ought to follow *Hughes* v *Lord Advocate* and hold the defendants liable. I cannot accept this. In my opinion, the damage here was of an entirely different kind from the foreseeable splash. Indeed, the evidence showed that any disturbance of the material resulting from the immersion of the hard-board was over an appreciable time before the explosion happened. This latter was caused by the distintegration of the hard-board under the great heat to which it was subjected and the consequent release of the moisture enclosed within it. This had nothing to do with the agitation caused by the dropping of the board into the cyanide. I am of opinion that it would be wrong on these facts to make another inroad on the doctrine of foreseeability which seems to me to be a satisfactory solvent of this type of difficulty.'

Commentary

Applied: *Overseas Tankship (UK) Ltd* v *Morts Dock & Engineering Co Ltd (The Wagon Mound)* [1961] 2 WLR 126.

Distinguished: *Hughes* v *Lord Advocate* [1963] 2 WLR 779.

Edison, The [1933] AC 449 House of Lords (Lord Buckmaster, Lord Warrington, Lord Tomlin, Lord Russell of Killowen and Lord Wright)

Negligence – measure of damages

Facts

The Edison, in leaving the port of Patras, caught the anchor ropes of *The Liesbosch* and dragged *The Liesbosch* out to sea where it sank. The plaintiffs were using *The Liesbosch* to dredge; they could not afford to buy another dredger so they had to hire one at a high rate. How should their damage be assessed?

Held

The plaintiffs were entitled to the market price of a dredger comparable to *The Liesbosch,* the cost of adapting a new vessel and transporting it to the port in question and insuring it for the voyage, and compensation for their loss in respect of their inability to carry out their contract between the sinking of *The Liesbosch* and the date on which the new dredger could reasonably have been available. Interest on this sum would run from the date of the loss. No account would be taken of any special loss due to the financial position of the owners of *The Liesbosch* as their impecuniosity was not traceable to the acts of the owners of *The Edison.*

Commentary

Distinguished in *Martindale* v *Duncan* [1973] 1 WLR 574 and *Dodd Properties (Kent) Ltd* v *Canterbury City Council* [1980] 1 WLR 433.

Hughes v *Lord Advocate* [1963] 2 WLR 779 House of Lords (Lord Reid, Lord Jenkins, Lord Morris of Borth-y-Gest, Lord Guest and Lord Pearce)

Negligence – foreseeability of damage

Facts

Post Office employees had opened a manhole in order to carry out repairs on the highway. A tent was placed over the open manhole and there were paraffin lamps around the tent. The entrance to the tent was blocked by a ladder and a tarpaulin. In the absence of the employees, the plaintiff, aged ten, went into the tent with a paraffin lamp. He fell and dropped the lamp into the hole. An explosion resulted and he was severely burned.

Held

The plaintiff's injuries were of the same kind as those which were reasonably foreseeable and thus not too remote: he could recover damages for negligence.

Lord Pearce:

'The dangerous allurement was left unguarded in a public highway in the heart of Edinburgh. It was for the respondent to show by evidence that, although this was a public street, the presence of children there was so little to be expected that a reasonable man might leave the allurement unguarded. But in my opinion their evidence fell short of that ...

The defenders are therefore liable for all the foreseeable consequences of their neglect. When an accident is of a different type and kind from anything that a defender could have foreseen he is not liable for it ... But to demand too great precision in the test of foreseeability would be unfair to the pursuer since the facets of misadventure are innumerable ... In the case of an allurement to children it is particularly hard to foresee with precision the exact shape of the disaster that will arise. The allurement in this case was the combination of a red paraffin lamp, a ladder, a partially closed tent, and a cavernous hole within it, a setting well-fitted to inspire some juvenile adventure that might end in calamity. The obvious risks were burning and conflagration and a fall. All these in fact occurred, but unexpectedly the mishandled lamp instead of causing an ordinary conflagration produced a violent explosion. Did the explosion create an accident and damage of a different type from the misadventure and damage that could be foreseen? In my judgment it did not. The accident was but a variant of the foreseeable … No unforeseeable extraneous, initial occurrence fired the train. The children's entry into the tent with the ladder, the descent into the hole, the mishandling of the lamp, were all foreseeable. The greater part of the path to injury had thus been trodden, and the mishandled lamp was quite likely at that stage to spill and cause a conflagration. Instead, by some curious chance of combustion, it exploded and no conflagration occurred, it would seem, until after the explosion. There was thus an unexpected manifestation of the apprehended physical dangers. But it would be, I think, too narrow a view to hold that those who created the risk of fire are excused from the liability for the damage by fire, because it came by way of explosive combustion. The resulting damage, though severe, was not greater than or different in kind from that which might have been produced had the lamp spilled and produced a more normal conflagration in the hole.'

Lord Reid:

'The cause of the accident – the lamp – was a known source of danger, but the way in which it behaved was unforeseeable. This does not absolve the defendant because the accident was caused by a known danger, but caused in a way which could not have been foreseen. That is no defence.'

Commentary
Applied in *Bradford* v *Robinson Rentals Ltd* [1967] 1 WLR 337 and *Doughty* v *Turner Manufacturing Co Ltd* [1964] 2 WLR 240.
    Distinguished: *Glasgow Corporation* v *Muir* [1943] AC 448.

Jones v *Boyce* (1816) 1 Stark 493 Court of King's Bench (Lord Ellenborough CJ)

Negligence – alarm and apprehension

Facts
The plaintiff was a passenger on the defendant's coach. Due to a defective coupling, one of the reins broke, the wheel came off the coach and it veered to the side of the road. The plaintiff, who was on the outside of the coach, feared it was about to overturn and jumped off, severely injuring his leg. In the event, the driver managed to bring the coach to a halt. The defendant alleged that as there had been no need for the plaintiff to jump off, his own action was the main cause of his injury and his claim should fail.

Held
The plaintiff succeeded.

Lord Ellenborough CJ:

'If I place a man in such a situation that he must adopt a perilous alternative, I am responsible for the consequences.'

Knightley v *Johns* [1982] 1 WLR 349 Court of Appeal (Stephenson and Dunn LJJ and Sir David Cairns)

Negligence – remoteness of damage

Facts
A serious road accident had occurred near the exit of a tunnel which carried one-way traffic. The accident had been caused by the negligence of the first defendant. The police inspector in charge at the scene realised that he had forgotten to close the tunnel to oncoming traffic. This was particularly important as

there was a sharp bend in the middle of the tunnel which obscured the exit, as well as the site of the first defendant's accident, to drivers entering the tunnel. The police inspector ordered two officers on motor cycles to go back and close off the tunnel. The two officers, one of whom was the plaintiff, rode into the tunnel against the oncoming traffic. Near the tunnel entrance the plaintiff collided with a motorist who, on the facts, was held not to have been negligent. Both the inspector in giving the order and the plaintiff in obeying the order were acting contrary to Standing Orders. The plaintiff claimed damages from, inter alia, the first defendant.

Held

The inspector had been guilty of negligence and this had been the real cause of the plaintiff's injuries. It was also a new cause, disturbing and interrupting the sequence of events between the first defendant's accident and that of the plaintiff. The inspector (and his chief constable) were liable in respect of the plaintiff's injuries; the first defendant was not.

Stephenson LJ:

'In the long run the question is ... one of remoteness of damage, to be answered, as has so often been stated, not by the logic of philosophers but by the common sense of plain men ... In my judgment, too much happened here, too much went wrong, the chapter of accidents and mistakes was too long and varied, to impose on [the first defendant] liability for what happened to the plaintiff in discharging his duty as a police officer, although it would not have happened had not [the first defendant] negligently overturned his car. The ordinary course of things took an extraordinary course.'

Liesbosch Dredger v SS Edison see Edison, The

Lord v Pacific Steam Navigation Co Ltd, The Oropesa [1943] P 32 Court of Appeal (Lord Wright, Scott and MacKinnon LJJ)

Negligence – chain of causation

Facts

Due to the negligence of *The Oropesa,* the ship collided with *The Manchester Regiment* and caused it serious damage. Most of the crew of the latter took to the lifeboats and the captain decided to go to *The Oropesa* in one of them in the hope of obtaining assistance of various kinds. This lifeboat capsized and nine of the crew lost their lives.

Held

The owners of *The Oropesa* were liable in respect of this loss of life as there had been no break in the chain of causation.

Lord Wright:

'In all these cases the question is not whether there was what one may call negligence or not. Negligence involves a breach of duty as between the plaintiff and the defendant. The captain or Lord, or whoever was deciding what to do, were not then owing a duty to anybody except, possibly, a duty to minimise damage so far as they could; but that is not a point which is relevant here. They were acting in an emergency. If they did something which was outside the exigencies of the emergency, whether it was from miscalculation or from error, or, if you like, from mere wilfulness, they would be debarred from saying that there had not intervened a new cause. The question is not whether there was new negligence, but whether there was a new cause ... It must always be shown that there is something which I will call ultroneous, something unwarrantable, a new cause coming in disturbing the sequence of events, something that can be described as either unreasonable or extraneous or extrinsic. I doubt very much whether the law can be stated more precisely than that ...

The real difficulty here is the application of the principle, which is a question of fact ... I am not prepared to say, and I do not say in this case that the fact that Lord's death was due in the circumstances to his leaving the ship in a boat, and to the unexpected and very unfortunate capsizing of that boat, prevented his death being a direct consequence of the casualty. It was a risk, no doubt; but a boat would not generally capsize in those circumstances; and I cannot think that that prevents it being held that his death was a direct consequence of the casualty.'

McKew v *Holland & Hannen & Cubitts (Scotland) Ltd* [1969] 3 All ER 1621 House of Lords (Lord Reid, Lord Hodson, Lord Guest, Viscount Dilhorne and Lord Upjohn)

Damages – subsequent further injury

Facts
Due to the defendants' negligence, the plaintiff's leg was injured. As a result, he occasionally lost the control of his left leg and it 'buckled'. Before the trial, the plaintiff went to visit a flat and while descending a steep staircase, his leg gave way; he attempted to avoid falling head-first and jumped, landing on his right leg and breaking it. The plaintiff claimed in respect of both injuries.

Held
The injuries from the second incident were the result of a novus actus interveniens (the attempt to descend a steep staircase without a handrail or adult assistance) and, therefore, too remote.

Lord Guest:

'The appellant was still convalescent from his first accident when the second accident occurred. He was limping. He had the experience of his leg giving way. Yet he chose without assistance, without hanging on to the wall, to commence to descend those steep stairs holding his young daughter by the hand. Like the Lord Justice-Clerk I could not characterise such conduct as other than unreasonable in the circumstances. If this be so, then the chain of causation between the first and second accident is broken and the appellant must fail.'

Oropesa, The see *Lord v Pacific Steam Navigation Co Ltd, The Oropesa*

Overseas Tankship (UK) Limited v *The Miller Steamship Pty Ltd (The Wagon Mound No 2)* [1966] 3 WLR 498 Privy Council (Lord Reid, Lord Morris of Borth-y-Gest, Lord Pearce, Lord Wilberforce and Lord Pearson)

Negligence – foreseeability of damage

Facts
On October 30 1951 the defendants' ship, the *Wagon Mound,* was loading oil in Sydney Harbour. Due to the negligence of the ship's engineers, a large quantity of the oil was spilt and floated on the surface of the water. The plaintiffs' vessels were being repaired at a wharf some 200 yds away, and oil began to accumulate there. The wharf owners were using welding equipment and, fearing the danger of fire, their manager made enquiries and was told it was safe to continue. On November 1, the oil ignited and both the plaintiffs' ship and the wharf were severely damaged by fire. The plaintiffs claimed damages in negligence and nuisance: the central issue was whether the risk of fire was foreseeable.

Held

The defendants were liable in negligence as a reasonable man in the position of the engineers would have thought that there was a real risk of fire and that it was not justifiable to neglect to take steps to eliminate that risk.

Lord Reid:

'... a person must be regarded as negligent if he does not take steps to eliminate a risk which he knows or ought to know is a real risk and not a mere possibility which could never influence the mind of a reasonable man ... it is justifiable not to take steps to eliminate a real risk if it is small and if the circumstances are such that a reasonable man, careful of the safety of his neighbour, would think it right to neglect it.'

Commentary

Distinguished: *Overseas Tankship (UK) Ltd* v *Mort Docks & Engineering Co Ltd (The Wagon Mound No 1)* [1961] 2 WLR 126 and *Bolton* v *Stone* [1951] AC 850.

Overseas Tankship (UK) Ltd v *Morts Dock & Engineering Co Ltd (The Wagon Mound No 1)* [1961] 2 WLR 126 Privy Council (Viscount Simonds, Lord Reid, Lord Radcliffe, Lord Tucker and Lord Morris of Borth-y-Gest)

Negligence – remoteness of damages

Facts

For the facts of this case see *The Wagon Mound No 2*, above. The present case concerned the claim by the wharf-owners, whose wharf was also destroyed by fire. The evidence in the present case differed in two material respects from that in *The Wagon Mound No 2*:

a) Some damage to the wharf-owners' property was reasonably foreseeable from the fouling of their slipways through oil;

b) It was *not* reasonably foreseeable that the oil on the water would catch fire.

The defendants here contended, inter alia, that the plaintiffs' damage was too remote.

Held

The defendants were not liable. as a man is only liable for those consequences of his negligent act which a reasonable man would have foreseen.

Viscount Simonds:

'It is a principle of civil liability, subject only to qualifications which have no present relevance, that a man must be considered to be responsible for the probable consequences of his act. To demand more of him is too harsh a rule; to demand less is to ignore that civilised order requires the observance of a minimum standard of behaviour. This concept, applied to the slowly developing law of negligence, has led to a great variety of expressions which can, as it appears to their Lordships, be harmonised with little difficulty with the single exception of the so-called rule *Polemis*. For, if it is asked why a man should be responsible for the natural or necessary or probable consequences of his act (or any other similar description of them) the answer is that it is not because they are natural or necessary or probable, but because since they have this quality, it is judged by the standard of the reasonable man, that he ought to have foreseen them. Thus, it is that, over and over again, it has happened that in different judgments in the case and sometimes in a single judgment, liability for a consequence has been imposed on the ground that it was reasonably foreseeable, or alternatively on the ground that it was natural or necessary or probable. The two grounds have been treated as coterminous and so they largely are. But, where they are not, the question arises to which the wrong answer was given in *Polemis*. For, if some limitation must be imposed on the consequences for which the negligent actor is to be held responsible – and all are agreed that some limitation there must be – why should that test (reasonable foreseeability) be rejected which, since he is judged by what the reasonable man ought to foresee, corresponds with the common conscience of mankind and a test (the 'direct' consequence) be substituted which leads to nowhere but the never ending and insoluble problems of causation.'

Commentary
Disapproved: *Re Polemis and Furness, Withy & Co Ltd* [1921] 3 KB 560.

    Applied in *Doughty* v *Turner Manufacturing Co Ltd* [1964] 2 WLR 240.

    Distinguished in *Overseas Tankship (UK) Ltd* v *The Miller Steamship Co Pty Ltd (The Wagon Mound No 2)* [1966] 3 WLR 498.

Polemis and Furness, Withy & Co Ltd, Re [1921] 3 KB 560 Court of Appeal (Bankes, Warrington and Scrutton LJJ)

Negligence – consequences of negligent act

Facts
The plaintiffs were the owners of a ship under charter to the defendants. After the cargo of petrol had been unloaded, the defendants' servants, stevedores, negligently caused a wooden plank to drop into the hold of the ship. This caused a spark and, due to the presence of inflammable vapour in the hold, an explosion ensued and the ship was destroyed by fire. It was found as a fact that although the dropping of the plank was likely to cause some damage to the ship, the spark and explosion were not foreseeable.

Held
The defendants were liable for the loss of the ship. If a reasonable man would have foreseen any damage as likely to result from his breach of duty, he is liable for all the direct consequences whether foreseeable or not.

Scrutton LJ:

'The second defence is that the damage is too remote from the negligence, as it could not be reasonably foreseen as a consequence. On this head we were referred to a number of well-known cases in which vague language, which I cannot think to be really helpful, has been used in an attempt to define the point at which damage becomes too remote from, or not sufficiently directly caused by, the breach of duty, which is the original cause of action, to be recoverable. For instance, I cannot think it useful to say the damage must be the natural and probable result. This suggests that there are results which are natural but not probable, and other results which are probable but not natural. I am not sure what either adjective means in this connection; if they mean the same thing, two need not be used; if they mean different things, the difference between them should be defined. And as to many cases of fact in which the distinction has been drawn, it is difficult to see why one case should be decided one way and one another ... In this case, however, the problem is simpler. To determine whether an act is negligent, it is relevant to determine whether any reasonable person would foresee that the act would cause damage; if he would not, the act is not negligent. But if the act would or might probably cause damage, the fact that the damage it in fact causes is not the exact kind of damage one would expect is immaterial, so long as the damage is in fact caused sufficiently directly by the negligent act, and not by the operation of independent causes having no connection with the negligent act, except that they could not avoid its results. Once the act is negligent, the fact that its exact operation was not foreseen is immaterial ... In the present case it was negligent in discharging cargo to knock down the planks of the temporary staging, for they might easily cause some damage either to workmen, or cargo, or the ship. The fact that they did directly produce an unexpected result, a spark in an atmosphere of petrol vapour which caused a fire, does not relieve the person who was negligent from the damage which his negligent act directly caused.'

Commentary

Disapproved in *Overseas Tankship (UK) Ltd v Morts Docks and Engineering Co Ltd (The Wagon Mound No 1)* [1961] 2 WLR 126.

Robinson v The Post Office [1974] 1 WLR 1176 Court of Appeal (Davies, Buckley and Orr LJJ)

Negligence – remoteness of damages

Facts

Due to Ds' negligence, P cut his leg at work. At hospital, P was given an anti-tetanus injection by Dr X without first being tested for allergy. In fact, P was allergic and suffered brain damage. A test would not have revealed the allergy.

Held

The defendants were liable for all P's damage – they must take P as they find him, including allergy. Dr X was also negligent, but this was not a cause of P's injury.

Commentary

Applied: *Smith v Leech Brain & Co Ltd* [1962] 2 WLR 148.

Rouse v Squires [1973] 2 WLR 925 Court of Appeal (Buckley and Cairns LJJ and MacKenna J)

Negligence – causation – contributory negligence

Facts

Due to the negligence of Allen, his lorry 'jack-knifed' on a motorway on a frosty night. Rouse was one of those who stopped to assist. Five or ten minutes later, Squires negligently collided with another lorry which had stopped to help and this lorry knocked down and killed Rouse. Rouse's widow was awarded damages against Squires: could Squires obtain contributions from Allen and the owners of the 'jack-knifed' lorry?

Held

He could and 25 per cent of the blame was attributed to them. There was no breach in the chain of causation between the original negligent driving and the killing of Mr Rouse.

Cairns LJ:

'If a driver so negligently manages his vehicles as to cause it to obstruct the highway and constitute a danger to other road users, including those who are driving too fast or not keeping a proper look-out, but not those who deliberately or recklessly drive into the obstruction, then the first driver's negligence may be held to have contributed to the causation of an accident of which the immediate cause was the negligent driving of the vehicle which because of the presence of the obstruction collides with it or with some other vehicle or some other person. Accordingly, I would hold in this case that Mr Allen's negligence did contribute to the death of Mr Rouse.'

Commentary
Distinguished: *Dymond* v *Pearce* [1972] 2 WLR 633.

Scott v *Shepherd* (1773) 2 Wm Bl 892 Court of Common Pleas (De Grey CJ, Nares, Blackstone and Gould JJ)

Squib – chain of causation

Facts
The defendant threw a lighted squib into a covered market: it fell on Yates's gingerbread stall and to save himself and the wares Willis picked it up and threw it across the market house. It landed on Ryal's stall and he, to save his goods, threw it away: it struck the plaintiff in the face, exploded and put out one of his eyes. The plaintiff sought damages for trespass and assault.

Held (Blackstone J dissenting)
His action would be successful.

Nares J:

> 'I am of opinion that trespass would well lie in the present case. The natural and probable consequence of the act done by the defendant was injury to somebody, and, therefore, the act was illegal at common law ... Being, therefore, unlawful, the defendant was liable to answer for the consequences, be the injury mediate or immediately ... malus animus is not necessary to constitute a trespass ... The principle I go on is ... that if the act in the first instance be unlawful, trespass will lie. Wherever, therefore, an act is unlawful at first, trespass will lie for the consequences of it ... I do not think it necessary, to maintain trespass, that the defendant should personally touch the plaintiff; if he does it by a mean it is sufficient. Qui facit per aliud facit per se. He is the person who, in the present case, gave the mischievous faculty to the squib. That mischievous faculty remained in it until the explosion. No new power of doing mischief was communicated to it by Willis or Ryal. It is like the case of a mad ox turned loose in a crowd. The person who turns him loose is answerable in trespass for whatever mischief he may do. The intermediate acts of Willis and Ryal will not purge the original tort in the defendant. But he who does the first wrong is answerable for all the consequential damages ...'

Smith v *Leech Brain & Co Ltd* [1962] 2 WLR 148 High Court (Lord Parker CJ)

Negligence – remoteness of damages

Facts
Due to the failure of the defendant employers to provide a safe system of working, the plaintiff's husband was burnt on the lip by a piece of molten metal. Soon after, the lip began to swell and cancer was diagnosed. Despite treatment, the plaintiff's husband died of the cancer some three years later. The evidence showed that the deceased had a pre-malignant condition, promoted into cancer by the burn.

Held
The plaintiff's claim against the defendants in respect of her husband's death succeeded.

Lord Parker CJ:

> 'The test is not whether these defendants could reasonably have foreseen that a burn would cause cancer and that Mr Smith would die. The question is whether these defendants could reasonably foresee the

type of injury which he suffered, namely, the burn. What, in the particular case, is the amount of damage which he suffers as a result of that burn, depends on the characteristics and constitution of the victim.'

Commentary

Applied in *Robinson* v *The Post Office* [1974] 1 WLR 1176.

Stansbie v *Troman* [1948] 2 KB 48 Court of Appeal (Tucker and Somervell LJJ and Roxburgh J)

Negligence – duty of care

Facts

The plaintiff, a painter and decorator, was working on the defendant's premises. One day when the house was unoccupied, the plaintiff left to buy some more wallpaper, leaving the front door unlocked. In his absence, a thief entered and stole some of the defendant's property. On a claim by the plaintiff for work done, the defendant counter-claimed alleging negligence.

Held

The theft was not too remote a consequence of the plaintiff's negligence in leaving the house unlocked. The entry of the thief was a direct result of his negligence and not a *novus actus interveniens*.

Wieland v *Cyril Lord Carpets Ltd* [1969] 3 All ER 1006 High Court (Eveleigh J)

Negligence – remoteness of damage

Facts

The plaintiff injured her neck due to the defendants' negligence and had to wear a neck-collar: this made it difficult to use her bi-focal spectacles. Next day, she fell down steps.

Held

The defendants were liable for the second injury also. The plaintiff was not acting unreasonably so soon after the first accident and the chain of causation had not been broken.

10 Contributory Negligence

Admiralty Commissioners* v *Volute (Owners), The Volute [1922] 1 AC 129 House of Lords (Viscount Birkenhead LC, Viscount Cave, Viscount Finlay, Lord Shaw and Lord Phillimore)

Negligence – contributory negligence

Facts

There was a collision between HMS Radstock, a destroyer, and the Volute, an oil tanker. If the Volute had signalled, there would have been no collision: similarly if, in its position of danger brought about by the Volute, the Radstock had not gone full steam ahead, a collision would have been avoided.

Held

The Volute was partly to blame for the collision.

Viscount Birkenhead LC:

> 'Upon the whole I think that this question of contributory negligence must be dealt with somewhat broadly and upon common-sense principles as a jury would probably deal with it. While, no doubt, where a clear line can be drawn, the subsequent negligence is the only one to look to, there are cases in which the two acts come so closely together, and the second act of negligence is so much mixed up with the state of things brought about by the first act that the party secondly negligent, while not held free from blame … might, on the other hand, invoke the prior negligence as being part of the cause of the collision so as to make it a case of contribution.'

Alliance & Leicester Building Society* v *Edgestop [1993] 1 WLR 1462 High Court (Mummery J)

Availability of defence in action for deceit

Facts

A private unlimited company of estate agents were sued by the plaintiff building society claiming that the estate agents were vicariously liable for the deceit of one of its former employees. The estate agents pleaded contributory negligence to claims in deceit. The question arose on a striking out application as to whether in law it was entitled to plead such a defence to a claim in deceit. The master held that this was not possible, and the plaintiffs appealed.

Held

That a person liable for deceit, whether personally or vicariously, was not entitled either at common law or under the Law Reform (Contributory Negligence) Act 1945 to plead as a defence that his victim was guilty of contributory negligence.

Fitzgerald v *Lane* [1989] AC 328 House of Lords (Lord Bridge of Harwich, Lord Brandon of Oakbrook, Lord Templeman, Lord Ackner and Lord Oliver of Aylmerton)

Contributory negligence – apportionment

Facts

Although the lights were green to traffic and red against pedestrians, the plaintiff walked on to a pelican crossing. He was struck by the first defendant's car and thrown across the road where he was struck by the second defendant's car travelling in the opposite direction. As a result of these collisions he suffered multiple injuries.

Held

As the plaintiff's responsibility for his injuries had been at least as great as that of the defendants jointly, he was entitled to no more than 50 per cent of his claim, the amount awarded by the Court of Appeal.

Lord Ackner:

'*The correct approach to the determination of contributory negligence, apportionment and contribution*
It is axiomatic that, whether the plaintiff is suing one or more defendants for damages for personal injuries, the first question which the judge has to determine is whether the plaintiff has established liability against one or other or all the defendants, ie that they, or one or more of them, were negligent (or in breach of statutory duty) and that that negligence (or breach of statutory duty) caused or materially contributed to his injuries. The next step, of course liability has been established, is to assess what is the total of the damage that the plaintiff has sustained as a result of the established negligence. It is only after these two decisions have been made that the next question arises, namely whether the defendant or defendants have established (for the onus is on them) that the plaintiff, by his own negligence, contributed to the damage which he suffered. If, and only if, contributory negligence is established does the court then have to decide, pursuant to s1 of the Law Reform (Contributory Negligence) Act 1945, to what extent it is just and equitable to reduce the damages which would otherwise be recoverable by the plaintiff, having regard to his "share in the responsibility for the damage".

All the decisions referred to above are made in the main action. Apportionment of liability in a case of contributory negligence between plaintiff and defendants must be kept separate from apportionment of *contribution between the defendants inter se*. Although the defendants are each liable to the plaintiff for the whole amount for which he has obtained judgment, the proportions in which, as between themselves, the defendants must meet the plaintiff's claim do not have any direct relationship to the extent to which the total damages have been reduced by the contributory negligence, although the facts of any given case may justify the proportions being the same.

Once the questions referred to above in the main action have been determined in favour of the plaintiff to the extent that he has obtained a judgment against two or more defendants, then and only then should the court focus its attention on the claims which may be made between those defendants for contribution pursuant to the Civil Liability (Contribution) Act 1978, re-enacting and extending the court's powers under s6 of the Law Reform (Married Women and Tortfeasors) Act 1935. In the contribution proceedings, whether or not they are heard during the trial of the main action or by separate proceedings, the court is concerned to discover what contribution is just and equitable, having regard to the responsibility between the tortfeasors inter se, for the damage which the plaintiff has been adjudged entitled to recover. That damage may, of course, have been subject to a reduction as a result of the decision in the main action that the plaintiff, by his own negligence, contributed to the damage which he sustained.

Thus, where the plaintiff successfully sues more than one defendant for damages for personal injuries and there is a claim between co-defendants for contribution, there are two distinct and different stages in the decision-making process, the one in the main action and the other in the contribution proceedings.'

Froom v *Butcher* [1975] 3 WLR 379 Court of Appeal (Lord Denning MR, Lawton and Scarman LJJ)

Negligence – contributory negligence

Facts

Due to the negligent driving of the defendant, he collided with the plaintiff's car. At the time of the accident, the plaintiff was not wearing a seat-belt. Had he done so, most of his injuries, which were largely to the head and chest, would have been avoided.

Held

The plaintiff's damages would be reduced by 25 per cent for contributory negligence.

Lord Denning MR:

'The question is not what was the cause of the accident. It is rather what was the cause of the damage. In most accidents on the road the bad driving which causes the accident also causes the ensuing damage. But, in seat-belt cases, the cause of the accident is one thing. The cause of the damage is another. The accident is caused by the bad driving. The damage is caused in part by the bad driving of the defendant and in part by the failure of the plaintiff to wear a seat belt. If the plaintiff was to blame in not wearing a seat-belt, the damage is in part the result of his own fault. He must bear some share in the responsibility for the damage and his damages fall to be reduced to such extent as the court thinks just and equitable.'

Commentary

Applied in *Eastman* v *South West Thames Health Authority* (1991) The Times 22 July

Gough v *Thorne* [1966] 1 WLR 1387 Court of Appeal (Lord Denning MR, Danckwerts and Salmon LJJ)

Negligence – contributory negligence – child

Facts

The plaintiff, aged 13, was waiting to cross the road. A lorry which was about to turn stopped, and the driver beckoned her to cross the road. As she did so, a 'bubble car' drove through a small gap between the lorry and a bollard in the centre of the road and collided with the plaintiff, causing her serious injuries. The trial judge found the car-driver to blame, but reduced the plaintiff's damages by 33 per cent finding that she was contributorily negligent in not stopping to look for other traffic after passing the lorry.

Held

The plaintiff had not been negligent in relying entirely on the lorry driver's signal and the finding of contributory negligence could not therefore be upheld.

Lord Denning MR:

'A very young child cannot be guilty of contributory negligence. An older child may be; but, it depends on the circumstances. A judge should only find a child guilty of contributory negligence if he or she is of such an age as reasonably to be expected to take precautions for his or her own safety; and then he or she is only to be found guilty if blame should be attached to him or her.'

Harrison v *British Railways Board* [1981] 3 All ER 679 High Court (Boreham J)

Negligence – injury to rescuer

Facts

The plaintiff was a guard on a passenger train. The second defendant, a Mr Howard, attempted to board the train while it was moving out of the station. The plaintiff gave an incorrect signal to the driver of the train to stop; the train kept accelerating. The plaintiff then attempted to grab the second defendant and pull him onto the train; in consequence, the second defendant fell off the train pulling the plaintiff with him. The plaintiff suffered injuries and brought an action in negligence against, amongst others, the second defendant. The second defendant argued that he was not liable on the ground that a person being rescued owed no duty to his rescuer, or, if he did owe the plaintiff a duty, the plaintiff had been contributorily negligent in giving the wrong signal to the driver to stop or failing to apply the emergency brake himself.

Held

The plaintiff would succeed, but his damages would be reduced by 20 per cent.

Boreham J:

> 'Thus, two questions arise: had the second defendant, Mr Howard, by a lack of reasonable care for his own safety, created a situation of danger? I have no doubt that he had. The second question: ought he, as a reasonable man, to have foreseen that the plaintiff might very well come to his aid? I have said enough already to indicate that in my view he should have foreseen, and he probably did foresee, the probability of the plaintiff's intervention. In these circumstances I hold that the second defendant is liable in negligence to the plaintiff ... It was the plaintiff's duty, according to the rules, to apply the brake in an emergency; he knew it and I think he was negligent in not doing so. Had he done so, the speed of the train would have been reduced. He should have known it was his duty, and I believe he did know it. As it was, he gave (no doubt in the heat of the moment) a meaningless signal and the train continued to accelerate. In these circumstances, I have come to the conclusion that had he acted as he should have done it is probable, though not certain, that both the chance of his being injured at all and the severity of his injuries would have been reduced. He should, therefore, bear some of the blame for those injuries.
>
> One has a feeling of distaste about finding a rescuer guilty of contributory negligence. It can rarely be appropriate to do so, in my judgment. Here, however, the contributory negligence which is alleged does not relate to anything done in the course of the actual rescue. What is alleged is the failure by the man in authority to reduce the danger by doing what he was duty-bound to do. The major responsibility must, of course, be borne by the second defendant. I assess the plaintiff's share at 20 per cent.'

Commentary

Applied: *Videan* v *British Transport Commission* [1963] 3 WLR 374.

Jones v *Livox Quarries Ltd* [1952] 2 QB 608 Court of Appeal (Singleton, Denning and Hodson LJJ)

Negligence – contributory negligence

Facts

The plaintiff was riding on the back of his employers' traxcavator (a slow-speed tracked excavator) when, due to the negligence of another employee, it was struck in the rear by another vehicle. The plaintiff sued the defendants, his employers, as being vicariously liable for the negligence of the second driver.

Held

Although the defendants were liable, the plaintiff's damages would be reduced by 20 per cent for contributory negligence.

Denning LJ:

'A person is guilty of contributory negligence if he ought reasonably to have foreseen that, if he did not act as a reasonable, prudent man, he might be hurt himself; and in his reckonings he must take into account the possibility of others being careless.'

Morales v *Eccleston* [1991] RTR 151 Court of Appeal (Staughton and McCowan LJJ and Sir John Megaw)

Contributory negligence – child

Facts

An 11-year-old boy, who ran into the road without looking to retrieve a ball, was struck by a car. At trial it was accepted that there was some degree of contributory negligence.

Held

That the child's contributory negligence would be assessed at 75 per cent.

Nance v *British Columbia Electric Railway Co Ltd* [1951] AC 601 Privy Council (Viscount Simon, Lord Porter, Lord Morton of Henryton, Lord Reid and Lord Asquith of Bishopstone)

Negligence – contributory negligence

Facts

Late at night the appellant and her husband were crossing a road. The respondents' street-car, having stopped to pick up passengers, restarted without warning and knocked down and killed the appellant's husband. The respondents pleaded contributory negligence.

Held

The respondents were solely to blame.

Viscount Simon:

'The statement that, when negligence is alleged as the basis of an actionable wrong, a necessary ingredient in the conception is the existence of a duty owed by the defendants to the plaintiff to take due care, is, of course, indubitably correct. But when contributory negligence is set up as a defence, its existence does not depend on any duty owed by the injured party to the party sued and all that is necessary to establish such a defence is to prove to the satisfaction of the jury that the injured party did not in his own interest take reasonable care of himself and contributed, by this want of care, to his own injury. For when contributory negligence is set up as a shield against the obligation to satisfy the whole of the plaintiff's claim, the principle involved is that, where a man is part author of his own injury, he cannot call on the other party to compensate him in full.'

Commentary

Applied: *Davies* v *Swan Motor Co (Swansea) Ltd* [1949] 2 KB 291.

O'Connell v *Jackson* [1971] 3 WLR 463 Court of Appeal (Russell, Edmund-Davies and Cairns LJJ)

Negligence – contributory negligence – failure to wear crash helmet

Facts

The plaintiff's moped collided with the defendant's motor car. The defendant admitted negligence: had the plaintiff been guilty of contributory negligence because, at the time of the accident, he had not been wearing a crash helmet?

Held

He had and his damages would be reduced by 15 per cent.

Edmund-Davies LJ:

' … in the present case the probable effectiveness of crash helmets in reducing the risk of a serious head injury was solidly established. It is true that no use has yet been made of the power conferred by s41 of the Road Traffic Act 1962 to make regulations requiring the wearing of protective headgear in such cases as the present. We would welcome such a regulation if economic considerations permit, for the possibility of serious injury resulting from failure to do so is manifest. More to the point, the evidence of the plaintiff himself in the present case establishes that he was alive to this risk and had only himself to blame for failing to remedy the omission. In these circumstances, we respectfully dissent from the judge's complete exculpation of the plaintiff, and we hold that he should bear part of the responsibility for the severe consequences of the accident.'

Owens v *Brimmell* [1977] 3 WLR 943 High Court (Tasker Watkins J)

Negligence – contributory negligence

Facts

The plaintiff and the defendant went out for an evening's drinking in the defendant's car. They visited several public houses and consumed a considerable amount of beer. On the return journey, due to the defendant's admitted negligence, there was an accident in which the plaintiff was severely injured. At the time of the accident, the plaintiff was not wearing a seat-belt, although given the severity of the impact, he would still have been injured even if he had worn one. The plaintiff claimed damages and the defendant pleaded contributory negligence.

Held

The plaintiff's damages would be reduced by 20 per cent for his contributory negligence in travelling with a driver whom he knew to be under the influence of alcohol. He was aware of the amount consumed and must have realised it was likely substantially to impair the defendant's driving ability. However, there would be no reduction for the plaintiff's failure to wear a seat-belt. Much of his injuries were to the head and face, but there are several ways in which these could have been sustained: it could have been that the plaintiff was thrown forward onto the fascia, in which case the belt might have restrained him. It is just as possible that the fascia was pushed back into him by the force of the impact, in which case the belt would have been of little, if any, assistance. If a defendant raises the defence of contributory negligence, the burden is upon him to prove, by evidence, that the plaintiff's act was a cause of his injury. This the defendant has not done.

11　Volenti Non Fit Injuria

Bowater* v *Rowley Regis Corporation [1944] KB 476 Court of Appeal (Scott, Goddard and du Parcq LJJ)

Negligence – volenti non fit injuria

Facts
The plaintiff rubbish collector was provided by his employers, the defendants, with a horse and cart. He was ordered to take a horse which was known to be restive and to have run away on previous occasions. He protested, but eventually obeyed. The horse ran away and the plaintiff was thrown from the cart and injured.

Held
The plaintiff was entitled to damages as the defendants had been guilty of negligence. He had not been contributorily negligent and, as it was not part of his employment to manage unruly horses, he had not accepted the risk.

Goddard LJ:

'The maxim volenti non fit injuria is one which in the case of master and servant is to be applied with extreme caution. Indeed, I would say that it can hardly ever be applicable where the act to which the plaintiff is said to be "volens" arises out of his ordinary duty, unless the work for which the plaintiff is engaged is one in which danger is necessarily involved. Thus a man in an explosives factory must take the risk of an explosion occurring in spite of the observance and provision of all statutory regulations and safeguards. A horse-breaker must take the risk of being thrown or injured by a restive or unbroken horse; it is an ordinary risk of his employment. But a man whose occupation is not one of a nature inherently dangerous but who is asked or required to undertake a risky operation is in a different position. To rely on this doctrine the master must show that the workman undertook that the risk should be on him. It is not enough that, whether under protest or not, he obeyed an order or complied with a request which he might have declined as one which he was not bound either to obey or to comply with. It must be shown that he agreed that what risk there was should lie on him. I do not mean that it must necessarily be shown that he contracted to take the risk, as that would involve consideration, though a simple case of showing that a workman did take a risk upon himself would be that he was paid extra for so doing, and in some occupations "danger money" is often paid ...

For this maxim or doctrine to apply it must be shown that a servant who is asked or required to use dangerous plant is a volunteer in the fullest sense; that, knowing of the danger, he expressly or impliedly said that he would do the job at his own risk and not at that of his master. The evidence in this case fell far short of that and, in my opinion, the plaintiff was entitled to recover.'

Cutler* v *United Dairies (London) Ltd [1933] 2 KB 297 Court of Appeal (Scrutton and Slesser LJJ and Eve J)

Negligence – volenti non fit injuria

Facts

The defendants' milkman left his horse and cart unattended. The horse bolted and ran off down a country road. The plaintiff was injured whilst trying to catch and control the horse.

Held

The plaintiff's action was unnecessary; his assistance had not been requested; there was no danger to others; volenti non fit injuria barred his claim.

Commentary

Distinguished: *Haynes* v *G Harwood & Son* [1935] 1 KB 146.

Dann v *Hamilton* [1939] 1 KB 509 High Court (Asquith J)

Negligence – volenti non fit injuria – intoxicated driver

Facts

The defendant's husband drove the plaintiff and her mother out for the evening. A considerable amount of alcohol was drunk and on the return, another passenger, T, was given a lift. When T was let out of the car, he commented on the bad state of the defendant's husband's driving and said to the plaintiff and her mother, 'You two have more pluck than I have'. The plaintiff replied, 'You should be like me. If anything is going to happen, it will happen.' A few minutes later, an accident occurred in which the defendant's husband and the plaintiff's mother were killed and the plaintiff herself injured. The plaintiff brought this action against the defendant representing the estate. Negligence was admitted and the defence of volenti non fit injuria relied upon.

Held

The plaintiff would be awarded damages. For the defence to succeed, there must be not only complete knowledge of the danger, but also consent: the maxim says volenti not scienti and knowledge does not necessarily imply consent.

Asquith J:

'I find it difficult to believe, although I know of no authority directly in point, that a person who voluntarily travels as a passenger in a vehicle driven by a driver who is known by the passenger to have driven negligently in the past is *volens* as to future negligent acts of such driver, even though he could have chosen some other form of transport if he had wished. Then, to take the last step, suppose that such a driver is likely to drive negligently on the material occasion, not because he is known to the plaintiff to have driven negligently in the past, but because he is known to the plaintiff to be under the influence of drink. That is the present case. Ought the result to be any different? After much debate, I have come to the conclusion that it should not, and that the plaintiff, by embarking in the car, or re-entering it, with knowledge that through drink the driver had materially reduced his capacity for driving safely, did not impliedly consent to, or absolve the driver from liability for, any subsequent negligence on his part whereby the plaintiff might suffer harm.

There may be cases in which the drunkenness of the driver at the material time is so extreme and so glaring that to accept a lift from him is like engaging in an intrinsically and obviously dangerous occupation, inter-meddling with an unexploded bomb or walking on the edge of an unfenced cliff. It is not necessary to decide whether in such a case the maxim *volenti non fit injuria* would apply, for in the present case I find as a fact that the driver's degree of intoxication fell short of this degree. I therefore conclude that the defence fails, and the claim succeeds.'

Commentary
Applied in *Nettleship* v *Weston* [1971] 3 WLR 370.

Morris v *Murray* [1991] 2 WLR 195 Court of Appeal (Fox, Stocker LJJ and Sir George Waller)

Volenti non fit injuria – aircraft joyride

Facts
The plaintiff was a passenger in an aeroplane which crashed because the pilot was drunk. The plaintiff had, in fact, been out drinking with the pilot, had driven to the airport with him and had assisted in the preparations for the flight. The plaintiff brought a claim against the estate of the deceased pilot claiming damages for personal injury. An autopsy on the pilot showed that he had consumed the equivalent of 17 whiskies. The trial judge gave judgment for the plaintiff; he held that the defence of volenti could not succeed, although he did reduce the damages payable by 20 per cent because of the plaintiff's contributory negligence in participating in this enterprise.

Held
The defendant's appeal would be allowed on the ground that the plaintiff was volens. The present case was distinguishable from *Dann* v *Hamilton* [1939] 1 All ER 59 on the very inception (which was not the case in *Dann* because there the driver did not get drunk until a late stage in the social outing at a time when it might not have been very easy for the plaintiff 'to extricate herself without giving offence'). Sir George Waller was also of the opinion that there was a fundamental difference between driving a car and piloting an aeroplane; the latter being more risky and requiring greater accuracy of control than the former. Nor was the plaintiff so drunk that he was incapable of appreciating the risks involved in the enterprise. He was sufficiently aware of what was going on that he drove the car to the airport and assisted in the preparations for the flight.

Pitts v *Hunt* [1990] 3 WLR 542 Court of Appeal (Dillon, Balcombe and Beldam LJJ)

Negligence – joint illegal enterprise

Facts
The plaintiff was 18 and his friend Mark 16. Mark owned a motor cycle which he used as a trail bike, but he was not, as the plaintiff was aware, insured to use it on a road and he did not have a licence. After spending the evening drinking, they set off for home on Mark's bike with the plaintiff on the pillion. Encouraged by the plaintiff, Mark rode in a fast, reckless and hazardous manner, intending to frighten members of the public. They collided with a car; the plaintiff was severely injured and Mark (more than twice over the legal limit) was killed. The plaintiff claimed damages in negligence against, inter alia, Mark's personal representative. The judge held that the claim was barred by the maxim ex turpi causa non oritur actio and public policy; he also decided that volenti non fit injuria would have defeated the claim, but for s148(3) of the Road Traffic Act 1972, and that in any case the plaintiff had been 100 per cent contributorily negligent. The plaintiff appealed.

Held
The appeal would be dismissed on grounds of public policy and the application of the maxim ex turpi causa non oritur actio and because the circumstances precluded the court from finding that Mark had owed the plaintiff a duty of care.

Beldam LJ:

'On the facts found by the judge in this case the plaintiff was playing a full and active part in encouraging the young rider to commit offences which, if a death other than that of the young rider himself had occurred, would have amounted to manslaughter. And not just manslaughter by gross negligence on the judge's findings. It would have been manslaugther by the commission of a dangerous act either done with the intention of frightening other road users or when both the plaintiff and the young rider were aware or but for self-induced intoxication would have been aware that it was likely to do so and nevertheless they went on and did the act regardless of the consequences. Thus on the findings made by the judge in this case I would hold that the plaintiff is precluded on grounds of public policy from recovering compensation for the injuries which he sustained in the course of the very serious offences in which he was participating.'

Dillon LJ:

'I feel unable to draw any valid distinction between the reckless riding of the motor cycle in the present case by the deceased boy, Hunt, and the plaintiff under the influence of drink, and the reckless driving of the cars, albeit stolen, in *Smith* v *Jenkins and Bondarenko* v *Sommers* (1968) 69 SR(NSW) 269. The words of Barwick CJ in *Smith* v *Jenkins* (1970) 119 CLR 397 at 399-400:

"The driving of the car by the appellant, the manner of which is the basis of the respondent's complaint, was in the circumstances as much a use of the car by the respondent as it was a use by the appellant. That use was their joint enterprise of the moment."

apply with equal force to the riding of the motor cycle in the present case. This is a case in which ... the plaintiff's action in truth arises directly ex turpi causa.'

Balcombe LJ:

'In a case of this kind I find the ritual incantation of the maxim ex turpi causa non oritur actio more likely to confuse than to illuminate. I prefer to adopt the approach of the majority of the High Court of Australia in the most recent of the several Australian cases to which we were referred, *Jackson* v *Harrison* (1978) 138 CLR 438. That is to consider that what would have been the cause of action had there been no joint illegal enterprise, that is the tort of negligence based on the breach of a duty of care owed by the deceased to the plaintiff, and then to consider whether the circumstances of the particular case are such as to preclude the existence of that cause of action ... I prefer to found my judgment on the simple basis that the circumstances of this particular case were such as to preclude the court from finding that the deceased owed a duty of care to the plaintiff.

I agree ... that s148(3) of the Road Traffic Act 1972 does not affect the position under this head ...

Counsel for the first defendant sought to persuade us that the application of the volenti doctrine is to extinguish liability and, if liability has already been extinguished, there is nothing on which s148(3) of the Road Traffic Act 1972 can bite. As Dillon LJ says, if this argument were to be accepted, it would mean that s148(3) could never apply to a normal case of volenti, although that was clearly its intention ... I agree that the effect of s148(3) is to exclude any defence of volenti which might otherwise be available. On this issue I agree with the judge below that Ewbank J's decision in *Ashton* v *Turner* [1981] QB 137 at 148 was incorrect ...

I agree that the judge's finding that the plaintiff was 100 per cent contributorily negligent is logically unsupportable and, to use his own words, "defies common sense". Such a finding is equivalent to saying that the plaintiff was solely responsible for his own injuries, which he clearly was not.'

Commentary

Section 148(3) of the Road Traffic Act 1972 has been replaced by s149 of the Road Traffic Act 1988 but its effect is unchanged.

12 Breach of Statutory Duty

Atkinson v ***Newcastle Waterworks Co*** (1877) 2 Ex D 441 Court of Appeal (Lord Cairns LC, Cockburn CJ and Brett LJ)

Breach of statutory duty – civil action

Facts
The plaintiff's house, timber yard and saw mills caught fire and were burnt down. By statute, the defendants were obliged to supply water and keep the mains charged to a prescribed pressure: on the occasion in question they had failed to do so: for this the Act provided penalties.

Held
No action for damages lay for the defendants' breach of statutory duty.

Lord Cairns LC:

'The proposition a priori appears to be somewhat startling that a company supplying a town with water – although they are willing to be put under obligation to keep up the pressure, and to be subject to penalties if they fail to do so – should further be willing to assume, or that Parliament should think it necessary to subject them to liability to individual actions by any householder who could make out a case. In the one case they are merely under liability to penalties if they neglect to perform their duty, in the other case they are practically insurers, so far as water can produce safety from damage by fire. It is necessary to look at the provisions of s43 [of the Waterworks Clauses Act 1847]. Four cases are there specified, which cover all the duty imposed by the former sections, and for neglect of any one of these duties, there is a penalty of £10. For neglect of two of them, viz, to furnish to the town commissioners a sufficient supply of water for public purposes, and to furnish a supply of water to the owner or occupier, there is a further penalty of 40s a day, payable to every person who has paid or tendered the rate, for as long as such neglect or refusal continues after notice in writing has been given of the want of supply. It is not material to say, but it is possible that it might be held that neglect or refusal to fix fire-plugs whould also subject the company to the 40s penalty. If so that penalty would be applicable in three cases out of the four. We have to consider why in some cases the penalty should go into the pocket of the individuals injured, and not in others. In the case of the obligation to keep the pipes charged, and allow all persons to use the water for the purpose of extinguishing fires, the provision is for the benefit of the public, and not of any individual specially, and the guarantee for the performance of the obligation is the liability to the public penalty of £10.'

CBS Songs Ltd v ***Amstrad Consumer Electronics plc*** [1988] AC 1013 House of Lords (Lord Keith of Kinkel, Lord Templeman, Lord Griffiths, Lord Oliver of Aylmerton and Lord Jauncey of Tullichettle)

Breach of copyright? – injunction

Facts

The first and second defendants made and sold respectively tape recording machines with a 'tape-to-tape' facility which were advertised in a manner likely to encourage home taping and copying of copyright material. The plaintiff record companies and copyright owners sought an injunction and the judge allowed them to amend their statement of claim to allege that the selling and advertising were an unlawful incitement to members of the public to commit an offence under s21(3) of the Copyright Act 1956. This decision was reversed on appeal: the plaintiffs appealed.

Held

The appeal would be dismissed.

Lord Templeman:

'BPI's [the plaintiff's] initial submissions are that Amstrad "authorised" infringement and that Amstrad is a joint infringer together with any person who uses an Amstrad machine for the purpose of making an infringing reproduction of a recording in which copyright subsists ... No manufacturer and no machine confers on the purchaser authority to copy unlawfully. The purchaser or other operator of the recorder determines whether he shall copy and what he shall copy. By selling the recorder Amstrad may facilitate copying in breach of copyright but do not authorise it.

BPI's next submission is that Amstrad by their advertisement authorise the purchaser of an Amstrad model to copy records in which copyright subsists. Amstrad's advertisement drew attention to the advantages of their models and to the fact that the recorder incorporated in the model could be employed in the copying of modern records. But the advertisement did not authorise the unlawful copying of records; on the contrary, the footnote warned that some copying required permission and made it clear that Amstrad had no authority to grant that permission ... The Amstrad advertisement is open to serve criticism but no purchaser of an Amstrad model could reasonably deduce from the facilities incorporated in the model or from Amstrad's advertisement that Amstrad possessed or purported to possess the authority to grant any required permission for a record to be copied ...

In the present case, Amstrad did not sanction, approve or countenance an infringing use of their model and ... in the context of the Copyright Act 1956 an authorisation means a grant or purported grant, which may be express or implied, of the right to do the act complained of ... Amstrad conferred on the purchaser the power to copy but did not grant or purport to grant the right to copy ...

BPI next submitted that Amstrad were joint infringers; they became joint infringers if and as soon as a purchaser decided to copy a record in which copyright subsisted; Amstrad could become a joint infringer not only with the immediate purchaser of an Amstrad model but also with anyone else who at any time in the future used the model to copy records. My Lords, Amstrad sells models which include facilities for receiving and recording broadcasts, disc records and taped records. All these facilities are lawful although the recording device is capable of being used for unlawful purposes. Once a model is sold Amstrad had no control over or interest in its use. In these circumstances the allegation that Amstrad is a joint infringer is untenable ...

My Lords, joint infringers are two or more persons who act in concert with one another pursuant to a common design in the infringement. In the present case there was no common design. Amstrad sold a machine and the purchaser or the operator of the machine decided the purpose for which the machine should from time to time be used. The machine was capable of being used for lawful or unlawful purposes. All recording machines and many other machines are capable of being used for unlawful purposes but manufacturers and retailers are not joint infringers if purchasers choose to break the law. Since Amstrad did not make or authorise other persons to make a record embodying a recording in which copyright subsisted, Amstrad did not entrench on the exclusive rights granted by the 1956 Act to copyright owners and Amstrad was not in breach of the duties imposed by the Act.

BPI submit, however, that, if the 1956 Act is defective to protect them, they are entitled to the protection of the common law ... in *Macmillan & Co Ltd* v *K & J Cooper* (1923) LR 51 Ind App 109 at 118, Lord

Atkinson said that an infringer of copyright disobeyed the injunction, "Thou shalt not steal." My Lords, these considerations cannot enhance the rights of owners of copyright or extend the ambit of infringement. The rights of BPI are derived from statute and not from the Ten Commandments. Those rights are defined by Parliament, not by the clergy or the judiciary. The rights of BPI conferred by the 1956 Act are in no way superior or inferior to any other legal rights; if BPI prove that on the true construction of the Act Amstrad and Dixons have infringed the rights conferred on BPI by the Act, the court will grant appropriate and effective reliefs and remedies. But the court will not invent additional rights or impose fresh burdens.

On behalf of BPI it was submitted that even if Amstrad did not authorise infringement and were not themselves infringers, nevertheless the activities of Amstrad in the sale and advertisement of Amstrad's models constitute a common law tort. The suggested torts were three in number, namely incitement to commit a tort, incitement to commit a criminal offence and negligence ...

My Lords, I accept that a defendant who procures a breach of copyright is liable jointly and severally with the infringer for the damages suffered by the plaintiff as a result of the infringement. The defendant is a joint infringer; he intends and procures and shares a common design that infringement shall take place. A defendant may procure an infringement by inducement, incitement or persuasion. But in the present case Amstrad does not procure infringement by offering for sale a machine which may be used for lawful or unlawful copying and it does not procure infringement by advertising the attractions of its machine to any purchaser who may decide to copy unlawfully. Amstrad is not concerned to procure and cannot procure unlawful copying ...

The next tort suggested by BPI was incitement to commit a criminal offence ... It is said that when a purchaser of an Amstrad model has in his possession a record in which copyright subsists that record becomes a "plate" and the purchaser commits an offence under s21(3) [of the 1956 Act] as soon as he forms the intention of copying that record.

There are two answers to this submission. First, as a matter of construction a record is not a plate but the product of the master recording which is a plate and from which the record is derived. Second, it is a mistake to compare crime and tort. If three persons are incited by a fourth to break into a house and cause damage each will be guilty of a crime and will receive separate punishment. The inciter will be guilty of the criminal offence of inciting others to commit crime. The other three will be guilty of the crime of breaking in. If the damage caused amounts to £5,000 then in a civil action the three who caused the damage will be jointly and severally liable for £5,000 and no more. The inciter will also be jointly and severally liable for the damage if he procures the commission of the tort and is a joint tortfeasor.'

Commentary
The Copyright Act 1956 has been repealed and replaced by the Copyright, Designs and Patents Act 1988 from various appointed days.

Cutler v *Wandsworth Stadium Ltd* [1949] AC 398 House of Lords (Lord Simonds, Lord du Parcq, Lord Normand, Lord Morton of Henryton and Lord Reid

Breach of statutory duty – civil action

Facts
By statute, so long as a totalisator was in operation, space had to be made available for bookmakers at dog racing tracks. A bookmaker brought an action for an alleged breach of this obligation.

Held
As the statutory provision was intended to benefit the public as opposed to bookmakers, a breach of it was a public and not a private wrong. The bookmaker therefore had no right of civil action against the occupier.

Lord Reid:

'The occupier is required to take such steps as are necessary to secure "that there is available for bookmakers space on the track where they can conveniently carry on bookmaking". This cannot mean that space must be provided on every occasion for as many bookmakers as wish to carry on business on that occasion. It cannot mean that, after the allotted space is fully occupied, an individual bookmaker who cannot find room there can demand further space where he can conveniently carry on business. The occupier must provide a space which is adequate in all the circumstances and which is in a convenient situation, but if he does that he has fulfilled his statutory obligation. He is not required by anything in the Act to find a place for each bookmaker who presents himself. If the Act does not give to an individual bookmaker a right to demand a place for himself, I find nothing to suggest that it gives him any other right enforceable by civil action. The sanction of prosecution appears to me to be appropriate and sufficient for the general obligation imposed by the sub-section.'

Commentary

Applied in *Thornton* v *Kirklees Metropolitan Borough Council* [1979] 3 WLR 1 and *Davis* v *Radcliffe* [1990] 1 WLR 821.

Gorris v *Scott* (1874) LR 9 Exch 125 Court of Exchequer (Kelly CB, Pigott and Pollock BB)

Breach of statutory duty – civil action

Facts

Contrary to their statutory obligation, the defendants, shipowners and carriers, did not provide separate pens for cattle and sheep which they were transporting. The object of this requirement was to prevent the spread of disease amongst the animals. The plaintiff's sheep were swept overboard by high seas and he claimed damages on the defendants' breach of statutory duty.

Held

The plaintiff's damage was entirely different from that which the statute sought to prevent: its object was to prevent disease, not accidents such as that which had occurred. The plaintiff's claim therefore failed.

Groves v *Lord Wimborne* [1898] 2 QB 402 Court of Appeal (A L Smith, Rigby and Vaughan Williams LJJ)

Breach of statutory duty – civil action

Facts

The plaintiff employee was injured by reason of the defendant factory owner's failure to fence machinery in accordance with statutory regulations made under the Factories Acts. For this breach, the defendant was fined the statutory £100.

Held

The plaintiff could recover damages for his personal injuries.

A L Smith LJ:

' ... unless it can be found from the whole purview of the Act that the legislature intended that the only remedy for a breach of the duty created by the Act should be the infliction of a fine upon the master, it seems clear to me that upon proof of such a breach of duty and of an injury done to the workman, a cause of action is given to the workman against the master.'

Lonrho Ltd v *Shell Petroleum Co Ltd* [1981] 3 WLR 33 House of Lords (Lord Diplock, Lord Edmund-Davies, Lord Keith of Kinkel, Lord Scarman and Lord Bridge of Harwich)

Breach of statutory duty – conspiracy

Facts
Lonrho owned an oil pipeline from Beira to Umtali and Shell and BP used it. After UDI, by statute the United Kingdom prohibited the supply of oil to Rhodesia, as it then was. Lonrho alleged that, before UDI, Shell and BP had assured the illegal Rhodesian regime that it would continue to be supplied with oil and that this had influenced the decision to declare independence and prevented the sanctions from being effective.

Held
Contravention of the sanctions order did not give Lonrho a right to recover in tort any loss caused by it. Further, Lonrho could not claim in conspiracy as any agreement to contravene the sanctions would have been to further the commercial interests of Shell and BP, not to injure Lonrho.

Lord Diplock:

'The sanctions order thus creates a statutory prohibition on the doing of certain classes of acts and provides the means of enforcing the prohibition by prosecution for a criminal offence which is subject to heavy penalties including imprisonment. So one starts with the presumption laid down originally by Lord Tenterden CJ in *Doe d Bishop of Rochester* v *Bridges* (1831) 1 B & Ad 847, where he spoke of the "general rule" that "where an Act creates an obligation, and enforces the performance in a specified manner … that performance cannot be enforced in any other manner", a statement that has frequently been cited with approval ever since, including on several occasions in speeches in this House. Where the only manner of enforcing performance for which the Act provides is prosecution for the criminal offence of failure to perform the statutory obligation or for contravening the statutory prohibition which the Act creates, there are two classes of exception to this general rule.

The first is where on the true construction of the Act is apparent that the obligation or prohibition was imposed for the benefit or protection of a particular class of individuals, as in the case of the Factories Acts and similar legislation.

… The second exception is where the statute creates a public right (ie a right to be enjoyed by all those of Her Majesty's subjects who wish to avail themselves of it) and a particular member of the public suffers what Brett J in *Benjamin* v *Storr* (1874) LR 9 CP 400 described as "particular, direct and substantial" damage "other and different from that which was common to all the rest of the public".

… My Lords, it has been the unanimous opinion of the arbitrators with the concurrence of the umpire, of Parker J and of each of the three members of the Court of Appeal that the sanctions orders made pursuant to the Southern Rhodesia Act 1965 fell within neither of these two exceptions. Clearly they were not within the first category of exception. They were not imposed for the *benefit* or *protection* of a particular class of individuals who were engaged in supplying or delivering crude oil or petroleum products to Southern Rhodesia. They were intended to put an end to such transactions. Equally plainly they did not create any public right to be enjoyed by all those of Her Majesty's subjects who wished to avail themselves of it. On the contrary, what they did was to withdraw a previously existing right of citizens of, and companies incorporated in, the United Kingdom to trade with Southern Rhodesia in crude oil and petroleum products.

… In agreement with all those present and former members of the judiciary who have considered the matter I can see no ground on which contraventions by Shell and BP of the sanctions orders, though not amounting to any breach of their contract with Lonrho, nevertheless constituted a tort for which Lonrho could recover in a civil suit any loss caused to them by such contraventions ...

This House, in my view, has an unfettered choice whether to confine the civil action of conspiracy to the narrow field to which alone it has an established claim or whether to extend this already anomalous tort beyond those narrow limits that are all that common sense and the application of the legal logic of the decided cases require.

My Lords, my choice is unhesitatingly the same as that of Parker J and all three members of the Court of Appeal. I am against extending the scope of the civil tort of conspiracy beyond acts done in execution of an agreement entered into by two or more persons for the purpose not of protecting their own interests but of injuring the interests of the plaintiff.'

Commentary
Applied in *RCA Corp v Pollard* [1982] 3 WLR 1007.
Explained in *Lonrho plc v Fayed* [1991] 3 WLR 188.

McCall v *Abelesz* [1976] 2 WLR 151 Court of Appeal (Lord Denning MR, Ormrod and Shaw LJJ)

Breach of statutory duty – civil liability

Facts
The plaintiff was tenant of a room in the defendant's house. At times, the gas, electricity and water supplies were cut off. The plaintiff sought damages for breach of the defendants' statutory duty not to harass him.

Held
His claim would fail as the relevant statutory duty did not give rise to a civil remedy in addition to imposing a criminal sanction.

Richardson v *Pitt-Stanley* [1995] 2 WLR 26 Court of Appeal (Russell and Stuart-Smith LJJ and Sir John Megaw)

Whether breach of Employers' Liability (Compulsory Insurance) Act 1969 gives right of action to injured worker

Facts
The plaintiff was severely injured during the course of his employment. The company had not taken out insurance as required by s1 Employers' Liability (Compulsory Insurance) Act 1969. The plaintiff successfully sued the company, but the company went into liquidation with no assets to satisfy the judgment. The plaintiff then brought an action against the company's directors and secretary claiming, inter alia, that they had committed an offence under s5 of the 1969 Act by having knowingly consented to or connived at the failure to insure, and the plaintiff had suffered loss equivalent to the sum he would have recovered had the company been properly insured. The master struck this out but the judge allowed the appeal, holding that the 1969 Act created a civil liability upon directors and officers not to consent to or connive at a breach of duty to insure.

Held

The appeal would be allowed (Sir John Megaw dissenting). Whether a breach of statutory duty which involved criminal liability also gave rise to a civil cause of action was a question of construction as to whether the relevant statutory provision as a whole, by express provision or by necessary implication, created such a civil liability. There was no express provision in the 1969 Act creating civil liability and the Act was intended to lie within the criminal law. Hence no civil liability could attach to the company or its directors or officers.

Per Sir John Megaw: The obligation on an employer to insure against injury sustained by its employees was imposed by Parliament to give protection to a particular class of individuals, the employees, to eliminate or reduce the risk to an injured employee of finding that he was deprived of his lawful compensation because of the financial position of the employer. Failure to perform this obligation should give rise to civil liability.

Commentary

Although the leading judgments in this case involve detailed consideration of the law, there is much force in Sir John Megaw's dissenting judgment. In it he noted that the statute in question imposed a criminal penalty and that under Lord Diplock's general rule in *Lonrho* v *Shell Petroleum* [1982] AC 173 performance could not be enforced in any other manner. Lord Diplock went on to say that there was an exception to this general rule where the obligation was imposed for the benefit or protection of a particular class of individuals. Sir John Megaw thought that this exception 'undoubtedly' applied in the present case.

T v *Surrey County Council* [1994] 4 All ER 577 High Court (Scott Baker J)

Local authority's breach of Nurseries and Child Minders' Regulation Act 1948 – whether duty owed to child

Facts

The plaintiff was seriously injured while in the care of a registered child-minder. Some three months earlier another child had suffered similar serious injuries while in the care of the same child-minder, but the local authority were unable to decide whether the child-minder had caused the injury. As a result the local authority did not deregister the child-minder. The child sued the local authority claiming, inter alia, damages for breach of statutory duty in failing to cancel the child-minder's registration pursuant to s5 Nurseries and Child Minders' Regulation Act 1948.

Held

The claim for breach of statutory duty failed. It was clearly the intention of Parliament in enacting the 1948 Act that only fit persons should be registered as child-minders. A person could not be so fit where there was an unresolved question concerning a non-accidental injury suffered by a child who had been in that person's care. Nevertheless, the local authority's failure to meet its statutory obligations to suspend the registration while further investigations were made did not confer a private law right of action for breach of statutory duty upon the injured child, since the courts were reluctant to impose on local authorities any liability for breach of statutory duty other than that expressly imposed in the statute.

Commentary

The above three cases show a marked reluctance by the courts to allow an action for damages for breach of statutory duty where the duty is imposed by the statute in very wide and general terms.

Thornton v *Kirklees Metropolitan Borough Council* [1979] 3 WLR 1 Court of Appeal (Megaw and Roskill LJJ)

Breach of statutory duty – civil action

Facts

The plaintiff alleged that the defendant housing authority was in breach of its duty under the Housing (Homeless Persons) Act 1977 and claimed damages for the distress and inconvenience which he alleged he had suffered.

Held

Such an action – which would be treated as an action in tort – would lie. The Act had imposed a duty on the housing authority for the benefit of a specified category of persons, but it had prescribed no special remedy for breach of that duty.

Commentary

Applied: *Cutler* v *Wandsworth Stadium Ltd* [1949] AC 398.

Wentworth v *Wiltshire County Council* [1993] 2 WLR 175 Court of Appeal (Parker, Stuart-Smith and Beldam LJJ)

Breach of statutory duty – remedies

Facts

The plaintiff's dairy farm was served by a road used by the Milk Marketing Board's tankers. The road having become dangerous to traffic because of its disrepair, the Board refused to use it and to collect the plaintiff's milk. As a result, the plaintiff gave up his dairy herd and suffered financial loss. Resorting to procedures under the Highways Act 1959, the plaintiff established that the defendant highway authority had been under a duty to repair the road. In the present action, he sued the defendants, maintaining that s1(1) of the Highways (Miscellaneous Provisions) Act 1961 had removed highway authorities' exemption from liability for non-repair and therefore that the defendants were liable for breach of statutory duty.

Held

The plaintiff's action would fail and his only remedy was in accordance with the 1959 Act's procedures.

Parker LJ:

'The sole question is whether the respondent can claim for the economic loss which admittedly flowed from the breach. This depends upon the construction of certain provisions of the 1959 Act and of the Highways (Miscellaneous Provisions) Act 1961, which, by s16, is to be construed as one with the 1959 Act.

Prior to the 1959 Act no civil action for damages resulting from non-repair (non-feasance) lay against the inhabitants at large or their successors who were responsible for repair, although at common law an indictment based on public nuisance could be brought if the lack of repair was sufficiently serious. An action for damages also lay for damages including financial loss directly flowing from obstruction to a highway.

The 1959 Act, as appears from its long title, was designed to consolidate with amendments earlier enactments relating to highways, streets and bridges and make consequential amendments to the common law. Part I created various highway authorities. Part IV deals with the maintenance of highways. It begins with s38, which by sub-s (1) abolishes the pre-existing duty with respect to the maintenance of highways, which lay upon the inhabitants at large of any area. The common law duty is thus swept away. There then follows provisions creating or providing for the creation of categories of highways maintainable at the public expense. The first of such categories is, by s38(2)(a), any highway which immediately prior to the commencement of the Act was maintainable by the inhabitants at large of any area or maintainable by a highway authority.

I go next to s44(1), which creates the statutory duty upon which the respondent founds his claim. It provides:

"The authority who are for the time being the highway authority for a highway maintainable at the public expense shall, subject to the following subsection, be under a duty to maintain the highway."

Since, by s295, "maintenance" includes "repair" the duty is clear.

The next relevant, and in my view vital, section is s59. Subsection (1) provides:

"After the commencement of this Act, no indictment shall be preferred in respect of neglect to maintain a highway."

Thereby the only pre-existing means of enforcing the duty to repair was removed. This must be coupled with the provisions of s298, which, subject to s89(1) to which I refer next, preserves from being affected by the Act the pre-existing exemption from liability for non-repair "available to a highway authority immediately before the commencement of this Act as the successor to the inhabitants at large".

Subject to s89(1) therefore it would at this point appear that the new statutory duty was without teeth. The remedy by indictment had gone and the exemption for non-repair had been preserved. That subsection provides that cattle-grids provided under the 1959 Act for a highway (and certain other works) -

"shall be maintainable by the highway authority for the highway; and they shall not be entitled to rely on any exemption from liability for non-repair available to a highway authority as the successor to the inhabitants at large."

There is, however, still even in such case an apparent absence of teeth.

This is plainly intended to be cured by the provisions of s59(2) to (10), which enable any person who alleges that a way or bridge is a highway maintainable at the public expense and is out of repair to establish those matters (if not admitted) by application to quarter sessions (now the Crown Court) and obtain an order that it be put in proper repair by the highway authority within such reasonable period as may be specified in the order. In cases where both matters are admitted a similar order may be made by a magistrates' court. If the order is not complied with within the time specified the complainant must be authorised by the court to carry out such works as may be necessary to put the highway in proper repair and to recover any expenses reasonably incurred in carrying out the works so authorised from the highway authority as a civil debt. The 1959 Act thus provides a specific and very detailed means of enforcing the statutory duty which it has placed on the highway authority.

This in my judgment indicates that no other means of enforcement was intended by Parliament: see *Doe d Bishop of Rochester v Bridges* (1831) 1 B & Ad 847 at 859, per Lord Tenterden CJ, *Pasmore v Oswaldtwistle UDC* [1898] AC 387 at 394 and *Lonrho Ltd v Shell Petroleum Co Ltd* [1981] [1982] AC 173 at 185 per Lord Diplock. The indication is of course not conclusive, for there are exceptions as appears clearly from Lord Diplock's speech in the *Lonrho* case and also from the speech of Lord Simonds in *Cutler v Wandsworth Stadium Ltd (in liq)* [1949] AC 398 at 407. If however the 1959 Act stood alone I would have no hesitation in concluding that, as a matter of construction, no other method of enforcement was available. It does not however stand alone, and it is necessary to see what is the effect of construing it as one with the 1961 Act.

Section 1(1) of that Act abolished the exemption of liability for non-repair which had been preserved, save as to cattle grids etc, by s298 of the earlier Act, and s1(6) repealed that section and also the concluding words of s89(1), which had abolished the exemption in relation to cattle-grids. The situation thus becomes one in which the highway authority is under a general duty to repair and has no exemption from liability for breach of that duty. At the same time, however, s1(2) provided a defence to any action against a highway authority in respect of damage resulting from failure to maintain. That defence consisted in proof

> "that the authority had taken such care as in all the circumstances was reasonably required to secure that the part of the highway to which the action relates was not dangerous for traffic."

It is in my view clear from the nature of the defence that it is an essential part of *any* claim for non-repair to establish that the relevant part of the highway was dangerous to traffic. This is, indeed, well settled by authority: see *Meggs* v *Liverpool Corp* [1968] 1 WLR 689, *Burnside* v *Emerson* [1968] 1 WLR 1490 ... amongst others. Further light is shed on the nature of the action contemplated by the provisions of s1(3), which prescribes the matters to which the court is to have particular regard when considering a defence under s1(2). They are five in number. The first three are of no particular significance but I regard the last two as important. They are:

> "(d) whether the highway authority knew, or could reasonably have been expected to know, that the condition of the part of the highway to which the action relates was likely to cause danger to users of the highway; (e) where the highway authority could not reasonably have been expected to repair that part of the highway before the cause of action arose, what warning notices of its condition had been displayed ..."

Both of those provisions indicate that the contemplated action is one for damage to a road user or his property from a condition of the highway making it dangerous to road users, ie such an action as was previously unavailable by reason of the non-repair exemption, but which now became available for the first time.

... the matter is in the end one of statutory construction and in my judgment the intention of Parliament, to be gathered from the wording of the two Acts and the pre-existing state of the law, is clear. It is (1) to replace the remedy for non-repair by way of indictment by the new remedy under s59 and (2) to replace the previous exemption from civil liability for damage resulting from non-repair by an action for damage to the person or property of a road user from the dangerous condition of a highway, subject only to the statutory defence.

I accept at once that, in one sense, the [plaintiff] was a road user even when himself not using the road for passage. The purpose of many highways is, inter alia, to enable traffic to deliver goods to, or visit, or collect goods from, or leave commercial premises. The owners of such premises might therefore be regarded as making use of the road for the purposes of their business although not themselves using the road for passage. In the light, however, of the fact that such persons are provided with the s59 remedy to replace the former remedy by way of indictment I do not regard them as being within the scope of those intended to have a civil remedy for breach of statutory duty going beyond that.

If [counsel for the plaintiff] were right, a person such as the [plaintiff] would be, and indeed the [plaintiff] was, in the position of being able to bring an action for large, perhaps very large, damages, notwithstanding that he could have avoided the damage by taking action under s59. Parliament did not in my view intend any such thing. In my judgment the [defendants] are not liable ...'

West Wiltshire District Council v Pugh [1993] NLJ 546 High Court (Morritt J)

Scope of statutory duty – lack of co-existence of common law duty of care

Facts

The plaintiff brought an action against, inter alia, two of its senior officers claiming that they were in breach of their duty by procuring payments to be made by the council without proper authority. The officers issued third party notices against three district auditors employed by the Audit Commission who, under the Local Government Finance Act 1982, had been responsible for auditing the council accounts during the relevant period. The officers claimed that they had merely followed the district auditors' advice in carrying out the transactions in question, and that the district auditors owed them a duty of care under statute and at common law. The auditors applied to have the notices set aside.

Held

That a district auditor acting under the Local Government Finance Act 1982 owed a statutory duty not to the officers of the local authority, but to the authority itself, since the purpose of the audit was to protect the authority. Thus any breach of this statutory duty would not give rise to any cause of action on the part of the officers. Also, it would not be fair, just or equitable to impose a duty of care on the district auditors towards the officers at common law when Parliament when enacting the 1982 Act had not chosen so to do.

X v *Bedfordshire County Council; M* v *Newham London Borough Council; E* v *Dorset County Council; Christmas* v *Hampshire County Council; Keating* v *Bromley London Borough Council* [1995] 3 WLR 152 House of Lords (Lord Jauncey, Lord Lane, Lord Ackner, Lord Browne-Wilkinson and Lord Nolan)

Breach of statutory duty

Facts

This case concerns five appeals to the House of Lords regarding breach of statutory duty, negligence in the exercise of a statutory power and the co-existence of a common law duty of care.

Held

1. 'That a breach of statutory duty did not, by itself, give rise to any private law cause of action, but such a right might arise where, on its true construction, the statute imposed a duty for the limited class of the public and there was a clear parliamentary intention to confer a private right of action for breach on members of that class; that there was no general rule for ascertaining whether a statute conferred such a right of action, but the absence of another remedy for breach and a clear intention to protect the limited class, were indications that a private right of action existed, and the mere existence of some other remedy was not necessarily decisive that no private right existed.'
2. 'That a plaintiff basing his claim on a careless exercise of a statutory duty had to show the existence of circumstances giving rise to a duty of care at common law.'
3. 'That in the performance of statutory functions a common law duty of care might arise, but the manner in which a discretion was exercised had to be distinguished from the implementation of the discretionary decision in practice; that where a statutory discretion was conferred on a public authority nothing done by the authority within the ambit of the discretion was actionable at common law, but where the decision complained of fell outside the statutory discretion it could give rise to common law liability; that the court could not adjudicate on the factors relevant to the exercise of the discretion in so far as they included matters of policy; that where such matters were justiciable the ordinary principles of negligence applied, but that a common law duty could not be imposed if it was inconsistent with, or had a tendency to discourage, the due performance of a statutory duty; and that, even where the defendant's servant was not alleged to owe a separate duty to the plaintiff, his negligent acts could constitute a breach of the duty of care, if any, owed directly by the defendant to the plaintiff.'

Commentary

This is now the leading case in this area. It is a long case (some 54 pages) and factually complex, involving as it does five appeals. However, that part of the speech of Lord Browne-Wilkinson in which he discusses the law is admirably lucid and concise for such a wide-ranging review and should be studied.

13 Employers' Liability

Coltman* v *Bibby Tankers Ltd, The Derbyshire [1987] 3 WLR 1181 House of Lords (Lord Keith of Kinkel, Lord Roskill, Lord Griffiths, Lord Oliver of Aylmerton and Lord Goff of Chieveley)

Employers' liability – defective equipment

Facts
A 90,000 ton bulk carrier owned by the defendants sank off the coast of Japan with the loss of all hands. The plaintiffs, personal representatives of a crew member, alleged that the ship had been unseaworthy because of defects in its hull and that the ship was defective 'equipment' within s1 of the Employer's Liability (Defective Equipment) Act 1969.

Held
The ship was 'equipment' in this sense, regardless of its size. Accordingly, where a seaman suffered in consequence of the unseaworthiness of a ship its owner was liable in negligence for that injury or loss of life.

Lord Oliver:

'My Lords, it is common ground that the 1969 Act was introduced with a view to rectifying what was felt to be the possible hardship to an employee resulting from the decision of this House in *Davie* v *New Merton Board Mills Ltd* [1959] 2 WLR 331. In that case an employee was injured by a defective drift supplied to him by his employers for the purpose of his work. The defect resulted from a fault in manufacture but the article had been purchased by the employers without knowledge of the defect from a reputable supplier and without any negligence on their part. It was held that the employers' duty was only to take reasonable care to provide a reasonably safe tool and that that duty had been discharged by purchasing from a reputable source an article whose latent defect they had no means of discovering. Thus the action against them failed although judgment was recovered against the manufacturer. Clearly this opened the door to the possibility that an employee required to work with, on or in equipment furnished by his employer and injured as a result of some negligent failure in design or manufacture might find himself without remedy in a case where the manufacturer and the employer were, to use the words of Viscount Simonds, "divided in time and space by decades and continents" so that the person actually responsible was no longer traceable or, perhaps, was insolvent or had ceased to carry on business ... Parliament accordingly met this by imposing on employers a vicarious liability and providing, in a case where injury was due to a defect caused by the fault of the third party, that the employer should, regardless of his own conduct, be liable to his employee as if he had been responsible for the defect, leaving it to him to pursue against the third party such remedies as he might have whether original or by way of contribution.'

Cook* v *Square D Ltd [1992] IRLR 34 Court of Appeal (Mustill, Mann and Farquharson LJJ)

Delegation of employer's duty to provide safe system of work

Facts

The plaintiff was sent by the defendants, his employers, to work as a computer consultant in Saudi Arabia. While working there he slipped into a small hole in the tiled floor of the control room and suffered injury. The plaintiff argued that the duty to provide a safe system of work was non-delegable, that the defendants were in breach of it and that the facts were analagous to those in *McDermid* v *Nash Dredging and Reclamation Co Ltd* [1987] AC 906 where the plaintiff's claim had succeeded.

Held

Rejecting the analogy, there had been no breach of duty by the defendants: the site was some 8,000 miles away and both the site occupiers and the general contractors were reliable companies who were aware of their responsibility for the safety of workers on site. However, there was not ruled out the possibility that circumstances might require employers in the UK to take steps to satisfy themselves as to the safety of foreign sites, for example where a number of their employees were going to work on a foreign site or where one or two employees were going to work there for a considerable period of time.

General Cleaning Contractors Ltd v *Christmas* [1953] 2 WLR 6 House of Lords (Earl Jowitt, Lord Oaksey, Lord Reid and Lord Tucker)

Employers' liability – safe system of working

Facts

The plaintiff, a window-cleaner for twenty years, was employed as such by the defendants. In cleaning sash windows, he followed the usual practice of standing on the outside sill and cleaning first the top half: this was then pushed up so as to leave just enough hand-hold while cleaning the bottom half. On one occasion the sash fell shut, dislodging the plaintiff's hand and causing him to fall. He sued his employers in negligence.

Held

The plaintiff's claim would succeed. The method of cleaning windows, although customary, was known to be dangerous and the employers were under a duty to devise a safer system.

Lord Reid:

'It is the duty of the employer to consider the situation, to devise a suitable system, to instruct his men what they must do, and to supply any implements that may be required such as in this case wedges or objects to be put on the window sill to prevent the window from closing. No doubt, he cannot be certain that his men will do as they are told when they are working alone. But, if he does all that is reasonable to ensure that his safety system is operated, he will have done what he is bound to do. In this case the appellants do not appear to have done anything as they thought they were entitled to leave the taking of precautions to the discretion of each of their men. In this I think that they were in fault, and I think that this accident need not have happened if the appellants had done as I hold they ought to have done.'

Commentary

Applied in *Pape* v *Cumbria County Council* [1992] 2 All ER 211.

Hewett v *Alf Brown's Transport Ltd* (1992) The Times 4 February Court of Appeal (Nourse, Taylor and Scott LJJ)

Lead poisoning from spouse's overalls – liability of spouse's employer

Facts

The plaintiff suffered lead poisoning as a result of coming into contact with lead oxide powder while washing her husband's overalls. Her husband worked for the defendants and his job required him to drive a lorry containing waste, including lead oxide, from a large gasworks which was being dismantled to a tip. However, her husband's exposure to lead was no more than one hour a day.

Held

There was such a low level of exposure to lead that no duty of care to the husband arose, nor was there any duty to provide washing facilities or to warn him of the risk of taking his overalls and boots home with him. Given that the exposure of the husband was minimal, the exposure of the plaintiff was also minimal and there had therefore been no breach by the defendants of their statutory obligations or of their common law duty to her. However, the court did accept that an employer owed a duty of care to members of an employee's family in respect of foreseeeable risk.

Hudson v *Ridge Manufacturing Co Ltd* [1957] 2 WLR 948 High Court (Streatfield J)

Employers' liability – competent staff

Facts

Over the years, Chadwick had indulged in horseplay at the expense of his fellow employees. The defendant employers were aware of this and had frequently issued reprimands and warnings. On the occasion in question Chadwick's prank caused the plaintiff a fractured wrist.

Held

The employers were liable as they had been in breach of their duty at common law to provide competent staff.

Streatfield J:

> 'It is really unarguable that here is a case where there did exist, as it were in the system of work, a source of danger, through the conduct of one of the employers' workmen, of which the employers knew: repeated conduct which went on over a long space of time, and which they did nothing whatever to remove, except to reprimand and go on reprimanding to no effect whatever ... whatever steps were taken, it was the duty of the employers to put a stop to such conduct. By that time they must have known that one day there might be injury if Mr Chadwick went on with this sort of conduct. He had done it before, he went on doing it and still he was allowed to remain in their employment and was not removed from it. In my judgment, therefore, the injury was sustained as a result of the employers' failure to take proper steps to put an end to that conduct, to see that it would not happen again and, if it did happen again, to remove the source of it. It was for that reason that this injury resulted. In those circumstances, although it is an unusual type of case, I have come to the conclusion that counsel for the plaintiff is right in his contention and that the employers are liable for the plaintiff's injuries.'

Knowles v *Liverpool City Council* [1993] 4 All ER 321 House of Lords (Lord Keith, Lord Templeman, Lord Jauncey, Lord Browne-Wilkinson and Lord Mustill)

Whether flagstones equipment

Facts

The plaintiff, who was employed by the defendant council to lay flagstones, was injured when a flagstone he was handling broke. He claimed damages for his injury alleging, inter alia, that the council had been negligent under s1 Employers' Liability (Defective Equipment) Act 1969 in providing him with equipment in a defective condition. The recorder held that the flagstone was 'equipment' within the meaning of the Act, and the Court of Appeal dismissed the appeal. The council appealed to the House of Lords.

Held

That the purpose of the 1969 Act was to protect employees where the employer, despite having exercised all proper care and relying on a reputable supplier, had exposed his employee to dangerous material. It was thus consistent with the purpose of the Act to construe the word 'equipment' widely so that it included every article provided by an employer to an employee for the purpose of the employer's business. The House applied its earlier wide approach in *Coltman* v *Bibby Tankers* [1988] AC 276.

McDermid v *Nash Dredging and Reclamation Co Ltd* [1987] AC 906 House of Lords (Lord Hailsham of St Marylebone LC, Lord Bridge of Harwich, Lord Brandon of Oakbrook, Lord Mackay of Clashfern and Lord Ackner)

Employers' liability – duty of care

Facts

The defendants employed the plaintiff as a deckhand for dredging operations carried out by the defendants and their parent company. Working on a tug which was owned by the parent company and controlled by one of their employees, the tug-master, the plaintiff suffered serious injuries. The accident had been caused by the tug-master's negligence.

Held

The defendants were liable as their duty of care was personal or non-delegable, but they had delegated both their duty of devising a safe system of work, and its operation, to the tug-master.

Lord Hailsham of St Marylebone LC:

'The plaintiff's claim in the proceedings was based on the allegation inter alia, of a "non-delegable" duty resting on his employers to take reasonable care to provide a "safe system of work" … The defendants did not, and could not, dispute the existence of such a duty of care, nor that it was 'non-delegable' in the special sense in which the phrase is used in this connection. This special sense does not involve the proposition that the duty cannot be delegated in the sense that it is incapable of being the subject of delegation, but only that the employer cannot escape liability if the duty has been delegated and then not properly performed. Equally the defendants could not and did not attempt to dispute that it would be a central and crucial feature of any safe system on the instant facts that it would prevent so far as possible the occurrence of such an accident as actually happened, viz injury to the plaintiff as the result of the use of Ina's engine so as to move the Ina before both the ropes were clear of the dredger and stowed safely in board and the plaintiff was in a position of safety.

Since such a system could easily have been designed and put in operation at the time of the accident in about half a dozen different ways, and since it is quite obvious that such a system would have prevented the accident had it been in operation, and since the duty to provide it was "non-delegable" in the sense that the defendants cannot escape liability by claiming to have delegated performance of their duty, it is a little difficult to see what possible defence there could ever have been to these proceedings.'

Lord Brandon:

'A statement of the relevant principle of law can be divided into three parts. First, an employer owes to his employee a duty to exercise reasonable care to ensure that the system of work provided for him is a safe one. Second, the provision of a safe system of work has two aspects: (a) the devising of such a system and (b) the operation of it. Third, the duty concerned has been described alternatively as either personal or non-delegable. The meaning of these expressions is not self-evident and needs explaining. The essential characteristic of the duty is that, if it is not performed, it is no defence for the employer to show that he delegated its performance to a person, whether his servant or not his servant, whom he reasonably believed to be competent to perform it. Despite such delegation the employer is liable for the non-performance of the duty.'

Pape v *Cumbria County Council* [1992] ICR 132 High Court (Waite J)

Employer's liability – duty to warn of dangers

Facts

The plaintiff aged 57 was employed as a part-time cleaner by the defendants and was required to use various detergents and chemical cleaning products in the course of her employment. The defendants supplied the plaintiff with gloves, which she used occasionally, but they did not warn her of the dangers of irritant dermatitis from sustained exposure of skin to cleaning products. The plaintiff later began to suffer from irritated skin on her hands and wrists, which developed into acute dermatitis affecting her entire skin, and she claimed damages for personal injuries.

Held

Her action would be successful as the defendants had been under a duty to warn her of the dangers and, as no attempt had been made to give her any such warning, the defendants had been in breach of their duty of care.

Waite J:

[Counsel] are both satisfied that there is no English authority precisely on this point. I do not think there is any difficulty about tackling this case from first principles. The question to be answered here is the same as the question that was exposed by the House of Lords in *General Cleaning Contractors Ltd* v *Christmas* [1953] AC 180 at 193, namely, reading from the speech of Lord Reid, the following:

"... whether it is the duty of the appellants to instruct their servants what precautions they ought to take, and to take reasonable steps to see that those instructions are carried out."

The House held in that case in the context of a claim against a window cleaning company that it had a duty not only to provide a safe system of work but to instruct employees in the use of it. The answer to that question was Yes. So it is in my judgment in the present case. The dangers of dermatitis or acute eczema from the sustained exposure of unprotected skin to chemical cleansing agents is well known, well enough known to make it the duty of a reasonable employer to appreciate the risks it presents to members of his cleaning staff but at the same time not so well known as to make it obvious to his staff without any necessity for warning or instruction.

There was a duty on the defendants to warn their cleaners of the dangers of handling chemical cleaning materials with unprotected hands and to instruct them as to the need to wear gloves at all times. It is common ground that no such warning or instruction was given and that is sufficient to place the defendants in breach of their duty of care. Since that is enough to establish liability I think it undesirable that I should attempt to answer the question, to which any reply would perforce be obiter in the present case, as to whether the placing of rubber gloves in the cleaning cupboard with a facility for replacement on demand was sufficient to discharge the defendants' further duty of care to ensure that any warning and instruction had it been given was observed and carried out ...

It remains to deal with damages. Counsel have already been able to agree a formula for the assessment of special damages ... subject to only one outstanding issue, namely the multiplier to be applied to the figure which is the already agreed multiplicand for lost future earnings ... The plaintiff enjoyed her work and apart from her eczema is in basic good health. She might reasonably have expected had it not been for the defendants' breach of duty to carry on working for someone, even if retired from the defendants' employment at 60, in a job for which there always seems to be a demand whatever the fortunes of the economy as a whole. All in all I consider that the multiplier of five would be appropriate.

As for general damages, pain and suffering and loss of amenity, counsel are once again agreed that there is no reported decision on facts sufficiently similar to provide an analogy for the instant case. Dealing with the matter at large, therefore, and remembering this is a case where the plaintiff's pain, embarrassment and discomfort were of a severe order when at their height and her symptoms will to some extent at least as regards her hands remain with her for ever, I have decided an appropriate figure to award under this head would be £22,000.'

Walker v *Northumberland County Council* [1994] NLJ 1659 High Court (Colman J)

Safe system of work – duty not to cause psychiatric damage

Facts
The plaintiff was employed by the defendant council as an area social services officer, responsible for managing four teams of social workers in an area with a high proportion of child-care problems. In 1986, the plaintiff suffered a nervous breakdown because of the stress and pressure of work, and was off work for three months. Before he returned to work it was agreed assistance would be provided to lessen his work burden, but in the event only limited assistance was provided. Six months later the plaintiff suffered a second breakdown and was forced to cease work permanently. The plaintiff sued his employer claiming damages for breach of its duty of care to take reasonable steps to avoid exposing him to a health-endangering work-load.

Held
Where it is reasonably foreseeable to an employer that an employee might suffer a nervous breakdown because of the stress and pressures of his work-load, the employer is under a duty of care, as part of his duty to provide a safe system of work, not to cause the employee psychiatric damage by the volume and character of the work which the employee is required to perform.

Colman J:

'In the present case, the mental illness and the lasting impairment of his personality which Mr Walker sustained in consequence of the 1987 breakdown was so substantial and damaging that the magnitude of the risk to which he was exposed must be regarded as relatively large. Moreover, there can, in my judgment, be no doubt on the evidence that by 1985 at the latest, it was reasonably foreseeable to Mr Davison [the plaintiff's superior], given the information which I have held that he then had, that by reason of stress of work there was in general *some* risk that Mr Walker might sustain a mental breakdown of some sort in consequence of his work. ...

I have no doubt that it ought to have been foreseen by Mr Davison that if Mr Walker was again exposed to the same work-load as he had been handling at the time of his breakdown in October 1986 there was risk that he would once again succumb to mental illness and that such illness would be likely to end his career as an area manager and perhaps his career in the social services ... In my judgment [Mr Davison] should have appreciated that Mr Walker was a man distinctly more vulnerable to psychiatric damage than he had appeared to be in 1986 ... In my judgment, once [support staff were] not fully available to assist Mr Walker, it was quite likely, if not inevitable, that he would again break down. I find that the failure ... to provide continuous and effective back-up for Mr Walker was fatal to Mr Walker's ability to survive ... In the result, it is established that by April 1987 Mr Walker was exposed in his job to a reasonably foreseeable risk to his mental health which materially exceeded the risk to be anticipated in the ordinary course of an area officer's job. Was it in those circumstances reasonable for the council to take action to alleviate or remove that risk? In my view, the only course which would have had a reasonable probability of preventing another mental breakdown was the provision of continuous or at least substantial back-up for Mr Walker ... Having regard to the reasonably foreseeable size of the risk of repetition of Mr Walker's illness if his duties were not alleviated by effective additional assistance and to the reasonably foreseeable gravity of the mental breakdown which might result if nothing were done, I have come to the conclusion that the standard of care to be expected of a reasonable local authority required that in March 1987 such additional assistance should be provided ... In the event, there will be judgment for the plaintiff on liability with damages yet to be assessed.'

14 Product Liability

Evans v *Triplex Safety Glass Co Ltd* [1936] 1 All ER 283 High Court (Porter J)

Negligence – liability of manufacturer

Facts

The plaintiff was injured when, for no apparent reason, his car windscreen shattered. He had had the car over a year and the windscreen had been fitted by the car-makers. The plaintiff sued the manufacturers of the windscreen.

Held

The plaintiff's claim would fail as, in the circumstances, it could not be presumed that the manufacturers had been at fault.

Grant v *Australian Knitting Mills Ltd* [1936] AC 85 Privy Council (Lord Hailsham LC, Lord Blanesburgh, Lord Macmillan, Lord Wright and Sir Lancelot Sanderson)

Negligence – liability of manufacturer

Facts

The plaintiff contracted a skin disease after wearing underpants manufactured by the defendants. The disease was due to an excess of chemical left in the garment during manufacture.

Held

The defendants were liable to the plaintiff on the principle of *Donoghue (or McAlister)* v *Stevenson.*

Lord Wright:

'The presence of the deleterious chemical in the pants, due to negligence in manufacture, was a hidden and latent defect, just as much as were the remains of the snail in the opaque bottle : it could not be detected by any examination that could reasonably be made. Nothing happened between the making of the garments and their being worn to change their condition. The garments were made by the manufacturers for the purpose of being worn exactly as they were worn in fact by the appellant: it was not contemplated that they should be first washed. It is immaterial that the appellant has a claim in contract against the retailers, because that is a quite independent cause of action, based on different considerations, even though the damage may be the same. Equally irrelevant is any question of liability between the retailers and the manufacturers on the contract of sale between them. The tort liability is independent of any question of contract.

It was argued, but not perhaps very strongly, that *Donoghue's* case was a case of food or drink to be consumed internally, whereas the pants here were to be worn externally. No distinction, however, can be logically drawn for this purpose between a noxious thing taken internally and a noxious thing applied externally: the garments were made to be worn next the skin: indeed Lord Atkin specifically puts as examples of what is covered by the principle he is enunciating things operating externally, such as "an ointment, a soap, a cleaning fluid, or cleaning powder" ... The decision in *Donoghue's* case did not depend on the bottle being stoppered and sealed; the essential point in this regard was that the article should reach the consumer or user subject to the same defect as it had when it left the manufacturer. That this was true of the garments is in their Lordships' opinion beyond question. At most there might in other cases be a greater difficulty of proof of that fact.'

15 Occupiers' Liability

Andrews* v *Schooling [1991] 1 WLR 783 Court of Appeal (Balcombe and Beldam LJJ and Sir Denys Buckley)

Section 1 of the Defective Premises Act 1972

Facts
The third defendants granted the plaintiffs a 199 year lease of a ground floor flat including a cellar. Extensive work had been done to the flat itself but the only work which had been done in the cellar was the painting of the walls. The plaintiff later discovered that the flat suffered from penetrating dampness which she alleged emanated from the cellar. She claimed damages from the defendants, alleging, inter alia, that the defendants were in breach of the duty which they owed to her under s1 of the 1972 Act. The defendants argued that they were not liable because they had not done any relevant work on the flat so that it could not be said that they had taken on work in relation to the cellar. Thus they argued that the Act applied only to cases of misfeasance and not to non-feasance.

Held
This argument would be rejected and the plaintiff awarded damages. A dwelling was unfit for habitation when it was without some essential attribute when the works were completed, even though the problems arising therefrom had not then been patent.

Beldam LJ:

'In my view, s1 of the Defective Premises Act 1972 applies to the failure to carry out necessary work as well as carrying it out badly. The evidence before the court establishes that the plaintiff's flat was not fit for habitation. That was due to the manner in which the work undertaken by the defendants for or in connection with the provision of the flat had been carried out.'

Billings (AC) & Sons Ltd* v *Riden [1957] 3 WLR 496 House of Lords (Viscount Simonds, Lord Reid, Lord Cohen, Lord Keith of Avonholm and Lord Somervell of Harrow)

Occupier's liability – independent contractor

Facts
The appellants had been employed by the occupier of a house to reconstruct the front pathway. In the course of carrying out this work, they laid a foundation of stones, bordered by a muddy area. On this was laid a plank which, for the time being, was the only means of access to the house. This plank passed alongside some railings which guarded it from a sunken basement next door. The appellants removed these railings also. One night the respondent, a lawful visitor to the premises, fell into the basement and was injured. She claimed against the appellants.

Held

The appellants, who were independent contractors of the occupier, owed a duty to take reasonable care for the safety of visitors. They had been in breach of this duty as they had made the route to the house unsafe: they were therefore liable. Her damages were reduced by 50 per cent for contributory negligence: she knew the path was dangerous, but refused assistance and did not have a torch, despite the fact that it was dark.

Commentary

Overruled: *Malone* v *Laskey* [1907] 2 KB 141 so far as it dealt with negligence.

British Railways Board v *Herrington* [1972] 2 WLR 537 House of Lords (Lord Reid, Lord Morris of Borth-y-Gest, Lord Wilberforce, Lord Pearson and Lord Diplock)

Negligence – duty owed to trespasser

Facts

The respondent, a six year old boy, was playing in a field beside which ran the appellants' railway line. The fence between the field and the line was in a bad state of repair and in fact, people often broke through it to cross the railway line. Some weeks before the appellants had been told of the presence of children on the line. The respondent passed through the fence and was electrocuted on the live rail.

Held

The appellants owed the respondent a duty of common humanity and though he was a trespasser, he was entitled to recover damages.

Lord Reid:

'So the question whether an occupier is liable in respect of an accident to a trespasser on his land would depend on whether a conscientious humane man with his knowledge, skill and resources could reasonably have been expected to have done or refrained from doing before the accident something which would have avoided it. If he knew before the accident that there was a substantial probability that trespassers would come, I think that most people would regard as culpable failure to give any thought to their safety. He might often reasonably think, weighing the seriousness of the danger and the degree of likelihood of trespassers coming against the burden he would have to incur in preventing their entry or making his premises safe, or curtailing his own activities on his land, that he could not fairly be expected to do anything. But, if he could at small trouble and expense take some effective action, again I think that most people would think it inhumane and culpable not to do that. If some such principle is adopted, there will no longer be any need to strive to imply a fictitious licence. It would follow that an impecunious occupier with little assistance at hand would often be excused from doing something which a large organisation with ample staff would be expected to do.'

Lord Morris of Borth-y-Gest:

'The duty that lay on the appellants was a limited one. There was no duty to ensure that no trespasser could enter on the land. And, certainly, an occupier owes no duty to make his land fit for trespassers to trespass in. Nor need he make surveys of his land in order to decide whether dangers exist of which he is unaware. The general law remains that one who trespasses does so at his peril. But, in the present case, there were a number of special circumstances: (a) the place where the fence was faulty was near to a public path and public ground; (b) a child might easily pass through the fence; (c) if a child did pass through and go on to the track, he would be in grave danger of death or serious bodily harm; (d) a child might not realise the risk involved in touching the live rail or being in a place where a train might pass at speed. Because of these circumstances (all of them well known and obvious) there was, in my view, a duty which, while not amounting to the duty of care which an occupier owes to a visitor, would be a duty to take such steps as common sense or common humanity would dictate; they would be steps calculated to exclude or to warn or otherwise within reasonable and practicable limits to reduce or avert danger.'

Lord Diplock:

'I would then seek to summarise the characteristics of an occupier's duty to trespassers ... First, the duty does not arise until the occupier has actual knowledge either of the presence of the trespasser on his land or of facts which make it likely that the trespasser will come on to his land; and has also actual knowledge of facts as to the condition of his land or of activities carried out on it which are likely to cause personal injury to a trespasser who is unaware of the danger. He is under no duty to the trespasser to make any enquiry or inspection to ascertain whether or not such facts do exist. His liability does not arise until he actually knows of them.

Secondly, once the occupier has actual knowledge of such facts, his own failure to appreciate the likelihood of the trespasser's presence or the risk to him involved, does not absolve the occupier from his duty to the trespasser if a reasonable man possessed of the actual knowledge of the occupier would recognise that likelihood and that risk.

Thirdly, the duty when it arises is limited to taking reasonable steps to enable the trespasser to avoid the danger. Where the likely trespasser is a child too young to understand or heed a written or a previous oral warning, this may involve providing reasonable physical obstacles to keep the child away from the danger.

Fourthly, the relevant likelihood to be considered is of the trespasser's presence at the actual time and place of danger to him. The degree of likelihood needed to give rise to the duty cannot, I think be more closely defined than as being such as would compel a man of ordinary humane feelings to take some steps to mitigate the risk of injury to the trespasser to which the particular danger exposes him. It will thus depend on all the circumstances of the case: the permanent or intermittent character of the danger; the severity of the injuries which it is likely to cause; in the case of children, the attractiveness to them of that which constitutes the dangerous object or condition of the land; the expense involved in giving effective warning of it to the kind of trespasser likely to be injured, in relation to the occupier's resources in money or in labour.'

Commentary
Distinguished: *Edwards* v *Railway Executive* [1952] AC 737.
    Not followed: *Addie (R) & Sons (Collieries) Ltd* v *Dumbreck* [1929] AC 358.
    Applied in *Pannett* v *P McGuinness & Co Ltd* [1972] 3 WLR 386.

Cunningham v *Reading Football Club Ltd* [1991] PIQR 141 High Court (Drake J)

Football club – duty to visitor policeman

Facts
As the defendants were aware, at a match on their ground only four months earlier spectators had loosened concrete by kicking and jumping on it and had then thrown concrete missiles at the police. After that match no measures had been taken to make it more difficult to loosen the concrete. On this occasion, the plaintiff police officers had all been struck by pieces of concrete loosened from the terraces and thrown at them by spectators. The defendants had known in advance that crowd trouble might well occur.

Held
The plaintiffs were entitled to damages for personal injury caused by the defendants' negligence and

breach of statutory duty under the Occupiers' Liability Act 1957. Drake J said that, given the appallingly dilapidated state of the ground, the conduct of the spectators was easily foreseeable by the defendants and was a strong probability. A reasonably prudent occupier would have realised the concrete in the ground was dangerous, because it might supply a source of missiles, and would have taken steps to remove or minimise the risk.

Ferguson v *Welsh* [1987] 1 WLR 1553 House of Lords (Lord Keith of Kinkel, Lord Brandon of Oakbrook, Lord Griffiths, Lord Oliver of Aylmerton and Lord Goff of Chieveley)

Occupier's liability – duty to contractor's employee

Facts

As part of a council's sheltered housing scheme, it was necessary to demolish a building and Spence's tender for this aspect of the work was accepted on condition, amongst others, that the council's approval must be obtained before subcontractors were employed on the site. Without obtaining such approval, Spence subcontracted the work to the Welsh brothers and, as they adopted an unsafe system of work, the appellant, their employee, was injured. The judge held that the Welsh brothers were liable and the Court of Appeal ordered a new trial against Spence. Were the council also liable?

Held

No, because the appellant had been unable to show that the council knew or ought to have known that Spence would subcontract the work without authority to persons who would employ an unsafe system of work. The council had not been in breach of the common duty of care owed to visitors under s2(2) of the Occupiers' Liability Act 1957 or the ordinary common law duty of care.

Lord Keith of Kinkel:

'It would not ordinarily be reasonable to expect an occupier of premises having engaged a contractor whom he has reasonable grounds for regarding as competent, to supervise the contractor's activities in order to ensure that he was discharging his duty to his employees to observe a safe system of work. In special circumstances, on the other hand, where the occupier knows or has reason to suspect that the contractor is using an unsafe system of work, it might well be reasonable for the occupier to take steps to see that the system was made safe.

The crux of the present case therefore, is whether the council knew or had reason to suspect that Mr Spence, in contravention of the terms of his contract, was bringing in cowboy operators who would proceed to demolish the building in a thoroughly unsafe way. The thrust of the affidavit evidence admitted by the Court of Appeal was that Mr Spence had long been in the habit of sub-contracting his demolition work to persons who proceeded to execute it by the unsafe method of working from the bottom up. If the evidence went the length of indicating that the council knew or ought to have known that this was Mr Spence's usual practice, there would be much to be said for the view that they should be liable to Mr Ferguson. No responsible council should countenance the unsafe working methods of cowboy operators. It should be clearly foreseeable that such methods exposed the employees of such operators to very serious dangers. It is entirely reasonable that a council occupying premises where demolition work is to be executed should take steps to see that the work is carried out by reputable and careful contractors. Here, however, the council did contract with Mr Spence subject to the condition that sub-contracting without their consent was prohibited. The fresh evidence sought to be adduced by Mr Ferguson does not go the length of supporting any inference that the council or their responsible officers knew or ought to have known that Mr Spence was likely to contravene this prohibition.'

Gitsham v *C H Pearce & Sons plc* [1992] PIQR 57 Court of Appeal (Glidewell and Stocker LJJ)

Occupier's liability – snow on factory road

Facts

The plaintiff fell outside his place of work on a roadway which was covered with ice and snow. He brought an action against his employers alleging that they were in breach of their statutory duty (under s29 of the Factories Act 1961) in failing to ensure that all means of access to his place of work had been gritted by the start of the working day.

Held

The plaintiff's appeal would be dismissed as the employers had an extensive procedure for clearing snow and ice which was being properly carried out on the morning of the accident and the defendants had done all that was reasonably practicable in the severe weather conditions to ensure that the access roads were safe. Glidewell LJ said that even if the particular area had not been gritted, on the evidence, particularly the severity of the weather, it had been open to the judge to conclude that the employers were not in breach of their statutory duty.

Glasgow Corporation v *Taylor* [1922] 1 AC 44 House of Lords (Lord Buckmaster, Lord Atkinson, Lord Shaw, Lord Sumner and Lord Wrenbury)

Occupier's liability – children

Facts

A boy of seven went with some other children to the defendant's recreation ground where, easily accessible, were shrubs with poisonous berries looking like grapes or cherries. The boy ate some – and died as a result.

Held

If the basic facts were proved, the defendants would be guilty of negligence.

Lord Atkinson:

'The liability of defendants in cases of this kind rests, I think, in the last resort upon their knowledge that by their action they may bring children of tender years, unable to take care of themselves, yet inquisitive and easily tempted, into contact, in a place in which they, the children, have a right to be, with things alluring or tempting to them, and possibly in appearance harmless, but which, unknown to them and well known to the defendants, are hurtful or dangerous if meddled with... I think, in the latter case, as much as in the former, the defendant would be bound, by notice or warning or some other adequate method, to protect the children from injury. In this case the averments are that the appellants did nothing of the kind. If that be true they were in my view guilty of negligence, giving the plaintiff a right of action.'

Harris v *Birkenhead Corporation* [1976] 1 WLR 279 Court of Appeal (Megaw, Lawton and Ormrod LJJ)

Negligence – occupation or control

Facts

The defendants acquired X's house by compulsory purchase order which stated that within a specified time they would enter and take possession. X vacated the house, but did not inform the defendants of the date of her departure. The defendants knew that property in the area was likely to be vandalised if left vacant and although they generally boarded up empty houses, they did not do so to X's house. The house was left empty by the defendants for three months, during which time it was ruined by vandals. The plaintiff, aged four and a half, wandered into the house from a nearby playground and was severely injured when she fell from a window.

Held

The defendants were occupiers of the premises and liable because they had been in breach of their duty to the plaintiff.

Ormrod LJ:

'The only question on the first part of this case is whether the corporation is properly regarded in law as a person occupying or in control of the premises in which the accident happened... there is, in my judgment, only one possible answer to that question. They were at all material times the persons with the right to control that property. It would have been almost absurd to suggest that, in the circumstances of this case, the second defendant [the previous owner] could have been expected by the law to go to expense in securing these premises against the damage which was inevitable and was bound to happen to them immediately or very soon after the tenant had vacated them. In those circumstances it would be a disastrous injustice to her to hold her liable for this appalling accident.'

Lawton LJ:

'... a man cannot claim that he has no knowledge when he has shut his eyes to the obvious.'

McAuley v *Bristol City Council* [1992] 1 All ER 749 Court of Appeal (Neill and Ralph Gibson LJJ)

Landlord's duty under Defective Premises Act 1972

Facts

The plaintiff and her husband were weekly tenants of a house owned by the defendants. The tenancy agreement required the defendants to keep the structure and exterior of the property in good repair while the plaintiffs were required to keep the premises, including the garden, in a clean and orderly condition. Under condition 6(c) of the agreement the plaintiffs were required to give the defendants access 'for any purpose which may from time to time be required ...' The plaintiff fell and sustained injury because a concrete garden step was unstable and, in an action for damages, she alleged, inter alia, that the defendants had been in breach of the duty of care imposed by s4(1) of the Defective Premises Act 1972.

Held

Her action would be successful.

Ralph Gibson LJ:

'Section 4(1) [of the 1972 Act] applies where the landlord is under an obligation to repair. A duty of care is imposed upon the landlord, assuming proof of knowledge or means of knowledge under subs(2) in respect of a "relevant defect", that is to say a defect which constitutes a failure to carry out the repairing obligation. Subsection (4) extends the basis of liability by treating the landlord as being under an obligation to repair, when in fact he is not. The extension is made when the landlord is given a right to enter "to carry out any description of maintenance or repair" but the extension of liability is not general. The landlord, when he is given a right to enter to carry out "any description of maintenance or repair" is to be treated as if he were under an obligation to the tenant "for that description of maintenance or repair", not all and any description of maintenance or repair.

Thus, in this case, assuming that there was no actual obligation, contractual or statutory, to repair the garden step, the plaintiff, to succeed under s4, must show that the defect in the garden step was a "relevant defect", ie that it was a defect in the state of the premises which constituted a failure by the council to carry out repair of a description for which the council had a right to enter the premises.

There is, I think, no warrant for a wide construction of the words of the section. They apply to all landlords, and not merely to local authorities, and can operate so as to impose a substantial burden upon a landlord in respect of premises under the immediate control of the tenant and in respect of which the landlord has assumed no contractual obligation.

Condition 6(c) applies to "any purpose which may from time to time be required by the council"; it does not say "for any purpose for which the council may be required to enter". I do not accept that the right of entry is limited to entry for the purpose of discharging the obligations of the council. The words are not, I think, perfectly drafted but the meaning seems to me to be clear, namely "any purpose for which from time to time entry may be required by the council" ...

In imposing the obligations stated in s4 of the 1972 Act where there is no obligation to repair, whether contractual or statutory, Parliament required proof of a tenancy which "expressly or impliedly gives the landlord the right to enter the premises to carry out any description of maintenance or repair". If such a right is proved, the landlord is, if the other conditions are satisfied, to be treated as under an obligation to the tenant for that description of repair. Parliament thus legislated by reference to the common law. If the common law says that the right to repair is implied, the statute imposes the obligation. The provisions apply to any tenancy agreement. The fact that, for this purpose, it would suit the tenants very well to have implied against them a right in favour of the landlord enforceable against the tenants does not, in my judgment, enable the court to imply such a right in circumstances where it could not properly do so upon the relevant principles ...

The decisive question in this case, therefore, is whether the court can properly hold that the council impliedly reserved a right against the tenant to carry out repair to the garden ... After some hesitation, I have reached the conclusion that the necessary reservation should be implied in restricted terms. The defect in the step exposed the tenants and visitors to the premises to the risk of injury. In this case ... the basis of the agreement was that the premises would be kept in reasonable and habitable condition and that, apart from interior decorative work and work to keep the garden in a clean and orderly condition, the work would be done by the council. The council had expressly reserved the right to enter "for any purpose for which from time to time entry may be required", if I have correctly construed the term, and the agreement did not expressly identify those purposes. If there should be a defect in the garden which exposed the tenants and lawful visitors to the premises to significant risk of injury, then I think that, to give business efficacy to the agreement ... a right should be implied in the council to carry out repairs for the removal of that risk of injury. A reasonable tenant could not sensibly object to such a right. If the council became aware of a dangerous defect in the steps of a steep garden, as in this case, and asked the tenant for access to repair it, in the interest of all persons who might be expected to be affected by the defect, the court could, in my judgment, properly require the tenant to allow such access upon the basis of an implied right in the council to do the work. So limited, I would hold that the implied right to enter to do the necessary repair was proved and the [defendants'] appeal should be dismissed.'

McGeown v Northern Ireland Housing Executive [1994] 3 All ER 53 House of Lords (Lords Keith, Goff, Browne-Wilkinson, Mustill and Lloyd)

Liability of owner of land to persons using right of way

Facts

The appellant was using a public right of way when she tripped in a hole and was injured. She sued the owner of the land over which the right of way ran. The trial judge and Court of Appeal in Northern Ireland dismissed her action and she appealed to the House of Lords claiming (a) that the rule that the owner of land over which a public right of way ran was under no liability for negligent nonfeasance towards members of the public using it was no longer good law and (b) that the appellant was not merely a member of the public but a visitor to whom a duty was owed under s2 Occupiers' Liability Act (Northern Ireland) 1957 (which is identical to s2 Occupiers' Liability Act 1957).

Held

The rule that the owner of the land over which a public right of way passed was under no liability for negligent nonfeasance towards members of the public was good law. Rights of way passed over many different types of terrain and it would be unreasonable if landowners were to owe a duty of care to members of the public, who needed no permission of the owner to use the right of way, to maintain the rights in good condition.

Furthermore, a person using a public right of way was neither the licensee nor invitee of the occupier, and any licence to use the way formerly granted by the owner before it became subject to the right of way was merged in the right of way and extinguished, because once a public right of way had been established there was no question of permission being granted and users used it as of right and not by virtue of any licence or invitation. Hence the appellant could not succeed at either common law or under the 1957 Act.

Murphy v *Bradford Metropolitan Council* [1992] PIQR 68 Court of Appeal (Glidewell and Stocker LJJ)

Occupier's liability – snow on school path

Facts

The plaintiff teacher fell on a path leading to a school run by the council and she suffered injury. The path was notoriously slippery but on the morning of the accident the school caretaker had cleared the path of snow at 6.20 am and treated it with rock salt and had done so again at 8 am, on being told that the path was still slippery. Despite these efforts the plaintiff still slipped on the path half an hour later.

Held

The defendants had not discharged their duty under s2(2) of the Occupiers' Liability Act 1957 because the path was a likely place for an accident to occur and they had failed to lay grit and cinders on it. Stocker LJ said that the trial judge had considered all the relevant facts and there was ample evidence on which he could conclude that the plaintiff's injuries from her fall were a result of the council's failure to take reasonable care to see that she would be reasonably safe when using the path in the school grounds.

Ogwo v *Taylor* [1987] 3 WLR 1145 House of Lords (Lord Mackay of Clashfern LC, Lord Bridge of Harwich, Lord Elwyn-Jones, Lord Templeman and Lord Ackner)

Negligence – duty of care to fireman

Facts

The defendant negligently set the roof of his house on fire whilst trying to burn off old paintwork on the eaves and guttering with a blow-lamp. The plaintiff, a fireman, came to put out the fire and whilst doing so he entered the loft of the house with a water hose. The intense heat in the confined loftspace caused much steam and afterwards the plaintiff discovered that he had suffered severe steam burns. The question was whether the defendant was liable for the plaintiff's burns, and whether a person who negligently starts a fire owes a duty of care to the firemen who come to put it out.

Held

The plaintiff should succeed as the defendant had been in breach of his duty of care.

Lord Bridge:

'Of course, I accept that not everybody, whether professional fireman or layman, who is injured in a fire negligently started will *necessarily* recover damages from the tortfeasor. The chain of causation between the negligence and the injury must be established by the plaintiff and may be broken in a number of ways. The most obvious would be where the plaintiff's injuries were sustained by his foolhardy exposure to an unnecessary risk either of his own volition or acting under the orders of a senior fire officer. But, subject to this, I can see no basis of principle which would justify denying a remedy in damages against the tortfeasor responsible for starting a fire to a professional fireman doing no more and no less than his proper duty and acting with skill and efficiency in fighting an ordinary fire who is injured by one of the risks to which the particular circumstances of the fire give rise. Fire out of control is inherently dangerous. If not brought under control, it may, in most urban situations, cause untold damage to property and possible danger to life. The duty of professional firemen is to use their best endeavours to extinguish fires and it is obvious that, even making full use of all their skills, training and specialist equipment, they will sometimes be exposed to unavoidable risks of injury, whether the fire is described as "ordinary" or "exceptional". If they are not to be met by the doctrine of volenti, which would be utterly repugnant to our contemporary notions of justice, I can see no reason whatever why they should be held at a disadvantage as compared to the layman entitled to invoke the principle of the so-called "rescue" cases.

Counsel for the defendant suggested it would be anomalous that a fireman should recover damages for injuries sustained in fighting a fire caused by negligence when his colleague who suffers similar injuries in fighting another fire of which the cause is unknown has no such remedy. If this be an anomaly, it is one which is common to most, if not all, injuries sustained by accident and is inevitable under a system which requires proof of fault as the basis of liability. The existence of the suggested anomaly is the strongest argument advanced by those who support the introduction of a "no fault" system of compensation. But it has no special application to the case of firemen.

At the end of the day I am happy to find my views in full accord with those expressed in the latest authority directly in point, which is the decision at first instance of Woolf J in *Salmon v Seafarer Restaurants Ltd*.'

Commentary

Approved: *Salmon v Seafarer Restaurants Ltd* [1983] 1 WLR 1264.

Phipps v *Rochester Corporation* [1955] 2 WLR 23 High Court (Devlin J)

Occupier's liability to child

Facts

The plaintiff, aged five, and his sister, aged seven, crossed the defendants' land, having implied permission to do so. The land was being developed for house building and in one place a deep trench had been dug. The plaintiff fell in and was injured.

Held

To a young child, the trench was a concealed danger, but his claim failed as the defendants had not been in breach of their duty towards him.

Devlin J:

'... the responsibility for the safety of little children must rest primarily upon the parents; it is their duty to see that such children are not allowed to wander about by themselves, or at least to satisfy themselves that the places to which they do allow their children to go unaccompanied are safe for them to go to. It would not be socially desirable if parents were, as a matter of course, able to shift the burden of looking after their children from their own shoulders to those of persons who happen to have accessible bits of land. Different considerations may well apply to public parks or to recognised playing grounds where parents allow their children to go unaccompanied in the reasonable belief that they are safe.'

Revill v *Newbury* (1995) The Independent 10 November Court of Appeal (Neill, Evans and Millett LJJ)

Occupiers' liability – duty of care owed to a trespasser

Facts

The plaintiff attempted to break into the defendant's property. The defendant loaded a shotgun, poked the barrel through a small hole in the door, and fired and hit the plaintiff at a range of around five feet. The plaintiff pleaded guilty to the relevant criminal offences, and claimed against the defendant under s1 Occupiers' Liability Act (OLA) 1984 and in negligence. At first instance the plaintiff succeeded, the judge rejecting the defences of ex turpi causa non omitar acto, accident and self-defence. The defendant appealed to the Court of Appeal.

Held

The appeal failed. On the facts, the negligence issue was identical to the issue of a breach of duty under s1 OLA 1984. Section 1 shows that an occupier cannot treat a burglar as an outlaw and defines the scope of the duty owed in s1(4). There was no room for a two-stage determination in first considering whether there had been a breach of duty, and second whether, despite this breach, the plaintiff was barred from recovering. The question at both common law and under s1(3)(b) OLA 1984 was: did the defendant have reasonable grounds to believe that the plaintiff was in the vicinity of the danger? On the facts the judge was entitled to treat the gunshot not as merely a warning shot but as a shot likely to strike anyone in the vicinity of the door. If the ex turpi defence applied, any claim by a trespasser would be barred, no matter how excessive or unreasonable the force used against him.

Note: a high level of contributory negligence was found on the part of the plaintiff.

Robson v *Hallett* [1967] 3 WLR 28 High Court (Lord Parker CJ, Diplock LJ and Ashworth J)

Police – trespassers

Facts

Three police officers without warrant were making inquiries at Ds' house. D1 ordered them to leave and as one PC was departing, he was leapt upon and assaulted by D2. D2 claimed that this assault was lawful because the police officer was trespassing.

Held

When a licence is revoked, a reasonable time must be given for the person requested to leave. Here, that time had not been allowed and the assault was therefore unlawful.

Roles v *Nathan* [1963] 1 WLR 1117 Court of Appeal (Lord Denning MR, Harman and Pearson LJJ)

Occupier's liability – warnings disregarded

Facts

The plaintiffs were the widows of two chimney-sweeps who had been called in by the defendant occupier to service and clean a central heating boiler and who were overcome by fumes whilst working in the boiler-room. They had been advised not to enter or remain in the room when the boiler was alight, but had disregarded this advice and a warning about the dangers of carbon monoxide.

Held (Pearson LJ dissenting)

The defendant was not in breach of his duty of care, by virtue of s2(4)(a) of the Occupiers' Liability Act 1957, and he was not therefore liable.

Lord Denning MR:

'When a householder calls in a specialist to deal with a defective installation on his premises, he can reasonably expect the specialist to appreciate and guard against the dangers arising from the defect. The householder is not bound to watch over him to see that he comes to no harm. I would hold, therefore, that the occupier here was under no duty of care to these sweeps. At any rate, in regard to the dangers which caused their deaths. If it had been a different danger, as for instance if the stairs leading to the celler had given way, the occupier might no doubt be responsible, but not for these risks which were special risks ordinarily incidental to their calling.

We all know the reason for this subsection. It was inserted so as to clear up the unsatisfactory state of the law as it had been left by the decision of the House of Lords in *London Graving Dock Co* v *Horton* [1951] AC 737. That case was commonly supposed to have decided that, when a person comes onto premises as an invitee and is injured by the defective or dangerous condition of the premises (due to the default of the occupier) it is nevertheless a complete defence for the occupier to prove that the invitee knew of the danger, or had been warned of it. Suppose, for instance, that there was only one way of getting into and out of premises and it was by a footbridge over a stream which was rotten and dangerous. According to *Horton's* case, the occupier could escape all liability to any visitor by putting up a notice: "this bridge is dangerous", even though there was no other way by which the visitor could get in or out; and he had no option but to go over the bridge. In such a case, s2(4) makes it clear that the occupier would nowadays be liable. But, if there were two footbridges, one of which was rotten and the other safe, a hundred yards away, the occupier could still escape liability, even today, by putting up a notice: "Do not use this footbridge. It is dangerous. There is a safe one further upstream". Such a warning is sufficient because it does enable the visitor to be reasonably safe.'

Salmon v *Seafarer Restaurants Ltd* [1983] 1 WLR 1264 High Court (Woolf J)

Occupier's liability to fireman

Facts

The plaintiff, a fireman, was injured by an explosion on premises occupied by the defendants as a fish and chip shop when a fire in the premises melted a seal on a gas meter thus allowing gas to escape. The fire was caused by the negligence of an employee of the defendants. P contended that because the fire had been started negligently he was entitled to recover damages from the Ds. The defendants, however, argued that the occupier's duty of care to firemen attending his premises in the course of their work was limited to protecting the fireman from any special or exceptional risks over and above the ordinary risks necessarily incidental to a fireman's job and did not extend to protecting firemen from such ordinary risks which included an explosion of the kind which had taken place on the Ds' premises.

Held

The defendants were liable to P. An occupier of premises owes the same duty of care to a fireman attending his premises to extinguish a fire as he owed to other visitors under s2 of the Occupiers' Liability Act 1957, subject to the fact that in determining whether the occupier was in breach of that duty a fireman was expected to exercise those skills which could be expected to be shown by firemen. Negligence was the cause of the fire in this case and since it was reasonably foreseeable that firemen would attend the fire and that an explosion of the kind which occurred might result from the fire, the Ds were liable to P for his consequent injury. The Ds' third party action against the British Gas Corporation was dropped for lack of evidence of any negligence against the latter.

Woolf J:

'Having found nothing in the authorities to which I was referred which is inconsistent with the ordinary approach to liability in these circumstances, I go on to consider, in the absence of authority, whether there is any basis for limiting the duty which is owed to firemen. It is true that their very occupation is one where they are specially trained to deal with the dangers inherent in any outbreak of fire. However, it seems to me that their consequent special skills should not change the normal approach to the establishing of liability. It is only a factor to take into account in seeing whether a liability is established and their calling is not in itself a defence. In deciding whether the negligent act could foreseeably cause injury to a fireman, it is necessary to take into account the skills that are ordinarily expected to be shown by firemen. To decide whether there has been any breach of the duty, which in my view undoubtedly exists, in certain cases it will be very relevant to consider whether or not the danger to the fireman requires the taking of precautions. Here again it is proper to take into account the special skills of the fireman. Where it can be foreseen that the fire which was negligently started is of the type which could, first of all, require firemen to attend to extinguish that fire, and where, because of the very nature of the fire, when they attend they will be at risk even though they exercise all the skill of their calling, there seems no reason why a fireman should be at any disadvantage when the question of compensation for his injuries arises.

I make the remarks which I have made, with regard to the position of firemen, because it was submitted by counsel on behalf of the defendants, in his very careful and helpful submissions, that in the case of firemen there were good public policy reasons why there should be a restriction on the extent of the duty owed to them, and that they should be treated differently from other "rescuers" (I here use the expression to identify the category of cases which I have in mind). Notwithstanding the submissions of counsel for the defendants, I find no principle of public policy which requires the ordinary rules to be limited, and it seems to me that the same principles disclosed by the "rescue" cases should be applied to firemen, though taking into account, of course, in the way I have already indicated, the special skills of firemen.'

Commentary
Approved in *Ogwo* v *Taylor* [1987] 3 WLR 1145.

Simkiss v *Rhondda Borough Council* (1983) 81 LGR 460 Court of Appeal (Waller, Dunn and Slade LJJ)

Occupier's liability – failure to fence

Facts

A seven-year-old girl, the plaintiff, lived opposite a mountain with a bluff abutting the road. She tried to slide down the bluff on a blanket and sustained severe injuries as a result. The land was occupied by the defendants and they had not fenced it. The girl alleged that they had been negligent.

Held

The defendants were not liable. Although an occupier had to be prepared for children to be less careful than an adult, the defendants did not have a higher duty of care than a reasonably prudent parent. They were entitled to assume that parents would warn their children and would not allow them to play there unless they appreciated the danger.

Simms v *Leigh Rugby Football Club Ltd* [1969] 2 All ER 923 High Court (Wrangham J)

Occupier's liability – injury to visiting player

Facts

During a rugby match, a visiting player was tackled and thrown towards a concrete wall 7 feet 3 inches from the touchline. Rugby Football League byelaws said that the distance had to be at least 7 feet. The player suffered a broken leg, but there was no evidence of a previous serious injury of this type. Was the club liable?

Held

No. On the balance of probabilities the injury had not arisen from contact with the concrete wall and having a leg broken in a tackle is one of rugby's accepted risks. Even if there had been contact with the wall, and the club owed the player the common duty of care under s2(1) of the Occupiers' Liability Act 1957, the injury, although foreseeable, was so improbable that it was not necessary to guard against it. Further, the club would have been saved by s2(5) of the 1957 Act.

Southern Portland Cement Ltd v *Cooper* [1974] 2 WLR 152 Privy Council (Lord Reid, Lord Morris of Borth-y-Gest, Lord Wilberforce, Lord Simon of Glaisdale and Lord Salmon)

Occupier's liability to trespasser

Facts

The defendants allowed a mound of waste from their limestone quarry so to grow that a high tension cable was within reach from the top of it. Children were in the habit of playing on adjoining land: they had been warned off the defendants' land and there had not been much trespassing, at least during working hours. One Sunday afternoon the plaintiff, aged 13, was playing on the mound: his arm came into contact with the electric cable and he suffered severe injuries.

Held

The defendants owed the plaintiff a duty to take steps to prevent the development of this dangerous situation and, as they were in breach of this duty, they were liable in respect of his injuries.

Lord Reid:

> 'The rights and interests of the occupier must have full consideration. No unreasonable burden must be put on him. With regard to dangers which have arisen on his land without his knowledge he can have no

obligation to make enquiries or inspection. With regard to dangers of which he has knowledge but which he did not create he cannot be required to incur what for him would be large expense.

If the occupier creates the danger when he knows that there is a chance that trespassers will come that way and will not see or realise the danger he may have to do more. There may be difficult cases where the occupier will be hampered in the conduct of his own affairs if he has to take elaborate precautions. But in the present case it would have been easy to prevent the development of the dangerous situation which caused the plaintiff's injuries. The more serious the danger the greater is the obligation to avoid it. And if the dangerous thing or something near it is an allurement to children that may greatly increase the chance that children will come there.

Next comes the question to whom does the occupier owes a duty. Their Lordships have already rejected the view that no duty is owed unless the advent of a trespasser is extremely probable. It was argued that the duty could be limited to cases where the coming of trespassers is more probable than not. Their Lordships can find neither principle nor authority nor any practical reason to justify such a limitation. The only rational or practical answer would seem to be that the occupier is entitled to neglect a bare possibility that trespassers may come to a particular place on his land but is bound at least to give consideration to the matter when he knows facts which shew a substantial chance that they may come there.

Such consideration should be all-embracing. On the one hand the occupier is entitled to put in the scales every kind of disadvantage to him if he takes or refrains from action for the benefit of trespassers. On the other hand he must consider the degree of likelihood of trespassers coming and the degree of hidden or unexpected danger to which they may be exposed if they come. He may have to give more weight to these factors if the potential trespassers are children because generally mere warning is of little value to protect children.

It is easy to be wise after an accident has occurred. In considering whether the occupier did all that he ought to have done before the accident the court or jury must endeavour to put itself back in the situation which confronted the occupier before the trespassers arrived. It is not enough to consider the point where the accident occurred if there are other danger points which the occupier would also have had to protect.

The problem then is to determine what would have been the decision of a humane man with the financial and other limitations of the occupier. Would he have done something which would or might have prevented the accident, or would he, regretfully it may be, have decided that he could not reasonably be expected to do anything... Once it is accepted that the nature of this duty cannot be determined without reference to such all embracing considerations as their Lordships have mentioned, the need for the imposition of two separate parallel duties disappears. Their Lordships believe that the above reformulation of the law would achieve results not substantially different from those achieved by recent decisions of the High Court. They believe moreover that it is substantially in line with the development in England law as expressed by the House of Lords in *British Railways Board* v *Herrington*.'

Commentary
Explained: *Commissioner for Railways* v *Quinlan* [1964] 2 WLR 817.
   Not followed: *Addie (R) and Sons (Collieries) Ltd* v *Dumbreck* [1929] AC 358.

Staples v *West Dorset District Council* (1995) The Times 28 April Court of Appeal (Nourse, Kennedy and Evans LJJ)

Occupiers' liability – breach of duty of care

Facts
The plaintiff, a visitor to the defendants, slipped on some visible algae that was an obvious danger and was injured. The plaintiff succeeded against the defendants in the High Court. On appeal to the Court of Appeal:

Held

The defendants owed the plaintiff a duty of care under s2(2) Occupiers' Liability Act 1957, but were not in breach of this duty. The plaintiff saw the algae before the accident and knew that it might well be slippery. He was well able to evaluate the danger and needed no warning.

Stone v *Taffe* [1974] 1 WLR 1575 Court of Appeal (Megaw, Stephenson LJJ and Sir Seymour Karminski)

Occupier's liability – duty to visitors

Facts

The second defendants were owners of public house run by the first defendant who, contrary to his employers' instructions, allowed guests to remain drinking after hours. The plaintiff left the pub at 1.00 am, fell on unlit stairs and was killed.

Held

At the time of the accident, the plaintiff was not a trespasser, but a lawful visitor, as no indication that his licence to be on the premises was withdrawn had been given. D1 was in breach of his duty under the Occupiers' Liability Act 1957 by failing to ensure the stairs were illuminated and D2 was vicariously liable.

Targett v *Torfaen Borough Council* [1991] NPC 126 Court of Appeal (Sir Donald Nicholls VC, Russell and Leggatt LJJ)

Negligence – personal injury – liability of landlord

Facts

The plaintiff was injured when he fell down stairs outside his council house. The house had been designed and built by the defendant council. There was no handrail for the lower steps, nor was there any lighting in the immediate vicinity of the steps. The recorder held that the council was liable for the plaintiff's injuries, although he reduced the damages payable by 25 per cent on the ground that the plaintiff had been guilty of contributory negligence. The council appealed. The difficulty facing them was that the Court of Appeal in *Rimmer* v *Liverpool City Council* [1984] 1 All ER 930 had held that a landowner, who designs or builds a house, is no more immune from personal responsibility for faults of construction than a building contractor, or from personal responsibility for faults of design than an architect, simply on the ground that he has disposed of the house by selling it or letting it. The defendant sought to get round *Rimmer* on two grounds. The first was that there was no defect in manufacture because the lack of a handrail or of lighting did not render the steps of faulty manufacture. The second ground was that *Rimmer* could no longer be regarded as good law in the light of the decision of the House of Lords in *Murphy* v *Brentwood District Council* [1991] 1 AC 398.

Held

Both arguments would be rejected and the appeal dismissed. The first argument was rejected because the lack of a handrail and lighting constituted manufacturing and design defects respectively, the second because *Murphy* was a case in which the plaintiffs had suffered *economic* loss and it did not overrule cases in which plaintiffs had suffered personal injury as a result of the negligence of the defendant.

Wheat v E Lacon & Co Ltd [1966] 2 WLR 581 House of Lords (Viscount Dilhorne, Lord Denning, Lord Morris of Borth-y-Gest, Lord Pearce and Lord Pearson)

Negligence – occupation or control

Facts

The respondent brewery company owned a public house, the first floor of which was the living quarters of the resident manager and his wife, who occasionally took in paying guests. The appellant and her husband took a room there. At about 9.00 pm one evening, the appellant's husband slipped and fell down the stairs from the first floor and was killed. The cause of the accident was found to be a) that the handrail did not go right to the bottom of the stairs, and b) the light at the top of the stairs was missing. The appellant sued the respondents, alleging they were in breach of their common duty of care under the Occupiers' Liability Act 1957.

Held

The respondents, together with the manager and his wife, were occupiers of the premises and owed a duty of care to all lawful visitors. However, the facts disclosed no breach of duty so the appeal was dismissed.

Lord Denning:

'... wherever a person has a sufficient degree of control over premises that he ought to realise that any failure to use care of his part may result in injury to a person coming lawfully there, then he is an "occupier" and the persons coming there are his "visitors"; and the "occupier" is under a duty to the "visitor" to use reasonable care. In order to be an occupier, it is not necessary for a person to have entire control over the premises. He need not have exclusive occupation. Suffice it that he has some degree of control. He may share control with others. Two or more may be occupiers. And, whenever this happens, each is under a duty to use care towards persons coming lawfully on the premises, dependent on his degree of control... any degree of control over the state of the premises may be enough (to make a person an occupier).'

Commentary

Applied in *Emanuel (H & N) Ltd* v *Greater London Council* [1971] 2 All ER 835.

White v Blackmore [1972] 3 WLR 296 Court of Appeal (Lord Denning MR, Buckley and Roskill LJJ)

Occupier's liability – exclusion

Facts

The plaintiff's husband entered as a competitor in a jalopy-race and took his wife as a spectator. At the entrance to the course were several notices stating 'Warning to the Public: Motor racing is dangerous' and exempting all persons involved in the racing from liability for loss or injuries however caused. Whilst standing by a safety rope watching the race, the plaintiff's husband received fatal injuries when a wheel of a competitor's car became tangled with the rope and caused the rope to spring forward, catapulting her husband some distance. The plaintiff sued, inter alia, the organisers of the race.

Held (Lord Denning MR dissenting)

The plaintiff's claim would fail, although the defendants had been negligent, because they had excluded their liability, as they were entitled to do under s2(1) of the Occupiers' Liability Act 1957. All the judges agreed that the maxim volenti non fit injuria did not apply here because the deceased could not have known the nature or extent of the risk created by the defendants' negligence.

Commentary
Applied: *Wooldridge* v *Sumner* [1962] 3 WLR 616 and *Ashdown* v *Samuel Williams & Sons Ltd* [1956] 3 WLR 1104.

White v *St Albans City and District Council* (1990) The Times 12 March Court of Appeal (Neill, Nicholls and Bingham LJJ)

Duty to trespasser under 1984 Act

Facts
The plaintiff, a trespasser, sustained injuries when he fell into a 12ft trench when walking across the defendants' fenced-off property while taking a short cut to a car park.

Held
The trial judge's rejection of the claim would be upheld as there was no evidence that people tended to use the land as a short cut.

Neill LJ said that the question for consideration under s1(3)(b) of the Occupiers' Liability Act 1984 had to be answered by looking at the actual state of affairs on the ground when the injury was met with and asking: had the occupiers reasonable grounds for believing someone would come into the vicinity of the danger? In the instant case the accident occurred on private land surrounded by a fence, which was insufficient to stop all but the elderly and disabled from entering the land. Nevertheless, the judge had been wholly justified in holding that the council had no reason to believe that the appellant would be in the vicinity of the trench.

Woollins v *British Celanese Ltd* (1966) 110 SJ 686 Court of Appeal (Lord Denning MR, Danckwerts and Salmon LJJ)

Occupier's liability – warning

Facts
The plaintiff was doing constructional work at a factory and he fell while on a roof. A warning that the roofing was unsafe without special caution had been put in the vicinity by the defendants, but it had been placed behind a door where it was not to be expected.

Held
The defendants had been in breach of s2 of the Occupiers' Liability Act 1957, although the plaintiff had been contributorily negligent.

Lord Denning MR:

'The defendants should have taken what care was reasonable in the circumstances. As they had put up a warning, but in the wrong place, they foresaw the risk and should have foreseen the accident. The risk was not a special risk ordinarily incident to the plaintiff's employment. It was a risk incident to the premises. Section 2(3)(b) did not apply to a place or means of access to a place, like this roofing, on to which a workman might clamber.'

16 Private Nuisance

Adams v *Ursell* [1913] 1 Ch 269 High Court (Swinfen Eady J)

Nuisance – smells

Facts

Using 'the most approved appliances', the defendant established a fried fish shop in a working-class district but next to the plaintiff's house which was rather superior.

Held

The plaintiff was entitled to an injunction to restrain the nuisance caused by odour and vapour from the defendant's premises.

Swinfen Eady J:

'It does not follow that because a fried fish shop is a nuisance in one place it is a nuisance in another.'

Allen v *Gulf Oil Refining Ltd* [1981] 2 WLR 188 House of Lords (Lord Wilberforce, Lord Diplock, Lord Edmund-Davies, Lord Keith of Kinkel and Lord Roskill)

Nuisance – statutory authority

Facts

The Gulf Oil Refining company wished to construct an oil refinery at Milford Haven. They were given wide authority under the provisions of the Gulf Oil Refining Act 1965 to undertake all necessary preliminaries to the creation of the refinery, including compulsory purchase. The plaintiff, who lived in the vicinity of the refinery, brought an action against Gulf Oil claiming damages or compensation, alleging that the operation of the refinery was a nuisance, or, in the alternative, that Gulf Oil were guilty of negligence in the method of construction and operation of the refinery. Gulf Oil defended the claim by a plea of statutory authority. On a preliminary issue, the judge ordered that Gulf Oil could rely on the 1965 Act as having authorised the construction of the oil refinery. The plaintiff appealed to the Court of Appeal which reversed the judge's ruling. Gulf Oil appealed to the House of Lords.

Held (Lord Keith dissenting)

The 1965 Act bestowed a wide authority upon Gulf Oil to construct a refinery, and to take all necessary preliminary steps necessary for that construction. Accordingly, Gulf Oil were entitled to statutory immunity in respect of any nuisance which was an inevitable result of the constructing and operating of the refinery which conformed with the intention of Parliament. The fact that the nuisance was an inevitable result of a refinery on that site was, as a matter of defence, for Gulf Oil to prove. However, to the extent that the actual nuisance caused by the refinery exceeded the nuisance which inevitably resulted from any refinery on that site, the statutory immunity would not apply and Gulf Oil would be liable to the plaintiff. Appeal allowed.

Lord Wilberforce:

'We are here in the well-charted field of statutory authority. It is now well settled that where Parliament by express direction or by necessary implication has authorised the construction and use of an undertaking or works, that carries with it an authority to do what is authorised with immunity from any action based on nuisance. The right of action is taken away .. To this there is made the qualification, or condition, that the statutory powers are exercised without 'negligence', that word here being used in a special sense so as to require the undertaker, as a condition of obtaining immunity from action, to carry out the work and conduct the operation with all reasonable regard and care for the interests of other persons .. It is within the same principle that immunity from action is withheld where the terms of the statute are permissive only, in which case the powers conferred must be exercised in strict conformity with private rights.'

Bridlington Relay Ltd v *Yorkshire Electricity Board* [1965] 2 WLR 349 High Court (Buckley J)

Nuisance – electrical interference

Facts

The plaintiffs operated a TV relay system and erected a mast on their own land for that purpose. A year later, the defendants proceeded to erect an overhead power line placing two pylons within 250 yards of Ps' mast. Ps sought a quia timet injunction to restrain the erection in so far as it interfered with Ps' reception and transmission.

Held

The injunction would not be granted as the defendants were already willing to do their best to suppress the interference.

Buckley J:

'On the evidence the interference was caused by defects in the power lines which could be remedied. If this was not the case, the plaintiffs were, in any event, only entitled to the same immunity from interference as a domestic user ... For myself, however, I do not think that it can at present be said that the ability to receive television free from occasional, even if recurrent and severe, electrical interference is so important a part of an ordinary householder's enjoyment of his property that such interference should be regarded as a legal nuisance, particularly perhaps if such interference affects only one of the suitable alternative programmes.'

Commentary

Applied: *Hunt* v *Canary Wharf Ltd* (1995) NLJ 1645.

British Celanese Ltd v *A H Hunt (Capacitors) Ltd* [1969] 1 WLR 959 High Court (Lawton J)

Nuisance – escape of metal foil

Facts

The defendants were manufacturers of electrical components and had on their land strips of metal foil. The plaintiffs were manufacturers of yarn whose premises were 150 yards from Ds' on the same industrial estate. Electricity on the estate came from a sub-station nearby. Some of the strips of metal foil were blown from Ds' land to this sub-station, where they hit the bus-bars and caused a power failure. A similar, though less serious, occurrence had taken place some three and a half years previously. The plaintiffs lost time, profits, etc; material solidified in machines and they had to be cleared. The Ps sued under three heads:

a) *Rylands* v *Fletcher*;
b) negligence;
c) nuisance.

Held

a) There was no special use of the property and hence no liability under *Rylands* v *Fletcher*;
b) the defendants were liable in negligence, and the damage was not too remote to be recovered;
c) the defendants were liable in nuisance and damages could be recovered. Ds' method of storing metal foil amounted to an interference with Ps' use of their property.

Lawton J:

'Most nuisances do arise from a long continued condition and many isolated happenings do not constitute a nuisance. It is, however, clear from the authorities that an isolated happening by itself can create an actionable nuisance.'

Commentary

Followed: *Midwood & Co Ltd* v *Manchester Corporation* [1905] 2 KB 597.
  Distinguished: *Cattle* v *Stockton Waterworks Co* (1875) LR 10 QB 453.
  Approved in *SCM (UK) Ltd* v *WJ Whittall & Son Ltd* [1970] 1 WLR 1017.
  But see *Cambridge Water Company* v *Eastern Counties Leather plc* [1994] 2 WLR 53 regarding liability in *Rylands* v *Fletcher*.

Christie v *Davey* [1893] 1 Ch 316 High Court (North J)

Nuisance – 'retaliation'

Facts

The plaintiff was a music teacher living with her husband, daughter (who studied at the Royal Academy of Music and was also a teacher) and a lodger friend of the daughter with like qualifications. The son of the house played the cello (badly!). The defendant lived next door and wrote to P, requesting that the amount of music played be curbed. When he received no reply, D commenced 'retaliation' by shrieking, banging and howling. This disrupted P's professional music lessons and she sued for an injunction, claiming the retaliation amounted to nuisance.

Held

While the playing of music was not here a nuisance, the defendant's behaviour did amount to a nuisance and it would be restrained by injunction.

North J:

'If what has taken place had occurred between two sets of persons both perfectly innocent, I should have taken an entirely different view of the case. But, I am persuaded that what was done by D was done solely for the purpose of annoyance and, in any view, it was not a legitimate use of D's house.'

Davey v Harrow Corporation [1957] 2 WLR 941 Court of Appeal (Lord Goddard CJ, Jenkins and Morris LJJ)

Nuisance – roots of trees

Facts
Roots of the defendants' trees penetrated into the plaintiff's land and caused subsidence to his house.

Held
The defendants were liable and it was immaterial whether the trees were planted or self-sown.

Lord Goddard CJ:

' .. it must be taken to be established law that, if trees encroach whether by branches or roots and cause damage, an action for nuisance will lie.'

Commentary
Approved in *Leakey v National Trust for Places of Historic Interest or Natural Beauty* [1980] 2 WLR 265.

Goldman v Hargrave [1966] 3 WLR 513 Privy Council (Lord Reid, Lord Morris of Borth-y-Gest, Lord Pearce, Lord Wilberforce and Lord Pearson)

Negligence – damage by fire

Facts
The defendant had a Redgum tree on his land 100 feet high. It was struck by lightning and caught fire. Nothing could be done while it was standing, so instead of calling the Fire Brigade, a space was cleared and the local tree-feller contacted. The tree was then felled and was allowed to burn in the expectation that the fire would burn itself out. The wind then increased and revived the fire. It spread and damaged the plaintiff's property next door.

Held
The defendant was liable in negligence. The fire did not 'accidentally begin' within the meaning of the Fires Prevention (Metropolis) Act 1774.

Lord Wilberforce:

'Their Lordships propose to deal with the issues as stated without attempting to answer the disputed question whether if responsibility is established it should be brought under the heading of nuisance or put in a separate category. As this board recently explained in *The Wagon Mound (No 2)*, the tort of nuisance uncertain in its boundary may comprise a wide variety of situations in some of which negligence plays no part, in others of which it is decisive. The present case is one where liability, if it exists, rests upon negligence and nothing else; whether it falls within or overlaps the boundaries of nuisance is a question of classification which need not be resolved here.'

Commentary
Applied in *Leakey v National Trust* [1980] 2 WLR 65.

Halsey v Esso Petroleum Co Ltd [1961] 1 WLR 683 High Court (Veale J)

Nuisance – oil depot

Facts

The plaintiff lived in Fulham in an area zoned for residential purposes. The defendants operated an oil distribution depot nearby in an industrial zone. They worked day and night in a boiler house with chimneys. The plaintiff claimed for the following: (i) Acid smuts came from chimney and damaged clothes and car paint on highway. (ii) A pungent/nauseating smell was emitted. (iii) Noise throughout night shook windows. (iv) Noise from tankers leaving and arriving throughout night on the road outside.

Held

The defendants were: (i) liable in damages for: (a) escape of harmful substances under *Rylands* v *Fletcher*; (b) as a private nuisance for damage to clothing; (c) as a public nuisance for damage to car; (ii) liable in damages for private nuisance; (iii) liable in damages for private nuisance and liable in damage for public nuisance; (iv) liable in damages for private nuisance.

Harrison v *Southwark and Vauxhall Water Co* [1891] 2 Ch 409 High Court (Vaughan Williams J)

Nuisance – noise and vibration

Facts

The defendants in the exercise of statutory powers sank a shaft beneath land adjacent to the plaintiff's house and employed lift pumps. The plaintiff commenced an action for nuisance based on noise and vibration from these pumps. The defendants then installed new centrifugal pumps and the nuisance was abated.

Held

The defendants were not liable in nuisance as they had used reasonable skill and care in the exercise of their statutory powers.

Vaughan Williams J:

'It frequently happens that the owners or occupiers of land cause in the execution of lawful works in the ordinary user of land a considerable amount of temporary annoyance to their neighbours, but they are not necessarily on that account held to be guilty of causing an unlawful nuisance. The business of life could not be carried on if it were so .. a man who pulls down his house for the purpose of building a new one no doubt causes considerable inconvenience to his next door neighbours during the process of demolition, but he is not responsible as for a nuisance if he uses all reasonable care and skill to avoid annoyance. This is so even though the noise and dust and consequent annoyance be such as would constitute a nuisance if the same, instead of being created for the purpose of the demolition, had been created .. in the execution of works for a purpose involving the permanent continuance of the noise and dust.'

Hoare & Co Ltd v *Sir Robert McAlpine, Sons & Co* [1923] 1 Ch 167 High Court (Astbury J)

Nuisance – vibration

Facts

The defendants prepared a city centre site for a large building. They drove heavy piles into the soil which caused serious structural damage to an old house owned by the plaintiffs. The plaintiffs sued in nuisance and under the principle in *Rylands* v *Fletcher*.

Held

The defendants were liable under *Rylands* v *Fletcher* for the escape of vibrations. They were also liable in nuisance because the instability of the house was not so great as to be abnormal.

Astbury J:

'In my judgment, *Rylands* v *Fletcher* applies in this case, though I do not wish to be understood as indicating that the law as to legal nuisance does not also apply. The plaintiffs' proposition was – a man cannot limit the operation of his neighbour on his own land, or increase his neighbour's liability by putting his own property into a structural condition in which it is more than ordinarily liable to be affected by legitimate operations. In some cases, this may be accurate.'

Hollywood Silver Fox Farm Ltd v *Emmett* [1936] 2 KB 468 High Court (Macnaghten J)

Nuisance – unreasonable acts

Facts

The plaintiff purchased land next to the defendant's in order to breed silver foxes. He erected a sign saying 'Hollywood Silver Fox Farm' which was visible both from D's field and from the road which bounded them both. D was developing his land as a building estate and objected to the sign. P refused to remove it and D, knowing that silver foxes are unusually sensitive to noise during the breeding season, threatened to fire a shot gun near to P's pens and prevent the foxes breeding. D's son carried out the threat and it was at least in part successful. The plaintiff sued in nuisance for the damage the farm had suffered.

Held

The firing was a nuisance for which the defendant was liable in damages and an injunction was granted restraining firing or other noises during the breeding season.

Hunter v *Canary Wharf Ltd* [1995] NLJ 1645 Court of Appeal (Neill, Waite and Pill LJJ)

Nuisance – interference with television reception – interest required to sue in nuisance

Facts

The defendants built a large tower in East London. The plaintiffs claimed damages for interference with their television reception which they claimed was caused by the tower. At first instance it was held that this was capable of constituting a nuisance. The defendants appealed to the Court of Appeal.

Held

That although television plays an important part in the lives of very many people, interference with television reception did not constitute an actionable nuisance, either private or public. The plaintiffs relied on the dicta of Buckley J in *Bridlington Relay Ltd* v *Yorkshire Electricity Board* [1965] 1 All ER 264 where, although holding that interference with television reception did not constitute a nuisance, he stated:

'I do not think that it can at present be said that the ability to receive television free from … interference is so important a part of an ordinary householder's enjoyment of his property that such interference should be regarded as a legal nuisance …!

The plaintiffs argued that in 1995 the ability to receive interference-free television did play an important part in people's lives, as was held in the Canadian case of *Nor-Video Services Ltd* v *Ontario Hydro* (1978) 84 DLR (3d) 231. However the Court of Appeal held that the presence of a high building between a television transmitter and a property leading to loss of quality of reception was analogous to loss of prospect or view and was hence not actionable.

Interestingly, however, the court held that the defence of statutory authority would not have protected the defendants if a nuisance had been established.

The court went on to consider whether an interest in property was necessary to claim in private nuisance. Following *Khorasandjian* v *Bush* [1993] 3 All ER 669 the court held that a proprietary or possessory interest in land was no longer necessary, but that a substantial link between the person enjoying the land and the land in question was required. Mere occupation of the property was insufficient, but occupation of the property as a home was sufficient.

Kennaway v *Thompson* [1980] 3 WLR 361 Court of Appeal (Lawton and Waller LJJ and Sir David Cairns)

Nuisance – private against public interest

Facts
The plaintiff built a house on land where the defendant club organised motor boat races and water skiing. When she began to build, she felt that the club's activities would not interfere with her enjoyment of her new house, but those activities developed and boats became more powerful and noisy.

Held
Despite the public interest in the club's activities, an injunction would be granted restricting the club's racing and the noise level of boats at other times.

Lawton J:

'The principles enunciated in *Shelfer's* case, which is binding on us, have been applied time and time again during the past 85 years. The only case which raises a doubt about the application of the *Shelfer* principles to all cases is *Miller* v *Jackson*, a decision of this court. The majority, Geoffrey Lane and Cumming-Bruce LJJ, Lord Denning MR dissenting, adjudged that the activities of an old-established cricket club which had been going for over seventy years, had been a nuisance to the plaintiffs by reason of cricket balls landing on their garden. The question then was whether the plaintiffs should be granted an injunction. Geoffrey Lane LJ was of the opinion that one should be granted. Lord Denning MR and Cumming-Bruce LJ though otherwise. Lord Denning MR said that the public interest should prevail over the private interest. Cumming-Bruce LJ stated that a factor to be taken into account when exercising the judicial discretion whether to grant an injunction was that the plaintiffs had bought their house knowing that it was next to the cricket ground. He thought that there were special circumstances which should inhibit a court of equity from granting the injunction claimed. The statement of Lord Denning MR that the public interest should prevail over the private interest runs counter to the principles enunciated in *Shelfer's* case and does not accord with the reason of Cumming-Bruce LJ for refusing an injunction. We are of the opinion that there is nothing in *Miller* v *Jackson*, binding on us, which qualifies what was decided in *Shelfer*. Any decisions before *Shelfer's* case (and there were some at first instance as counsel for the defendants pointed out) which give support for the proposition that the public interest should prevail over the private interest must be read subject to the decision in *Shelfer's* case.

It follows that the plaintiff was entitled to an injunction .. But she was only entitled to an injunction restraining the club from activities which caused a nuisance, and not all of their activities did.'

Commentary

Distinguished in *Tetley* v *Chitty* [1986] 1 All ER 663.

Applied: *Shelfer* v *City of London Electric Lighting Co* [1895] 1 Ch 287.

Khorasandjian v *Bush* [1993] 3 WLR 476 Court of Appeal (Dillon and Rose LJJ and Peter Gibson J)

Whether interest in land required to sustain an action in nuisance

Facts

The plaintiff, whose friendship with the defendant had broken down, claimed relief in respect of her complaints that the defendant had, inter alia, pestered her with unwanted telephone calls to her parents' home. An injunction was granted to restrain this activity at first instance, and the defendant appealed on the grounds that as the plaintiff had no interest in the land affected she could not maintain an action based on private nuisance.

Held

That harassment by unwanted telephone calls amounting to interference with the ordinary and reasonable enjoyment of property which the recipient of the calls had a right to occupy was actionable as a private nuisance, notwithstanding that she had no proprietary interest in the property. The Court refused to be bound by its earlier decision in *Malone* v *Laskey* [1907] 2 KB 141, and adopted instead the reasoning of the Appellate Division of the Alberta Supreme Court in *Motherwell* v *Motherwell* (1976) 73 DLR (3d) 62.

Dillon LJ:

'That a legal owner of property can obtain an injunction, on the ground of private nuisance, to restrain persistent harassment by unwanted telephone calls to his home was decided by the Appellate Division of the Alberta Supreme Court in *Motherwell* v *Motherwell* (1976) 73 DLR (3d) 62. The court there rejected, by reference to English authority, a submission, at p67:

"that the common law does not have within itself the resources to recognise invasion of privacy as either included in an existing category or as a new category of nuisance, and that it has lost its original power, by which indeed it created itself, to note new ills arising in a growing and changing society and pragmatically to establish a principle to meet the need for control and remedy; and then by categories to develop the principle as the interests of justice make themselves sufficiently apparent."

Consequently, notwithstanding *Malone* v *Laskey*, the court held that the wife of the owner had also the right to restrain harassing telephone calls to the matrimonial home. Clement JA who delivered the judgment of the court said, at p78:

"Here we have a wife harassed in the matrimonial home. She has a status, a right to live there with her husband and children. I find it absurd to say that her occupancy of the matrimonial home is insufficient to found an action in nuisance. In my opinion she is entitled to the same relief as is her husband, the brother."

I respectfully agree, and in my judgment this court is entitled to adopt the same approach.'

Laws v *Florinplace Ltd* [1981] 1 All ER 659 High Court (Vinelott J)

Nuisance – sex shop

Facts

The defendants purchased a shop in Longmore Street, Pimlico. They proceeded to convert the shop into a 'sex centre', for the sale of pornographic magazines and films; they also installed seating for the purpose of enabling customers to view pornographic films. They advertised the enterprise with a large illuminated sign, warning that explicit sex acts were to be shown on the premises. The plaintiffs, being a small residential association led by Mr Laws, a barrister, sought an injunction and damages; they further sought interlocutory relief pending trial. The defendants argued that the centre would not harm the vicinity, and alleged that on the contrary it would have a therapeutic effect. The plaintiffs contended that the existence of the centre would adversely affect property prices in the area, and would attract undesirables to the area who might make indecent suggestions to young girls living in the area.

Held

It was established law that cases of nuisance were not confined to cases where there was some physical emanation of a damaging kind from the defendants' premises which had happened, or was reasonably feared but included cases where the use made by the defendant of his property was such that, while not necessarily criminal, was such as to affront ordinary reasonably people. In the circumstances of the case it was not possible to say that there was not at least a triable issue whether the existence of the centre was not a nuisance independently of any risk of undesirables being attracted to the area. The fact that the centre was proposing to sell hard core pornography and would thus be a business repugnant to the sensibilities of ordinary men and women could not be disregarded. Since the danger that might be suffered by the defendants upon grant of interlocutory relief which was afterwards found to be unjustified was quantifiable, and since there were strong factors which favoured the grant of interlocutory relief, not least of which was the fact that the centre would be operating near the boundary of the criminal law, the balance of convenience lay in favour of granting the interim relief sought by the plaintiffs.

Leakey v National Trust for Places of Historic Interest or Natural Beauty [1980] 2 WLR 65 Court of Appeal (Megaw, Shaw and Cumming-Bruce LJJ)

Nuisance – national process

Facts

The defendants owned and occupied a parcel of land consisting of a conical shaped hill 'Burrow Hump' next to P's houses which were situated effectively at the base of the hill being separated from it only by a narrow strip of land. The hill was composed of keaper marl which made it prone to cracking and slipping. In the past weathering had caused soil slides onto P's property. After the long drought in 1976, a large crack appeared. The plaintiff notified Ds of this and Ds, having taken legal advice, refused to act. A large slide of earth onto P's property then occurred, the soil in fact reaching P's houses. The plaintiff sued for a mandatory injunction to get it removed. Pursuant to this, Ds spent £2,000 removing the material. The action then proceeded to trial and before O'Connor J P succeeded in establishing nuisance. Between the first instance decision and the Court of Appeal hearing, Ds spent a further £4,000 on protective works. The purpose of the appeal was to establish whether the case of *Goldman* v *Hargrave* represented the law of England.

Held

a) There is a general duty imposed on occupiers in relation to hazards occurring on their land whether natural or man-made. A person on whose land a natural hazard develops which threatens to encroach on another's land must do all that is reasonable to prevent it;

b) this was properly described as a claim in nuisance;

c) the defendants were liable for nominal damages.

Megaw LJ:

'In my judgment, there is, in the scope of the duty as explained in *Goldman* v *Hargrave*, a removal, or at least a powerful amelioration, of the injustice which might otherwise be caused in such a case by the recognition of the duty of care. Because of that limitation on the scope of the duty, I would say that, as a matter of policy, the law ought to recognise such a duty of care.

This leads on to the question of the scope of the duty. This is discussed, and the nature and extent of the duty is explained, in the judgment in *Goldman* v *Hargrave*. The duty is a duty to do that which is reasonable in all the circumstances, and no more than what, if anything, is reasonable, to prevent or minimise the known risk of damage or injury to one's neighbour or to his property. The considerations with which the law is familiar are all to be taken into account in deciding whether there has been a breach of duty, and, if so, what that breach is, and whether it is causative of the damage in respect of which the claim is made. Thus, there will fall to be considered the extent of the risk. What, so far as reasonably can be foreseen, are the chances that anything untoward will happen or that any damage will be caused? What is to be foreseen as to the possible extent of the damage if the risk becomes a reality? Is it practicable to prevent, or to minimise, the happening of any damage? If it is practicable, how simple or how difficult are the measures which could be taken, how much and how lengthy work do they involve, and what is the probable cost of such works? Was there sufficient time for preventive action to have been taken, by persons acting reasonably in relation to the known risk, between the time when it became known to, or should have been realised by, the defendant, and the time when the damage occurred? Factors such as these, so far as they apply in a particular case, fall to be weighed in deciding whether the defendant's duty of care requires, or required, him to do anything, and, if so, what.'

Commentary

Applied: *Goldman* v *Hargrave* [1966] 3 WLR 513 and *Sedleigh-Denfield* v *O'Callagan* [1940] AC 880.

Approved: *Davey* v *Harrow Corporation* [1957] 2 WLR 941.

Distinguished: *Rylands* v *Fletcher* (1868) LR 3 HL 330.

Overruled: *Giles* v *Walker* (1890) 24 QBD 656 and *Pontardawe Rural District Council* v *Moore-Gwyn* [1929] 1 Ch 656.

Applied in *Home Brewery plc* v *William Davis & Co (Loughborough) Ltd* [1987] 2 WLR 117.

Lemmon v *Webb* [1895] AC 1 House of Lords (Lord Herschell LC, Lord Macnaghten and Lord Davey)

Nuisance – overhanging trees

Facts

The plaintiff had trees growing on his land, the branches of which overhung the defendant's property. The defendant, without notice to P, cut these branches off at the boundary, alleging they were a nuisance. P claimed: (i) a declaration that D could not cut the branches except for any recent growth; (ii) an injunction restraining D from cutting any more; (iii) damages.

Held

Providing there was no trespass on the neighbour's land, D could cut the branches without notice to P because they constituted a nuisance.

Malone v *Laskey* [1907] 2 KB 141 Court of Appeal (Sir Gorell Barnes P, Fletcher Moulton and Kennedy LJJ)

Nuisance – vibration

Facts
The defendants were trustees of a building society which owned a great deal of property. X was a sub-tenant of one of Ds' properties. On their property next door, Ds placed machinery for the purpose of generating electricity to light their premises. This machinery caused much vibration which in turn caused a water tank in the lavatory of X's premises to become insecure. This tank fell on X's wife and seriously injured her. She sued Ds in nuisance.

Held
She had no cause of action against Ds on the ground of nuisance because she had no interest in the premises or any right of occupation. On the evidence Ds were not liable in negligence.

Sir Gorell Barnes P:

'Many cases were cited in the course of the argument in which it had been held that actions for nuisance could be maintained where a person's rights of property had been affected by the nuisance, but no authority was cited nor, in my opinion, could any principle of law be formulated to the effect that a person who has no interest in property, no right of occupation in the proper sense of the term can maintain an action in nuisance.'

Commentary
Overruled in *Billings (AC) & Sons Ltd* v *Riden* [1957] 3 WLR 496 in so far as it deals with negligence.

See *Khorasandjian* v *Bush* [1993] 3 WLR 476 regarding the requirements for an interest in land in nuisance actions.

Matania v *The National Provincial Bank Ltd* [1936] 2 All ER 633 Court of Appeal (Slesser and Romer LJJ and Finlay J)

Nuisance – building operations

Facts
Premises were demised to the defendant bank, who let the second and third floors to the plaintiffs. They then let the first floor to the defendant syndicate. The latter wished to make extensive alterations and obtained the permission of the bank for this purpose. The plaintiffs suffered greatly from dust and noise caused by the contractors employed.

Held
Although the defendant syndicate had employed independent contractors to carry out the work, they were liable for damages in nuisance.

Slesser LJ:

'We are not here concerned with danger, such as might found an action for negligence; we are here concerned with danger such as might found an action for nuisance, but the principles are in my view the same .. that is to say that if the act done is one in its very nature that involves a special danger of nuisance being complained of then it is one which falls within the exception for which the employer of the contractor will be responsible.

It seems to me that in the present case, looking at all the facts of the case, it is not possible to say that here (the builders) did use all reasonable care and skill.'

Miller v *Jackson* [1977] 3 WLR 20 Court of Appeal (Lord Denning MR, Geoffrey Lane and Cumming-Bruce LJJ)

Nuisance – village cricket club

Facts
Cricket was played on a village ground since 1905. In 1970 houses were built in such a place that cricket balls would inevitably be hit into their gardens. The plaintiff, who bought one of the houses in 1972, sued the members of the cricket club for damages for negligence and nuisance, on the basis of incidents causing physical damage to the house and apprehension of personal injury.

Held
(1) The defendants were guilty of negligence, since the risk of injury was both foreseeable and foreseen. (2) The playing of cricket in the circumstances constituted an unreasonable interference with the plaintiff's enjoyment of land, and therefore a nuisance, since there was a real risk of serious injury. It was no defence that the plaintiff brought trouble on his own head by coming to live in the house. (3) By reason of special circumstances, namely the plaintiff's knowledge when he bought his house that cricket was played nearby, and the interest of the village as a whole in the existence of a cricket ground, no injunction should be granted to restrain the playing of cricket, and the plaintiff's only remedy was in damages.

Robinson v *Kilvert* (1889) 41 Ch D 888 Court of Appeal (Cotton, Lindley and Lopes LJJ)

Nuisance – heat-sensitive paper

Facts
The defendant owned a warehouse. He let a floor to the plaintiff for the latter to store paper. D later started a process of manufacturing paper boxes on the ground floor. This heated the first floor to 80CC. The plaintiff sued in nuisance on the grounds that this dried his brown paper. Evidence at trial showed that neither P's workforce nor normal paper was affected by the heat. Also, that D did not know at the time of letting that P would store heat-sensitive paper.

Held
There was no nuisance to P on these facts.

Cotton LJ:

'It would, in my opinion, be wrong to say that the doing of something not in itself noxious is a nuisance because it does harm to a particular trade in the adjoining property, although it would not prejudice or affect any adjoining trade carried on in the property and does not interfere with the ordinary enjoyment of life.'

St Helen's Smelting Co v *Tipping* (1865) 11 HL Cas 642 House of Lords (Lord Westbury LC, Lord Cranworth and Lord Wensleydale)

Nuisance – injurious vapour

Facts

The plaintiff bought an estate consisting of about 1,300 acres near to the defendants' copper smelting works. The vapour from the work proved injurious to the plaintiff's trees and crops and he claimed to be entitled to damages.

Held

The plaintiff would succeed. The jury was correctly directed that an actionable injury was one producing sensible discomfort and that every man, unless enjoying rights obtained by prescription or agreement, was bound to use his property in such a way as not to injure that of his neighbour. The law was not concerned with trifling inconvenience and everything had to be considered from a reasonable point of view. In this case the jury was asked to consider whether the injury was such as visibly diminished the value of the property and the comfort and enjoyment of it. Time and locality were factors to be taken into account.

Sedleigh-Denfield v *O'Callaghan* [1940] AC 880 House of Lords (Viscount Maugham, Lord Atkin, Lord Wright, Lord Romer and Lord Porter)

Nuisance by flooding

Facts

The plaintiff's land was next to defendants'. A ditch ran between their land and the end of his garden. Owners of other land agreed with the County Council that a pipe or culvert be put in. A grating should have been placed near the opening to prevent blockage. Instead, it was placed on top of the culvert. The opening was on defendants' land, although they had never given permission for the installation. However, their servants did clean it out bi-annually. In a heavy rainstorm, the pipe was blocked and plaintiff's land flooded.

Held

The defendants must be taken to have some knowledge of the existence of the pipe on their land and, consequently, they were liable for all damage caused.

Lord Wright:

'I do not attempt any exhaustive definition of that cause of action (nuisance) but it has never lost its essential character which was derived from its prototype, the Assize of Nuisance, and was maintained under the form of action on the case of Nuisance. The Assize of Nuisance was a real action supplementary to the Assize of Novel disseisin. The latter (ie Assize of Novel Disseisin) was devised to protect the plaintiff's seisin of his land, and the former (ie the Assize of Nuisance) aimed at vindicating the plaintiff's right to the use and enjoyment of his land. The Assize became .. superseded by the less formal procedure of an action on the case for Nuisance which lay for damages. This action was less limited in its scope for whereas the Assize was by a freeholder against a freeholder, the action lay also between possessors and occupiers of land. With possibly certain anomalous exceptions not here, material possession or occupation is still the test.

The forms which Nuisance may take are protean. Certain classifications are possible, but many reported cases are no more than illustrations of particular matters of fact that have been held to be Nuisances.

The liability for a nuisance is not, at least in modern law, a strict or absolute liability... it has, I think, been rightly established in the Court of Appeal that an occupier is not prima facie responsible for a nuisance created without his knowledge or consent. If he is to be liable, a further condition is necessary, namely that he had knowledge or means of knowledge, that he knew or should have known of the nuisance in time to correct it and obviate its mischievous effects.'

Commentary

Applied in *Leakey* v *National Trust* [1980] 2 WLR 65.

 Distinguished in *Mint* v *Good* [1951] 1 KB 517.

Shelfer **v** *City of London Electric Lighting Co* [1895] 1 Ch 287 Court of Appeal (Lord Halsbury LC, Lindley and A L Smith LJJ)

Nuisance – injunction

Facts

The defendant electricity company erected powerful engines and other works on land near to the house which the plaintiff had leased from a brewery. Both the brewery and the plaintiff sued the defendants. The brewery sued for physical damage to the house and thus to their reversion. The plaintiff sued for annoyance by noise. Before Kekewich J, both claims succeeded as to damages, but not as to an injunction.

Held

The claim for an injunction must also succeed.

A L Smith LJ:

 'In my opinion, it may be stated as a good working rule that: (i) if the injury to the P's legal rights is small; (ii) and is one which is capable of being estimated in money; (iii) and is one which can be adequately compensated by a small money payment; (iv) and the case is one in which it would be oppressive to D to grant an injunction; then damages may be given in substitution for an injunction.'

Commentary

Applied in *Kennaway* v *Thompson* [1980] 3 WLR 361.

Sturges **v** *Bridgman* (1879) 11 Ch D 852 Court of Appeal (Thesiger, James and Baggallay LJJ)

Nuisance – doctor's consulting room

Facts

The plaintiff was a doctor who bought premises in Wimpole Street. The defendant had a confectionery business in Wigmore Street, which runs at right angles to Wimpole Street. The defendant's kitchen abutted part of P's garden. In the kitchen, against the abutting wall, D had two mortars for pounding loaf sugar and meat: he had used them there for more than 20 years. Some eight years after he moved in, P built a consulting room on the abutting wall. He alleged that the noise from the mortars then became a nuisance to him and he sought an injunction.

Held

The injunction would be granted. The defendant was not protected by prescription as until the consulting room was built there was no actionable nuisance.

Thesiger LJ:

 'Whether anything is a nuisance or not is a question to be determined not merely by an abstract consideration of the thing itself, but with reference to its circumstances; what would be a nuisance in

Belgrave Square would not necessarily be so in Bermondsey or where a locality is devoted to a particular trade or manufacture carried on by the traders in a particular or established manner not constituting a public(?) nuisance. Judges and juries would be justified in finding and may be trusted to find, that the trade or manufacture so carried on in that locality is not a private or actionable wrong .. It would be on the one hand in a very high degree unreasonable and undesirable that there should be a right of action for acts which are not (in the present condition of the adjoining land) and perhaps never will be any inconvenience or annoyance and it would be on the other hand in an equal degree unjust that the use and value of the adjoining land should for all time and in all circumstances be diminished by reason of the continuance of acts incapable of physical interruption and which the law gives no power to prevent.'

Tetley v *Chitty* [1986] 1 All ER 663 High Court (McNeill J)

Nuisance – landlord's liability

Facts

The Medway Borough Council (the second defendants) leased to the Medway Kart Club premises to be used as a go-kart track. Local residents brought an action against the council and the first defendant, representing the club, and claimed damage for noise resulting from nuisance and an injunction restraining the operation of the track. The noise created varied according to the number of karts in operation, speed alterations and the direction of the wind, and technical evidence supported the assertion that the noise was excessive.

Held

The second defendants were liable in nuisance because the noise was an ordinary and necessary consequence, or a natural and necessary consequence, of the operation of go-karts on their land, and they as landlords had given express or at least implied consent to the nuisance on their land.

Commentary

Applied: *Harris* v *James* (1876) 45 LJQB 545.
    Distinguished: *Kennaway* v *Thompson* [1980] 3 WLR 361.

Wheeler v *JJ Saunders* [1995] 3 WLR 466 Court of Appeal (Staughton and Peter Gibson LJJ and Sir John May)

Nuisance – effect of planning permission

Facts

The plaintiffs and the defendants were neighbours. The defendants obtained planning permission to build two pig houses close to the plaintiffs' land, resulting in strong smells affecting the plaintiffs' property. The plaintiffs claimed that the defendants were liable in nuisance in respect of these odours. At first instance it was held that the smells amounted to an actionable nuisance. The defendants appealed.

Held

That the smells did amount to a nuisance. Although statutory authorisation for a development could confer immunity in respect of a nuisance inevitably arising from it, a planning authority could not authorise a nuisance other than by permitting a change in the character of the neighbourhood, which might render lawful activities that would have previously constituted a nuisance. Thus, although the smells were an inevitable result of the planning permission, that permission did not allow a change in character of the neighbourhood and thus the planning permission did not afford a defence.

Commentary
Compare this case with *Gillingham Borough Council* v *Medway (Chatham) Dock Co Ltd* [1993] QB 343. There the grant of planning permission did alter the character of the neighbourhood, and thus provided a defence, as the alleged nuisance had to be considered in the light of the change in character of the neighbourhood brought about by the planning permission.

Wringe v *Cohen* [1940] 1 KB 229 Court of Appeal (Slesser and Luxmoore LJJ and Atkinson J)

Nuisance – owner's liability

Facts
The plaintiff owned a lock-up shop in Sheffield. The defendant owned a house next door. D let the house to X some two years before. When one night in a storm the gable end of D's house fell through the roof of P's shop, P sued for repair cost in: (i) negligence; (ii) nuisance. There had been a bulge in the wall due to defective repair, especially poor pointing and collaring. Repairs were D's obligation under the lease. He said in defence that he did not appreciate the danger.

Held
This provided no defence to the action and D was liable.

Atkinson J:

'In our judgment if owing to want of repair premises on a highway become dangerous and therefore a nuisance and a passer-by or an adjoining owner suffers damage by their collapse, the occupier or owner who has undertaken the duty of repair is answerable whether he knew or ought to have known of the danger or not .. On the other hand, if the nuisance is created not by want of repair, but, for example, by the act of a trespasser or by a secret and unobservable operation of nature such as a subsidence under or near the foundation of the premises, neither an occupier nor an owner responsible for repair is answerable unless with knowledge or means of knowledge he allows the danger to continue.'

Commentary
Applied in *Mint* v *Good* [1951] 1 KB 517.

17 Public Nuisance

Attorney-General v *PYA Quarries Ltd* [1957] 2 WLR 770 Court of Appeal (Denning, Romer and Parker LJJ)

Public nuisance – definition

Facts

The Attorney General on the relation of a county council alleged that the defendants were committing a public nuisance at their quarries. Their system of blasting caused stones, splinters, dust and vibration. The plaintiffs got an injunction restraining Ds: (1) from causing stones and splinters to leave the quarry confines; and (2) from causing a nuisance to HM's subjects by dust/vibration. The defendants prevented stones leaving the quarry and appealed against (2) on the grounds that at most there was a private, not a public nuisance. There were two highways and 30 or so houses close to the quarry. Oliver J described these as 'a little colony'.

Held

There was a public nuisance and the injunction had been rightly granted.

Romer LJ:

'It is, however, clear in my opinion that any nuisance is public which materially affects the reasonable comfort and convenience of a class of Her Majesty's subjects. The sphere of nuisance may be described generally as "the neighbourhood", but the question whether the local community within that sphere comprises a sufficient number of persons to constitute a "class of the public" is a question of fact in every case. It is not necessary in any judgment to prove that every member of the class has been injuriously affected; it is sufficient to show that a representative cross-section of the class has been so affected.'

Denning LJ:

'So I here declined to answer the question how many people are necessary to make up Her Majesty's subjects generally. I prefer to look to the reason of the thing and say that a public nuisance is a nuisance which is so widespread in its range or so indiscriminate in its effect that it would not be reasonable to expect one person to take proceedings on his own responsibility to put a stop to it, but that it should be taken on the responsibility of the community as a whole.'

Gillingham Borough Council v *Medway (Chatham) Dock Co Ltd* [1993] QB 343 High Court (Buckley J)

Public nuisance – effect of planning permission

Facts

The defendants were lessees of a port. The plaintiffs alleged that the use of the roads around the port at night by numerous heavy goods vehicles (HGVs) constituted a public nuisance. The evidence established that in 1988 there were approximately 750 HGV 'movements' every night and that the sleep and comfort of the residents in the vicinity of the port were disturbed. The defendants conceded that these conditions constituted a substantial interference with the residents' enjoyment of their property up to June 1990 and that, subject to defences, enough residents were affected to constitute a public nuisance. However the defendants argued that they had been given planning permission to operate a commercial port, that such a port could operate viably only on a 24-hour basis, that no limits had been placed on the volume of traffic in the vicinity when they had been granted planning permission and that their estimate of the likely throughput of traffic had been remarkably accurate.

Held

The plaintiffs' action would not succeed.

Buckley J noted that planning legislation had been enacted by Parliament in an effort to balance the interests of the community and the interests of individuals likely to be adversely affected by the plans being put forward. He then asked himself the question whether residents could defeat the planning legislation by bringing an action in nuisance. His conclusion was that 'where planning consent is given for a development or change of use, the question of nuisance will thereafter fall to be decided by reference to a neighbourhood with that development or use and not as it was previously'. So planning permission was not, of itself, a defence to a nuisance action but it was a factor to be taken into account in identifying the character of the neighbourhood. So, on the facts, account had to be taken of the fact that planning permission had been given to use the dockyard as a commercial port. In the light of this fact, in his Lordship's view the disturbance experienced by the residents of the area was not an actionable nuisance.

Littler v *Liverpool Corporation* [1968] 2 All ER 343 High Court (Cumming-Bruce J)

Highway repairs – statutory duty

Facts

On his way to a shop carrying two empty lemonade bottles, a young man tripped on the paving stones, fell and suffered injury.

Held

His claim for damages could not succeed.

Cumming-Bruce J:

'The test in relation to a length of pavement is reasonable foreseeability of danger. A length of pavement is only dangerous if, in the ordinary course of human affairs, danger may reasonably be anticipated from its continued use by the public who usually pass over it. It is a mistake to isolate and emphasise a particular difference in levels between flagstones unless that difference is such that a reasonable person who noticed and considered it would regard it as presenting a real source of danger. Uneven surfaces and differences in level between flagstones of about an inch may cause a pedestrian temporarily off balance to trip and stumble, but such characteristics have to be accepted. A highway is not to be criticised by the standards of a bowling green.

In the present case the only significant defect in the pavement was the small triangular gap which at its deepest presented a trip of half-an-inch. This is the kind of imperfection which has to be accepted in a pavement used by children and adults. Its presence would not make a reasonable person ... think injury would ensue unless it was repaired ... it is important that all concerned in litigation should realise that there is not a cause of action whenever someone trips over an uneven pavement or as a result of a fractional difference in levels between flagstones.'

Lyons, Sons & Co v Gulliver [1914] 1 Ch 631 Court of Appeal (Cozens-Hardy MR, Swinfen Eady and Phillimore LJJ)

Nuisance – theatre crowd

Facts

Persons waiting for admission to the defendants' theatre formed a queue outside the plaintiffs' shop.

Held (Phillimore LJ dissenting)

This amounted to an actionable nuisance.

Swinfen Eady LJ:

'In my opinion, there can be no question about the law applicable to the present case. Collecting together a crowd of people to the annoyance of one's neighbours may be a nuisance ... If the natural and probable consequence of what the defendant is doing is to collect a crowd so as to obstruct the highway, that may be an indictable nuisance, and if damage is occasioned to an individual, he may have a right of action in respect of it.'

Mint v Good [1951] 1 KB 517 Court of Appeal (Somervell, Denning and Birkett LJJ)

Nuisance – premises adjoining highway

Facts

A wall in front of two houses which were let to weekly tenants collapsed on the public footpath and injured the plaintiff. The danger could have been ascertained by inspection. No express agreement existed between the landlord and his tenants as to liability to repair and no right of entry to carry out repairs had been reserved to him.

Held

The landlord was liable for the plaintiff's injuries as there was an implied term that he would keep the premises in a reasonable and habitable condition.

Lord Denning LJ:

'The law of England has always take particular care to protect those who use a highway. It puts on the occupier of adjoining premises a special responsibility for the structures which he keeps beside the highway. If those structures fall into disrepair so as to be a potential danger to passers-by, they become a nuisance, and, what is more, a public nuisance, and the occupier is liable to anyone using the highway who is injured by reason of the disrepair. It is no answer for him to say that he and his servants took reasonable care, for even if he has employed a competent independent contractor to repair the structure, and has every reason for supposing it to be safe, the occupier is still liable if the independent contractor did the work badly: see *Tarry v Ashton*. The occupier's duty to passers-by is to see that the structure is as safe as reasonable care can make it – a duty which is as high as the duty which an occupier owes to people who pay to come on his premises. He is not liable for latent defects which could not be discovered by reasonable care on the part of anyone nor for acts of trespassers of which he neither knew nor ought to have known ... but he is liable when structures fall into dangerous disrepair, because there must be some fault on the part of someone for that to happen and he is responsible for it to persons using the highway, even though he was not actually at fault himself. That principle was laid down in this court in *Wringe v Cohen*, where it is to be noted that the principle is confined to "premises on a highway".'

Commentary
Applied: *Wringe* v *Cohen* [1940] 1 KB 229.
   Distinguished: *Sedleigh-Denfield* v *O'Callaghan* [1940] AC 880.

R v *Shorrock* [1993] 3 WLR 698 Court of Appeal (Simon Brown LJ, Popplewell and Rattee JJ)

Public nuisance – mental element

Facts
The defendant granted a licence for the use of a field on which loud music was played, causing noise and disturbance to local residents. The question arose as to the necessary mental element required for public nuisance.

Held
That the mental element of the crime of public nuisance was the same as that of the tort of private and public nuisance, namely that liability would arise where the person knew or ought to have known, because the means of knowledge were available to him, that there was a real risk of a nuisance arising.

Commentary
Sedleigh-Denfield v *O'Callaghan* [1940] AC 880 applied.

Rose v *Miles* (1815) 4 M & S 101 Court of King's Bench (Lord Ellenborough CJ, Bayley and Dampier JJ)

Public nuisance – private injury

Facts
Wrongfully intending to injure the plaintiff, the defendant moored a barge across a creek of a public navigable river. As a result, the plaintiff had to carry the merchandise from his barges 'a great distance over land'.

Held
The plaintiff was entitled to damages.

Lord Ellenborough CJ:

> 'The is something substantially more injurious to this person, than to the public at large, who might only have it in contemplation to use [the river]. And he has been impeded in his progress by the defendants' wrongfully mooring their barge across and has been compelled to unload and to carry his goods over land, by which he has incurred expense, and that expense caused by the act of the defendants. If a man's time or his money are of any value, it seems to me that this plaintiff has shown a particular damage.'

Tarry v *Ashton* (1876) 1 QBD 314 High Court (Blackburn, Quain and Lush JJ)

Nuisance – negligent independent contractor

Facts
The defendant moved into a house which had a heavy lamp projecting from the front wall. After moving

in, D employed an experienced gas fitter, an independent contractor, to mend the lamp. Some months later, the lamp fell on and injured the plaintiff as she was walking along the pavement.

Held
D was liable for the plaintiff's injuries.

Lush J:

'The question is what is the duty of a person in the position of the defendant? Is it his duty to maintain his premises in good repair, or only to employ a competent person in the work of maintaining them? I think the mere statement of the case suggests its answer. A person who keeps a lamp of this kind puts the public in peril. He cannot get rid of his duty to put the public out of peril by employing another person to take the necessary steps for doing so.'

Thomas v *National Union of Mineworkers (South Wales Area)* [1985] 2 WLR 1081
High Court (Scott J)

Nuisance – obstruction of highway

Facts
During a strike, the plaintiffs decided to return to work, but 60-70 pickets outside the colliery gates sought to deter them by using abusive and violent language. The plaintiffs sought interlocutory injunctions.

Held
On the facts, and in the light of the relevant law, the injunctions would not be granted.

Scott J:

'The working miners are entitled to use the highway for the purpose of entering and leaving their respective places of work. In the exercise of that right they are at present having to suffer the presence and behaviour of the pickets and demonstrators. The law has long recognised that unreasonable interference with the rights of others is actionable in tort ... It is, however, not every act of interference with the enjoyment by an individual of his property rights that will be actionable in nuisance. The law must strike a balance between conflicting rights and interests ...

Nuisance is strictly concerned with, and may be regarded as confined to, activity which unduly interferes with the use or enjoyment of land or of easements. But there is no reason why the law should not protect on a similar basis the enjoyment of other rights. All citizens have the right to use the public highway. Suppose an individual were persistently to follow another on a public highway, making rude gestures or remarks in order to annoy or vex. If continuance of such conduct were threatened no one can doubt but that a civil court would, at the suit of the victim, restrain by an injunction the continuance of the conduct. The tort might be described as a species of private nuisance, namely unreasonable inference with the victim's rights to use the highway. But the label for the tort does not, in my view, matter.

In the present case, the working miners have the right to use the highway for the purpose of going to work. They are, in my judgment, entitled under the general law to exercise that right without unreasonable harassment by others. Unreasonable harassment of them in their exercise of that right would, in my judgment, be tortious.

A decision whether in this, or in any other similar case, the presence or conduct of pickets represents a tortious interference with the right of those who wish to go to work to do so without harassment must depend on the particular circumstances of the particular case. The balance to which I have earlier referred must be struck between the rights of those going to work and the rights of the pickets.'

18 The Rule in *Rylands* v *Fletcher*

Cambridge Water Company v ***Eastern Counties Leather plc*** [1994] 2 WLR 53
House of Lords (Lord Templeman, Lord Goff, Lord Jauncey, Lord Lowry and Lord Woolf)

Need for foreseeability of damage

Facts

The defendants used a chlorinated solvent at their tannery which was situated some 1.3 miles from the plaintiff's borehole where water was abstracted for domestic purposes. This water became unfit for human consumption by solvent contamination when the solvent seeped into the ground below the defendants' premises and then percolated into the borehole. The plaintiffs brought an action in, inter alia, *Rylands*. In the High Court this action was dismissed on the grounds that the defendants had not made a non-natural user of their land, which was situated in an industrial village. On appeal, the Court of Appeal declined to determine the matter on the basis of *Rylands* but imposed liability on other grounds. The defendants appealed.

Held

That foreseeability of harm of the relevant type by the defendants was required to recover damages under the rule in *Rylands* v *Fletcher* (and also in nuisance). The House of Lords also held, contrary to the finding at first instance, that the defendants had made a non-natural user of their land. However, on the facts of the case the contamination was not foreseeable and the appeal was allowed.

Lord Goff, with whose speech the other law Lords agreed, also briefly considered the meaning of the phrase 'natural use of the land', and doubted whether the storage of substantial quantities of chemicals on industrial premises could ever be a natural user. Lord Goff pointed out that now foreseeability of damage was an essential ingredient of the tort, courts might feel less inclined to extend the concept of natural use to circumstances such as those in the present case.

Lord Goff:

Foreseeability of damage under the rule in Rylands v Fletcher
'I start with the judgment of Blackburn J in *Fletcher* v *Rylands* (1866) LR 1 Ex 265 itself. His celebrated statement of the law is to be found at pp279–280, where he said:

> "We think that the true rule of law is, that the person who for his own purposes brings on his lands and collects and keeps there anything likely to do mischief if it escapes, must keep it in at his peril, and, if he does not do so, is prima facie answerable for all the damage which is the natural consequence of its escape. He can excuse himself by showing that the escape was owing to the plaintiff's default; or perhaps that the escape was the consequence of vis major, or the act of God; but as nothing of this sort exists here, it is unnecessary to inquire what excuse would be sufficient. The general rule, as above stated, seems on principle just. The person whose grass or corn is eaten down by the escaping cattle of his neighbour, or whose mine is flooded by the water from his neighbour's reservoir, or whose cellar is invaded by the filth of his neighbour's privy, or whose habitation is made unhealthy by the fumes and noisome vapours of his neighbour's alkali works, is damnified without any fault of his own; and it seems but reasonable and just

that the neighbour, who has brought something on his own property which was not naturally there, harmless to others so long as it is confined to his own property, but which he knows to be mischievous if it gets on his neighbour's, should be obliged to make good the damage which ensues if he does not succeed in confining it to his own property. But for his act in bringing it there no mischief could have accrued, and it seems but just that he should at his peril keep it there so that no mischief may accrue, or answer for the natural and anticipated consequences. And upon authority, this we think is established to be the law whether the things so brought be beasts, or water, or filth, or stenches."

In that passage, Blackburn J spoke of "anything *likely* to do mischief if it escapes"; and later he spoke of something "which he *knows* to be mischievous if it gets on his neighbour's [property]", and the liability to "answer for the natural *and anticipated* consequences". Furthermore, time and again he spoke of the strict liability imposed upon the defendant as being that he must keep the thing in at his peril; and, when referring to liability in actions for damage occasioned by animals, he referred, at p282, to the established principle that "it is quite immaterial whether the escape is by negligence or not". The general tenor of his statement of principle is therefore that knowledge, or at least foreseeability of the risk, is a prerequisite of the recovery of damages under the principle; but that the principle is one of strict liability in the sense that the defendant may be held liable notwithstanding that he has exercised all due care to prevent the escape from occurring.

There are however early authorities in which foreseeability of damage does not appear to have been regarded as necessary: see, eg, *Humphries* v *Cousins* (1877) 2 CPD 239. Moreover, it was submitted by Mr Ashworth for CWC that the requirement of foreseeability of damage was negatived in two particular cases, the decision of the Court of Appeal in *West* v *Bristol Tramways Co* [1908] 2 KB 14, and the decision of this House in *Rainham Chemical Works Ltd* v *Belvedere Fish Guano Co Ltd* [1921] 2 AC 465.

In *West* v *Bristol Tramways Co* the defendant tramway company was held liable for damage to the plaintiff's plants and shrubs in his nursery garden adjoining a road where the defendant's tramline ran, the damage being caused by fumes from creosoted wooden blocks laid by the defendants between the rails of the tramline. The defendants were so held liable under the rule in *Rylands* v *Fletcher*, notwithstanding that they were exonerated from negligence, having no knowledge of the possibility of such damage; indeed the evidence was that creosoted wood had been in use for several years as wood paving, and no mischief had ever been known to arise from it. The argument that no liability arose in such circumstances under the rule in *Rylands* v *Fletcher* was given short shrift, both in the Divisional Court and in the Court of Appeal. For the Divisional Court, it was enough that the creosote had been found to be dangerous by the jury, Phillimore J holding that creosote was like the wild animals in the old cases. The Court of Appeal did not call upon the plaintiffs, and dismissed the appeal in unreserved judgments. Lord Alverstone CJ relied upon a passage from *Garrett on the Law of Nuisances*, 2nd ed (1897), p129, and rejected a contention by the defendant that, in the case of non-natural use of land, the defendant will not be liable unless the thing introduced onto the land was, to the knowledge of the defendant, likely to escape and cause damage. It was however suggested, both by Lord Alverstone CJ (with whom Sir Gorell Barnes P agreed) and by Farwell LJ that, by analogy with cases concerning liability for animals, the defendant might escape liability if he could show that, according to the common experience of mankind, the thing introduced onto the land had proved not to be dangerous.

The *Rainham Chemical* case [1921] 2 AC 465 arose out of a catastrophic explosion at a factory involved in the manufacture of high explosive during the First World War, with considerable loss of life and damage to neighbouring property. It was held that the company carrying on the business at the premises was liable for the damage to neighbouring property under the rule in *Rylands* v *Fletcher*; but the great question in the case, at least so far as the appellate courts were concerned, was whether two individuals, who were shareholders in and directors of the company, could be held personally responsible on the same principle.

However, this House dismissed their appeal on a point of some technicality, viz that their Lordships could not satisfy themselves that the two individuals had sufficiently divested themselves of the occupation of the premises, so as to substitute the occupation of the company in the place of their own – notwithstanding that the company itself was also in occupation: see [1921] 2 AC 465, 478-479, per Lord

Buckmaster; pp480, 483-484, per Lord Sumner; p491, per Lord Parmoor; and pp492, 493-494, per Lord Carson.

I feel bound to say that these two cases provide a very fragile base for any firm conclusion that foreseeability of damage has been authoritatively rejected as a prerequisite of the recovery of damages under the rule in *Rylands* v *Fletcher*. Certainly, the point was not considered by this House in the *Rainham Chemical* case. In my opinion, the matter is open for consideration by your Lordships in the present case, and, despite recent dicta to the contrary (see, eg *Leakey* v *National Trust for Places of Historic Interest or Natural Beauty* [1980] QB 485, 519, per Megaw LJ), should be considered as a matter of principle. Little guidance can be derived from either of the two cases in question, save that it seems to have been assumed that the strict liability arising under the rule precluded reliance by the plaintiff on lack of knowledge or the means of knowledge of the relevant danger.

The point is one on which academic opinion appears to be divided: cf *Salmond & Heuston on the Law of Torts*, 20th ed (1992), pp324-325, which favours the prerequisite of foreseeability, and *Clerk & Lindsell on Torts*, 16th ed (1989), p1429, para 25.09, which takes a different view. However, quite apart from the indications to be derived from the judgment of Blackburn J in *Fletcher* v *Rylands*, LR 1 Ex 265 itself, to which I have already referred, the historical connection with the law of nuisance must now be regarded as pointing towards the conclusion that foreseeability of damage is a prerequisite of the recovery of damages under the rule. I have already referred to the fact that Blackburn J himself did not regard his statement of principle as having broken new ground; furthermore, Professor Newark has convincingly shown that the rule in *Rylands* v *Fletcher* was essentially concerned with an extension of the law of nuisance to cases of isolated escape. Accordingly since, following the observations of Lord Reid when delivering the advice of the Privy Council in *The Wagon Mound (No 2)* [1967] 1 AC 617, 640, the recovery of damages in private nuisance depends on foreseeability by the defendant of the relevant type of damage, it would appear logical to extend the same requirement to liability under the rule in *Rylands* v *Fletcher*.

Natural use of land
I turn to the question whether the use by ECL of its land in the present case constituted a natural use, with the result that ECL cannot be held liable under the rule in *Rylands* v *Fletcher*. In view of my conclusion on the issue of foreseeability, I can deal with this point shortly.

The judge held that it was a natural use. He said:

"In my judgment, in considering whether the storage of organochlorines as an adjunct to a manufacturing process is a non-natural use of land, I must consider whether that storage created special risks for adjacent occupiers and whether the activity was for the general benefit of the community. It seems to me inevitable that I must consider the magnitude of the storage and the geographical area in which it takes place in answering the question. Sawston is properly described as an industrial village, and the creation of employment is clearly for the benefit of that community. I do not believe that I can enter upon an assessment of the point on a scale of desirability that the manufacture of wash leathers comes, and I content myself with holdings that this storage in this place is a natural use of land."

It is commonplace that this particular exception to liability under the rule has developed and changed over the years. It seems clear that, in *Fletcher* v *Rylands*, LR 1 Ex 265 itself, Blackburn J's statement of the law was limited to things which are brought by the defendant onto his land, and so did not apply to things that were naturally upon the land. Furthermore, it is doubtful whether in the House of Lords in the same case Lord Cairns, to whom we owe the expression "non-natural use" of the land, was intending to expand the concept of natural use beyond that envisaged by Blackburn J. Even so, the law has long since departed from any such simple idea, redolent of a different age; and, at least since the advice of the Privy Council delivered by Lord Moulton in *Rickards* v *Lothian* [1913] AC 263, 280, natural use has been extended to embrace the ordinary use of land. I ask to be forgiven if I again quote Lord Moulton's statement of the law which has lain at the heart of the subsequent development of this exception:

"It is not every use to which land is put that brings into play at that principle. It must be some special use bringing with it increased danger to others, and must not merely be the ordinary use of the land or such a use as is proper for the general benefit of the community."

Rickards v *Lothian* itself was concerned with a use of a domestic kind, viz the overflow of water from a basin whose runaway had become blocked. But over the years the concept of natural use, in the sense of ordinary use, has been extended to embrace a wide variety of uses, including not only domestic uses but also recreational uses and even some industrial uses.

It is obvious that the expression "ordinary use of the land" in Lord Moulton's statement of the law is one which is lacking in precision. There are some writers who welcome the flexibility which has thus been introduced into this branch of the law, on the ground that it enables judges to mould and adapt the principle of strict liability to the changing needs of society; whereas others regret the perceived absence of principle in so vague a concept, and fear that the whole idea of strict liability may as a result be undermined. A particular doubt is introduced by Lord Moulton's alternative criterion – "or such a use as is proper for the general benefit of the community". If these words are understood to refer to a local community, they can be given some content as intended to refer to such matters as, for example, the provision of services; indeed the same idea can, without too much difficulty, be extended to, for example, the provision of services to industrial premises, as in a business park or an industrial estate. But if the words are extended to embrace the wider interests of the local community or the general benefit of the community at large, it is difficult to see how the exception can be kept within reasonable bounds. A notable extension was considered in your Lordships' House in *Read* v *J Lyons & Co Ltd* [1947] AC 156, 169-170, per Viscount Simon, and p174, per Lord Macmillan, where it was suggested that, in time of war, the manufacture of explosives might be held to constitute a natural use of land, apparently on the basis that, in a country in which the greater part of the population was involved in the war effort, many otherwise exceptional uses might become "ordinary" for the duration of the war. It is however unnecessary to consider so wide an extension as that in a case such as the present. Even so, we can see the introduction of another extension in the present case, when the judge invoked the creation of employment as clearly for the benefit of the local community, viz "the industrial village" at Sawston. I myself, however, do not feel able to accept that the creation of employment as such, even in a small industrial complex, is sufficient of itself to establish a particular use as constituting a natural or ordinary use of land.

Fortunately, I do not think it is necessary for the purposes of the present case to attempt any redefinition of the concept of natural or ordinary use. This is because I am satisfied that the storage of chemicals in substantial quantities, and their use in the manner employed at ECL's premises, cannot fall within the exception. ... Indeed I feel bound to say that the storage of substantial quantities of chemicals on industrial premises should be regarded as an almost classic case of non-natural use; and I find it very difficult to think that it should be thought objectionable to impose strict liability for damage caused in the event of their escape. It may well be that, now that it is recognised that foreseeability of harm of the relevant type is a prerequisite of liability in damages under the rule, the courts may feel less pressure to extend the concept of natural use to circumstances such as those in the present case; and in due course it may become easier to control this exception, and to ensure that it has a more recognisable basis of principle. For these reasons, I would not hold that ECL should be exempt from liability on the basis of the exception of natural use.

However, for the reasons I have already given, I would allow ECL's appeal with costs before your Lordships' House and in the courts below.'

Green v *Chelsea Waterworks Co* (1894) 70 LT 547 Court of Appeal (Lindley, Kay and A L Smith LJJ)

Statutory authority – burst water pipe

Facts
Acting under statutory powers, the defendants laid a main water pipe in a street near the plaintiffs' premises. Without negligence on the defendants' part, the pipe burst and water flowed into the plaintiffs' premises and damaged their stock.

Held
The defendants were not liable.

Lindley LJ:

'So far as the action is based on negligence it is not maintainable, because the jury have found that there was no negligence. Then on what principle can the defendants be held liable except negligence? It was argued that they were liable by reason of the doctrine in *Rylands* v *Fletcher*, and it was said that this was like the case of a landowner who stores water on his land so as to become a source of danger to his neighbours, and that, consequently, the defendants were bound to show that they were relieved by the Acts of Parliament under which they were constituted from the duty of keeping the water in their pipes. The fault of that argument is in the major proposition. *Rylands* v *Fletcher* was not a case of a company authorised to lay down water pipes by Act of Parliament. It was a case of a private individual storing water on his own land for his own purposes. There was no negligence on his part ... That case is not to be extended beyond the legitimate principle on which the House of Lords decided it. If it were extended as far as strict logic might require, it would be a very oppressive decision. Here the defendants were only doing what they were authorised to do by their Act, and, as they were not guilty of negligence, they are not liable for damage.'

Commentary
Distinguished: *Rylands* v *Fletcher* (1868) LR 3 HL 330.

Hale v *Jennings Brothers* [1938] 1 All ER 579 Court of Appeal (Slessor, Scott and Clauson LJJ)

Chair-o-plane injury

Facts
The defendants were the proprietors of a fairground. One of their attractions was a roundabout with planes on, which revolved at high speed. The plaintiff ran a stall as a tenant of the defendants. One of the planes came away and caused considerable injury to the plaintiff.

Held
The defendants were liable without proof of negligence under the *Rylands* v *Fletcher* principle.

Mason v *Levy Auto Parts of England Ltd* [1967] 2 WLR 1384 High Court (MacKenna J)

Escape of fire

Facts
The defendants' yard contained machinery, which was greased and stacked in wooden cases pending sale. There was also other inflammable material there. The defendants had installed fire-fighting equipment on the advice of the local fire brigade because of the considerable fire-risk. After a period of very dry weather, fire broke out in the yard; despite immediate steps taken to put the blaze out, it spread to the plaintiff's adjoining property where it destroyed trees and plants in his garden. The cause of the fire was unknown, but was probably caused by a workman's cigarette. The defendants disclaimed liability, inter alia, on the ground that the fire had 'accidentally begun' within s86 of the Fires Prevention (Metropolis) Act 1774.

Held

The defendants were liable under the principle in *Rylands* v *Fletcher*, because their use of the yard was non-natural user of the land, having regard to the material they had brought on to it, the manner in which it was stored and the character of the neighbourhood. As far as the statutory protection went, the defendants were not under any burden of disproving negligence when seeking its protection.

Nichols v *Marsland* (1876) 2 Ex D 1 Court of Appeal (Cockburn CJ, Mellish and James LJJ, Baggallay JA and Archibald J)

Flooding – Act of God

Facts

On the defendant's land were artificial pools containing large quantities of water connected by weirs. This was achieved by damming a stream and allowing the water to return to it further down its course. After a very heavy rain storm, the pools flooded and damaged the plaintiff's property.

Held

The rainstorm was an Act of God and the defendant was not liable.

Mellish LJ:

> 'The present case is distinguished from *Rylands* v *Fletcher* in that it is not the act of the defendants in keeping this reservoir, an act in itself lawful, which alone leads to the escape of the water, and so renders wrongful that which but for such escape would have been lawful. It is the supervening "vis major" of the water caused by the flood, superadded to the water in the reservoir, which of itself would have been innocuous, caused the disaster. A person cannot, in our opinion, be properly said to have caused or allowed the water to escape, if the act of God or the Queen's enemies was the real cause of its escaping without any fault on the part of the defendant. If a reservoir was destroyed by an earthquake, or the Queen's enemies destroyed it in conducting some warlike operation, it would be contrary to all reason and justice to hold the owner of the reservoir liable for any damage that might be done by the escape of the water. We are of opinion, therefore, that the defendant was entitled to excuse herself by proving that the water escaped through the act of God.'

North-Western Utilities Ltd v *London Guarantee and Accident Co Ltd* [1936] AC 108 Privy Council (Lord Hailsham LC, Lord Blanesburgh and Lord Wright)

Escape of gas – fire

Facts

The appellants laid gas pipes under a street in Edmonton. Eight years later the local authority constructed a storm sewer beneath the gas main. The following year gas escaped into a hotel where it ignited: the hotel was burned down. The gas had escaped because of a break in a welded joint which had occurred because of the local authority's sewer operations.

Held

The appellants were liable as their failure to know of the local authority's operations was not consistent with due care on their part.

Lord Wright:

> 'That gas is a dangerous thing within the rules applicable to things dangerous in themselves is beyond question. Thus the appellants, who are carrying in their mains the inflammable and explosive gas, are

prima facie within the principle of *Rylands* v *Fletcher*; that is to say, that, though they are doing nothing wrongful in carrying the dangerous thing so long as they keep it in their pipes, they come prima facie within the rule of strict liability if the gas escapes; the gas constitutes an extraordinary danger created by the appellants for their own purposes, and the rule established by *Rylands* v *Fletcher* requires that they act at their peril and must pay for damage caused by the gas if it escapes, even without any negligence on their part. The rule is not limited to cases where the defendant has been carrying or accumulating the dangerous thing on his own land; it applies equally in a case like the present where the appellants were carrying the gas in mains laid in the property of the city – that is, in the subsoil – in exercise of a franchise to do so ...

This form of liability is in many ways analogous to a liability for nuisance, though nuisance is not only different in its historical origin, but in its legal character and many of its incidents and applications. But the two causes of action often overlap, and in respect of each of these causes of action the rule of strict liability has been modified by admitting as a defence that what was being done was properly done in pursuance of statutory powers, and the mischief that has happened has not been brought about by any negligence on the part of the undertakers ...

By the same reasoning the rule has been held inapplicable where the casualty is due to the act of God; or to the independent or conscious volition of a third party ... and not to any negligence of the defendants.'

Perry v *Kendricks Transport Ltd* [1956] 1 WLR 85 Court of Appeal (Singleton, Jenkins and Parker LJJ)

Explosion caused by strangers

Facts
The plaintiff (a boy of ten) was seriously injured in the defendants' coach park when he approached two other boys who were near a coach, who jumped away having thrown a match into an empty petrol tank causing an explosion. The P sued the Ds on the grounds that the coach was a dangerous thing within *Rylands* v *Fletcher*.

Held
The defendants were not liable.

Singleton LJ:

'The principle laid down may cease to be applicable if the harm done was due to the act of a stranger. If the mischievous, deliberate and conscious act of a stranger causes the damage, the occupier can escape liability ... I am prepared to accept this position: if the person who interferes with something of the Ds' is a person whom they might expect to be upon their ground and the character of the interference is something they ought to anticipate, then they do owe some duty.'

Commentary
Applied: *Rickards* v *Lothian* [1913] AC 263.

Ponting v *Noakes* [1894] 2 QB 281 High Court (Charles and Henn Collins JJ)

Liability for horse's death

Facts
A yew tree grew on the defendants' land adjoining the plaintiff's field. The tree did not overhang the field, but the plaintiff's colt had reached its branches from the field, eaten some of its leaves – and died. The plaintiff sued to recover the colt's value.

Held

His action could not succeed.

Charles J:

'The poisonous tree was admitted to be wholly on the defendants' land, but, inasmuch as it was so near to the boundary that an animal could easily reach the branches, it was contended that the principle of *Rylands* v *Fletcher* was applicable. But this argument appears to me to rest on a misconception of what that case really decided. The decision only refers to the escape from a defendant's land of something which he has brought there, and which is likely to do mischief if it escapes ... The rule of law enunciated in *Rylands* v *Fletcher* I think therefore has no application ... The hurt which the animal received was due to his wrongful intrusion. He had no right to be there, and his owner therefore has no right to complain.'

Read v *J Lyons & Co Ltd* [1947] AC 156 House of Lords (Viscount Simon, Lord Macmillan, Lord Porter, Lord Simonds, and Lord Uthwatt)

Explosion – escape

Facts

The defendants manufactured high explosive shells for the Government and occupied factory premises as agents of the Minister for the purpose. The plaintiff was employed by the Ds at this factory as a supervisor in the shell-filling shop. While she was there, an explosion occured which injured her. She could prove no negligence and sued on the principle in *Rylands* v *Fletcher*.

Held

The defendants were not liable because there was no 'escape' of any dangerous thing from their premises.

Viscount Simon:

'It seems better therefore when a plaintiff relies on *Rylands* v *Fletcher* to take the conditions declared by this House to be essential for liability in that case and to ascertain whether these conditions exist in the actual case.

Now the strict liability recognised by this House to exist in *Rylands* v *Fletcher* is conditioned by two elements which I may call the condition of "escape" from the land of something likely to do mischief if it escapes and the condition of "non-natural use" of the land.'

Rickards v *Lothian* [1913] AC 263 Privy Council (Viscount Haldane LC, Lord Macnaghten, Lord Atkinson and Lord Moulton)

Overflow – act of third party

Facts

D was the tenant of a building. P was a sub-tenant of the second floor and various other of D's tenants occupied the floors above him. Someone on the floor above turned on a wash basin tap and plugged the sink so that water left the over-flow pipe and soaked into the second floor wall, damaging P's stock-in-trade.

Held

D was not liable either for negligence or nuisance.

Lord Moulton:

'The legal principle which underlies the decision in *Fletcher* v *Rylands* was well known in English law from a very early period, but it was explained and formulated in a strikingly clear and authoritative manner in that case and, therefore, is usually referred to by that name. It is nothing other than an application of the old maxim, sic utere tuo at aberum non laedas.

It is not every use to which land is put which brings into play that principle [in *Rylands* v *Fletcher*]. It must be some special use bringing with it increased danger to others and must not merely be the ordinary use of the land or such a use as is proper for the general benefit of the community ... The provision of a proper supply of water to the various parts of a house is not only reasonable, but has become in accordance with modern sanitary views, an almost necessity. It is recognised as being so desirable in the interests of the community that in some form or other it is usually made obligatory in civilized nations. Such a supply cannot be installed without causing some concurrent danger of leakage or overflow. It would be unreasonable for the law to regard those who instal or maintain such a system of supply as doing so at their own peril with an absolute liability for any damage resulting from its presence, even if there has been no negligence.'

Commentary

Applied in *Perry* v *Kendricks Transport Ltd* [1956] 1 WLR 85.

Rylands v *Fletcher* (1868) LR 3 HL 330 House of Lords (Lord Cairns LC and Lord Cranworth)

Escape of dangerous things

Facts

The plaintiff built a colliery on his land. One shaft was extended to join up with some old shafts which had been excavated under land adjacent to the plaintiff's. Using competent but, on this occasion, negligent independent contractors, the defendants constructed a reservoir on nearby land under which some of the old mine shafts were situated. When they filled the reservoir, the water entered the old shafts and, by that route, flooded the plaintiff's mine. The defendants themselves had not been negligent.

Held

The defendants were liable for the damage caused. Their Lordships approved the judgment of Blackburn J in the Court of Exchequer Chamber in which he said:

'The question therefore arises what is the obligation which the law casts upon a person who, like the defendants, lawfully brings onto his land something which though harmless while it remains there, will do mischief if it escapes ...

We think the true rule of law is that the person who for his own purposes brings onto his lands and collects and keeps there anything likely to do mischief if it escapes, must keep it in at his peril and if he does not do so, is prima facie liable for all the damage which is the natural consequence of its escape. He can excuse himself by showing that the escape was owing to the plaintiffs' default or, perhaps, that the escape was the consequence of vis major or Act-of-God but as nothing of this sort exists here, it is unnecessary to inquire what excuse would be sufficient.

The general rule as stated above, seems on principle just. The person whose grass or corn is eaten down by the escaping cattle of his neighbour or whose mine is flooded by water from his neighbour's reservoir or whose cellar is invaded by the filth of his neighbour's privy or whose habitat is made unhealthy by the fumes and noisome vapours of his neighbour's alkali works, is dominified without any fault of his own and it seems but reasonable and just that the neighbour who has brought something on his own property which was not naturally there, harmless to others so far as it is confined to his own property but which he knows will be mischievous if it gets on his neighbour's, should be obliged to make good the damage which ensues if he does not succeed in confining it to his own property.

... And upon authority this we think is established to be the law whether the things so brought be beasts or water or filth or stenches.'

Lord Cairns LC:

'... if the defendants not stopping at the natural use of their close (land) had desired to use it for any purpose which I may term non-natural use for the purpose of introducing into the close that which in its natural use was not in or upon it ... then it appears to me that that which the defendants were doing they were doing at their own peril.'

Commentary

Approved in *Leakey* v *National Trust* [1980] 2 WLR 65.

Distinguished in *Noble* v *Harrison* [1926] 2 KB 332 and *Green* v *Chelsea Waterworks Co* (1894) 70 LT 547.

Shiffman v *The Grand Priory in the British Realm of the Venerable Order of the Hospital of St John of Jerusalem* [1936] 1 All ER 557 (Atkinson J)

Flag pole accident

Facts

Here the defendants, at the request of the police, erected a casualty tent to cope with an anticipated public crowd. They also erected a flag pole, supported by four guy ropes. Children kept playing on this and, despite attempts to prevent them, they pulled it down onto the plaintiff.

Held

On the facts, the defendants had been negligent. Seemingly, the flag pole was within *Rylands* v *Fletcher* and was erected at the defendants' peril.

19 Fire

Emanuel (H & N) Ltd* v *Greater London Council [1971] 2 All ER 835 Court of
Appeal (Lord Denning MR, Edmund-Davies and Phillimore LJJ)

Escape of fire – act of third party

Facts
An arrangement was made whereby a firm of independent contractors, engaged by the Ministry of
Works, would remove two war-time bungalows and all materials and rubbish from a site owned by the
defendant Council. The contractors started a fire to burn unwanted materials. Sparks blew on to the
plaintiffs' property and the resulting fire caused damage.

Held
The council as occupier was liable for the escape of fire caused by the negligence of anyone other than
a stranger. The contractors were on the land with the Council's leave, and although the contractors were
forbidden by the terms of their contract from starting fires on the land, the Council could reasonably have
anticipated that they might start a fire.

Lord Denning MR:

'There has been much discussion about the exact legal basis of liability for fire. The liability of the
occupier can be said to be a strict liability in this sense that he is liable for the negligence not only of his
servants but also of independent contractors and, indeed, of anyone except a "stranger". By the same token
it can be said to be a "vicarious liability", because he is liable for the defaults of others as well as his
own. It can also be said to be a liability under the principle of *Rylands* v *Fletcher*, because fire is
undoubtedly a dangerous thing which is likely to do damage if it escapes. But I do not think it necessary
to put it into any one of these three categories. It goes back to the time when no such categories were
thought of. Suffice it to say that the extent of the liability is now well defined as I have stated it. The
occupier is liable for the escape of fire which is due to the negligence of anyone other than a stranger.'

Commentary
Applied: *Balfour* v *Barty-King* [1957] 2 WLR 84 and *Wheat* v *E Lacon & Co Ltd* [1966] 2 WLR 581.

Sochacki v *Sas* [1947] 1 All ER 344 High Court (Lord Goddard CJ)

Accidental fire

Facts
Fire broke out in a lodger's room. There was no evidence of negligence on his part; the fire was probably
caused by a spark from his fire setting alight the floorboards.

Held

Neither the rule in *Rylands* v *Fletcher* nor the doctrine of res ipsa loquitur applied and the lodger was not liable.

Spicer v *Smee* [1946] 1 All ER 489 High Court (Atkinson J)

Nuisance – faulty wiring

Facts

The plaintiff's bungalow was destroyed by a fire which originated in the defendant's adjoining bungalow and was caused by faulty wiring. The defendant maintained that she was not liable for acts of an independent contractor (the electrician) and that she was protected by the Fires Prevention (Metropolis) Act 1774.

Held

There was a nuisance and the defendant was liable. As the fire was due to nuisance the 1774 Act did not apply.

Atkinson J:

'Nuisance and negligence are different in their nature and a private nuisance arises out of a state of things on one man's property whereby his neighbour's property is exposed to danger. I am satisfied that the state of the defendant's bungalow around that plug with a bare wire in contact with wet wood did constitute a nuisance and that it exposed the neighbouring property to danger.'

20 Animals

Bates* v *Director of Public Prosecutions (1993) The Times 8 March Queen's Bench Divisional Court (Rose LJ and Waller J)

Meaning of public place

Facts
The defendant was charged before the magistrates with the offence of having in his possession a dangerous dog (a pit bull terrier) in a public place when the dog was unmuzzled and not on a lead as required by s1(2) of the 1991 Act. The defendant was convicted and appealed.

Held
That a dangerous dog (as defined by s1 of the 1991 Act) in a private car which was on a public highway was in a public place within the meaning of s10(2) of the Act. The appeal was therefore dismissed.

Cummings* v *Grainger [1977] QB 397 Court of Appeal (Lord Denning MR, Ormrod and Bridge LJJ)

Liability and defences under the Animals Act 1971

Facts
The defendant was the occupier of a breaker's yard in the East End of London. At night the yard was locked up and the defendant's untrained Alsatian dog was turned loose to deter intruders. One night an associate of the defendant, who had access to a key, unlocked the side gate and, accompanied by the plaintiff, who knew about the dog, entered the yard. The dog attacked the plaintiff causing her serious injury. The plaintiff brought an action for damages based on, inter alia, breach of the duty contained in s2(2) of the Animals Act 1971. At the trial expert evidence was given that the dog's behaviour in the circumstances was normal for an untrained Alsatian with a territory to defend. The judge held that the defendant was liable under s2(2) of the Act and that he did not come within any of the exceptions in section 5 but that the plaintiff was 50 per cent to blame for her injuries.

On the defendant's appeal:

Held
(1) That if the dog were to bite anyone the damage was likely to be severe; that the likelihood of such damage was due to characteristics not normally found in Alsatians except in the 'particular circumstances', namely, an untrained dog roaming a yard which it regarded as its territory that it could be assumed that those characteristics were known to the defendant and, accordingly, that the requirements of s2(2) were satisfied.

But (2), allowing the appeal, that in all the circumstances it was not unreasonable for the defendant to keep the dog in the yard to protect his property that, accordingly, as the plaintiff was a trespasser, the defendant was excepted from liability under s2 by s5(3)(b); and, further, that as the plaintiff entered the yard knowing all about the dog she must be taken to have voluntarily accepted the risk of damage, thereby absolving the defendant of liability as provided by s5(2).

Cunningham v *Whelan* (1917) 52 Ir LT 67 High Court (Ireland) (Moloney LJ)

Animals on highway – nuisance

Facts

The plaintiff was driving an empty cart when he saw 24 bullocks and heifers (a 'mass' of cattle), the property of the defendant, on the highway in front of him. There was no one in charge of the animals and, although the plaintiff stopped his horse, they pressed in on the cart and upset it, causing injury to both the cart and the plaintiff.

Held

The plaintiff was entitled to damages as an owner is bound to use care and caution to prevent his animals from straying in such numbers as to render the highway positively unsafe or dangerous to those who use it.

Curtis v *Betts* [1990] 1 WLR 459 Court of Appeal (Slade, Nourse and Stuart-Smith LJJ)

Dangerous dog – liability

Facts

The plaintiff, aged 10, had known the defendants' bull mastiff Max since it was a puppy and he was very friendly with it. When the dog was being loaded into the back of the defendants' Land Rover, the boy called its name and approached it. Although the dog was on a lead held by the first defendant, it leapt at the plaintiff and bit him on the face: the plaintiff had been in no way to blame.

Held

The plaintiff was entitled to damages as the requirements of s2(2)(a)(b) and (c) of the Animal Act 1971 had been satisfied.

Stuart-Smith LJ:

'Like Slade and Nourse LJJ and others before me, I have not found s2(2) of the Animals Act 1971 easy to construe ...

Paragraph (a) is concerned with the type of damage that it is foreseeable that the animal may cause. It may be of two types: the first is of a kind that the animal unless restrained, is likely to cause; the second is if it is likely to be severe. In each case the question relates to the animal in question ... I can see no reason for ... limiting the plain words of the paragraph. Moreover, it seems to me to be contrary to the decision of this court in *Cummings* v *Granger* [1976] 3 WLR 842 ... At the time of this incident Max was a big dog: he weighed about 10 stone and he had big teeth and a large mouth ... if he did bite anyone the damage was likely to be severe.

Paragraph (b) presents more difficulty. Here again there are two limbs to the subsection. The first deals with what may for convenience be called permanent characteristics, the second, temporary characteristics. Dogs are not normally fierce or prone to attack humans; a dog which has a propensity to do this at all times and in all places and without discrimination as to persons would clearly fall within the first limb. One that is only aggressive in particular circumstances, for example when guarding its territory or, if a bitch, when it had a litter of pups, will come within the second limb. In the present case the judge concluded that Max fell within the second limb. He said that he was –

"satisfied on the balance of probabilities that the defendants knew of the tendency of these dogs to be what one may term fierce, when protecting the boundaries of what they considered their territory, which expression may have included the rear of the Land Rover" ...

In my judgment the judge correctly directed himself on this aspect of the matter ... he was ... justified in concluding that the place and circumstances of the attack were within the ambit of the dog protecting its territory ...

Counsel for the defendants did not seek to challenge the judge's finding that the defendants knew of Max's propensity to be fierce in defence of his territory; but he submitted that this did not extend to knowledge of such a propensity with regard to the place and circumstances of the attack. But counsel for the defendants realistically accepted that this submission was dependent on the last. If the judge was justified in holding, as in my view he was, that the attack was part and parcel of defence of territory, then it seems to me to follow that the characteristic of the dog to act as it did at the place and in the circumstances of the attack were within the ambit of the defendants' knowledge and para (c) was satisfied.

I would only add this. In my view it is desirable, when judges have to decide cases under this subsection, that they should consider each part of the subsection in turn and satisfy themselves that the plaintiff has made out his case on one or other of the limbs of each part.'

Fellowes v *Director of Public Prosecutions* (1993) The Times 1 February Queen's Bench Divisional Court (Kennedy LJ and Clarke J)

Meaning of public place

Facts

The defendant was charged before the magistrates with the offence of having a dog which was dangerously out of control in a public place and which had caused injury, contrary to s3(1) of the Dangerous Dogs Act 1991. The place in question was the defendant's garden path, and the magistrates held that it was a 'street, road or other place' within s10(2). The defendant appealed against his conviction.

Held

That the path was private property, and that anyone who went along it went as a visitor to the house and not as a member of the public. Thus the path was not a public place within s10(2), and the appeal was allowed.

Leeman v *Montagu* [1936] 2 All ER 1677 High Court (Greaves-Lord J)

Nuisance – cockerels

Facts

The plaintiff purchased a house in a partly rural, but largely residential, area. Adjoining the house was a poultry farm. Here the defendant kept large numbers of cockerels. P complained of the noise made by them in the early morning and threatened proceedings unless they were removed. D did remove them, but they returned later.

Held

This constituted a nuisance and an injunction would be granted, suspended for one month to allow further steps to be taken.

R v *Bezzina* (1993) The Times 7 December Court of Appeal (Kennedy LJ, Waterhouse and Ebsworth JJ)

Whether mens rea required for contravention of Dangerous Dogs Act 1991

Facts

The defendant, along with others, was convicted at the Crown Court of being the owner of a dog which was dangerously out of control in a public place and while so out of control injured a person contrary to s3(1) of the Dangerous Dogs Act 1991. The defendant appealed on the grounds that the prosecution had failed to establish any mens rea.

Held

Section 3(1) of the 1991 Act imposed strict liability on the owners or handlers of dogs of any breed which were dangerously out of control in public places, and there was no requirement of mens rea.

R v *Knightsbridge Crown Court, ex parte Dunne* [1993] 4 All ER 491 Queen's Bench Divisional Court (Glidewell LJ and Cresswell J)

'Type' not synonymous with 'breed'

Facts

The defendant had been convicted before the magistrates of the offence of permitting a pit bull terrier to be in a public place without being muzzled. His appeal to the Crown Court was dismissed and he appealed to the Divisional Court, on the grounds that the dog in question was not a pit bull terrier.

Held

Section 1 of the Dangerous Dogs Act 1991 which prohibits, inter alia, allowing 'any dog of the type known as the pit bull terrier' to be in public without being muzzled and kept on a lead, does not just apply to the breed of dogs known as pit bull terriers, since the word 'type' is not synonymous with the word 'breed'. Section 1 applies to any dog having a substantial number, or most, of the physical characteristics of a pit bull terrier. Whether a dog is of that 'type' is a question of fact for the court to decide.

Smith v *Ainger* (1990) The Times 5 June Court of Appeal (Neill, Woolf and Butler-Sloss LJJ)

Aggressive dog – liability

Facts

The second defendant had Sam on a lead: Sam lunged at the plaintiff's dog: the second defendant fell: Sam knocked the plaintiff to the ground and he (the plaintiff) suffered a broken leg: it was an attack by dog on dog to which the plaintiff's accident was incidental.

Held

The plaintiff was entitled to damages by virtue of s2(2) of the Animals Act 1971. Neill LJ said that the kind of damage concerned was personal injury to a human being caused by the direct application of force, and if the personal injury was the result of an attack by a dog it was unrealistic to distinguish between a bite and the consequences of a buffet. On the facts (Sam had been reported twice for attacks on other dogs) both limbs of s2(2)(a) of the 1971 Act had been satisfied: *Cummings* v *Granger* [1976] 3 WLR 842 and *Curtis* v *Betts* [1990] 1 All ER 769 both indicated that damage caused by a large dog such as an alsation was likely to be 'severe'.

Wallace v *Newton* [1982] 1 WLR 375 High Court (Park J)

Animals – violent horse

Facts

The plaintiff was a groom employed by the defendant to care for several horses. One of the horses, named 'Lord Justice', was known to have a nervous and unpredictable temperament. One day while the plaintiff was attempting to load the horse into a horse box it became violent and uncontrollable and jumped forward, crushing the plaintiff's arm against the breast bar. The plaintiff sued the defendant for damages for breach of duty under (inter alia) s2(2) of the Animals Act 1971.

Held

The plaintiff was entitled to damages.

Park J:

'Under s2(2)(a) of the Animals Act 1971 the plaintiff has to establish first that the damage which she suffered was of a kind which Lord Justice was likely to cause, and on this part of the case there is no dispute. Under s2(2)(b) the plaintiff has to establish that the likelihood of the damage was due to characteristics of Lord Justice which were not normally found in horses. The question is whether the words "characteristics which are not normally found in horses" have to be interpreted as meaning that Lord Justice must be shown to have had a vicious tendency to injure people by attacking them or whether the words have to be given their ordinary natural meaning, that is that Lord Justice had characteristics of a kind not usually found in horses. If the plaintiff has to establish that her injuries were due to Lord Justice's vicious tendency to injure people, then her claim would fail. He was not, as the plaintiff herself agreed, a vicious horse or a dangerous horse in the way in which the defendant understood that word. On the other hand, if she has to establish that her injuries were due to a characteristic of Lord Justice which was unusual in a horse, then she would establish this limb of her case. I think this is the meaning to be given to the words in s2(2)(b).

On the evidence I am satisfied that, certainly during the period that the plaintiff had Lord Justice in her charge, the horse was unpredictable and unreliable in his behaviour, and in that way he was, as the plaintiff said, dangerous. The injury to her arm was due to this characteristic, which is not normally found in a horse. So, in my judgment, the plaintiff has established the second limb of her case.

Under s2(2)(c) the plaintiff has to prove that these characteristics were known to the defendant, as Lord Justice's keeper, or at any time known to a person who at that time had charge of Lord Justice as the defendant's servant. I have no doubt at all that Tom Read [the head man in charge of the defendant's horses] well knew about Lord Justice's unpredictability and unreliability and because of that knowledge he very properly warned the plaintiff about the horse. The defendant says that she knew nothing of the incident a week before the plaintiff's accident and of the consequent change of procedure. I am sure that her evidence is honest, but ... to me it is inconceivable that Tom Read did not tell her everything about Lord Justice and in particular about the incident which occurred a week before the accident. I think that the defendant at the material time knew as much about the horse as Tom Read.

For these reasons I am satisfied that the defendant is liable to the plaintiff under the provisions of s2(2) of the Act.'

21 Defamation

Alexander v *North Eastern Railway Co* (1865) 6 B & S 340 Court of Queen's Bench (Cockburn CJ, Blackburn, Mellor and Shee JJ)

Libel – justification

Facts
The defendant published a notice saying "Caution, JA was charged before the magistrates at Darlington for riding in a train from Leeds, for which his ticket was not available and refusing to pay the proper fare. He was convicted in the penalty of £9 1s 10d including costs or three weeks imprisonment." In fact, the plaintiff (JA) had been sentenced to 14 days imprisonment in default of payment of the fine and costs.

Held
The defence of justification would be successful. It is sufficient if the substance of the libellous statement is justified ... 'As much must be justified as meets the sting of the charge and if anything be contained in a charge which does not add to the sting of it, that need not be justified'.

Browne v *D C Thomson & Co Ltd* 1912 SC 359 Court of Session (Lord Dunedin, Lord Kinnear and Lord Mackenzie)

Libel – members of class

Facts
The defenders' newspaper published an article stating that in Queenstown the Roman Catholic authorities had instructed that all Protestant shop assistants should be dismissed. The seven persons who alone exercised religious authority on behalf of the Roman Catholic Church in Queenstown sued for libel.

Held
They were entitled to do so.

Lord Dunedin:

' ... if a certain set of people are accused of having done something, and if such accusation is libellous, it is possible for the individuals in that set of people to show that they have been damnified, and it is right that they should have the opportunity of recovering damages as individuals.'

Bryanston Finance Ltd v *de Vries* [1975] 2 WLR 718 Court of Appeal (Lord Denning MR, Lord Diplock and Lawton LJ)

Defamation – privilege

Facts

The defendant and C prepared circulars to be sent to the shareholders of B (a public company), accusing S, the chairman both of B and B's banking subsidiary, of defalcation. The circulars were dictated to shorthand typists, but they were sent only to S, in order to induce him to settle a separate action. B, the subsidiary and S sued the defendant and C for libel. C submitted to a consent judgment. At the trial, the judge rejected the defence of privilege and awarded the plaintiffs £500 damages against the defendant.

Held

Lord Denning MR:

'The actionable publication was on an occasion of qualified privilege, since it is in accord with the reasonable and usual course of business for a businessman to dictate letters to a typist; the former has an interest in dictating the letter, and the latter has a duty to take it down.'

Lawton LJ:

'The judge misdirected himself on qualified privilege. Publication to typists attracts privilege only if such privilege would have protected publication to the intended recipients. The publication to the shareholders of B would have been privileged, but not the publication to S, since it involved threats and was not fairly warranted. The damages were too high in any event.'

Lawton LJ:

'Nominal damages are appropriate where publication is only to clerks. Where one of two joint tortfeasors has consented to judgment, judgment cannot be given against the other, if the first judgment has been satisfied. The plaintiffs had not told the judge whether the judgment against C had been satisfied, and therefore judgment should not have been entered against the defendant.'

Byrne v *Deane* [1937] 1 KB 818 Court of Appeal (Greer, Slesser and Greene LJJ)

Libel – report to police

Facts

For many years gambling machines had been installed in the local golf club. Someone informed the police. The machines were removed and a notice appeared on the board, saying:

'He who gave the game away, may he byrnn in hell and rue the day.'

The plaintiff brought an action in libel, saying that the words implied he had reported the matter to the police and was guilty of underhand disloyalty to the defendant club proprietors and fellow members.

Held

The words were not defamatory as it is not defamatory to say of someone that he has reported a crime to the police.

Slesser LJ:

'We have to consider in this connection the arbitrium boni, the view which would be taken by the ordinary good and worthy subject of the King ... such a good and worthy subject would not consider such an allegation in itself to be defamatory.'

Cassidy v *Daily Mirror Newspapers Ltd* [1929] 2 KB 331 Court of Appeal (Scrutton, Greer and Russell LJJ)

Libel – defamatory meaning

Facts
The plaintiff was and was generally well known as the lawful wife of C, a race horse owner. They did not live together, but he occasionally stayed with her. P sued the defendants for libel for publishing a photograph of her husband in the 'Gossip' column. Under the photograph was the caption 'Mr C, the race horse owner, and Miss X, whose engagement has been announced'. P claimed she had suffered damage in that people would believe she was not C's wife, but was living with him in immoral cohabitation.

Held (Greer LJ dissenting)
The words involved were capable of the defamatory meaning alleged by P, especially to people who knew P. It was for the jury to decide whether the inference alleged could be reasonably inferred, and they had so decided, so P was entitled to recover.

Commentary
See now s4 of the Defamation Act 1952.

Charlton v *EMAP plc* (1993) The Times 11 June High Court (Judge Previté QC)

Statement of reasons for payment into court

Facts
The plaintiff sued the defendants, who published a newspaper, claiming that seven articles in the newspaper were libellous. The defendants made a series of payments into court, and when this total reached £75,000 the plaintiff accepted the payment in. The defendants wished to make a statement in open court in terms approved by the judge, stating that the payment into court was made without admission of liability and also that it was made for commercial reasons. The plaintiff objected to the latter part of the proposed statement.

Held
The defendants in a libel action were not entitled to say in such a statement that a substantial payment into court was made for commercial reasons. Such an explanation detracted from the value of money paid in as being in itself a vindication.

Taking all the circumstances of the case into account, the plaintiff was entitled to a statement which wholly vindicated and exonerated her in respect of the allegations made in the articles.

Church of Scientology of California v *Johnson-Smith* [1971] 3 WLR 434 High Court (Browne J)

Libel – privilege

Facts
The defendant, a member of Parliament, gave an interview to the press during which he made remarks which the plaintiffs alleged were defamatory of them. D pleaded fair comment and privilege. In order to defeat the defence, P sought to prove malice and to that end sought to cite Hansard as evidence.

Held

Although the comments were made outside Parliament and therefore outside the protection of Parliamentary privilege, evidence which was absolutely privileged could not be adduced as it was not open to either party to go directly or indirectly into anything said or done in Parliament. Therefore, without more, the allegation of malice failed.

Derbyshire County Council v *Times Newspapers Ltd* [1993] 2 WLR 449 House of Lords (Lord Keith of Kinkel, Lord Griffiths, Lord Goff of Chieveley, Lord Browne-Wilkinson and Lord Woolf)

Local authorities – actions for libel

Facts

The Sunday Times, one of the defendants' newspapers, published articles questioning the propriety of certain investments involving the plaintiffs' superannuation fund. The preliminary point arose as to whether the plaintiff council could maintain an action for libel for any words which reflected upon it as the county council for Derbyshire in relation to its governmental and administrative functions in Derbyshire, including its statutory responsibility for the investment and control of the superannuation fund.

Held

A local authority cannot maintain an action for defamation in respect of its governing reputation.

Lord Keith of Kinkel:

'The authorities ... clearly establish that a trading corporation is entitled to sue in respect of defamatory matters which can be seen as having a tendency to damage it in the way of its business. Examples are those that go to credit such as might deter banks from lending to it, or to the conditions experienced by its employees, which might impede the recruitment of the best qualified workers, or make people reluctant to deal with it. The *South Hetton Coal Co* case would appear to be an instance of the latter kind, and not ... an authority for the view that a trading corporation can sue for something that does not affect it adversely in the way of its business ... Similar considerations can no doubt be advanced in connection with the position of a local authority. Defamatory statements might make it more difficult to borrow or to attract suitable staff and thus affect adversely the efficient carrying out of its functions.

There are, however, features of a local authority which may be regarded as distinguishing it from other types of corporation, whether trading or non-trading. The most important of these features is that it is a governmental body. Further, it is a democratically elected body, the electoral process nowadays being conducted almost exclusively on party political lines. It is of the highest public importance that a democratically elected governmental body, or indeed any governmental body, should be open to uninhibited public criticism. The threat of a civil action for defamation must inevitably have an inhibiting effect on freedom of speech ...

It is of some significance to observe that a number of departments of central government in the United Kingdom are statutorily created corporations, including the Secretaries of State for Defence, Education and Science, Energy, Environment and Social Services. If a local authority can sue for libel there would appear to be no reason in logic for holding that any of these departments (apart from two which are made corporations only for the purposes of holding land) were not also entitled to sue. But as is shown by the decision in *A-G* v *Guardian Newspapers Ltd (No 2)* [1988] 2 WLR 805, a case concerned with confidentiality, there are rights available to private citizens which institutions of central government are not in a position to exercise unless they can show that it is [in] the public interest to do so. The same applies, in my opinion, to local authorities. In both cases I regard it as right for this House to lay down that not only is there no public interest favouring the right of organs of government, whether central or local, to sue for libel, but that it is contrary to the public interest that they should have it. It is contrary to the public interest because to admit such actions would place an undesirable fetter on freedom of speech ...

In the case of a local authority temporarily under the control of one political party or another it is difficult to say that the local authority as such has any reputation of its own. Reputation in the eyes of the public is more likely to attach itself to the controlling political party, and with a change in that party the reputation itself will change. A publication attacking the activities of the authority will necessarily be an attack on the body of councillors which represents the controlling party, or on the executives who carry on the day-to-day management of its affairs. If the individual reputation of any of these is wrongly impaired by the publication any of these can himself bring proceedings for defamation. Further, it is open to the controlling body to defend itself by public utterances and in debate in the council chamber.

The conclusion must be, in my opinion, that under the common law of England a local authority does not have the right to maintain an action of damages for defamation. That was the conclusion reached by the Court of Appeal, which did so principally by reference to art 10 of the European Convention on Human Rights ... , to which the United Kingdom has adhered but which has not been enacted into domestic law.

My Lords, I have reached my conclusion upon the common law of England without finding any need to rely upon the European convention. Lord Goff of Chieveley in *A-G v Guardian Newspapers Ltd (No 2)* expressed the opinion that in the field of freedom of speech there was no difference in principle between English law on the subject and art 10 of the convention. I agree, and can only add that I find it satisfactory to be able to conclude that the common law of England is consistent with the obligations assumed by the Crown under the treaty in this particular field ... It follows that *Bognor Regis UDC v Campion* [1972] 2 WLR 983 was wrongly decided and should be overruled.'

Hayward v Thompson [1981] 3 WLR 470 Court of Appeal (Lord Denning MR, Sir George Baker and Sir Stanley Rees)

Libel – murder plot

Facts
The plaintiff was a well-known supporter of the Liberal Party and contributor to charity. On 9 April 1978 an article appeared in a national newspaper stating that the names of two more people 'connected with' an alleged murder plot had been given to the police, one of them 'a wealthy benefactor of the Liberal Party'. That article did not name the plaintiff but the newspaper published a second article which did name the plaintiff and connected him with the investigations. The plaintiff brought a libel action against the newspaper. He contended that the words in the article were meant and understood to mean that the plaintiff was guilty of, or suspected of being involved in, the murder plot and that the subsequent article identified the plaintiff as being the person referred to in the first article. At trial, the judge directed that the words complained of in the articles were capable of being defamatory, and the jury could properly read the two articles together and properly come to the conclusion that the second article identified the plaintiff as the person referred to in the first article, and if they found in favour of the plaintiff, they could make one award of damages in respect of both articles. The jury found in favour of the plaintiff and awarded £50,000. The defendant appealed.

Held
The appeal would be dismissed. The words used in the first article were clearly capable of being defamatory of the plaintiff and the judge had properly left it to the jury to say whether they were.

Lord Denning MR:

'One thing is of the essence in the law of libel. It is that the words should be defamatory and untrue and should be published "of and concerning the plaintiff". That is, the plaintiff should be aimed at or intended by the defendant. If the defendant intended to refer to the plaintiff, he cannot escape liability simply by not giving his name. He may use asterisks or blanks. He may use initials or words with a hidden meaning. He may use any other device. But still, if he intended to refer to the plaintiff, he is liable. He is to be given credit for hitting the person whom he intended to hit. The law goes further. Even if he did not aim at the plaintiff or intend to refer to him, nevertheless if he names the plaintiff in such a way that other persons will read it as intended to refer to the plaintiff, then the defendant is liable.'

Commentary
Applied: *Hulton (E) & Co* v *Jones* [1910] AC 20.

Horrocks v *Lowe* [1974] 2 WLR 282 House of Lords (Lord Wilberforce, Lord Hodson, Viscount Dilhorne, Lord Diplock and Lord Kilbrandon)

Defamation – malice

Facts
The plaintiff, a conservative councillor, claimed he was slandered at a meeting by the defendant, a labour councillor. The trial judge found the occasion privileged, but that the defendant acted with express malice. The Court of Appeal allowed the defendant's appeal.

Held
The appeal would be dismissed. The occasion had been privileged and there was not sufficient evidence on which to find malice.

Lord Diplock:

'So, the motive with which the defendant on a privileged occasion made a statement defamatory of the plaintiff becomes crucial. The protection might, however, be illusory if the onus lay on him to prove that he was actuated solely by a sense of the relevant duty or a desire to protect the relevant interest. So he is entitled to be protected by the privilege unless some other dominant and improper motive on his part is proved. "Express malice" is the term of art descriptive of such a motive. Broadly speaking, it means malice in the popular sense of a desire to injure the person who is defamed and this is generally the motive which the plaintiff sets out to prove. But to destroy the privilege the desire to injure must be the dominant motive for the defamatory publication; knowledge that it will have that effect is not enough if the defendant is nevertheless acting in accordance with a sense of duty or in bona fide protection of his own legitimate interests.'

Hulton (E) & Co v *Jones* [1910] AC 20 House of Lords (Lord Loreburn LC, Lord Atkinson, Lord Gorell and Lord Shaw)

Libel – defendant unaware of plaintiff's existence

Facts
The plaintiff, Thomas Artemus Jones, barrister, brought an action for libel against a newspaper, the Sunday Chronicle, which published an article saying of a Dieppe Motor Show ... 'Whilst ... there is Artemus Jones with a woman who is not his wife ...' The editor of the paper said he knew nothing of the plaintiff and that he did not intend to refer to him.

Held
The article designated the plaintiff in such a way as to let those who knew him understand that he was the person meant. Accordingly, he was entitled to succeed.

Lord Shaw:

> 'With regard to this whole matter I should put my propositions in a threefold form ... In the publication of matter of a libellous character – that is, matter which would be libellous if applying to an actual person – the responsibility is as follows. In the first place, there is responsibility for the words used being taken to signify that which readers would reasonably understand by them; in the second place, there is responsibility also for the names used being taken to signify those whom the readers would reasonably understand by those names; and, in the third place, the same principle is applicable to persons unnamed, but sufficiently indicated by designation or description.'

Commentary
Applied in *Haywood* v *Thompson* [1981] 3 WLR 470.

John v *Mirror Group Newspapers Ltd* [1995] NLJ 13 December Court of Appeal (Sir Thomas Bingham MR, Neill and Hirst LJJ)

Defamation – damages

Facts
The plaintiff brought an action against the defendants, publishers of the *Sunday Mirror* newspaper, alleging defamation. The jury awarded damages of £350,000, comprising £75,000 compensatory damages and £275,000 exemplary damages. The defendants appealed against, inter alia, the amount of damages.

Held
The Court of Appeal stated that it was rightly offensive to public opinion that a plaintiff should recover damages for injury to his reputation which were greater, perhaps by a significant factor, than the sum he might have been awarded for personal injuries, rendering him helplessly crippled or insensate.

The court held that some guidance should be provided for juries in assessing compensatory damages and that:

1. No reference should be made to previous jury defamation awards.
2. Awards approved or substituted by the Court of Appeal should be referred to, although it would take time for a framework of such awards to be established.
3. Juries could be referred to damages in personal injury actions. This was not intended to promote equality of damages in defamation and personal injuries, but to point out to the jury when considering a serious libel that the maximum conventional award for pain, suffering and loss of amenity for severe brain damage was around £125,000, which the jury might wish to take into account.
4. Reference to an appropriate award. It was the invariable practice that neither counsel nor the judge could suggest any award to the jury. However, in personal injury actions both sides may address the judge on quantum, and the Court of Appeal thought that in defamation actions both counsel and the judge should indicate to the jury an award which they considered appropriate.

As regards exemplary damages, such an award should never exceed the minimum sum necessary to meet its underlying public purpose, namely that the defendant should be punished, that the tort should be shown not to pay and that others should be deterred from acting similarly. The court also held that the jury should be told before awarding such damages that they had to be satisfied that the publisher had no genuine belief in the truth of the material published.

Kemsley v *Foot* [1952] AC 345 House of Lords (Lord Porter, Lord Goddard, Lord Oaksey, Lord Radcliffe and Lord Tucker)

Defamation – fair comment

Facts

Under the title 'Lower than Kemsley', *Tribune* published an article by Michael Foot which, without making any other direct reference to Lord Kemsley, suggested that he was a newspaper proprietor who prostituted his position by conducting his newspapers or permitting them to be conducted in an undesirable manner.

Held

The defence of fair comment was available as the article contained sufficient facts to form the basis of comment.

Lord Porter:

'The question, therefore, in all cases is whether there is a sufficient substratum of fact stated or indicated in the words which are the subject-matter of the action ... I am of the opinion that in this case a sufficient substratum of fact is to be found in the words complained of.'

Kerr v *Kennedy* [1942] 1 KB 409 High Court (Asquith J)

Slander – lesbianism alleged

Facts

The defendant said to another that the plaintiff 'used to live with other women – she is a lesbian'.

Held

The imputation of lesbianism is an imputation of unchastity within the meaning of the Slander of Women Act 1891 and it followed that it was not necessary for the plaintiff to prove actual pecuniary damage.

Knupffer v *London Express Newspapers Ltd* [1944] AC 116 House of Lords (Viscount Simon LC, Lord Atkin, Lord Thankerton, Lord Russell of Killowen and Lord Porter)

Libel – words referring to class

Facts

The respondents newspaper published an article referring to an association of political refugees which, it was admitted, would have been defamatory if it had been written about a named individual. The appellant was the head of the United Kingdom branch of the association which consisted of some 24 members.

Held

The appellant was not entitled to damages as the words were written of a class and he had failed to show that they were pointed at him as an individual.

Lewis v *Daily Telegraph Ltd* [1963] 2 WLR 1063 House of Lords (Lord Reid, Lord Jenkins, Lord Morris of Borth-y-Gest, Lord Hodson and Lord Devlin)

Libel – innuendo

Facts

The Daily Telegraph published a report headed 'Inquiry on firm by City Police', the gist being that the City Fraud Squad was inquiring into the firm's affairs and identified the firm and the plaintiff, its chairman. The defendants admitted that the words in their ordinary meaning were capable of being libellous, but contended that they were simply reporting there was a police inquiry on foot. P contended the words meant he was a fraud, and the jury awarded him damages.

Held

There should be a new trial.

Lord Reid:

'In this case it is, I think, sufficient to put the test in this way. Ordinary men and women have different temperaments and outlooks. Some are unusually suspicious and some are unusually naive. One must try to envisage people between these two extremes and see what is the most damaging meaning that they would put on the words in question. So let me suppose a number of ordinary people discussing one of these paragraphs which they had read in the newspaper. No doubt one of them might say – "Oh, if the fraud squad are after these people you can take it they are guilty". But I would expect the others to turn on him, if he did say that, with such remarks as – "Be fair. This is not a police state. No doubt their affairs are in a mess or the police would not be interested. But that could be because Lewis or the cashier has been very stupid or careless. We really must not jump to conclusions. The police are fair and know their job and we shall know soon enough if there is anything in it. Wait till we see if they charge him. I wouldn't trust him until this is cleared up, but it is another thing to condemn him unheard."

What the ordinary man, not avid for scandal, would read into the words complained of must be a matter of impression. I can only say that I do not think that he would infer guilt of fraud merely because an inquiry is on foot. And if that is so then it is the duty of the trial judge to direct the jury that it is for them to determine the meaning of the paragraph but that they must not hold it to impute guilt of fraud because as a matter of law the paragraph is not capable of having that meaning. So there was here, in my opinion, misdirection of the two juries sufficiently serious to require that there must be new trials.'

London Artists Ltd v *Littler* [1969] 2 WLR 409 Court of Appeal (Lord Denning MR, Edmund-Davies and Widgery LJJ)

Defamation – fair comment

Facts

Four actors terminated their contracts in a play. The impresario, L, was convinced there was a plot to stop the play. He wrote to each artiste and the press in which he said that each of the four had taken part in a plot to end a successful play. In an action for libel, L pleaded inter alia, fair comment on a matter of public interest, ie the fate of the play.

Held

The allegation that there was a plot was a statement of fact not of opinion and the defendant could therefore not avail himself of the defence of fair comment.

Lucas-Box v *News Group Newspapers Ltd* [1986] 1 WLR 147 Court of Appeal (Ackner, Mustill and Nourse LJJ)

Libel – justification

Facts

The defendants were newspaper proprietors and the publishers of two articles which claimed that the plaintiff had assisted and cohabited with Italian terrorists in particular Petrone, who was wanted by Italian police for robbery and murder. They issued defences to the statements of claim which denied that the words referred to the plaintiff or that they were defamatory. Two years later the defendants wished to amend their defence by pleading justification. They were given leave to do so. However, they did not plead the defamatory meanings in relation to which their defence of justification was directed.

Held

A defendant who is relying on a plea of justification must make it clear to the plaintiff what is the case which he is seeking to set up. This may be clear from the particulars but if the particulars are ambiguous then the situation must be made unequivocal.

Ackner LJ:

'It would be odd to say the least if the current practice, which obliges the plaintiff to plead the nature and ordinary meaning of the words complained of, where that meaning is not clear and explicit, should treat as frivolous or vexatious or likely to embarrass or delay the trial of the action a similar such helpful definition by the defendant.'

Commentary

Applied in *Morrell* v *International Thomson Publishing Ltd* [1989] 3 All ER 733 and *Control Risks Ltd* v *New English Library Ltd* [1990] 1 WLR 183 (defence of fair comment).

Lyon v *Daily Telegraph Ltd* [1943] KB 746 Court of Appeal (Scott, MacKinnon and Goddard LJJ)

Libel – fair comment

Facts

The Daily Telegraph, which was owned by the defendants, published a letter which was highly critical of a radio entertainment called 'Hi Gang' in which the plaintiffs were the principal artistes. The letter bore the address of a vicarage and was signed "A Winslow". The address was a false one and there was no clergyman of that name. In an action for libel the defendants pleaded fair comment.

Held

This defence would be upheld and the fact that the name and address of the correspondent were fictitious was not evidence of malice on the part of the defendants.

Scott LJ:

'It seems to me contrary to common sense to say that the annoymous writer (who may have been absolutely single-minded in his comment) must in law be regarded for the purpose of that contention as if he had been co-defendant and his oblique motive had been exposed in the trial, with the consequence that the newspaper must lose the protection of the defence.'

Metropolitan Saloon Omnibus Co v Hawkins (1859) 4 H & N 87 Court of Exchequer (Pollock CB, Martin and Watson BB)

Libel of company by shareholder

Facts

The defendant shareholder libelled the plaintiff company by imputing insolvency, amongst other things.

Held

The action could be maintained and it was no answer for the defendant to say that he was a shareholder.

Commentary

See also *Derbyshire County Council v Times Newspapers Ltd* [1993] 2 WLR 445.

Monson v Madame Tussaud Ltd [1894] 1 QB 671 Court of Appeal (Lord Halsbury LC, Lopes and Davey LJJ)

Libel – Whether a wax effigy could constitute a statement

Facts

The plaintiff had been tried in Scotland for the murder of H. His defence that the gun had gone off accidentally led to a jury verdict of 'not proven'. Shortly after, P's wax figure was put on display by defendants, in the room containing Napoleon I, a convicted murderer, a suicide and another person who had been charged along with P. The room gave access to the 'Chamber of Horrors'. P applied for an interim injunction to restrain the public display of the wax figure until the trial of a libel action.

Held

Although an interlocutory injunction ought not to be granted, this was a matter capable of being the subject of a libel action.

Lopes LJ:

> 'Libels are generally in writing or printing, but this is not necessary; the defamatory matter may be conveyed in some other permanent form, eg a statue, a caricature, an effigy, chalk marks on a wall, signs, or pictures may constitute a libel ...'

Morgan v Odhams Press Ltd [1971] 1 WLR 1239 House of Lords (Lord Reid, Lord Morris of Borth-y-Gest, Lord Guest, Lord Donovan and Lord Pearson)

Libel – reference to the plaintiff

Facts

The plaintiff complained he was libelled by an article in *The Sun* which said: 'A girl who is likely to be a key witness in a dog doping scandal went into hiding yesterday after threats were made on her life ... Miss M ... was kidnapped last week by members of the gang when they heard she had made a statement to the police. She was kept at a house in Finchley, but was eventually allowed to leave'. Only Miss M's name was used in the article. P, in whose flat Miss M had stayed a week before the article was published, relied on extrinsic evidence which he said would entitle an ordinary reader to understand the article referred to him. Six witnesses gave evidence to this effect.

Held (Lord Guest and Lord Donovan dissenting)

The judge was right to leave the question to the jury whether readers having knowledge of the circumstances would reasonably have understood that the article referred to P. The jury had so decided, but a new trial was ordered as to quantum of damages.

Rantzen v *Mirror Group Newspapers* [1993] 3 WLR 953 Court of Appeal (Neill, Roch and Staughton LJJ)

Libel – damages – excessive award – court's power to order a new trial or substitute another award – guidelines

Facts

The plaintiff was a well-known television presenter and the founder and chairperson of the 'Childline' charity for sexually abused children. She sued the defendants in libel in respect of four articles in *The People* newspaper which she claimed bore the meaning that her activities on behalf of sexually abused children were insincere and hypocritical as she had protected a known abuser of children. The defendants pleaded justification and fair comment, but the jury found for the plaintiff and awarded her £250,000 damages. The defendants appealed, seeking a reduction in damages under s8 of the Courts and Legal Services Act 1990 and article 10 of the European Convention on Human Rights.

Held

Allowing the appeal, that the court's power under s8 of the 1990 Act to order a new trial or to substitute another award in any case where the damages awarded by a jury were 'excessive' should be construed in a manner which was not inconsistent with article 10 of the European Convention. An almost unlimited discretion in a jury to award damages for defamation was not a necessary restriction in a democratic society on the exercise of the right to freedom of expression under article 10 to protect the reputation of others; the common law therefore required that large awards of damages by a jury should be more closely scrutinised by the Court of Appeal than hitherto. In all the circumstances the award should be reduced to £110,000.

The Court went on to hold that, while at the present time it would not be right to allow juries to be referred to awards made by juries in previous cases, awards substituted by the Court of Appeal under s8 of the 1990 Act were different and could be relied on as establishing a norm. Juries should also be invited to consider the purchasing power of any award they make, and to ensure that it is proportionate to the damage which the plaintiff has suffered and necessary to provide adequate compensation and to re-establish his or her reputation.

Sim v *Stretch* [1936] 2 All ER 1237 House of Lords (Lord Atkin, Lord Russell of Killowen and Lord Macmillan)

Libel – defamatory meaning

Facts

The defendant sent the plaintiff a telegram concerning a housemaid who had left P's employment to work for D. It read:

'Edith has resumed her service with us today. Please send her possessions and the money you borrowed, also her wages to Old Barton – Sim.'

P claimed these words were defamatory and that D intended them to mean P was in financial difficulty, had to borrow money from his housemaid, failed to pay her wages and that he was not someone to whom credit should be given.

Held

The words, in their ordinary signification, were not capable of defamatory meaning and, therefore, no libel was committed.

Lord Atkin:

> 'I propose in the present case the test: would the words tend to lower P in the estimation of right-thinking members of society generally?'

Slim v Daily Telegraph Ltd [1968] 2 WLR 599 Court of Appeal (Lord Denning MR, Diplock and Salmon LJJ)

Libel – innuendo – fair comment

Facts

The defendants published a letter from one of their readers which contained a statement which might have been capable of imputing dishonesty and insincerity to the plaintiffs. The defendants pleaded fair comment.

Held

Allowing the defendants' appeal from a judgment awarding damages to the plaintiffs, the defence was entitled to succeed. If a person expresses an honest opinion about a matter of public interest, then, even though the words used might convey derogatory imputations, in the absence of malice no action for defamation will lie.

Lord Denning MR:

> 'These comments are capable of various meanings. They may strike some readers in one way and others in another way. One person may read into them imputations of dishonesty, insincerity and hypocrisy (as the judge did). Another person may only read into them imputations of inconsistency and want of candour (as I would). In considering a plea of fair comment, it is not correct to canvass all the various imputations which different readers may put on the words. The important things is to determine whether or not the writer was actuated by malice. If he was an honest man expressing his genuine opinion on a subject of public interest, then no matter that his words conveyed derogatory imputations: no matter that his opinion was wrong or exaggerated or prejudiced; and no matter that it was badly expressed so that other people read all sorts of innuendoes into it; nevertheless, he has a good defence of fair comment. His honesty is the cardinal test. He must honestly express his real view. So long as he does this, he has nothing to fear, even though other people may read more into it ... I stress this because the right of fair comment is one of the essential elements which go to make up our freedom of speech. We must ever maintain this right intact. It must not be whittled down by legal refinements. When a citizen is troubled by things going wrong, he should be free to "write to the newspaper": and the newspaper should be free to publish his letter. It is often the only way to get things put right. The matter must, of course, be one of public interest. The writer must get his facts right: and he must honestly state his real opinion. But that being done, both he and the newspaper should be clear of any liability. They should not be deterred by fear of libel actions.'

Slipper v *British Broadcasting Corp* [1990] 3 WLR 967 Court of Appeal (Slade, Stocker and Bingham LJJ)

Press reviews – relevance to assessment of general damages

Facts

The defendants made a film about the plaintiff police officer's unsuccessful attempt to bring back from Brazil one of 'The Great Train Robbers'. They showed the film at a press preview and a week later broadcast it to the public at large: after the transmission reviews appeared in the national press allegedly repeating the sting of the alleged libel of the plaintiff contained in the film. The defendants sought to have struck out the claim based on the repetition of the libel in the reviews.

Held

Their application had correctly been dismissed.

Stocker LJ:

'The conclusion I draw from *Weld-Blundell* v *Stephens* [1920] AC 956 is that it was concerned with the question whether or not on the facts the acts of the manager, Hurst, broke the chain of causation and was a novus actus which rendered Stephens no longer liable for the publication of the libel to the officers. It was not concerned with any other issue and in particular was not concerned to establish *Ward* v *Weeks* (1830) 7 Bing 211 as a principle of law in defamation actions ... In my view this case [*Weld-Blundell*] does not establish the law relating to republication of libel. Further, in my view, the law relating to republication in defamation cases is but an example of the rules of novus actus in all cases of tort or, where applicable, breaches of contract where that issue arises. In a defamation case where there has been republication the question whether or not there has been a breach in the chain of causation inevitably arises but such cases are not in a special category related to defamation actions but are examples of the problem and will fall to be decided on general principles and in the light of their own facts as established. ... In this case, therefore, the questions raised on this appeal are, in my opinion: (i) did the reviews reproduce the sting of the libel? This is a question of fact for the jury. (ii) Did the defendants invite such reviews? The answer to this question depends on the facts concerning all the circumstances in which the preview was given to the press and, again, is a matter of fact for the jury. (iii) Did the defendants anticipate that such reviews would repeat the sting of the libel? It is at this point that the issue of natural and probable consequence or foreseeability arises. In my opinion this is a question of remoteness of damage and not liability and raises an issue of fact for the jury. I have no doubt at all that, to put it no higher, it could not be said that this was a "plain and obvious case" so as to justify striking out. I would go further and say that the matter cannot be resolved without the findings of fact by the jury to which I have referred. This includes the question of whether or not it was foreseeable or a natural and probable consequence of the invitation to review that such reviews would include the sting of the libel.'

South Hetton Coal Co Ltd v *North-Eastern News Association Ltd* [1894] 1 QB 133 Court of Appeal (Lord Esher MR, Lopes and Kay LJJ)

Defamation – fair comment

Facts

The plaintiffs owned a number of cottages in connection with their collieries and it was found that the defendants had published a libel in their newspaper by suggesting that most of the cottages were in a highly insanitary state.

Held

The plaintiffs were entitled to damages.

Lord Esher MR:

'In my opinion, the statements complained of, if not fair coment upon a matter of public interest, were such as to entitle the jury to find that they were defamatory of the plaintiffs.

   Then comes the question whether this is a matter of public interest. The Lord Chief Justice held that it was a matter of public interest, and I agree with him. The matter regarded so many people, and people of such a class, and the matter itself was so important, as, in my opinion, to make it matter of public interest that the conduct of the colliery proprietors should be criticised. Yet, if the matter is one of public interest, the person who criticises must do so with moderation, and if it is shown that the criticism was malicious, or so unfair as to be exaggerated, then such criticism is not fair comment upon a matter of public interest, but is a libel for which damages can be recovered. If, however, it is a fair comment upon a matter of public interest, then it is not a libel at all, and the defendant is entitled to a verdict. If the matter complained of is fair comment upon a matter of public interest, that takes it out of the category of libels. Then comes the question whether there was in this case a sufficient exaggeration of description to entitle the jury to say that the matter published went beyond a fair comment upon a matter of public interest. I am not prepared to say whether, if I had been on the jury, I would not have found that this was within the bounds of fair comment. I am inclined to think that it was, but I cannot say that the jury were not entitled to take a different view, and to say that so exaggerated and florid a description went beyond the limit, and was unfair, and that damages ought to be awarded. I think that we cannot interfere with the verdict of the jury, and that this appeal must be dismissed.'

Commentary

Distinguished in *Derbyshire County Council* v *Times Newspapers Ltd* [1992] 2 WLR 449.

Stuart v *Bell* [1891] 2 QB 341 Court of Appeal (Lindley, Kay and Lopes LJJ)

Defamation – qualified privilege

Facts

Stanley, the explorer, was the guest of the defendant, the Major of Newcastle. The latter received information tending to suggest that the plaintiff (Stanley's valet) was a thief. The defendant passed this information to Stanley and Stanley then dismissed the plaintiff.

Held (Lopes LJ dissenting)

In the absence of malice, the defendant's plea of qualified privilege should succeed.

Lindley LJ:

'The question of moral or social duty being for the judge, each judge must decide it as best he can for himself. I take moral or social duty to mean a duty recognised by English people of ordinary intelligence and moral principle, but at the same time not a duty enforceable by legal proceedings whether civil or criminal. My own conviction is that all, or at all events, the great mass of right-minded men in the position of the defendant would have considered it their duty, under the circumstances, to inform Stanley of the suspicion which had fallen on the plaintiff.'

Sun Life Assurance Co of Canada v *W H Smith & Son Ltd* (1933) 150 LT 211 Court of Appeal (Scrutton, Lawrence and Greer LJJ)

Libel – dissemination

Facts

The defendants, who were newsagents, displayed a poster which contained a libel of the plaintiffs. The poster had been supplied to the defendants by a third party and they did not know that its contents were defamatory.

Held

The plaintiffs were entitled to judgment. In such a case, the jury should be asked: (i) did the defendant know, or (ii) ought he to have known, ie if he carried on his business carefully, that the publication was one which was likely to contain a libel?

Telnikoff **v** *Matusevitch* [1991] 3 WLR 952 House of Lords (Lord Keith of Kinkel, Lord Brandon of Oakbrook, Lord Templeman, Lord Ackner and Lord Oliver of Aylmerton)

Libel – fair comment

Facts

A newspaper published an article written by the plaintiff: the defendant had been incensed by it and he wrote a letter which the newspaper published. The plaintiff had taken exception to the letter and issued a writ for libel. The defendant pleaded fair comment on a matter of public interest (the Russian service of the BBC) and, in reply, the plaintiff alleged that the defendant had been actuated by express malice. The judge (Drake J) upheld the defendant's submission that there was no case to go to the jury.

Held (Lord Ackner dissenting)

The letter should be considered on its own and, since a reasonable jury could properly find that it contained statements of fact, the question whether they constituted pure comment or contained defamatory statements of fact should have been left to the jury. However, on the facts (Lord Ackner concurring) there was no evidence of express malice fit to go to the jury and the judge had been right to withdraw that issue from them.

Lord Keith of Kinkel:

'The first matter considered by Drake J and the Court of Appeal was whether those parts of the defendant's letter which were defamatory in character ... were capable of being regarded as statements of fact or could only properly be held to be comment. Since justification was not pleaded the plaintiff would necessarily succeed if the jury, the issue being left to them, were to decide that these paragraphs contained statements of fact. Drake J said that on a consideration of the letter as a whole he had no doubt that these paragraphs constituted comment. If he had felt any doubt about the matter he would presumably have left it to the jury to decide ... I am of the opinion, in common I understand with the majority of your Lordships, that if the letter alone is looked at it would be open to a reasonable jury properly to find that the offending paragraphs contained statements of fact ...

The question then arises whether it is permissible to have regard to the whole terms of the plaintiff's article, not only the sentence from it quoted in the letter, in determining whether ... the letter [contains] statements of fact or ... pure comment. In my opinion the letter must be considered on its own. The readers of the letter must have included a substantial number of persons who had not read the article or who, if they had read it, did not have its terms fully in mind. If to such persons the letter appeared ... to contain statements of fact about what the plaintiff had written in his article, which as I have already indicated might well be the case, then in the eyes of those persons the plaintiff would clearly be defamed. The matter cannot turn on the likelihood or otherwise of readers of the letter having read the article. In some cases many readers of a criticism of some subject matter may be familiar with that subject matter but in other cases very few may be, for example where that subject matter is a speech delivered to a limited audience. The principle must be the same in either case.

Lloyd LJ, in the course of his judgment in the Court of Appeal, was troubled by what he regarded as the anomaly that the jury should not be allowed to consider the terms of the article in deciding whether or not the letter contained only comment, but should be allowed to look at the article, if they decided that question affirmatively, for the purpose of deciding whether or not the comment was fair. For my part, I can see nothing undesirable about that situation. The jury would simply be directed, in deciding the first question, to consider the effect of the letter on the mind of a person who had not read the article …

There can be no doubt that where the words complained of are clearly to be recognised as comment, and the subject matter commented on is identified, then that subject matter must be looked at to determine whether the comment is fair …

I conclude that Drake J was wrong in failing to leave to the jury the question whether … the defendant's letter contained statements of fact.

Drake J also refused to leave to the jury the question whether, assuming that [the offending paragraphs] were pure comment, they constituted fair comment on a matter of public interest, and the Court of Appeal upheld his decision on this matter also. Both took the view that on an application of the normal objective test of fair comment any reasonable jury would be bound to hold that it was satisfied. Lloyd LJ correctly stated the test as being whether any man, however prejudiced and obstinate, could honestly hold the view expressed by the defendant in his letter (see [1991] 1 QB 102 at 112-113). I agree with Drake J and the Court of Appeal as to the only reasonable outcome of a proper application of that test, and find it unnecessary to elaborate the matter. It was, however, argued by counsel for the plaintiff before the Court of Appeal and in your Lordships' House that in addition to satisfying the objective test a defendant pleading fair comment must prove affirmatively that the comment represented his own honest opinion, which the present defendant failed to do, since the case was withdrawn from the jury before any evidence had been given by him. Lloyd LJ, after an extensive review of the authorities, concluded that this argument was unsound (see [1991] 1 QB 102 at 114-119) … I find myself in respectful agreement with him and feel that to repeat his review would be a work of supererogation. The law is correctly stated in *Gatley on Libel and Slander* (8th edn, 1981) p348, para 792 as follows:

> "*Onus of proof of malice: fair comment.* In the same way, the defendant who relies on a plea of fair comment does not have to show that the comment is an honest expression of his views. 'In alleging any unfairness the plaintiff takes on him or herself the onus, also taken by an allegation of malice, to prove that the criticism is unfair either from the language used or from some extraneous circumstance.'"

Finally, it was argued for the plaintiff that Drake J was wrong to decide that there was no evidence of express malice fit to go before the jury, and that the Court of Appeal was wrong in upholding that decision. I am satisfied that the decision was correct, and find it unnecessary to go into any detail upon this matter.'

Theaker v *Richardson* [1962] 1 WLR 151 Court of Appeal (Ormerod, Harman and Pearson LJJ)

Libel – letter opened by plaintiff's husband

Facts
The defendant wrote a defamatory letter to plaintiff, a married woman and a fellow-member of the council. The letter was placed in a sealed manila envelope which was addressed to P. P's husband, seeing the letter on the mat, thought it was an election address and opened it.

Held (Ormerod LJ dissenting)
It had been right for the jury to be left with the question 'was P's husband acting reasonably when opening the letter?' and, in the light of the finding that he was, there was a publication.

Pearson LJ:

> 'The plaintiff's husband acting carelessly and thoughtlessly, but meaning no harm, picked up, opened and read the letter ... was his conduct unreasonable or unnatural ... or was it to be expected in the ordinary course of events? This is a question of fact which, in a trial with a jury, can and should be left to the jury.'

Tolley v *J S Fry and Sons Ltd* [1931] AC 333 House of Lords (Lord Hailsham, Lord Dunedin, Lord Buckmaster, Lord Blanesburgh and Lord Tomlin)

Libel – defamatory meaning

Facts
The plaintiff was a well-known amateur golfer, the defendants manufacturers of chocolate. In June 1928, D published in the *Daily Sketch* and *Daily Mail* a caricature of P which showed him in golfing gear having just completed a drive with a packet of Ds' chocolate protruding from his pocket. His caddie, too, held a packet of Ds' chocolate and below there was a limerick:

> 'My word how it flies ... Like a Frys ... etc.'

P alleged there was a defamatory innuendo that P had agreed to pose for an advertisement for reward, that he had prostituted his reputation as an amateur golfer and was guilty of conduct unworthy of amateur status.

Held (Lord Blanesburgh dissenting)
Although the words were not libellous, the imputation from them was and the plaintiff was entitled to succeed.

Truth (NZ) Ltd v *Holloway* [1960] 1 WLR 997 Privy Council (Viscount Simonds, Lord Reid, Lord Tucker, Lord Denning and Lord Morris of Borth-y-Gest)

Defamation – publication

Facts
A newspaper article calling for a public inquiry into import licences included a report of a defamatory statement made about the responsible minister. The trial judge directed the jury that the fact that the article was calling for an inquiry was no defence to the minister's action against the newspaper and that the matter should be dealt with as if the newspaper had itself originated the defamatory matter.

Held
There had been no misdirection by the trial judge.

Vizetelley v *Mudie's Select Library Ltd* [1900] 2 QB 170 Court of Appeal (A L Smith, Vaughan Williams and Romer LJJ)

Libel – dissemination

Facts
The proprietors of a circulating library, the defendants, lent and sold copies of a book which, unknown to them, contained a libel on the plaintiff. The publishers of the book had previously advertised in the

recognised trade papers asking that all copies should be returned to them in order that one page should be cancelled and replaced, but this advertisement had been overlooked by the defendants.

Held

The plaintiff's action for libel would succeed.

Watt v *Longsdon* [1930] 1 KB 130 Court of Appeal (Scrutton, Greer and Russell LJJ)

Libel – privilege

Facts

The Scottish Petroleum Company had in Casablanca a manager (Browne) and a managing director (Watt). Browne wrote to Longsdon (a director in London) stating, inter alia, that Watt had left to look for a job, leaving a whisky bill unpaid, and that Watt had been in immoral relations with his housemaid. Longsdon sent the letter on to Singer, the chairman, and on the same day wrote to Browne saying, inter alia, that he had long suspected Watt of immorality. After a further week, Longsdon sent Browne's letter to Watt's wife. Watt sued Longsdon for libel: the trial judge dismissed the claim: Watt appealed.

Held

The appeal would be allowed and there should be a new trial.

'As regards the publication to Singer, we must act upon the view ... that at all material times the plaintiff, the defendant, and Browne were in the employ of the Scottish Petroleum Co. In these circumstances, and the defendant believing the truth of the libels, there was a duty on the defendant to make the communication to Singer, and an interest in Singer to receive it; hence was the occasion a privileged occasion. As regards the defendant's letter to Browne, this must also, I think, be held to have been written on a privileged occasion; the defendant having a duty to communicate to Singer, had an interest in asking Browne for further information, and so an interest in making the communication which Browne had a duty to receive. Accordingly, I agree with the learned judge that, as regards these two publications, the occasions of them were privileged occasions. In regard to the question of evidence of malice .... I would have thought that the conduct of the defendant in making his hasty communication to the wife, and his subsequent conduct, and the language used by him in his letter to Browne, was some evidence to go to the jury. No doubt the necessity of accepting the view that the defendant did, in fact, believe the truth of all the defamatory matters alleged diminishes the weight of the other matters which might be relied upon by the jury as indicating express malice. The question should, however, in my opinion, have been left to them to consider and determine. As regards the communication to the plaintiff's wife, I am unable to say that, in the circumstances of the present case, there existed any duty on the defendant to communicate to the plaintiff's wife Browne's letter .... The question whether any duty lies on a third party to communicate to one spouse the delinquencies of the other can never be answered by reference to a fixed test or rule. The answer in each case must always depend upon the actual facts of that case. After carefully considering the proved facts of the present case I agree with the other members of the court that the publication made by the defendant to the plaintiff's wife of Browne's letter was not made upon a privileged occasion.'

Watts v *Aldington* (1993) The Times 16 December Court of Appeal (Neill, Steyn and Simon Brown LJJ)

Settlement agreement with one loser of defamation case – effect on other loser

Facts

The defendant had previously successfully sued the plaintiff, together with another person, for defamation and had been awarded £1,500,000. Some time later the defendant agreed a settlement with the plaintiff whereby a payment of £10,000 was accepted in full and final settlement, providing certain conditions were kept. The question arose as to whether this agreement constituted a release by the defendant of all his rights against either the plaintiff or the other person arising out of the defamation case. At first instance it was held that the agreement did not release the plaintiff, but was merely an agreement not to sue him and that the second person had not been discharged by it. The plaintiff (and the other person) appealed.

Held

The appeal was dismissed; the agreement by a winner in a defamation case with one of two losers did not constitute a release but merely an agreement by the defamed party not to sue for the remainder of the judgment, and thus did not discharge the other loser from liability.

Youssoupoff v *Metro-Goldwyn-Mayer Pictures Ltd* (1934) 50 TLR 581 Court of Appeal (Scrutton, Slesser and Greer LJJ)

Libel – film

Facts

The plaintiff claimed damages for a libel which she claimed was contained in a sound film called 'Rasputin, the Mad Monk'. She said that the defendant alleged that she, referred to as 'Princess Natasha', had been seduced by Rasputin. The jury awarded her £25,000. D appealed.

Held

The action was properly framed in libel and there was no reason for allowing the appeal.

Slesser LJ:

'The action was properly framed in libel. There can be no doubt that, so far as the photographic part of the exhibition is concerned, that is a permanent matter to be seen by the eye and is the proper subject of an action for libel, if defamatory. I regard the speech which is synchronised with the photographic reproduction and forms part of one complex, common exhibition as an ancillary circumstance, part of the surroundings explaining that which is to be seen.'

22 Trespass to the Person

Bird v Jones (1845) 7 QB 742 Queen's Bench Division (Denman CJ and Patteson and Coleridge JJ)

False imprisonment – way of escape

Facts
Part of Hammersmith Bridge which was ordinarily used as a public footway was appropriated for seats to view a regatta and separated for that purpose by a temporary fence from the carriageway. The plaintiff insisted on passing along the appropriated part and tried to climb over the fence. D, a Bridge clerk, tried to stop him by pulling his coat, but P got over whereupon D directed two policemen who prevented P from going on, but said he could pass over by going back to the carriageway. P refused and stayed where he was for half an hour. He tried to force his way through; assaulted D and was arrested.

Held (Denman CJ dissenting)
Mere obstruction of a person in one direction leaving him free to go in another direction is not false imprisonment.

Patteson J:

> 'In general, if one man compels another to stay in any given place against his will, he imprisons him ... and it is not necessary ... to touch him ... But, I cannot bring my mind to the conclusion that if one man merely obstructs the passage of another in a particular direction whether by threat of personal violence or otherwise, leaving him at liberty to stay where he is or to go in any other direction if he pleases, he can be said thereby to imprison him. Imprisonment is ... a total restraint upon the liberty of the person and not a partial obstruction of his will.'

Collins v Wilcock [1984] 1 WLR 1172 High Court (Robert Goff LJ and Mann J)

Trespass to the person – taking hold of arm

Facts
Wishing to question the appellant about suspected prostitution, a policewoman took hold of her arm to detain her. At the time, the policewoman was not exercising a power of arrest.

Held
The policewoman's conduct had gone beyond acceptable lawful physical contact between two citizens and it followed that her act constituted a battery on the appellant.

Davidson v Chief Constable of North Wales Police (1993) The Times 26 April Court of Appeal (Sir Thomas Bingham MR, Staughton and Waite LJJ)

Person giving incorrect information to police – whether liable in false imprisonment

Facts

A store detective incorrectly informed police officers that the plaintiff had been involved in shoplifting and she was arrested. No charge was brought against the plaintiff, and it was accepted that she was entirely innocent of any allegation of dishonesty. The plaintiff sued the defendant store detective for damages in false imprisonment, and this claim was dismissed at first instance. The plaintiff appealed.

Held

A defendant was not liable in false imprisonment if he merely gave information to the prosecuting authority which effected a plaintiff's arrest and detention, and had not himself instigated or procured it. Although the store detective in question expected her information to carry weight with the police who had always acted on it, and she regarded the arrest as being made on her behalf, the police officers had exercised their own judgment in making the arrest.

Commentary

Compare: *Martin* v *Watson* [1995] 3 WLR 318

F v West Berkshire Health Authority [1989] 2 WLR 1025 House of Lords (Lord Bridge of Harwich, Lord Brandon of Oakbrook, Lord Griffiths, Lord Goff of Chieveley and Lord Jauncey of Tullichettle)

Operation – consent

Facts

Did the court have power to declare that the sterilisation of a woman suffering from a serious mental disability, without her consent, would not be unlawful?

Held

The court did have such power, under its inherent jurisdiction, provided the operation was in the patient's best interests, ie that the operation was accepted as appropriate treatment by a reasonably body of medical opinion skilled in that particular form of treatment.

Lord Bridge of Harwich:

'The issues canvassed in argument before your Lordships revealed the paucity of clearly defined principles in the common law which may be applied to determine the lawfulness of medical or surgical treatment given to a patient who for any reason, temporary or permanent, lacks the capacity to give or to communicate consent to that treatment. It seems to me to be axiomatic that treatment which is necessary to preserve the life, health or well-being of the patient may lawfully be given without consent. But, if a rigid criterion of necessity were to be applied to determine what is and what is not lawful in the treatment of the unconscious and the incompetent, many of those unfortunate enough to be deprived of the capacity to make or communicate rational decisions by accident, illness or unsoundness of mind might be deprived of treatment which it would be entirely beneficial for them to receive.

Moreover, it seems to me of first importance that the common law should be readily intelligible to and applicable by all those who undertake the care of persons lacking the capacity to consent to treatment. It would be intolerable for members of the medical, nursing and other professions devoted to the care of the sick that, in caring for those lacking the capacity to consent to treatment, they should be put in the dilemma that, if they administer the treatment which they believe to be in the patient's best interests, acting with due skill and care, they run the risk of being held guilty of trespass to the person, but, if they withhold that treatment, they may be in breach of a duty of care owed to the patient. If those who undertake responsibility for the care of incompetent or unconscious patients administer curative or prophylactic [tending to prevent disease] treatment which they believe to be appropriate to the patient's existing condition of disease, injury or bodily malfunction or susceptibility to such a condition in the future, the lawfulness of that treatment should be judged by one standard, not two. It follows that if the professionals in question have acted with due skill and care, judged by the well-known test laid down in *Bolam* v *Friern Hospital Management Committee* [1957] 1 WLR 582, they should be immune from liability in trespass, just as they are immune from liability in negligence. The special considerations which apply in the case of sterilisation of a woman who is physically perfectly healthy or of an operation on an organ transplant donor arise only because such treatment cannot be considered either curative or prophylactic.'

Commentary
Applied in *Airedale NHS Trust* v *Bland* [1993] 2 WLR 316.

Fowler v *Lanning* [1959] 2 WLR 241 High Court (Diplock J)

Trespass to the person – intent

Facts
The plaintiff claimed damages for trespass to the person committed by the defendant at Corfe Castle. The plaintiff was shot by the defendant whilst on a shoot, but in his statement of claim the plaintiff did not state that the defendant was negligent, merely that 'the defendant shot the plaintiff'.

Held
No cause of action was disclosed. Negligence or intention must be proved in trespass to the person and the burden of proof is on the plaintiff.

Diplock J:

'It is fashionable to regard trespass to the person as representing the historic principle that every man acts at his peril and is liable for all the consequences of his acts ... But, however true this may have been of trespass in medieval times ... the strict principle that every man acts at his peril was not applied in trespass even as long ago as 1617.'

Hague v *Deputy Governor of Parkhurst Prison*

See *R* v *Deputy Governor of Parkhurst Prison, ex parte Hague*, below.

Janvier v *Sweeney* [1919] 2 KB 316 Court of Appeal (Bankes and Duke LJJ and A T Lawrence J)

Threats causing shock

Facts
The plaintiff, a Frenchwoman, was engaged to a German who was interned in the Isle of Man. One of the defendants called at her house and falsely told her that he was representing the military authorities and that she was the woman they wanted as she had been corresponding with a German spy. In consequence the plaintiff suffered severe nervous shock.

Held
The plaintiff was entitled to damages.

Commentary
Applied: *Wilkinson* v *Downton* [1987] 2 QB 57 and *Dulieu* v *White & Sons* [1901] 2 KB 669.

Lane v *Holloway* [1967] 3 WLR 1003 Court of Appeal (Lord Denning MR, Salmon and Winn LJJ)

Trespass to the person – disproportionate response

Facts
L & H got into an argument. H approached L in a manner which caused L to fear a blow. L threw a blow at H's shoulder. H replied with a severe blow to L's eye: the wound needed 19 stitches and L was in hospital for a month.

Held
This was a proper case for a civil action and there was no defence of 'Ex turpi causa ...' available to H. He responded out of all proportion to the blow he had received.

Lord Denning MR:

'The man who strikes a blow of such severity is liable in damages unless he can prove accident or self-defence. The sum of £75 was far too little compensation for L. It should be £300 given the circumstances and H's defence of self-defence fails.'

Commentary
Applied: *Fontin* v *Katapodis* (1962) 108 CLR 177.

Letang v *Cooper* [1964] 3 WLR 573 Court of Appeal (Lord Denning MR, Danckwerts and Diplock LJJ)

Trespass to the person without intent

Facts
The plaintiff was on holiday at a hotel in Cornwall. She decided to sunbathe in some grass where cars were parked. The defendant drove his Jaguar over her legs; he had not seen her. More than three years passed before the plaintiff sued the defendant.

Held
The cause of action was statute barred as, where the injury is not inflicted intentionally but negligently, the only cause of action is negligence. Even if the cause of action had been trespass to the person, it would still have been statute barred.

Lord Denning MR:

'The truth is that the distinction between trespass and case is obsolete. We have a different sub-division altogether. Instead of dividing actions for personal injuries into *trespass* (direct damage) or *case* (consequential damage), we divide the causes of action now according as the defendant did the injury intentionally or unintentionally. If one man intentionally applies force directly to another, the plaintiff has a cause of action in assault and battery, or, if you so please to describe it, in trespass to the person. "The least touching of another in anger is a battery." If he does not inflict injury intentionally, but only unintentionally, the plaintiff has no cause of action today in trespass. His only cause of action is in negligence, and then only on proof of want of reasonable care. If the plaintiff cannot prove want of reasonable care, he may have no cause of action at all. Thus, it is not enough nowadays for the plaintiff to plead that "the defendant shot the plaintiff". He must also allege that he did it intentionally or negligently. If intentional, it is the tort of assault and battery. If negligent and causing damage, it is the tort of negligence.'

Commentary
See also *Stubbings* v *Webb* [1993] 2 WLR 120.

Meering v *Grahame-White Aviation Co Ltd* (1919) 122 LT 44 Court of Appeal (Atkin, Duke and Warrington LJJ)

False imprisonment

Facts
The plaintiff was taken to a police station and put into a waiting room. He said that unless he was told why, he would leave, but was told he was wanted in connection with inquiries into thefts. He stayed. Three policemen stayed on duty in the vicinity of the waiting room. P sued for false imprisonment.

Held (Duke LJ dissenting)
The plaintiff was entitled to judgment as it is perfectly possible for a person to be imprisoned in law without his knowing the fact and appreciating that he is imprisoned.

Atkin LJ:

'I think a person can be imprisoned whilst asleep, whilst in a state of drunkenness, whilst unconscious and whilst he is a lunatic. Those are cases where it seems to me a person might properly complain if he were imprisoned, though the imprisonment began and ceased while he was in that state.'

Murphy v *Culhane* [1976] 3 WLR 458 Court of Appeal (Lord Denning MR, Orr LJ and Waller J)

Trespass to the person – contributory negligence

Facts
The defendant pleaded guilty to the manslaughter of the plaintiff's husband and was convicted of that offence. In the plaintiff's civil action, the defendant sought to avail himself of the defences ex turpi causa non oritur actio and volenti non fit injuria: alternatively, he alleged that the deceased had been guilty of contributory negligence.

Held
He was entitled to raise these pleas and the facts should be investigated.

R v *Deputy Governor of Parkhurst Prison, ex parte Hague; Weldon* v *Home Office* [1991] 3 WLR 340 House of Lords (Lord Bridge of Harwich, Lord Ackner, Lord Goff of Chieveley, Lord Jauncey of Tullichettle and Lord Lowry)

Breach of prison rules – private law remedies

Facts

In both cases the question arose whether a prisoner who had been restrained in breach of the Prison Rules 1964 had a private law cause of action for breach of statutory duty or false imprisonment. In the first case the breach involved segregation from other prisoners, in the second removal to the punishment block.

Held

A claim could not be sustained in either case.

Lord Bridge of Harwich:

'*Breach of statutory duty ...*

... like any other question of statutory construction, the question whether an enactment gives rise to a cause of action for breach of statutory duty is a question of ascertaining the intention of the legislature.

The Prison Rules 1964 are made under s47 of the Prison Act 1952 ...

In *Arbon* v *Anderson* [1943] KB 252 the question at issue was whether a cause of action arose from a breach of the Prison Rules 1933, made under the Prison Act 1898. Goddard LJ said ([1943] KB 252 at 254):

"The real question which falls to be determined is whether it is intended by the statute to confer an individual right. I am clearly of opinion that neither the Prison Act nor the rules were intended to confer any such right."

In *Becker* v *Home Office* [1972] 2 QB 407 both Lord Denning MR and Edmund Davies LJ expressed their conclusion that a breach of the Prison Rules 1964 creates no civil liability in equally general terms. [Counsel for Hague] submits that such a general approach is erroneous and that each provision in the rules must be considered separately. Whilst I do not accept this criticism of the earlier authorities, I do accept that we may properly be invited in asking the question whether the breach of a particular provision of the rules gives rise to a cause of action to examine that provision in its context. Adopting that course, I can find nothing in r43 or in any context that is relevant to the construction of r43 which would support the conclusion that it was intended to confer a right of action on an individual prisoner. The purpose of the rule, apart from the case of prisoners who need to be segregated in their own interests, is to give an obviously necessary power to segregate prisoners who are liable for any reason to disturb the orderly conduct of the prison generally. The rule is a purely preventive measure. The power is to be exercised only in accordance with the procedure prescribed by sub-r(2). But where the power has been exercised in good faith, albeit that the procedure followed in authorising its exercise was not in conformity with r43(2), it is inconceivable that the legislature intended to confer a cause of action on the segregated prisoner.

False imprisonment

The tort of false imprisonment has two ingredients: the fact of imprisonment and the absence of lawful authority to justify it. In *Meering* v *Grahame-White Aviation Co Ltd* (1919) 122 LT 44 at 54 Atkin LJ said that "any restraint within defined bounds which is a restraint in fact may be an imprisonment". Thus if A imposes on B a restraint within defined bounds and is sued by B for false imprisonment, the action will succeed or fail according to whether or not A can justify the restraint imposed on B as lawful. A child may be lawfully restrained within defined bounds by his parents or by the schoolmaster to whom the parents have delegated their authority. But if precisely the same restraint is imposed by a stranger without authority, it will be unlawful and will constitute the tort of false imprisonment.

I shall leave aside initially questions arising from the situation where a convicted prisoner serving a sentence is restrained by a member of the prison staff acting in bad faith, by a fellow prisoner or any other third party, or in circumstances where it can be said that the conditions of his detention are intolerable. I shall address first what I believe to be the primary and fundamental issue, viz whether any restraint within defined bounds imposed upon a convicted prisoner whilst serving his sentence by the prison governor or by officers acting with the authority of the prison governor and in good faith, but in circumstances where the particular form of restraint is not sanctioned by the Prison Rules, amounts for that reason to the tort of false imprisonment.

The starting point is s12(1) of the Prison Act 1952 which provides:

"A prisoner, whether sentenced to imprisonment or committed to prison on remand pending trial or otherwise, may be lawfully confined in any prison."

This provides lawful authority for the restraint of the prisoner within the defined bounds of the prison by the governor of the prison, who has the legal custody of the prisoner under s13, or by any prison officer acting with the governor's authority. Can the prisoner then complain that his legal rights are infringed by a restraint which confines him at any particular time within a particular part of the prison? It seems to me that the reality of prison life demands a negative answer to this question ...

In my opinion, to hold a prisoner entitled to damages for false imprisonment on the ground that he has been subject to a restraint upon his movement which was not in accordance with the Prison Rules would be, in effect, to confer on him under a different legal label a cause of action for breach of statutory duty under the rules. Having reached the conclusion that it was not the intention of the rules to confer such a right, I am satisfied that the right cannot properly be asserted in the alternative guise of a claim to damages for false imprisonment ...

I turn next to the question posed by the example given in the judgment of Parker LJ in *Weldon*'s case [1990] 3 WLR 465 at 480, of a prisoner locked in a shed by fellow prisoners. I think the short answer to this question is given by Taylor LJ who said in *Hague*'s case [1990] 3 WLR 1210 at 1267:

"In such a situation an action for false imprisonment would surely lie (for what it was worth), since the fellow prisoners would have no defence under s12 of the Prison Act 1952."

The prisoner locked in the shed is certainly restrained within defined bounds and it is nihil ad rem that if he were not locked in the shed, he would be locked in his cell or restrained in accordance with the prison regime in some other part of the prison. The restraint in the shed is unlawful because the fellow prisoners acted without the authority of the governor and it is only the governor, who has the legal custody of the prisoner, and persons acting with the authority of the governor who can rely on the provisions of s12(1).

This consideration also leads to the conclusion that a prison officer who acts in bad faith by deliberately subjecting a prisoner to a restraint which he knows he has no authority to impose may render himself personally liable to an action for false imprisonment as well as committing the tort of misfeasance in public office. Lacking the authority of the governor, he also lacks the protection of s12(1). But if the officer deliberately acts outside the scope of his authority, he cannot render the governor or the Home Office vicariously liable for his tortious conduct ...

There remains the question whether an otherwise lawful imprisonment may be rendered unlawful by reason only of the conditions of detention ...

I sympathise entirely with the view that the person lawfully held in custody who is subjected to intolerable conditions ought not to be left without a remedy against his custodian, but the proposition that the conditions of detention may render the detention itself unlawful raises formidable difficulties. If the proposition be sound, the corollary must be that when the conditions of detention deteriorate to the point of intolerability, the detainee is entitled immediately to go free. It is impossible, I think, to define with any precision what would amount to intolerable conditions for this purpose. ...

The logical solution to the problem, I believe, is that if the conditions of an otherwise lawful detention are truly intolerable, the law ought to be capable of providing a remedy directly related to those conditions without characterising the fact of the detention itself as unlawful. I see no real difficulty in saying that the law can provide such a remedy. Whenever one person is lawfully in the custody of another, the custodian owes a duty of care to the detainee. If the custodian negligently allows, or a fortiori, if he deliberately causes, the detainee to suffer in any way in his health he will be in breach of that duty. But short of anything that could properly be described as a physical injury or an impairment of health, if a person lawfully detained is kept in conditions which cause him for the time being physical pain or a degree of discomfort which can properly be described as intolerable, I believe that could and should be treated as a breach of the custodian's duty of care for which the law should award damages. For this purpose it is quite unnecessary to attempt any definition of the criterion of intolerability. It would be a question of fact and degree in any case which came before the court to determine whether the conditions to which a detainee had been subjected were such as to warrant an award of damages for the discomfort he had suffered. In principle I believe it is acceptable for the law to provide a remedy on this basis ... In practice the problem is perhaps not very likely to arise.'

R v *St George* (1840) 9 C & P 483 Court of Exchequer (Parke B)

Assault – unloaded pistol

Facts

On the trial of an indictment for feloniously attempting to discharge loaded arms, the court considered whether by pointing an unloaded pistol a common law assault had been committed.

Held

It had if the weapon had the appearance of being loaded, thus causing fear and alarm, and the range was such that it would have endangered life if it had been fired.

R v *Self* [1992] 1 WLR 657 Court of Appeal (Watkins LJ, Swinton Thomas and Garland JJ)

Lawful citizen's arrest – requirement

Facts

A store detective and a sales assistant followed the appellant out of a store and accused him of shoplifting. During a scuffle the appellant scratched, punched and kicked the sales assistant. Another man grabbed the appellant, saying that he was making a citizen's arrest, and the appellant kicked him. The appellant was acquitted on a count of theft but was convicted on two counts of assault with intent to resist arrest.

On appeal against conviction:

Held

Allowing the appeal, that it was clear from the words of s24(5) of the Police and Criminal Evidence Act 1984 that the powers of arrest without warrant under that subsection required, as a condition precedent, an arrestable offence committed: that where an appellant was acquitted of the alleged offence for which he had been arrested he had committed no arrestable offence so that no one was entitled under the subsection to apprehend or detain him without a warrant; and that, accordingly, his convictions of assault with intent to resist his lawful apprehension must be quashed (post p661 A-B, I-G).

Commentary

Walters v *W H Smith & Sons Ltd* [1914] 1 KB 595 applied.

Robinson v *Balmain New Ferry Co Ltd* [1910] AC 295 Privy Council (Lord Loreburn LC, Lord Macnaghten, Lord Collins and Sir Arthur Wilson)

False imprisonment – turnstile

Facts

The plaintiff paid one penny to enter a wharf to get a boat to the other side. Then P changed his mind and decided to go back. The rules of the wharf required a further one penny to get through the turnstile. P refused to pay and was restrained from leaving. He claimed damages for false imprisonment.

Held

There was no false imprisonment.

Lord Loreburn:

'P was merely called upon to leave the wharf in the way in which he contracted to leave it … Ds were entitled to resist a forcible passage through their turnstile … The payment of one penny was a quite fair condition and if he did not choose to comply with it, Ds were not bound to let him through.'

Stanley v *Powell* [1891] 1 QB 86 High Court (Denman J)

Trespass to the person – accident

Facts

The defendant, a member of a shooting party, fired at a pheasant. A shot glanced off the bough of a tree and wounded the plaintiff in the eye. The defendant had not been negligent.

Held

As the defendant had not intended to injure the plaintiff he was not liable in respect of his injury

Commentary

Approved in *National Coal Board* v *JE Evans & Co (Cardiff) Ltd* [1951] 2 KB 861.

Tuberville v *Savage* (1699) 1 Mod Rep 3 Court of King's Bench (Kelynge CJ, Twiden, Moreton and Rainsford JJ)

Assault by word of mouth?

Facts

The defendant said 'If it were not Assize time, I would not take such language from you'. It was Assize time – were these words an assault?

Held

They were not.

'The declaration of the defendant was that he would not assault him, the judges being in town; and the *intention* as well as the *act* makes an assault. Therefore, if one strike another upon the hand or arm … in discourse it is no assault; but if one, intending to assault, strike at another and miss him, this is an assault; so, if he hold up his hand against another in a threatening manner and say nothing, it is an assault.'

Wilkinson v *Downton* [1897] 2 QB 57 High Court (Wright J)

Damages – nervous disorders

Facts

The defendant, as a practical joke, falsely told the plaintiff that the plaintiff's husband had been smashed up in an accident and was lying at a pub with both legs broken and that she was to take a car and fetch him home. As a result, the plaintiff suffered severe nervous disorders, she vomited and needed medical treatment.

Held

The plaintiff could recover damages for her injuries.

Wright J:

'This claim cannot succeed on the basis of fraud, but it can succeed on the ground that the defendant has wilfully done an act calculated to cause physical harm to the plaintiff – that is to infringe her legal right to personal safety and has, in fact, thereby caused physical harm to her ... Such an intention can be imputed on the facts. The injuries were not too remote.

Suppose that a person is in a precarious and dangerous condition and another person tells him that his physician has said he has but a day to live ... if a serious aggravation of illness ensued, damages might be recovered.'

Commentary

Applied in *Janvier* v *Sweeney* [1919] 2 KB 316.

Wilson v *Pringle* [1987] QB 237 Court of Appeal (O'Connor, Croom-Johnson and Balcombe LJJ)

Trespass to the person – hostility

Facts

The defendant and plaintiff were both schoolboys. The defendant jumped on the plaintiff whilst playing around and caused the plaintiff to sustain injury. The plaintiff claimed damages for battery. The plaintiff claimed that as the defendant had admitted jumping on the plaintiff there could be no defence.

Held

The defendant also had to show hostility on the part of the defendant. The question of hostility was a question of fact and therefore the case should be remitted for trial.

Croom-Johnson LJ:

'In our view ... in a battery there must be an intentional touching or contact in one form or another of the plaintiff by the defendant. That touching must be proved to be a hostile touching.'

23 Trespass to Land

Bernstein of Leigh (Lord) v *Skyviews & General Ltd* [1977] 3 WLR 136 High Court (Griffiths J)

Facts

The defendants flew over the plaintiff's property for the purpose of taking aerial photographs of P's country house which they then offered to sell him. P claimed damages, alleging that by entering airspace above his property, Ds were guilty of trespass or were guilty of an actionable invasion of P's right to privacy by taking the photographs without his consent.

Held

Judgment would be given for the defendants because an owner's rights to airspace above his land was limited to such light as was necessary for the ordinary use and enjoyment of the land and of the structures upon it. These rights had not been infringed by the defendants.

Griffiths J:

'I can find no support in authority for the view that a landowner's rights in the air space above his property extend to an unlimited height ... The problem is to balance the rights of an owner to enjoy the use of his land against the rights of the general public to take advantage of all that science now offers in the use of air space. This balance is in my judgment best struck in our present society by restricting the rights of an owner in the air space above his land to such height as is necessary for the ordinary use and enjoyment of his land and the structures on it, and declaring that above that height he has no greater rights in the air space than any other member of the public.'

Cinnamond v *British Airports Authority* [1980] 1 WLR 582 Court of Appeal (Lord Denning MR, Shaw and Brandon LJJ)

Trespass ab initio

Facts

Six minicab drivers were prohibited from entering Heathrow. They appealed against that decision.

Held

Their appeal would be dismissed.

Lord Denning MR:

'... when one of these car-hire drivers picks up a passenger at a London hotel and drives to the airport he has a right to enter so as to drop his passenger and luggage. But the driver has no right whatever to hang about there so as to "tout" for a return fare. By so doing he is abusing the right which is given to him by the law, and that automatically makes him a trespasser from the beginning ... These car-hire drivers abused the authority given to them by the law by hanging about and "touting". So they become trespassers from the beginning, and can be turned out. Whether they come with a passenger and then stop to "tout", or whether they come with a faked slip, they are abusing the authority given by the law. They become trespassers from the beginning and can be turned out.'

Graham v *Peat* (1801) 1 East 244 Court of King's Bench (Lord Kenyon CJ)

Trespass – possession

Facts
The rector of a parish had demised some land to the plaintiff, although the lease was void by statute because the rector no longer lived in the parish. The defendant trespassed on the land.

Held
The plaintiff's possession was sufficient to maintain an action against the defendant.

Lord Kenyon CJ:

'Any possession is a legal possession against a wrong-doer.'

Harrison v *Duke of Rutland* [1893] 1 QB 142 Court of Appeal (Lord Esher MR, Lopes and Kay LJJ)

Trespass on highway

Facts
The defendant owned a grouse moor across which ran a highway the soil of which he also owned, while a shoot was in progress, the plaintiff went on to the highway and waved his handkerchief and opened and shut his umbrella with a view to diverting the grouse from the butts. The defendant's servants held him down to prevent further interference until the drive was over. The plaintiff claimed damages for assault and false imprisonment.

Held
His action could not succeed as he was a trespasser on the highway.

Kay LJ:

'The plaintiff went upon this highway, not for the purpose of exercising as one of the public his right of passage, but of interfering with the grouse drive by placing himself upon the soil of the highway so as to prevent the grouse from flying over the butts. ... I am unable to agree that this was a use of the right of passing along the highway. I think it was an abuse of that right. In other words, it was a use of the soil of the highway for another purpose, which use interfered, and was intended to interfere, with a right which was then being exercised by the owner of the soil, and was incident to that ownership. Such a misuse of the soil of a highway is a trespass. There seems to have been sufficient evidence that the plaintiff was not only asserting a right to do what he did, but also that his intention was to repeat his interference. This strictly would entitle the defendants to the assistance of the court by injunction to prevent a repetition of the act. But this is not pressed for; and I think that the defendants are entitled at any rate to a declaration ... that under the circumstances the plaintiff ... when stopped by the duke's keepers, was trespassing upon the soil of the highway.'

Hemmings v *Stoke Poges Golf Club Ltd* [1920] 1 KB 720 Court of Appeal (Bankes, Scrutton and Duke LJJ)

Removal of trespasser

Facts

The plaintiffs, husband and wife, were employed by the defendant golf club, and to enable them to perform their duties properly they were required to live in a cottage owned by the defendants. The plaintiffs left the service of the defendants and the defendants gave them notice to quit. The plaintiffs refused to go so the defendants broke into the cottage and ejected them. The plaintiffs sued for trespass, assault and battery.

Held

The action would fail as it was found that the defendants had used no more force than was necessary.

Bankes LJ:

'In the present case the defendants were undoubtedly entitled to possession of the cottage. The plaintiffs had no right and did not pretend they had any right to remain there. Assuming, but without deciding, that the entry by the defendants was a forcible entry, the right to possession was in the defendants, and the acts which are alleged as giving the plaintiffs a right of action were done in defence of their right to possession ... and of the possession which they had acquired by the alleged forcible entry. I have no fear that the present decision will encourage lawlessness as was suggested for the plaintiffs. A person who makes a forcible entry upon lands and tenements renders himself liable to punishment, and he exposes himself also to the civil liability to pay damages in the event of more force being used than was necessary to remove the occupant of the premises, or in the event of any want of proper care in the removal of his goods.'

Hickman v *Maisey* [1900] 1 QB 752 Court of Appeal (Collins, Romer and A L Smith LJJ)

Trespass on the highway

Facts

The defendant, a 'racing tout', used a highway which ran across the plaintiff's land for the purpose of watching P's horses in training and using the information thereby obtained for the purposes of his business. The effect was to depreciate the value of P's land as a place for the training of race horses.

Held

The defendant was liable for trespass as his use of the highway was unreasonable.

A L Smith LJ:

'The question is ... what is the lawful use of a highway? Many authorities show ... that prima facie the right of the public is to pass and repass along the highway ... but I quite agree with Lord Esher MR in *Harrison* v *Duke of Rutland* that though it is a slight extension of the rule as previously stated namely that, though highways are dedicated prima facie for the purpose of passage 'things are done upon them by everybody which are recognised as being rightly done and as constituting a reasonable and usual mode of using the highway ... I cannot agree that in this case the defendant was using the highway in an ordinary and reasonable manner. I do not agree with the defendant's argument that the intention and object of the defendant in going upon the highway cannot be taken into account in determining whether he was using it in a lawful manner. His intention and object are all important.'

Hurst v Picture Theatres Ltd [1915] 1 KB 1 Court of Appeal (Buckley, Kennedy and Phillimore LJJ)

Licence – revocation

Facts
The plaintiff, having paid the entrance fee, entered the defendants' cinema and took a seat. The attendant thought he had not paid and asked him to leave. When P refused, he was forcibly ejected.

Held (Phillimore LJ dissenting)
The plaintiff would succeed in his action for assault as he had a licence to stay until the end of the film and this could not be revoked at will.

Jones v Llanrwst Urban District Council [1911] 1 Ch 393 High Court (Parker J)

Trespass to land – river deposits

Facts
Here the plaintiff was the owner of a farm on the banks of the river Conway. He still occupied the house, but a tenant occupied the fields. The defendants installed a sewage system which fouled the water and made it unsuitable for cattle, etc. The plaintiff sued for nuisance and also in trespass for sewage deposited on the river bank.

Held
The defendants were liable and the plaintiff was entitled to an injunction. The defendants had pleaded that P could not maintain an action in either trespass or nuisance because he was only the reversioner and his tenant was not his co-plaintiff.

Parker J:

> 'It is reasonably certain that a reversioner cannot maintain actions in the nature of trespass including action for infringement of natural rights arising out of his ownership of land without alleging and proving injury to the reversioner. If the thing complained of is of such a permanent nature that the reversion may be injured, the question of whether or not the reversion is injured is one for the jury. I take "permanent" in this sense to mean such as will continue indefinitely, unless something is done to remove it ... a noisy trade and the exercise of an alleged right of way are not in their nature permanent within the rule, for they cease of themselves unless there be someone to continue them ... In my opinion, what is complained of in the present case is of a permanent nature within the rule. The sewage will continue to be turned into the Conway unless and until something is done to divert it elsewhere.'

Kelsen v Imperial Tobacco Co (of Great Britain and Ireland) Ltd [1957] 2 WLR 1007 High Court (McNair J)

Trespass – air space

Facts
The plaintiff had a lease on a tiny corner shop in Islington; it was only one storey high. The neighbouring shop was two storeys higher and had three metal signs on the wall advertising the defendants' wares. Ds obtained permission to replace these with new signs which encroached very slightly on the airspace

above P's shop. Five years later, due to business differences, P demanded that Ds remove the sign. Ds refused and P sued for a mandatory injunction.

Held

This was a trespass of the column of air above the shop and, accordingly, a mandatory injunction would be granted.

Konskier v *B Goodman Ltd* [1928] 1 KB 421 Court of Appeal (Scrutton, Sargant and Greer LJJ)

Trespass to land – debris

Facts

The defendants, a firm of house-breakers, were engaged in demolition work on a house, the owner of which had obtained permission from the owner and occupier of the adjoining house to pull down a chimney stack. The defendants undertook to restore the chimney stack at any future period and to make good any damage caused to the adjoining premises by any of the works. The demolition work was completed by April, but the defendants had omitted to remove a quantity of debris which had been deposited on the roof of the adjoining premises. In July, the plaintiff became the tenant of those premises. In September, a heavy rain-storm washed the debris from the roof into the guttering and drain pipes so that it choked a gulley, flooded the basement, and damaged the plaintiff's goods.

Held

Although the defendants were not liable in negligence, they were liable on the grounds of trespass.

Greer LJ:

'It is quite clear that, in order to recover damages for negligence against the defendants, the plaintiff must prove that the defendants were under a duty towards the plaintiff himself and had committed a breach of such duty, but here there was no duty on the part of the defendants towards the plaintiff, and therefore, the claim in negligence fails ... But it is equally clear that, if the case is fought in trespass, the plaintiff ought to succeed. The dropping of the debris on the roof ... would have been a trespass but for the licence, which was a limited one. The act of leaving the debris there, or the omission to remove it at the completion of the demolition operations, was a trespass.'

League Against Cruel Sports Ltd v *Scott* [1985] 3 WLR 400 High Court (Park J)

Trespass to land – hurt

Facts

The plaintiff was an anti-blood sports organisation and it owned land on Exmoor which was unfenced where hunted wild deer could seek refuge. It refused permission to the local hunt to enter on that land, but the hunt disobeyed seven times during the space of one year. The plaintiff therefore sought an injunction restraining the masters and members of the hunt from further intrusions on to its land.

Held

The master of the hunt was liable for trespass if he (i) deliberately allowed the hounds to go after an animal and (ii) he knew there was 'a real risk' of the hounds entering land on which permission to hunt had been refused and (iii) either he *intentionally* let them enter the land or *negligently* did so by not controlling them. The injunction would be granted.

Ocean Estates Ltd v *Pinder* [1969] 2 AC 19 Privy Council (Lord Guest, Lord Upjohn and Lord Diplock)

Trespass to land – right to maintain action

Facts
Although the appellant development company could show a sufficient documentary title to certain land in the Bahamas, the respondent maintained that they could not bring an action for trespass to land because they had failed to show that, at the time the action was brought, they had sufficient possession of it.

Held
The appellants were entitled to succeed.

Lord Diplock:

'Put at its highest against the appellants, it was clear law that the slightest acts by the person having title to the land or by his predecessors in title, indicating his intention to take possession, were sufficient to enable him to bring an action for trespass against a defendant entering upon the land without any title, unless there could be shown a subsequent intention on the part of the person having the title to abandon the constructive possession so acquired.'

Six Carpenters' Case (1610) 8 Co Rep 146a Court of Common Pleas (Sir Edward Coke CJ and other judges)

Trespass ab initio

Facts
The defendant and five other carpenters entered the plaintiff's wine tavern and ordered and drank wine and food. They refused to pay for some of the food and drink. The question was 'Did their failure to pay … make them trespassers ab initio?'

Held
It did not.

Sir Edward Coke CJ:

' … when an entry, authority or licence is given to any one by the law and he abuses it, he shall be a trespasser ab initio; but where an entry, authority or licence is given by the party and he abuses it, there he must be punished for his abuse but shall not be a trespasser ab initio. The reason for this difference is that in the case of a general authority or licence of law, the law adjudges by the subsequent act, quo animo, or to what intent he entered.'

Swordheath Properties Ltd v *Tabet* [1979] 1 WLR 285 Court of Appeal (Megaw, Browne and Waller LJJ)

Trespass – damages

Facts
After a tenant had left a flat, the judge granted the landlord an order for possession against two other persons who were living there as licensees. However, he refused to award damages for trespass.

Held

The landlord's appeal would succeed.

Megaw LJ:

'It appears to me to be clear, both as a matter of principle and of authority, that in a case of this sort the plaintiff, when he has established that the defendant has remained on as a trespasser in residential property, is entitled, without bringing evidence that he could or would have let the property to someone else in the absence of the trespassing defendant, to have as damages for the trespass the value of the property as it would fairly be calculated; and, in the absence of anything special in the particular case it would be the ordinary letting value of the property that would determine the amount of damages.'

24 Deceit

Archer v *Brown* [1984] 3 WLR 350 High Court (Peter Pain J)

Misrepresentation – damages

Facts
The plaintiff was a victim of the defendant's fraud – he bought from him for £30,000 the share capital of a company when he had already sold the same shares several times over to other unsuspecting victims. The plaintiff sought the return of his £30,000 and damages: the defendant conceded that he was entitled to rescission and the return of the money.

Held
The concession as to rescission did not deprive the plaintiff of the right to damages in deceit and these would include bank interest on money borrowed to buy the shares and moderate (£500) aggravated damages. However, the plaintiff was not awarded exemplary damages, even if they could be awarded in deceit: the defendant had been imprisoned for his fraud and he should not be punished a second time.

Attwood v *Small* (1838) 6 Cl & Fin 232 House of Lords (Lord Cottenham LC, Earl of Devon, Lord Lyndhurst, Lord Brougham and Lord Wynford)

Misrepresentation – inducement

Facts
During negotiations for the sale by the appellant to the respondents of certain mines and iron works, the respondents asked questions and verified the appellant's answers. However, after completion of the sale, it appeared that the answers had been inaccurate.

Held
The respondents were without a remedy.

Lord Wynford:

'I say, if the parties are induced fraudulently in any way, although they may have other reasons for entering into the contract, if the strong grounds which prevailed on them to enter into the contract were fraudulent representations, that will give an action in a court of law for deceit, and, I should hope, would be considered as a sufficient ground in a court of equity to set aside the contract. The representations of course, must be material, and the party making them must know at the time that he was making representations which were false. I am aware that, if a party chooses to trust to the representations and does not make any inquiry, that reliance will be sufficient to make out a charge of false representations so as to set aside the contract. If the party thinks proper to inquire and to use his own eyes, and does not depend upon the representations, if the representations be of such a nature that by a view of the thing he can detect their falsehood, undoubtedly the party making the representations will not be answerable for that falsehood, but the other party must consider it as attributable to his own negligence if he thought proper to give weight to any such representations. But if a party who thinks proper not to trust entirely to the representations is prevented from making such full inquiry, as he otherwise would have made, by any artifice on the part of the person making these representations, in that case the contract ought to be set aside.'

Derry v *Peek* (1889) 14 App Cas 337 House of Lords (Lord Halsbury LC, Lord Watson, Lord Bramwell, Lord FitzGerald and Lord Herschell)

Deceit – belief in truth

Facts

A special Act incorporating a tramway company provided that the carriages might be moved by animal power and, with the consent of the Board of Trade, by steam power. The directors issued a prospectus containing a statement that by their special Act the company had the right to use steam instead of horses. P bought shares on the strength of this statement. The Board of Trade later refused to consent to the use of steam and the company was wound up. P brought an action for deceit.

Held

1. In an action for deceit, it is not enough to establish misrepresentation alone; something more must be proved to cast liability on D.
2. There is an essential difference between the case where D honestly believes in the truth of a statement although D is careless and where he is careless with no such honest belief.
3. A mere statement by D that he believed something to be true is not conclusive proof that it was so. Fraud is established where it is proved that a false statement is made:

   a) knowingly;
   b) without belief in its truth;
   c) recklessly, careless as to whether it be true or false. There must, to prevent fraud, always be an honest belief in its truth.

   If fraud is proved, the motive of the person making the statement is irrelevant. It matters not that there was no intention to cheat or injure the person to whom the statement was made.
4. The defendants were not fraudulent in this case. They made a careless statement but they honestly believed in its truth.

Edgington v *Fitzmaurice* (1885) 29 Ch D 459 Court of Appeal (Cotton, Bowen and Fry LJJ)

Company prospectus – misrepresentation

Facts

The defendant directors issued a prospectus inviting subscriptions for debenture bonds to complete works to buildings, to buy horses and vans and generally to develop the business. The plaintiff shareholder duly subscribed believing, for no good reason, that the advances were to be secured on the company's property. In fact, most of the money raised was used to discharge some of the company's existing liabilities. The plaintiff sought repayment of the amount which he subscribed in an action of deceit.

Held

He was entitled to succeed.

Fry LJ:

'...with respect to the statement of the objects for which the debentures were issued I have come to the conclusion that there was a misstatement of fact, that the statement contained in the circular was false in fact, and false to the knowledge of the defendants ... It is not necessary to call attention to the evidence that the defendants knew at the time that a large proportion of the loan would have to be expended in paying pressing liabilities. It is hardly denied by the defendants. I come, therefore, to the conclusion with regret that this false statement was not only false in fact, but was false to the knowledge of the defendants.

The next inquiry is, whether this statement materially affected the conduct of the plaintiff in advancing the money. He has sworn that it did, and the learned judge who tried the action has believed him ... the natural inference from the facts is in accordance with the judge's conclusion. The prospectus was intended to influence the mind of the reader.

Then this question has been raised. The plaintiff admits that he was induced to make the advance, not merely by this false statement, but by the belief that the debentures would give him a charge on the company's property, and it is admitted that this was a mistake of the plaintiff. Therefore it is said the plaintiff was the author of his own injury. It is quite true that the plaintiff was influenced by his own mistake, but that does not benefit the defendant's case. The plaintiff says: "I had two inducements, one my own mistake and the other the false statement of the defendants. The two together induced me to advance the money." But in my opinion, if the false statement of fact actually influenced the plaintiff, the defendants are liable, even though the plaintiff may have been also influenced by other motives. I think, therefore, the defendants must be held liable.'

Horsfall v *Thomas* (1862) 1 H & C 90 Court of Exchequer (Pollock CB and Bramwell B)

Misrepresentation

Facts
The defendant employed the plaintiff to make a steel gun. When the plaintiff delivered the gun it was defective in such a way as would have justified the defendant in refusing to accept delivery and this defect might have been apparent if the gun had been examined. The gun was fired by the defendant and after several shots it burst and became worthless. There was some evidence that the plaintiff had concealed the defect and when he sued to recover the cost of the gun the defendant maintained that he was entitled to rescind the contract as the plaintiff had induced him to accept delivery by fraud and misrepresentation.

Held
The plaintiff would succeed as the defendant's contention as to fraud and misrepresentation was defeated by the fact that the defendant had not examined the gun so that the concealment of the defect had not influenced his acceptance.

Peek v *Gurney* (1873) LR 6 HL 377 House of Lords (Lord Chelmsford, Lord Colonsay and Lord Cairns)

Misrepresentations in prospectus

Facts
A prospectus contained misrepresentations of fact and concealed the existence of a deed which, if known, would probably have prevented the formation of the company. A person who bought some of the shares from an allottee sought an indemnity against the loss which he suffered in consequence of his purchase.

Held

His claim would fail as when the allotment was completed the office of the prospectus was exhausted.

Lord Colonsay:

> 'Those who were concerned in issuing that prospectus can hardly be listened to when they say that they did not know what were the contents of it, or that they had not sufficiently examined into the matter before putting it forth. That would be a reckless putting forth of statements which they did not know to be true, and which were calculated to induce people to subscribe. But that does not solve this case ... the proper office of a prospectus is to invite persons to become original partners in a company, that is to say, allottees of shares; and I do not think that the responsibility towards those allottees which attached to the directors who issued the prospectus followed the shares when they were transferred to any number of persons however distant from the allottees, persons who ultimately purchased those shares. I think that the office of the prospectus was fulfilled when the allottee got his shares as far as regarded those shares. I think, further, that in a case of this kind it is necessary to make out some direct connection between the directors and the party who alleges that he was deceived.'

Commentary

Distinguished in *Andrews* v *Mockford* [1896] 1 QB 372.

Smith **v** *Chadwick* (1884) 9 App Cas 187 House of Lords (Earl of Selborne LC, Lord Blackburn, Lord Watson and Lord Bramwell)

Deceit – inducing cause

Facts

A prospectus contained a statement that 'the present value of the turnover or output of the entire works is over £1,000,000 sterling per annum'. This statement was ambiguous in that it could mean that in one year the works produced goods worth £1,000,000, in which case it was untrue, or that the works were capable of this output, in which case it was correct.

Held

In order to succeed in an action of deceit for fraudulent misrepresentation, the plaintiff had to prove that he had interpreted the statement in the sense in which it was false and that he had in fact been influenced by it in making his decision to take shares. The plaintiff failed to satisfy the court on these points.

Smith **v** *Land and House Property Corporation* (1884) 28 Ch D 7 Court of Appeal (Baggallay, Bowen and Fry LJJ)

Misrepresentation as to tenant

Facts

In the particulars of sale the plaintiffs said that their hotel was 'now held by a very desirable tenant ... for an unexpired term of twenty-eight years, at a rent of £400 pa'. The defendants resisted the plaintiffs' claim for specific performance on the ground of misdescription in that it afterwards appeared that the rent was in arrear at the time of the sale and the tenant shortly afterwards filed his petition for liquidation.

Held

The contract should be rescinded as the description of the tenant as 'very desirable' was not an expression of opinion but a misrepresentation on the faith of which the defendants contracted to purchase the hotel.

Smith Kline & French Laboratories Ltd v Long [1988] 3 All ER 887 Court of Appeal (Slade, Croom-Johnson and Ralph Gibson LJJ)

Measure of damages

Facts

The plaintiff drug manufacturers were induced by the fraudulent misrepresentations of the defendant managing director of Swift Exports Ltd (Swift) to sell to Swift a substantial quantity of tablets. Swift went into liquidation; the plaintiffs issued proceedings against the defendant claiming damages for deceit. On what basis should damages be assessed?

Held

Where a plaintiff has been permanently deprived of his goods as a result of the defendant's deceit, the proper measure of damages is the market value of the goods not the cost of replacing them.

Commentary

Considered: *Doyle* v *Olby (Ironmongers) Ltd* [1969] 2 QB 158.

Smith New Court Securities Ltd v Scrimgeour Vickers (Asset Management) Ltd [1994] 1 WLR 1271 Court of Appeal (Nourse, Rose and Hoffmann LJJ)

Damages in deceit

Facts

Following representations made by the second defendant, the plaintiff bought a large number of shares in a public company at 82.25p each. The plaintiff subsequently discovered that the representations were false. At first instance it was held that the plaintiff was entitled to recover from the second defendant damages equivalent to the difference between the purchase price and the 'true' value of the shares, which, after having heard expert evidence and by reason of another unconnected and then undiscovered fraud, he found to be 44p each. Had there been no misrepresentation, the judge found that the plaintiff would have paid 78p per share. The second defendant appealed.

Held

The appeal was allowed. In determining the loss incurred due to the fraudulent misrepresentation it was necessary to assume that the market knew everything it actually did know, but not to assume that the market knew of the existing but undiscovered and unconnected fraud. Hence the correct measure of damages was the difference between the price actually paid, 82.25p, and the price which in the absence of the misrepresentation the shares would have fetched in the open market, namely 78p.

25 Malicious Falsehood

De Beers Abrasive Products Ltd v *International General Electric Co of New York Ltd* [1975] 1 WLR 972 High Court (Walton J)

Slander of goods – puff

Facts
The parties both manufactured concrete abrasives and the defendants issued a pamphlet claiming that their product was superior. The plaintiffs sought, inter alia, damages for slander of goods.

Held
The defendants would be liable if the statements made in the pamphlet were false and the plaintiffs could show malice.

Walton J:

'… in the kind of situation where one expects, as a matter of ordinary common experience, a person to use a certain amount of hyperbole in the description of goods, property or services, the courts will do what any ordinary reasonable man would do, namely take it with a large pinch of salt.

Where, however, the situation is not that the trader is puffing his own goods, but turns to denigrate those of his rival, then, in my opinion, the situation is not so clear cut. Obviously the statement: "My goods are better than X's" is only a more dramatic presentation of what is implicit in the statement: "My goods are the best in the world". Accordingly, I do not think such a statement would be actionable. At the other end of the scale, if what is said is: "My goods are better than X's, because X's are absolute rubbish", then … the statement would be actionable.

Between these two kinds of statements there is obviously still an extremely wide field; and it appears to me that, in order to draw the line, one must apply this test, namely, whether a reasonable man would take the claim being made as being a serious claim or not. A possible alternative test is to ask whether the defendant has pointed to a specific allegation of some defect or demerit in the plaintiff's goods.'

Joyce v *Sengupta* [1993] 1 WLR 337 Court of Appeal (Sir Donald Nicholls V-C, Butler-Sloss LJ and Sir Michael Kerr)

Malicious falsehood – choice of action – damages

Facts
In an article on the front page of the defendants' newspaper it was alleged that the plaintiff was, inter alia, 'the thief who stole Princess Anne's intimate letters'. As legal aid is not available for defamation proceedings, the plaintiff sought damages for malicious falsehood, proceedings which could and did attract legal aid. The judge struck out the statement of claim as an abuse of the process of the court: the plaintiff appealed.

Held

The appeal would be allowed.

Sir Donald Nicholls V-C:

'Before turning to the issues raised by the appeal I should comment briefly on the difference between defamation and malicious falsehood. The remedy provided by the law for words which injure a person's reputation is defamation. Words may also injure a person without damaging his reputation. An example would be a claim that the seller of goods or land is not the true owner. Another example would be a false assertion that a person has closed down his business. Such claims would not necessarily damage the reputation of those concerned. The remedy provided for this is malicious falsehood, sometimes called injurious falsehood or trade libel. This cause of action embraces particular types of malicious falsehood such as slander of title and slander of goods, but it is not confined to those headings.

Falsity is an essential ingredient of this tort. The plaintiff must establish the untruth of the statement of which he complains. Malice is another essential ingredient. A genuine dispute about the ownership of goods or land should not of itself be actionable. So a person who acted in good faith is not liable. Further, since the object of this cause of action is to provide a person with a remedy for a false statement made maliciously which has caused him damage, at common law proof of financial loss was another essential ingredient. The rigour of this requirement was relaxed by statute. I shall have to return to the question of damages at a later stage. For present purposes it is sufficient to note that if a plaintiff establishes that the defendant maliciously made a false statement which has caused him financial damage, or in respect of which he is relieved from proving damage by the Defamation Act 1952, the law gives him a remedy. The false statement may also be defamatory, or it may not. As already mentioned, it need not be defamatory. Conversely, the fact that the statement is defamatory does not exclude a cause of action for malicious falsehood, although the law will ensure that a plaintiff does not recover damages twice over for the same loss.

Abuse of process: (1) no right to trial by jury
It is as plain as a pikestaff that, had legal aid been available for libel, this action would have been a straightforward defamation action. In an action for malicious falsehood the plaintiff has to take on the burden of proving that the words were false and that in publishing them the defendant was actuated by malice. It would make no sense for Miss Joyce to take on this burden. If this had been a defamation action she would not have to prove malice, and if the newspaper wished to put in issue the truth of the defamatory assertions it would have to plead and prove justification as a defence.

One consequence of this action being a claim for malicious falsehood and not defamation is that there is no absolute right to a trial by jury ... Against this background counsel submitted that the present action should be struck out by the court as an abuse of process because it is based on a secondary tort which deprives the defendants of their absolute right to have a jury trial. This right is a legitimate juridical advantage they would have had if the plaintiff had relied on the primary tort. By a "secondary tort" was meant a tort which would not be relied upon save for the plaintiff's need to secure a collateral purpose unrelated to the merits of her claim.

I am not able to accept this submission. The concept of a legitimate juridical advantage has been taken from the field of conflict of laws where an issue arises over the country in which a dispute between the parties should be determined. The issue there concerns which of two countries, with their different laws and legal systems, would be the more appropriate forum.

I can see no place for that concept in wholly domestic proceedings. English law has marked out causes of action on which plaintiffs may rely. Many causes of action overlap. On one set of facts a plaintiff may have more than one cause of action against a defendant. He may have a cause of action in tort and also for breach of contract. This is an everyday occurrence ... I have never heard it suggested before that a plaintiff is not entitled to ... take full advantage of the various remedies English law provides for the wrong of which he complains. I have never heard it suggested that he must pursue the most appropriate remedy, and if he does not do so he is at risk of having his proceedings struck out as a misuse of the court's procedures. In my view those suggestions are as unfounded as they are novel ...

Abuse of process: (2) "economic lunacy" and legal aid

[Counsel for the defendants'] second submission was as bold as his first. He submitted that another reason why this action is an abuse is that only nominal damages, or at best modest damages of a few hundred pounds, will be recoverable by the plaintiff. The amount she stands to obtain is wholly out of line with the costs each side will incur. In practice the defendants will never recover their costs even if they are successful in defending the actions and even if they make a payment into court of an amount in excess of any damages awarded at the trial. [Counsel] submitted that, so far as the plaintiff is concerned, the action is "economic lunacy", given that any damages awarded to her will be swallowed up by the Legal Aid Board's charge over them as property recovered in the proceedings. Public funds are being used to support the plaintiff in a wholly uneconomic way.

With all respect to counsel, this is a hopeless submission. I shall consider later the question of damages. For the moment let me assume that the defendants are correct in submitting that the plaintiff is unlikely to recover more than a few hundred pounds in damages. I shall make that assumption although I am not to be taken as indorsing it. Even so I do not see how it follows that this action should be struck out as an abuse. The plaintiff's main purpose in bringing this action is to clear her name. If she wins, she will succeed in doing so. Compared with a libel action, the amount of damages she may recover in malicious falsehood may be small, but there is no reason why she should not be entitled to pursue such a claim. I see no justification for the court stopping her action. The defendants, it must be borne in mind, are resisting her claim in its entirety. The prospect that they are unlikely to recoup their costs even if their defence is wholly successful is an unfortunate fact of everyday life for many defendants when sued by legally aided plaintiffs.

The reality here is that the defendants are unhappy that the plaintiff has obtained legal aid to pursue the action. They fear if this action is permitted to proceed, the floodgates will be opened. The Legal Aid Board will be flooded with applications for legal aid to pursue claims for malicious falsehood against newspapers. Newspapers will be faced with the prospect, not intended by Parliament, of legally aided plaintiffs pursuing claims against them founded on defamatory articles.

As to these fears, it is vital to keep in mind that the decision on whether or not to grant legal aid has been entrusted by Parliament to the Legal Aid Board, not the court. Parliament has prescribed a framework of limitations and conditions but the Legal Aid Board retains a discretion. A person whose financial resources make him eligible for legal aid must satisfy the board that he has reasonable grounds for taking, defending or being a party to the proceedings ...

Abuse of process: (3) the action is bound to fail

The defendant's third submission was that the action is incapable of success and should be struck out summarily. The jurisdiction the defendants invoke here is well established. The court will not permit an action to go to trial if plainly and obviously it cannot succeed. But when exercising this jurisdiction the court is careful not to conduct a summary trial on affidavit evidence without the benefit of discovery of documents and cross-examination of witnesses on disputed questions of fact. If there is an issue or dispute that ought to be tried, the action must go to trial ...

So far as the statement of claim is concerned I am satisfied that, although open to criticism here and there, it does disclose the essentials of a cause of action for malicious falsehood. It is susceptible to a request for further particulars in some respects, but the omissions are not so serious or incapable of being made good that the defendants will be embarrassed in the conduct of their defence ...

Damages

I turn to the points raised regarding damages. The plaintiff claims, first, that she suffered financial loss in consequence of the ... article. Having regard to the nature and prominence of the assertions in the article, her chances of finding work in any employment requiring trust and confidence have been diminished. Secondly, she relies on s3 of the Defamation Act 1952 ... She alleges that the article was likely to cause pecuniary damage to her by seriously prejudicing her opportunity to obtain other employment requiring trust and confidence.

On this interlocutory appeal it would be wholly inappropriate for us to attempt to go into the detail of the evidence which may properly be called in support of these claims. Suffice to say, on the first claim the plaintiff will need to give particulars of the financial loss she claims to have suffered sufficient to ensure that the defendants will not be taken by surprise by any evidence she may adduce on the amount of her loss.

As to the second claim, this is an allegation of general damage. In support of this claim the plaintiff cannot adduce evidence of actual loss ... I do not accept, however, that in consequence the award under this head must necessarily be nominal only ... The whole purpose of s3 was to give the plaintiff a remedy in malicious falsehood despite the difficulty of proving actual loss. A plaintiff is seldom able to call witnesses to say they ceased to deal with him because of some slander that had come to their ears. In consequence actions for malicious falsehood had become extremely rare ... Section 3 was enacted to right this injustice. The section would fail in its purpose if, whenever relied on, it could lead only to an award of nominal damages.

Damages for distress and injury to feelings
The plaintiff claims, thirdly, that as a consequence of the article she suffered anxiety, distress and injury to her feelings. [Counsel] submitted that this third head of damages is irrecoverable as a matter of law and should be struck out. [Counsel for the plaintiff] contended that, although at common law proof of pecuniary damage was an essential ingredient of the tort, once pecuniary loss is established, or a claim under s3 is made out, a plaintiff is entitled to recover his whole loss. If he suffered mental distress, the law will include an award of damages under this head also.

The point seems never to have been decided ... it is well settled that at common law proof of "special damage" is an essential ingredient in this cause of action. At common law if such damage is not established the action will fail ...

[The] state of the authorities suggests that damages for anxiety and distress are not recoverable for malicious falsehood. If that is the law it could lead to a manifestly unsatisfactory and unjust result in some cases. Take the example I gave earlier of a person who maliciously spreads rumours that his competitor's business has closed down. Or the rumour might be that the business is in financial difficulty and that a receiver will soon be appointed. The owner of the business suffers severe financial loss. Further, because of the effect the rumours are having on his business he is worried beyond measure about his livelihood and his family's future. He suffers acute anxiety and distress. Can it be right that the law is unable to give him any recompense for this suffering against the person whose malice caused it? Although injury to feelings alone will not found a cause of action in malicious falsehood, ought not the law to take such injury into account when it is connected with financial damage inflicted by the falsehood? ...

The point bristles with problems, not all of which were explored in argument. One possibility is that in an action for malicious falsehood damages are limited to financial loss. That would mark out a clear boundary, but it would suffer from the drawback of failing to do justice in the type of case I have mentioned. I instinctively recoil from the notion that in no circumstances can an injured plaintiff obtain recompense from a defendant for understandable distress caused by a false statement made maliciously. However, once it is accepted there are circumstances in which non-pecuniary loss, or some types of non-pecuniary loss, can be recovered in a malicious falsehood action, it becomes extremely difficult to define those circumstances or those types of loss in a coherent manner. It would be going too far to hold that all non-pecuniary loss suffered by a plaintiff is recoverable in a malicious falsehood action, because that would include injury to reputation at large. The history of malicious falsehood as a cause of action shows it was not designed to provide a remedy for such injury: the remedy for such loss is an action for defamation in which, incidentally, damages for injury to feelings may be included in a general award of damages ...

My conclusion is that, on the limited argument addressed to us, it would be undesirable to decide this point. It is an important point of law but only a minor point in the present application. The pleading should be left as it stands and, if need be, this issue can be pursued further at the trial.'

Ratcliffe **v** *Evans* [1892] 2 QB 524 Court of Appeal (Lord Esher MR, Bowen and Fry LJJ)

Malicious falsehood – general loss of business

Facts
This was an action for damages for injurious falsehoods for a statement in a newspaper that the plaintiff's firm had gone out of business. P proved a general loss of business as a result, but he could not prove the loss of any particular order or customer. The jury found the words were not libellous, but on the other hand were not published bona fide. The defendant had judgment entered against him and he appealed.

Held
The appeal would be dismissed as an action will lie for written or oral falsehoods not actionable per se where they are published maliciously and where they are calculated to and do cause damage. To support the action, actual damage must be proved and a general loss of business is sufficient to prove actual damage.

Commentary
See now s3 of the Defamation Act 1952

White **v** *Mellin* [1895] AC 154 House of Lords (Lord Herschell LC, Lord Watson, Lord Macnaghten, Lord Morris and Lord Shand)

Malicious falsehood – no injury

Facts
The defendant sold the plaintiff's 'Infants Foods' affixing a label to P's wrappers, stating that D's foods for infants and invalids were far more nutritious and healthful than any other. It was not proved that the statement was untrue or that it had caused any damage to P.

Held
The action in injurious falsehood would fail: there was no evidence that the statement had injured P or had been calculated to injure him.

26 Passing Off

Associated Newspapers plc v *Insert Media Ltd* [1991] 1 WLR 571 Court of Appeal
(Sir Nicolas Browne-Wilkinson VC, Stocker and Beldam LJJ)

Unauthorised advertising – insertions in newspapers

Facts
The defendant, without the consent of the plaintiff newspaper company, proposed to arrange for his customers to insert their own advertising material between the pages of the plaintiffs' national newspapers. The defendant offered to put a disclaimer on the inserts stating that 'this material does not appear with approval and/or knowledge of publishers of the newspaper with which it was delivered'. The plaintiffs sought an injunction to restrain such insertions.

Held
The injunction would be granted as, notwithstanding the offered disclaimer (which, in the unlikely event of it coming to readers' attention, would be likely to confuse them), there was a substantial body of the public at large which would perceive or assume that the inserts were made by the plaintiffs or with their authority.

Beldam LJ:

'The [plaintiffs], in taking advertisements for their publication, insist that their advertisers will meet recognised standards ... In addition they require that the advertiser warrants that any goods advertised will conform with the Trade Descriptions Act 1968 and, in the case of advertisements promoting investment opportunities, that the contents have been approved or authorised in accordance with the meaning of the Financial Services Act 1986. The [plaintiffs] regard the integrity of those who advertise in their publications as of such importance in maintaining their readership that they make a particular point of following up complaints by their readers and trying to secure that they are satisfactorily dealt with by the advertisers. Thus, if readers could reasonably believe that the appellant's inserts were included with the authority and approval of the respondents in their publications, they would believe that those inserts and the advertisements in them had the quality and backing of the [plaintiffs'] approved advertisements, whereas they did not in fact do so.

... I consider that the [plaintiffs'] readership could have readily believed that the inserts were included with the [plaintiffs'] approval and authority. I think therefore that there was an implied representation that the advertisements are approved by the [plaintiffs] and are of the quality associated with their advertisements with the backup that they provide. That representation is untrue. The acts of inserting such material within the [plaintiffs'] publications are clearly likely to cause loss of goodwill. Such an adverse effect on their goodwill is, in my judgment, readily foreseeable.

It is argued that there is no causal connection shown between the risk of losing goodwill and the implied representation ... I agree that the risk of loss of goodwill is directly connected with the misrepresentation made to the [plaintiffs'] readership ...'

British Vacuum Cleaner Co Ltd v *New Vacuum Cleaner Co Ltd* [1907] 2 Ch 312
High Court (Parker J)

Trade name – name of descriptive article and process

Facts
The plaintiffs had letters patent in respect of carpet cleaning machinery depending on suction. Some years later the defendant company was formed to exploit a similar (but materially different) invention. The plaintiffs sought to restrain the use by the defendants of the words 'vacuum cleaner' in their title.

Held
An injunction would not be granted as the words in question were merely descriptive and without secondary or subsidiary meaning.

Commentary
Distinguished: *Reddaway* v *Banham* [1896] AC 199.

Cadbury Schweppes Pty Ltd v *Pub Squash Co Pty Ltd* [1981] 1 WLR 193 Privy Council (Lord Wilberforce, Lord Edmund-Davies, Lord Fraser of Tullybelton, Lord Scarman and Lord Roskill)

Passing off – descriptive material

Facts
In 1974 the appellants began marketing a soft drink called 'Solo': it was sold in cans of a distinctive colour with a medallion and the marketing was accompanied by an intensive advertising campaign associating the drink with rugged masculine endeavour. By early 1975 'Solo' was selling well, but in that year the respondents launched a similar product called 'Pub Squash' and they sold it in cans of the same type and colour, also with a medallion on the label. Their more limited advertising also used the theme of masculine endeavour. Sales of 'Solo' dropped and the appellants sought, inter alia, an injunction in respect of the alleged passing off of 'Pub Squash' as 'Solo'.

Held
The injunction should not be granted as the trial judge had been entitled to find that the consuming public had not been deceived or misled and that a cause of action for passing off had not therefore been established.

Lord Scarman:

> 'The width of the principle now authoritatively recognised by the ... House of Lords is, therefore, such that the tort is no longer anchored, as in its early nineteenth century formulation, to the name or trade mark of a product or business. It is wide enough to encompass other descriptive material, such as slogans or visual images, which radio, television or newspaper advertising campaigns can lead the marker to associate with a plaintiff's product, provided always that such descriptive material has become part of the goodwill of the product. And the test is whether the product has derived from the advertising a distinctive character which the market recognises ... In reaching his conclusion of fact that the respondent had "sufficiently" distinguished its product from "Solo", the judge had not only to conduct an elaborate and detailed analysis of the evidence, which he certainly did, but to bear in mind the necessity in this branch of the law of the balance to be maintained between the protection of a plaintiff's investment in his product and the protection of free competition. It is only if a plaintiff can establish that a defendant

has invaded his "intangible property right" in his product by misappropriating descriptions which have become recognised by the market as distinctive of the product that the law will permit competition to be restricted. Any other approach would encourage monopoly. The new, small man would increasingly find his entry into an existing market obstructed by the large traders already well known as operating in it.'

Commentary
Applied: *Erven Warnink BV* v *J Townend & Sons (Hull) Ltd* [1979] 3 WLR 68.

Dalgety Spillers Foods Ltd v *Food Brokers Ltd* (1993) The Times 2 December High Court (Blackburne J)

Injunctions in passing-off actions

Facts
The defendants proposed to sell in England a product, Cup Noodles, which was similar in get up to the plaintiffs' product, Pot Noodles. The defendants, on the advice of leading counsel, wrote to the plaintiffs describing their intentions and enclosing sample containers. The letter was acknowledged but never answered, and some 12 months later the defendants launched their Cup Noodles product. The plaintiffs sought an injunction.

Held
The injunction would be refused on the balance of convenience. In informing the plaintiffs of their intentions and submitting samples, the defendants had demonstrated a wish to act with proper regard for the rights of others. The plaintiffs had effectively ignored the letter and the defendants had expended time, trouble and expense in their launch.

Erven Warnink BV v *J Townend & Sons (Hull) Ltd* [1979] 3 WLR 68 House of Lords (Lord Diplock, Viscount Dilhorne, Lord Salmon, Lord Fraser of Tullybelton and Lord Scarman)

Passing off – product's name

Facts
The plaintiffs manufactured and distributed 'advocaat', a drink containing eggs and spirits. It had become popular in England and its name had acquired a substantial reputation and goodwill. The plaintiffs had 75 per cent of the English market; the rest was held by other Dutch manufacturers. The defendants made a drink out of dried eggs and Cyprus sherry which they marketed as 'Old English Advocaat'. As excise duty was less on sherry than spirits it could be sold at a lower price. The alcoholic strength of the two drinks was much the same, although a regular (but not a casual) drinker could tell the difference between them. The plaintiffs sought an injunction to restrain the use of the word 'advocaat' in relation to any product which was not made out of eggs and spirits without the addition of wine.

Held
The injunction would be granted.

Lord Fraser of Tullybelton:

'It is essential for the plaintiff in a passing-off action to show at least the following facts: (1) that his business consists of, or includes, selling in England a class of goods to which the particular trade name applies; (2) that the class of goods is clearly defined, and that in the minds of the public, or a section of the public, in England, the trade name distinguishes that class from other similar goods; (3) that because of the reputation of the goods there is goodwill attached to the name; (4) that he, the plaintiff, as a member of the class of those who sell the goods, is the owner of goodwill in England which is of substantial value; (5) that he has suffered, or is really likely to suffer, substantial damage to his property in the goodwill by reason of the defendants selling goods which are falsely described by the trade name to which the goodwill is attached. Provided these conditions are satisfied, as they are in the present case, I consider that the plaintiff is entitled to protect himself by a passing-off action.'

Commentary
Applied in *Cadbury Schweppes Pty Ltd* v *Pub Squash Co Pty Ltd* [1981] 1 WLR 193.

Hodgkinson & Corby Ltd v *Wards Mobility Services Ltd* [1994] 1 WLR 1564 High Court (Jacob J)

Ingredients of tort – deception

Facts
The plaintiff marketed in the United Kingdom cushions under the trade name 'Roho' for use in wheelchairs. There was no United Kingdom patent for the cushions and the United States patent had expired. In 1993, the defendant sought to market in the United Kingdom, under the trade name 'Flo'Tair', cheaper cushions made to a design copied from and similar to Roho. The plaintiffs brought an action claiming that the defendant was passing off its cushions as those of the plaintiffs'. The evidence established that such cushions were invariably bought by healthcare professionals.

Held
That deception was an essential ingredient of the tort of passing off, and that if the ingredients of the tort were made out the defendant would not be liable in the absence of deceit. Where a defendant marketed copies of a plaintiff's goods, the plaintiff could only succeed if he could prove that purchasers were deceived into buying the defendant's product in the mistaken belief that they were buying the plaintiff's goods. On the facts the only purchasers of the goods were healthcare professionals who would not be so deceived, hence the action was dismissed.

Maxim's Ltd v *Dye* [1977] 1 WLR 1155 High Court (Graham J)

Passing off – trade name

Facts
The plaintiff, an English company, since 1907 had owned Maxim's, a famous restaurant in Paris. In 1975 the defendant opened a restaurant in Norwich under the name of Maxim's and she furnished it in such a style as to give it a French atmosphere. According to the plaintiff, the defendant's restaurant was run to a much lower standard than the plaintiff's and the defendant's conduct was calculated to injure the plaintiff's goodwill and reputation. The plaintiff sought an injunction: the defendant failed to deliver a defence.

Held
Since it had to be assumed that the plaintiff had proved that it had a reputation and goodwill in England derived from its restaurant business in Paris, the plaintiff was entitled to the relief claimed.

Graham J:

'True, the plaintiff is an English company but it is clear it has not and never has had any business in this country. Nevertheless I am bound on the statement of claim to hold that as a fact the plaintiff has a reputation in this country by virtue of its restaurant in Paris. If it is in law correct to say that a plaintiff cannot establish that he has goodwill in England which will be protected by our courts without actually showing that he has a business in England, then of course that is the end of the matter and the plaintiff cannot recover here, but in my judgment that is not the law.'

Commentary
Not followed: *Bernadin (Alain) et Compagnie* v *Pavilion Properties Ltd* [1967] RPC 581.

Reckitt & Colman Products Ltd v *Borden Inc* [1990] 1 WLR 491 House of Lords (Lord Bridge of Harwich, Lord Brandon of Oakbrook, Lord Oliver of Aylmerton, Lord Goff of Chieveley and Lord Jancey of Tullichettle)

Passing off – plastic lemon container

Facts
Effectively, the plaintiffs were the only company marketing in the United Kingdom lemon juice ('Jif') in lemon-like plastic containers, but the defendants adopted a similar approach. The plaintiffs sought an injunction to restrain the defendants from passing off their lemon juice as that of the plaintiffs by use of a get-up deceptively similar to that used by the plaintiffs. The trial judge found that although a careful shopper would conclude that the defendants' 'lemon' was not that of the plaintiffs, since it was merely a question of reading the label, nevertheless the evidence conclusively established that the introduction of the defendants lemons was bound to result in many shoppers purchasing them in the belief that they were purchasing the plaintiffs' well-known and liked lemons, since the crucial point of reference for a shopper who wished to purchase one of the plaintiffs' lemons was the lemon shape itself and no attention was paid to the label. Accordingly, he granted the injunction and his decision was upheld by the Court of Appeal. The defendants appealed.

Held
The appeal would be dismissed

Lord Oliver of Aylmerton:

'In the end, the question comes down not to whether the [plaintiffs] are entitled to a monopoly in the sale of lemon juice in natural-size lemon-shaped containers but whether the [defendants], in deliberately adopting, out of all the many possible shapes of container, a container having the most immediately striking feature of the [plaintiffs'] get-up, have taken sufficient steps to distinguish their product from that of the [plaintiffs] ... the trial judge was satisfied of the fact that a substantial part of the purchasing public requires specifically Jif lemon juice, associates it with the lemon-shape, lemon-size container which is the dominant characteristic of the get-up and pays little or no attention to the label. It is no answer to say that the diversion of trade which he was satisfied would take place would be of relatively short duration, since the public would ultimately become educated to the fact that there were two brands of lemon juice marketed in such containers and would then be likely to pay more attention to the labels to be sure that they got the brand which they required. His finding was that the diversion would be likely to run into millions of units. It inevitably follows from these findings that the [defendants] have not in fact sufficiently and effectively distinguished their goods from those of the [plaintiffs] and it is not for the [plaintiffs] or for the court to suggest what more they should do .... In the light of the trial judge's finding, I see no escape from the proposition that the [plaintiffs] were entitled to the injunction which they obtained in the form in which it was granted.'

Reddaway & Co v Banham & Co [1896] AC 199 House of Lords (Lord Halsbury LC, Lord Herschell, Lord Macnaghten and Lord Morris)

Passing off – trade description

Facts

For some years the plaintiff had manufactured machine belting which was known throughout the trade as 'Camel Hair Belting'. The defendant manufacturers began to stamp their product 'Camel Hair Belting' and the plaintiff sought an injunction to restrain them from using the words 'camel hair' so as to deceive purchasers and pass off their goods as those of the plaintiff.

Held

An injunction would be granted.

Lord Morris:

'I have felt some difficulty in concurring as I do in the judgment proposed to be given in favour of the [plaintiff] by your Lordships, for it established, and, in my opinion, for the first time, the proposition that a trader is not permitted merely to tell truthfully and accurately the material of which his goods are made. I find myself coerced, however, to a conclusion against the [defendants] by the finding of the jury, which amounts to this, that camel hair belting had become so identified with the name of the [plaintiff] Reddaway, as that camel hair belting had in the market obtained the meaning of Reddaway's belting, and there was sufficient evidence given at the trial to support that finding of the jury. That finding establishes as a fact that use of the words "camel hair belting" simpliciter deceives purchasers, and it becomes necessary for the [defendants] to remove that false impression so made on the public. That something, to my mind, is obviously done when the [defendants] put prominently and in a conspicuous place on the article the statement that it was camel hair belting manufactured by themselves. Having done so, they would, as it appears to me, fully apprise purchasers that it was not Reddaway's make, by stating that it was their own. A representation deceiving the public is and must be the foundation of the [plaintiff's] right to recover; [he is] not entitled to any monopoly of the name "camel hair belting", irrespective of its deceiving the public, and everyone has a right to describe truly his article by that name provided he distinguishes it from the [plaintiff's] make. In this case the [defendants] did not so distinguish it, because they omitted to state that it was their own make.'

Commentary

Distinguished in *British Vacuum Cleaner Co Ltd* v *New Vacuum Cleaner Co Ltd* [1907] 2 Ch 312.

Taittinger* v *Allbev Ltd (1993) The Times 26 June Court of Appeal (Sir Thomas Bingham MR, Mann and Peter Gibson LJJ)

Passing-off action – nature of actual damage

Facts

The defendant manufactured and marketed mostly traditional non-alcoholic drinks, and marketed a product described as 'Elderflower Champagne'. The product was sold in a bottle that looked like the usual champagne bottle with a wire retaining device attached to the cork. In the High Court the judge, following the approach in *Warnink* v *Townsend* [1979] AC 731, found that there was a misrepresentation made by a trader in the course of trade to prospective customers which was calculated to injure the goodwill of another trader in the sense that it was a reasonably foreseeable consequence but that it had caused no actual damage to the business or goodwill of the plaintiff. The plaintiff, acting on behalf of itself and other French champagne producers, appealed.

Held

The appeal was allowed, on the grounds that there was ample evidence that it was reasonably foreseeable that the plaintiffs would suffer injury to their goodwill; the defendant had accepted in evidence that confusion was likely if he continued to describe his product using the word 'champagne'. If the defendants were allowed to use the name 'Elderflower Champagne' the goodwill in the distinctive name 'champagne' would be eroded.

White Hudson & Co Ltd v *Asian Organisation Ltd* [1964] 1 WLR 1466 Privy Council (Lord Guest, Lord Pearce and Lord Upjohn)

Passing off – wrappings

Facts

Since 1953 the appellants had sold in Singapore medicated cough sweets called 'Hacks'. Each sweet was wrapped in red cellophane on which the name was printed, but the vast majority of non-English speaking customers simply asked for 'red paper cough sweets'. In 1958 the respondents began selling medicated cough sweets called 'Pecto': they also had red wrappers bearing the name. The appellants sought an injunction and the trial judge found that (a) the get-up of the appellants' sweets had become distinctive of the sweets and identified with them; (b) there was a probability of confusion and that the similarity of get-up was calculated to deceive.

Held

The appellants had been entitled to the injunction granted by the trial judge.

Lord Guest:

'The essence of a passing off action is that A is not entitled to represent his goods as the goods of B or to enable someone else to do so ... The first matter which a plaintiff must prove in a passing off action is that the get-up of his goods has become distinctive of these goods and that it was associated or identified with them. This is a question of fact ... The second matter which, in order to succeed, a plaintiff must establish is that in the circumstances there is a probability of confusion between the goods of the plaintiff and of the defendant. This again is a question of fact ... No case of actual deception was proved, but this was not necessary.'

27 The Economic Torts

Acrow (Automation) Ltd* v *Rex Chainbelt Inc [1971] 1 WLR 1676 Court of Appeal (Lord Denning MR, Phillimore and Megaw LJJ)

Unlawful interference with trade

Facts

SI Inc granted an English company a special right to manufacture automation equipment and gave the plaintiffs exclusive right of sale in England. The essential component, a chain, was made by R with whom SI Inc were already closely associated and reserved the rights to tell R to whom the chains should be sold. SI Inc purported to terminate the agreement with P and gave instructions to R *not* to supply belts to P. P obtained an injunction against SI Inc and R and both were informed. SI Inc ignored the injunction. When P ordered a chain from R, he was refused. R claimed it would jeopardise his contractual relations with SI Inc to supply P.

Held

Ordering R *not* to supply was both a contempt of court and a breach of an implied term in the combination made by R and SI Inc.

Lord Denning MR:

'I take the principle of law to be that which I stated in *Torquay Hotel Co Ltd* v *Cousins*, namely, that if one person, without just cause or excuse, deliberately interferes with the trade or business of another, and does so by unlawful means, that is, by an act which he is not at liberty to commit, then he is acting unlawfully. He is liable in damages; and, in a proper case, an injunction can be granted against him.'

Allen* v *Flood [1898] AC 1 House of Lords (Lord Halsbury LC, Lord Watson, Lord Ashbourne, Lord Herschell, Lord Macnaghten, Lord Morris, Lord Shand, Lord Davey and Lord James of Hereford)

Procurement of lawful act

Facts

The plaintiff shipwrights were skilled in both wood and iron work: on this assignment they were working in wood, employed by the day. Hearing of this, the boilermakers' union told the employees that, as the plaintiffs had previously worked in iron, unless they were dismissed, the boilermakers working on the same ship would leave off work. The plaintiffs were discharged, although it was reasonable for them to expect that the work would have lasted for about a fortnight: they sued the defendant, a representative of the union, for 'intimidating and coercing' the employers to terminate their employment.

Held (Lord Halsbury LC, Lord Ashbourne and Lord Morris dissenting)
Their action could not succeed.

Lord Shand:

' ... the argument of the plaintiffs ... [seems] to me to fail, because, although it is no doubt true that the plaintiffs were entitled to pursue their trade as workmen "without hindrance", their right to do so was qualified by an equal right, and, indeed, the same right, on the part of the other workmen. The hindrance must not be of an unlawful character. It must not be by unlawful action. Among the rights of all workmen is the right of competition. In the like manner and to the same extent as a workman has a right to pursue his work or labour without hindrance, a trader has a right to trade without hindrance. That right is subject to the right of others to trade also, and to subject him to competition – competition which is in itself lawful, and cannot be complained of where no unlawful means ... has been employed. The matter has been settled in so far as competition in trade is concerned by the decision of this House in *Mogul Steamship Co* v *McGregor, Gow & Co* [1892] AC 25. I can see no reason for saying that a different principle should apply to competition in labour. In the course of such competition, and with a view to secure an advantage to himself, I can find no reason for saying that a workman is not within his legal rights in resolving that he will decline to work in the same employment with certain other persons, and in intimating that resolution to his employers.

It is further to be observed, distinguishing the case from one in which a contract might have subsisted between the plaintiffs and their employers for a definite period, or for the work, it might be on a particular ship, until the whole was completed (in which case the refusal to continue to give the work would be a breach of contract on the employers' part) that there was here no such breach of contract. The employers' act in dispensing with the services of the plaintiffs at the end of any day was a lawful act on their part. The defendant only induced them to do what they were entitled to do, and in the absence of any fraud or other unlawful means used to bring this about, the actions fails. As already fully explained there was no case of malice in the ordinary sense of the term, as meaning personal ill-will, presented to the jury; but I agree with those of your Lordships who hold that, even if such a motive had existed in the mind of the defendant, this would not have created liability in damages.

... I think the defendant only exercised a legal right in intimating that the boilermakers would leave work if the plaintiffs were continued; he used no fraud or illegal means in the assertion of that right; and the exercise by a person of a legal right does not become illegal because the motive of action is improper or malicious: (*Bradford Corpn* v *Pickles* [1895] AC 587 and *Mogul Steamship Co Case*, already cited) ... It seems to me, with reference also to the decision in the latter case, bearing on the rights of competitors in trade, that on the same principle it may be affirmed that the exercise of any legal right in the course of competition in labour or in trade does not become illegal because it is prompted by a motive which is improper or even malicious.'

Belmont Finance Corporation v *Williams Furniture Ltd (No 2)* [1980] 1 All ER 393
Court of Appeal (Buckley, Goff and Waller LJJ)

Conspiracy – illegal transaction

Facts
The first defendant (Williams) owned all the shares in the second defendant (City) which in turn owned all the shares in the plaintiff company. A director of Williams and City was aware that an agreement between the two companies had the unlawful purpose of enabling another party to acquire Belmont using money provided by Belmont.

Held
Belmont was entitled to damages. Williams and City had been a party to a conspiracy and as a result of that conspiracy Belmont had suffered damage.

Brimelow v *Casson* [1924] 1 Ch 302 High Court (Russell J)

Inducement to break contract – chorus girls

Facts

The plaintiff, a theatrical manager, only paid his chorus girls £1 10s per week when the recommended minimum wage was £2 10s. One member of his company, a girl aged 18, was living with a deformed dwarf in immorality. She had to do this to avoid starvation. The defendants desired to stop this and organised a boycott of P's theatre. P sued them.

Held

The inducement to the girls was justified and, although there was a breach, it was genuinely in the interests of the girls and, therefore, justified.

Russell J:

> 'In these circumstances, have the defendants justification for their acts? That they would have the sympathy and support of decent men and women I can have no doubt. But have they in law justification for those acts? As has been pointed out, no general rule can be laid down as a general guide in such cases, but I confess that, if justification does not exist here, I can hardly conceive the case in which it would be present. These defendants, as it seems to me, owed a duty to their calling and to its members (and I am tempted to add to the public) to take all necessary peaceful steps to terminate the payment of this insufficient wage which in the plaintiff's company had apparently been in fact productive of those results which their past experience had led them to anticipate. "The good sense" of this tribunal leads me to decide that in the circumstances of the present case justification did exist.'

Cory Lighterage Ltd v *Transport and General Workers Union* [1973] 1 WLR 792 Court of Appeal (Lord Denning MR, Buckley and Orr LJJ)

Industrial dispute – action in tort

Facts

A lighterman was employed by the plaintiffs and he was a member of the defendant trade union. He left the union and an official of the union told the plaintiffs that if he was not withdrawn their tugs would not sail. The plaintiffs sent the lighterman home on full pay.

Held

The defendants' acts were actionable in tort, although it was doubtful whether the action would succeed in this case as the lighterman may have been so actuated by ill-will as to give the defendants sufficient justification or excuse for their actions.

Crofter Hand Woven Harris Tweed Co Ltd v *Veitch* [1942] AC 435 House of Lords (Viscount Simon LC, Viscount Maugham, Lord Thankerton, Lord Wright and Lord Porter)

Conspiracy – real purpose

Facts

In order to protect the interests of their members, a union imposed an embargo at the port of Stornaway on all Harris tweed woven from yarn imported from the mainland. Producers of tweed made from such yarn alleged that, in imposing the embargo, the union had conspired to injure them as the natural result of it was the destruction of their businesses.

Held
There had not been an unlawful conspiracy which was actionable at law.

Viscount Simon LC:

' ... the conclusion, in my opinion, is that the predominant object of the [union] in getting the embargo imposed was to benefit their trade union members by preventing under-cutting and unregulated competition, and so helping to secure the economic stability of the island industry. The result they aimed at achieving was to create a better basis for collective bargaining, and thus directly to improve wage prospects. A combination with such an object is not unlawful, because the object is the legitimate promotion of the interests of the combiners, and because the damage necessarily inflicted on the [producers] is not inflicted by criminal or tortious means and is not "the real purpose" of the combination. I agree ... that it is not for a court of law to consider in this connection the expediency or otherwise of a policy adopted by a trade union. Neither can liability be determined by asking whether the damage inflicted to secure the purpose is disproportionately severe. This may throw doubts on the bona fides of the avowed purpose, but, once the legitimate purpose is established an no unlawful means are involved, the quantum of damage is irrelevant.'

Commentary
See also *Lonrho plc* v *Fayed* [1991] 3 WLR 188.

Department of Transport v *Williams* (1993) The Times 7 December Court of Appeal (Dillon, Staughton and Mann LJJ)

Criminal obstruction and the tort of wrongful interference with business

Facts
The defendants were in breach of s303 of the Highways Act 1980 in that they wilfully obstructed a person carrying out his lawful duties under the Act. The question arose as to whether an injunction should be granted in respect of this obstruction. An injunction was granted at first instance and the defendant appealed.

Held
That an injunction could be granted, founded on the tort of interference with business by unlawful means, and as by virtue of s303 of the 1980 Act any wilful interference was unlawful, the elements of the tort were present. The criminal offence established by s303 of the Act, namely wilfully obstructing any person carrying out his lawful duties under the Act, also constituted the tort of wrongful interference with business.

Emerald Construction Co Ltd v *Lowthian* [1966] 1 WLR 691 Court of Appeal (Lord Denning MR, Diplock and Russell LJJ)

Trade union – inducement to breach of contract

Facts
Main contractors subcontracted with the plaintiffs for the supply of labour, but the defendant trade

union officials endeavoured by industrial action to have the subcontract terminated. When the industrial action began, the defendants did not know the subcontract's precise terms.

Held

An interlocutory injunction would be granted as ignorance of the subcontract's precise terms was not enough to show absence of intent to procure its breach.

Commentary

Applied in *Daily Mirror Newspapers Ltd* v *Gardner* [1968] 2 WLR 1239.

Huntley v *Thornton* [1957] 1 WLR 321 High Court (Harman J)

Conspiracy – trade union

Facts

The plaintiff, a fitter, was employed at a shipyard. He was a member of AEU. He was given a leaflet by his union ordering him to stop work over a wage claim. He refused. P later left the area, but returned to find work. On his return, a letter was sent to all shop stewards in the area that P be not allowed to start work 'under any consideration'. He started work with L, but L was shown the letter by T and dismissed P. P brought an action against T, L and the Union.

Held

The Executive Committee of the AEU were liable for conspiracy – they were motivated by spite. T and L were not a party to the Executive Committee's deliberations nor did they have their motivations; therefore, they were not liable.

Commentary

Applied: *Crofter Hand Woven Harris Tweed Co Ltd* v *Veitch* [1942] AC 435.

Law Debenture Trust Corporation v *Ural Caspian Oil Corporation Ltd* [1994] 3 WLR 1221 Court of Appeal (Sir Thomas Bingham MR, Beldam and Saville LJJ)

Inducing breach of contract – nature of right interfered with

Facts

The facts of this case are somewhat complicated, but basically four English companies traded in Russia until 1917 when their assets were confiscated. Following improved relations with the (then) Soviet Union it seemed likely that compensation would be paid in respect of these assets. A company, LI Ltd, acquired the shares of these companies, and LI Ltd and the four companies agreed with the plaintiff company that they would pay any compensation received to the plaintiff as trustee for the shareholders of the four companies. LI Ltd also agreed that it would not transfer the shares unless the transferee entered into a similar agreement. In breach of this agreement LI Ltd transferred the shares to the fifth defendant, who in turn transferred the shares to the sixth defendant.

The plaintiff sued, inter alia, the sixth defendant and applied for leave to amend the statement of claim to allege that the sixth defendant, by causing or procuring or accepting the transfer of shares from the fifth defendant had knowingly, intentionally and/or wrongfully, rendered ineffective the plaintiff's potential claims against the fifth defendant for the retransfer of the shares to LI Ltd, and had interfered with its remedies against the fifth defendant in respect of the fifth defendant's tortious conduct.

At first instance it was held that the general principle which gave a plaintiff a cause of action against a person who procured the violation, by an actionable wrong, of the plaintiff's right against a third party applied where the right violated was a secondary right to a remedy for the tortious inducement of a third party's breach of its primary obligation under a contract. It thus followed that the plaintiff could rely on its secondary right to injunctive relief arising from the sixth defendant's inducement of the breach by the fifth defendant of its contract with LI Ltd, and the facts disclosed a cause of action in tort against the sixth defendant. The sixth defendant appealed.

Held

The appeal was allowed. Although the fifth defendant was liable for its tortious conduct in procuring LI Ltd's breach of contract with the plaintiff so that the plaintiff might have obtained injunctive relief to restrain onward transfer of the shares and to secure their retransfer to LI Ltd, in fact no such injunction had been sought. There was, therefore, nothing unlawful in the transfer of the shares by the fifth defendant, and the sixth defendant's conduct in accepting the transfer did not constitute an actionable wrong which amounted to a violation of the plaintiff's rights. The plaintiff's proposed amendment thus disclosed no cause of action against the sixth defendant.

Sir Thomas Bingham MR:

'Caspian [the sixth defendant] can be liable to Law Debenture if an only if Hilldon's [the fifth defendant] transfer of the shares to it was tortious. But at the time this transfer was made Hilldon [the fifth defendant] was the full legal and beneficial owner of the shares. It had no contractual relationship of any kind with Law Debenture. It was liable to Law Debenture for its tortious conduct in procuring [LI Ltd's] breach of its contract with Law Debenture, but that was all. It was open to Law Debenture to seek an interlocutory injunction restraining Hilldon from making onward transfer and a final injunction ordering retransfer but application had not been made and injunctions had not been granted. Until some injunction was granted, Hilldon [the fifth defendant] was in my judgment entitled to do what it would with its own. I cannot regard the onward transfer as an actionable wrong, and it would in my view defeat the ingenuity of any pleader to frame a plausible statement of claim based on that transfer alone.'

Lonrho plc v *Fayed* [1991] 3 WLR 188 House of Lords (Lord Bridge of Harwich, Lord Brandon of Oakbrook, Lord Templeman, Lord Goff of Chieveley and Lord Jauncey of Tullichettle)

Tort of conspiracy – ingredients

Facts

There was a bitter dispute in relation to the take-over of House of Fraser plc, the owner of Harrods. While the plaintiffs' bid to purchase House of Fraser had been referred to the Monopolies and Mergers Commission (MMC) and they were the subject of an undertaking not to purchase any more shares in that company, the defendants made a bid for House of Fraser which was not referred to the MMC. The plaintiffs alleged that the defendants had influenced the decision of the Secretary of State not to refer the defendants' bid to MMC by fraudulent misrepresentations made about themselves which deprived the plaintiffs of the opportunity to bid for the company and claimed that the defendants had thereby committed, inter alia, the torts of wrongful interference with the plaintiffs' trade or business and conspiracy to injure. The judge struck out the claim: the plaintiffs appealed and the Court of Appeal allowed the appeal in relation to unlawful interference but dismissed it in relation to conspiracy. The parties appealed and cross-appealed.

Held

As the two causes of action stood or fell together, the case should proceed to trial.

Lord Bridge of Harwich:

'It was ... accepted in the Court of Appeal that the statement of claim had not alleged that the predominant purpose of the alleged conspiracy was to injure Lonrho and that accordingly the Court of Appeal were bound by their own decision in *Metall und Rohstoff AG* v *Donaldson Lufkin & Jenrette Inc* [1989] 3 WLR 563 to hold that the pleaded cause of action in conspiracy could not succeed ...

It will be convenient to consider first the clear-cut issue of law which arises on the cross-appeal. In the *Metall* case the Court of Appeal interpreted the decision of this House in *Lonrho Ltd* v *Shell Petroleum Co Ltd* [1981] 3 WLR 33 as holding it to be an essential ingredient in the civil tort of conspiracy to establish that the predominant purpose of the conspirators was to injure the plaintiff irrespective of whether the means they used to effect that purpose were lawful or unlawful ...

In *Rookes* v *Barnard* [1964] 2 WLR 269 Lord Devlin said:

"There are, as is well known, two sorts of conspiracies, the *Quinn* v *Leathem* ([1901] AC 495) type which employs only lawful means but aims at an unlawful end, and the type which employs unlawful means."

Of these two types of tortious conspiracy the *Quinn* v *Leathem* type, where no unlawful means are used, is now regarded as an anomaly for the reasons so clearly explained by Lord Diplock in *Lonrho Ltd* v *Shell Petroleum Co Ltd* ...

Where conspirators act with the predominant purpose of injuring the plaintiff and in fact inflict damage on him, but do nothing which would have been actionable if done by an individual acting alone, it is in the fact of their concerted action for that illegitimate purpose that the law, however anomalous it may now seem, finds a sufficient ground to condemn their action as illegal and tortious. But when conspirators intentionally injure the plaintiff and use unlawful means to do so, it is no defence for them to show that their primary purpose was to further or protect their own interests; it is sufficient to make their action tortious that the means used were unlawful.

Did the House in *Lonrho Ltd* v *Shell Petroleum Co Ltd* depart from this reasoning and lay down for the first time a new principle that a plaintiff, seeking to establish the tort of conspiracy to injure, must in every case prove that the intention to injure him was the predominant purpose of the defendants, whether the means used were lawful or unlawful? ...

My Lords, I am quite unable to accept that Lord Diplock or the other members of the Appellate Committee concurring with him, of whom I was one, intended the decision in *Lonrho Ltd* v *Shell Petroleum Co Ltd* to effect, sub silentio, such a significant change in the law as it had been previously understood. The House ... had never been invited to take such a step. Moreover, to do so would have been directly contrary to the view of Lord Denning MR expressed in the judgment which the House was affirming and inconsistent with the dicta in what Lord Diplock described as "Viscount Simon LC's now classic speech in *Crofter Hand Woven Harris Tweed Co Ltd* v *Veitch* [1942] AC 435 at 439". I would overrule the *Metall* case in this respect.

It follows from this conclusion that Lonrho's acceptance that the pleaded intention on the part of the defendants to cause injury to Lonrho was not the predominant purpose of their alleged unlawful action is not necessarily fatal to the pleaded cause of action in conspiracy and therefore affords no separate ground for striking out that part of the pleading. If the defendants fail to establish that Lonrho's primary pleading asserting the tort of interference with business by unlawful means should be struck out, they are in no stronger position in relation to the pleaded cause of action in conspiracy. It is not, I think, necessary for present purposes to consider whether the pleaded conspiracy adds anything of substance or raises any significantly different issues from those on which the rest of the pleading depends. At this interlocutory stage it is sufficient to say that the two pleaded causes of action must stand or fall together. Either both should be struck out or both should go to trial ... I have reached the conclusion that it would be inappropriate to strike out the statement of claim and that the case must accordingly proceed to trial ...

I would emphasise that the only question of law which, in my opinion, it is appropriate for the House to decide at this stage is that involved in overruling the *Metall* case. The facts pleaded in the statement of claim are strongly disputed. When the facts have been found at trial they may or may not give rise to important questions of law requiring resolution, but for the present purposes it suffices to say that the appellants fail to demonstrate that Lonrho's claim is obviously doomed to fail. Nothing in this opinion should be understood as saying any more than that.'

Lonhro v *Fayed (No 5)* [1993] 1 WLR 1489 Court of Appeal (Dillon, Stuart-Smith and Evans LJJ)

Whether damages for injury to reputation and to feelings can be recovered in conspiracy

Facts
The plaintiffs, two individuals and a company, claimed damages and an injunction for conspiracy, alleging that by conspiracy the defendants had sponsored and encouraged a third party to publish defamatory statements concerning the plaintiffs, and had financed and caused another party to bring an action against the plaintiffs, and that the plaintiffs had suffered damage. The damage was not particularised, and the judge struck out the action.

The plaintiffs appealed and applied for leave to amend the pleadings to give particulars of the injury to the plaintiffs' reputation and feelings and pecuniary loss to the company.

Held
The essential ingredient of the tort of conspiracy to injure by lawful means was an agreement by two or more persons to do acts, which were lawful in themselves, for the sole or predominant purpose of causing injury to the plaintiff and which in fact caused injury to the plaintiff. The tort could not found an action for damages for injury to reputation or injury to feelings since such damages could only be claimed in defamation, in which the defendant could plead justification as an absolute defence. The problems of countering a defence of justification could not be avoided by bringing an action for conspiracy to injure by lawful means: *Joyce* v *Sengupta* [1993] 1 WLR 337 and *Spring* v *Guardian Assurance* [1993] 2 All ER 273 applied.

Lumley v *Gye* (1853) 2 E & B 216 Court of Queen's Bench (Coleridge, Erle, Wightman and Crompton JJ)

Procurement of breach of contract

Facts
The plaintiff, the lessee and manager of the Queen's Theatre, claimed damages from the defendant for causing Johanna Wagner to break a contract by which she had undertaken to perform at the plaintiff's theatre for a specified time.

Held (Coleridge J dissenting)
His action would be successful.

Crompton J:

'Whatever may have been the origin or foundation of the law as to enticing of servants, and whether it be, as contended by the plaintiff, an instance and branch of a wider rule, or, as contended by the defendant, an anomaly and an exception from the general rule of law on such subjects, it must now be considered clear law that a person who wrongfully and maliciously, or, which is the same thing, with notice, interrupts the relation subsisting between master and servant by procuring the servant to depart from the master's service, or by harbouring and keeping him as servant after he has quitted it and during the time stipulated for as the period of service, whereby the master is injured, commits a wrongful act for which he is responsible at law. I think that the rule applies wherever the wrongful interruption operates to prevent the service during the time for which the parties have contracted that the service shall continue, and I think that the relation of master and servant subsists, sufficiently for the purpose of such action, during the time for which there is in existence a binding contract of hiring and service between the parties. I think that it is a fanciful and technical and unjust distinction to say that they not having actually entered into the service, or that the service is not actually continuing, can make any difference.'

Merkur Island Shipping Corp v *Laughton* [1983] 2 WLR 778 House of Lords (Lord Diplock, Lord Edmund-Davies, Lord Keith of Kinkel, Lord Brandon of Oakbrook and Lord Brightman)

Trade union – inducement to breach of contract

Facts
The International Transport Workers Federation, of which the defendants were officials, decided to black the plaintiffs' ship because of the low wages paid to an Asian crew. As a result, the ship could not leave port and the plaintiffs sought interlocutory injunctions.

Held
The injunctions had properly been granted. The plaintiffs had a cause of action at common law for interference with the performance of their contract with a third party (charterers of the ship) of which the defendants were, or were assumed to be, aware. Although the cause of action had been removed by s13(1)(a) of the Trade Union and Labour Relations Act 1974, it had been restored by s17 of the Employment Act 1980.

Middlebrook Mushrooms Ltd v *Transport and General Workers' Union* (1993) The Times 18 January Court of Appeal (Neill, Mann and Hoffmann LJJ)

Procuring breach of contract – scope of tort

Facts
The defendant trade union proposed to undertake a campaign of distributing leaflets outside supermarkets, urging members of the public to support dismissed employees of the plaintiffs by refusing to buy the plaintiffs' products which were on sale in the supermarkets. The plaintiffs obtained an interlocutory injunction restraining these actions, on the grounds that the defendant actions amounted to a direct interference with contracts with which the plaintiffs were parties, namely between the plaintiffs and the supermarkets. The defendants appealed.

Held
That as the plaintiffs alleged that the proposed actions would amount to a direct interference with contractual relations, they must show that their case fell within the principles established in *Lumley* v *Gye* (1853) 2 E & B 216. The persuasion thus had to be directed at one of the parties to the contract. In the present case the leaflet was directed to the customers; there was no message in the leaflets to the supermarkets who were not exhorted to take, or desist from taking, any action. The court refused to accept that it was enough for the plaintiffs to prove one of the supermarket managers might be influenced by the distribution of the leaflets. The court held that it was most important not to extend *Lumley* v *Gye* outside its proper limits.

Midland Bank Trust Co Ltd v *Green (No 3)* [1979] 2 WLR 594 Court of Appeal (Lord Denning MR, Fox LJ and Sir George Baker)

Conspiracy – husband and wife

Facts

A husband and wife conspired together to defraud a son by depriving him of an option to purchase his father's farm.

Held

For the purposes of the law of tort there was no rule that a husband and wife could not conspire together and damages had rightly been awarded against them.

Sir George Baker:

'The law is a living thing; it adapts and develops to fulfil the needs of living people whom it both governs and serves. Like clothes it should be made to fit people. It must never be strangled by the dead hand of long discarded custom, belief, doctrine or principle. The legal doctrine, in so far as there ever was one, of unity of husband and wife, whether founded originally on unity of flesh from Genesis 2:24 ... or on the subjugation of woman to man resulting in the submersion of the wife in the husband, he being the head, 'the two are one and that one is the husband', survives in the very limited rule now to be found in the exemptions from liability for conspiracy: see the sidenote to s2(2) of the Criminal Law Act 1977. To extend this rule or exemption to the tort of conspiracy because of the legal fiction of ancient times that husband and wife being one person could not agree or combine with each other would to my mind be akin to basing a judgment on the proposition that the Earth is flat, because many believed that centuries ago. We now know that the Earth is not flat. We now know that husband and wife in the eyes of the law and in fact are equal.'

Mogul Steamship Co Ltd v *McGregor, Gow & Co* [1892] AC 25 House of Lords (Lord Halsbury LC, Lord Watson, Lord Bramwell, Lord Macnaghten, Lord Morris, Lord Field and Lord Hannen)

Course of dealing unlawful?

Facts

An associated body of traders endeavoured to get the whole of the limited China tea trade into their own hands by offering exceptional and very favourable terms to customers who would deal exclusively with them. If their trading had been confined to one particular period they would have been trading at a loss, but they gave these terms in the belief that by such competition they would prevent rival traders competing with them and so receive themselves the whole profits of the trade. A shipping company alleged that this course of dealing was unlawful and constituted an actionable conspiracy.

Held

This was not the case.

Lord Halsbury LC:

'I am of opinion ... that the whole matter comes round to ... whether a combination to trade, and to offer, in respect of prices, discounts and other trade facilities, such terms as will win so large an amount of custom as to render it unprofitable for rival customers to pursue the same trade, is unlawful, and I am clearly of opinion that it is not.'

Morgan v *Fry* [1968] 3 WLR 506 Court of Appeal (Lord Denning MR, Davies and Russell LJJ)

Trade union – inducement to terminate contracts of employment

Facts

Being dissatisfied with a wage settlement, the plaintiff and three others decided to form a breakaway union. Their former union gave the employers over two weeks' notice that their members would be instructed not to work with the plaintiff and his colleagues: under their contracts of service their employment could be terminated by one week's notice. The employers sacked the plaintiff and he sued the union for intimidation and conspiracy.

Held

The union's notice to the employers was not unlawful, being longer than the requisite notice of one week, and it followed that the plaintiff's action would fail.

Lord Denning MR:

> 'In my opinion ... the defendants here did not use any unlawful means to achieve their aim. They were not guilty of intimidation: because they gave a "strike notice" of proper length. They were not guilty of conspiracy to use unlawful means: because they used none. They were not guilty of conspiracy to injure, because they acted honestly and sincerely in what they believed to be the true interests of their members. That is enought to decide this case.'

RCA Corp v *Pollard* [1982] 3 WLR 1007 Court of Appeal (Lawton, Oliver and Slade LJJ)

Unauthorised recordings

Facts

The plaintiff record companies alleged that the defendant had knowingly traded in bootleg records although they did not claim that he had made them. The plaintiffs sought, inter alia, an injunction.

Held

The defendant was entitled to judgment as he had not interfered with the performance of the plaintiffs' exclusive recording contracts.

Commentary

Applied: *Lonrho Ltd* v *Shell Petroleum Co Ltd* [1981] 3 WLR 33.
    Not followed: *Ex parte Island Records Ltd* [1978] 3 WLR 23.

Rookes v *Barnard* [1964] 2 WLR 269 House of Lords (Lord Reid, Lord Evershed, Lord Hodson, Lord Devlin and Lord Pearce)

Intimidation – trade union

Facts

The plaintiff, employed by BOAC, left his union – AESD – because of policy disagreements. The AESD had an informal agreement with BOAC that only their members would be employed by BOAC. B, F and D, local union officials, informed BOAC that unless P was removed within three days, all labour would be withdrawn. P was sacked; he sued B, F and D for conspiracy.

Held

The plaintiff was entitled to damages for the tort of intimidation, but this was not a suitable case for exemplary damages to be granted.

Commentary

Distinguished in *Stratford (JT) & Son Ltd* v *Lindley* [1964] 3 WLR 541.
   Followed in *AB* v *South West Water Services Ltd* [1993] 2 WLR 507.

Scala Ballroom (Wolverhampton) Ltd v *Ratcliffe* [1958] 1 WLR 1057 Court of Appeal (Hodson, Morris and Sellers LJJ)

Conspiracy – trade union

Facts

The plaintiffs decided to exclude 'coloured' persons from their ballroom and the Musicians' Union, with many coloured members, said none of its members would play there until the colour bar was lifted. The plaintiffs sought an injunction on grounds of conspiracy.

Held

The injunction would not be granted. There was no actionable conspiracy as the union's purpose (the protection of the interests of its members) was not illegal.

Hodson LJ:

   'I am not prepared ... to say that the interests which can lawfully be protected are confined to the material interests in the sense of interests which can be exchanged for cash.'

Sorrell v *Smith* [1925] AC 700 House of Lords (Viscount Cave LC, Lord Dunedin, Lord Atkinson, Lord Sumner and Lord Buckmaster)

Trade combination – legality

Facts

A trade union of retail newsagents wished to limit the number of retail newspaper shops in a certain area. This policy was enforced by inducing the members of the union to withdraw their custom from any wholesaler who supplied newspapers to a retailer who had opened a new shop within that particular area without first obtaining the union's consent. The appellant, who was a member of the union, obtained his supplies from Ritchie Brothers, but as they were also supplying newcomers who had opened shops without the union's permission, at the request of the union he transferred his custom to Watson & Sons. The respondents, who were the circulating managers of the principal London daily newspapers, threatened to withhold supplies to Watson & Sons unless the appellant returned his business to Ritchie Brothers. The appellant sought to restrain the respondents from interfering with his contractual relations with Watson & Sons.

Held

The action would fail as the respondents had not committed, or threatened to commit, any wrong.

Lord Dunedin:

   'The means were not illegal; all the means used were to tell Watson that if he did not cease supplying Sorrell, the newspaper proprietors would cease to supply him. To cease to supply Watson was just as legal in itself as Sorrell's leaving Ritchie, because he did not carry out the distance resolution. What I have to do is to fancy myself a juryman, faced with the question with which I began this opinion, and which, I think, still remains: Was there here a conspiracy to injury Sorrell? I hold there was not ... Sorrell had volunteered to take action as a piece of policy on behalf of the federation. The action of the circulation managers was a defensive action to protect their own trade against being dictated to by the federation; it was in no sense a conspiracy to injure Sorrell ... I look at the inquiry into the facts, not as a means of arriving at the conclusion whether there was justification of what, without justification, would be an illegal action, but as evidence of whether there was any proof of illegal action, ie a conspiracy to injure, and I find, as a juryman, that there was none. As I am attempting to deal with the whole subject, I should say something as to the meaning of the expression "threats" ... Expressing the matter in my own words, I would say that a threat is a pre-intimation of proposed action of some sort. That action must be either per se a legal action or an illegal, ie, a tortious action. If the threat used to effect some purpose is of the first kind, it gives no ground for legal proceeding; if of the second, it falls within the description of illegal means, and the right to sue of the person injured is established.'

South Wales Miners' Federation v *Glamorgan Coal Co Ltd* [1905] AC 239 House of Lords (Earl of Halsbury LC, Lord Macnaghten, Lord James of Hereford and Lord Lindley)

Miners – procurement of breach of contract

Facts
Miners' leaders ordered stop days. They did this intentionally, the object being to restrict output from the coal face which would increase the price of coal which, in turn, would mean that miners' wages would rise because their wages depended on the selling price of coal. The miners' leaders argued that although there was inducement to break contracts, they were justified in what they did.

Held
The miners were not justified in what they did and the mine owners were entitled to damages.

Lord Macnaghten:

'The intention of the defendants was directly to procure the breach of contracts. The fact that their motives were good in the interests of those whom they moved to action does not form any answer to those who have suffered from the unlawful act.'

Lord Lindley:

'A legal duty to do what is known to be illegal cannot arise in law; it is a contradiction in terms. I cannot find there was a moral or a social duty to do as they did which the law recognises.'

Stratford (JT) & Son Ltd v *Lindley* [1964] 3 WLR 541 House of Lords (Lord Reid, Viscount Radcliffe, Lord Pearce, Lord Upjohn and Lord Donovan)

Inducement to breach contract

Facts
B Ltd had consistently refused to recognise the Watermen's Union, but had come to a closed shop agreement with the TGWU: 45 of their 48 employees belonged to the TGWU. The defendants, officials of the Watermen's Union, decided to put pressure on S, the chairman of B Ltd and instructed their

members to refuse to take barges to B Ltd for repair, or to return barges hired out to customers. It brought B Ltd's trade to a standstill. B Ltd brought an action for an injunction for conspiracy.

Held

B Ltd was entitled to an injunction not for conspiracy, but for inducing breach of contract.

Commentary

Distinguished: *Rookes* v *Barnard* [1962] 3 WLR 260.

Thomson (DC) & Co Ltd v *Deakin* [1952] Ch 646 Court of Appeal (Sir Raymond Evershed MR, Jenkins and Morris LJJ)

Trade union – procuring breach of contract

Facts

The plaintiffs, publishers, employed non-union labour. Their paper was supplied by B Ltd under a contract. Ps dismissed W, who had become a member of NATSOPA and that union called out on strike Ps' employees. B Ltd's drivers also refused to deliver to Ps (on persuasion) and as a result, Ps could not perform their contract to their customers. Ps sought an injunction to restrain Ds, the officers of several unions concerned, from taking this action. Ps conceded that Ds had not entered into any conspiracy directed to injure Ps within the principle of *Sorrell* v *Smith*. Upjohn J dismissed Ps' claim.

Held

The High Court had been correct in its decision as the plaintiffs had not succeeded in showing that the unions, with actual knowledge of the contract in question and with the intention of damaging the plaintiffs, had, by means of a wrongful act, persuaded or procured the employees of the company which supplied the plaintiffs with paper to make it impossible for that company to carry out its contractual obligations.

28 Remedies

AB v *South West Water Services Ltd* [1993] 2 WLR 507 Court of Appeal (Sir Thomas Bingham MR, Stuart-Smith and Simon Brown LJJ)

Nuisance – exemplary and aggravated damages

Facts

Drinking water supplied by the defendants had been accidentally polluted by aluminium sulphate and the plaintiffs suffered ill effects in respect of which they sought damages for personal injuries. The defendants admitted liability for compensatory damages for breach of statutory duty but the judge refused to strike out the plaintiffs' claim for exemplary and/or aggravated damages for the tort of nuisance.

Held

This claim would be struck out.

Sir Thomas Bingham MR:

'A defendant accused of crime may ordinarily be ordered (if convicted) to pay a financial penalty. In such a case he will enjoy the constitutional safeguards afforded to defendants in criminal cases, which may include trial by jury,. and the sum he is ordered to pay is received by the state, not (even in the case of a private prosecution) by the prosecutor. In a civil case, arising out of a civil wrong (whether or not it is also a crime), the defendant may be ordered to pay damages. In the ordinary way, damages bear no resemblance to a criminal penalty. The damages awarded to a plaintiff will be such as will compensate him for the loss he has suffered as a result of the wrong, so far as money can. The court looks to the extent of the plaintiff's loss not to the quality of the defendant's conduct. Since the damages are awarded to compensate the plaintiff they are of course paid to him.

Exemplary (or, as they were once revealingly called, punitive) damages cut across this simple distinction. They are awarded in civil cases, so that the defendant does not enjoy the safeguards afforded to defendants in criminal cases including, save in a small minority of cases, trial by jury. They are paid to the plaintiff, not the state. But they are not paid to compensate the plaintiff, who will be fully compensated by the ordinary measure of damages. They are paid to punish or deter the defendant, to mark the disapproval which his conduct has provoked. For the plaintiff such damages represent a bonus, an addition to the sum needed to compensate him fully for the loss he has suffered as a result of the wrong done to him.

In his leading speech on this topic of *Rookes* v *Barnard* [1964] AC 1129 Lord Devlin recognised the law on exemplary damages as anomalous. But he (and the other members of the House, all of whom agreed with him) did not think it open to them to refuse to recognise the exemplary principle and in any event held that there were certain classes of case in which it served a valuable purpose. So the House ruled that awards of exemplary damages should not be abolished but should be curtailed or restricted ... It is the extent of that curtailment or restriction which raises the first, and major, issue in this appeal.

In his speech Lord Devlin was not, as I understand him, concerned to identify certain causes of action which could and others which could not properly ground claims for exemplary damages. His focus was not on causes of action at all. Rather, his concern was to identify those elements which had been present in claims which had led to awards of exemplary damages in the past and which served to justify retention of the principle. Statute apart, he identified two such elements giving rise to two categories or classes of case.

In the first category there had been what he variously described as an "arbitrary and outrageous use of executive power" and "oppressive, arbitrary or unconstitutional action by the servants of the government" ... there can be no doubt what Lord Devlin was speaking about. It was gross misuse of power, involving tortious conduct, by agents of government ...

The second category covered cases in which the defendant had acted tortiously on a calculation that the economic benefits to him of his unlawful conduct would outweigh any compensation he might be liable to pay the injured party. The rationale underlying this category was clearly stated: "Exemplary damages can properly be awarded whenever it is necessary to teach a wrongdoer that tort does not pay." This again suggests that it was the quality of the conduct complained of rather than the cause of action pleaded which governed the right to claim exemplary damages.

Lord Devlin's speech in *Rookes* v *Barnard* was the subject of detailed exegesis by an enlarged Appellate Committee of the House of Lords in *Cassell & Co Ltd* v *Broome* [1972] AC 1027 ... I cannot pretend to find the answer at all clear, but I incline to think that a majority of the House regarded an award of exemplary damages as permissible only where (a) a case fell within one or other of Lord Devlin's categories and (b) was founded on a tort for which exemplary damages had been awarded before *Rookes* v *Barnard*. This may involve a misreading of their Lordships' speeches in *Cassell & Co Ltd* v *Broome*, but I think it is the basis upon which the Court of Appeal should, until corrected, proceed.

If it is correct to import a cause of action test, this court is bound to hold that the plaintiffs' claims in negligence cannot found a claim for exemplary damages even if they fall within one or other of Lord Devlin's categories. Our attention has been drawn to no negligence claim leading to such an award before 1964 (or, I think, since). By contrast, I understand *Bell* v *Midland Rly Co* (1861) 10 CBNS 287, in which damages described as exemplary were awarded, to have been founded in private nuisance, possibly in addition to other causes of action. More recently, in *Guppys (Bridport) Ltd* v *Brookling*, *Guppys (Bridport) Ltd* v *James* (1983) 14 HLR 1 the Court of Appeal upheld an award of damages for private nuisance, although the present issue was not raised or addressed.

It does not, however, appear that there has ever, before *Rookes* v *Barnard* or since, been an award of exemplary damages for public nuisance. In one sense, public nuisance is private nuisance writ large. But there are significant differences. First, the causing of a public nuisance in a number of its forms is a crime (and a crime for which, in this case, the defendants were prosecuted) which a private nuisance will rarely, if ever, be. I describe this difference as significant because Lord Devlin in *Rookes* v *Barnard* regarded conduct falling within his two categories as not ordinarily falling within the criminal law. He would plainly have regarded the award of exemplary damages as even more anomalous in cases where the conduct in question already attracted the sanctions of the criminal law. Secondly, a public nuisance may lead to numerous complainants, which a private nuisance will not. I describe this difference as significant because it highlights an obvious and intractable difficulty: in the case of a public nuisance affecting hundreds or even thousands of plaintiffs, how can the court assess the sum of exemplary damages to be awarded to any one of them to punish or deter the defendant without knowing at the outset the number of successful plaintiffs and the approximate size of the total bill for exemplary damages which the defendant must meet? If, as I think, a claim in public nuisance falls foul of the cause of action test, assuming there is one, these seem to me good reasons for holding that it will not support an award of exemplary damages.

It is, however, necessary to consider whether the plaintiffs' claims for exemplary damages, if otherwise good on the facts as pleaded, fall within one or other or both of Lord Devlin's two categories ... If the defendants' conduct was as pleaded, as we must for present purposes assume, it was highly reprehensible, but the conduct complained of was quite unlike the abuses of power which Lord Devlin had in mind and I cannot regard the defendants, for any purposes relevant to these claims, as wielding executive or governmental power. They were a publicly owned utility acting as monopoly supplier of a necessary commodity, enjoying certain statutory powers and subject to certain obligations, but they were not acting as an instrument or agent of government. I regard this case as falling well outside the first category.

The plaintiffs have not in my opinion pleaded a claim arguably falling within the second category either. It is true that the defendants' conduct is said ... to have been "calculated by them to make a profit for themselves which may well exceed that payable to the plaintiffs". This is plainly directed towards establishing a second category claim. But [the statement of claim does] ... not in my opinion contain facts from which the necessary inference could be drawn. The plaintiffs say that when they obtain discovery they will either obtain material to support the allegation or they will drop it. That is not in my view a correct approach. Unless the plaintiffs already have enough material to plead a plausible (even if incomplete) case, the pleading should not be allowed to stand. It is not permissible to plead a bare assertion in the hope that material to support it will turn up on discovery.

I turn, lastly, to the claim ... for aggravated damages. The plaintiffs are of course entitled to be fully compensated for all they suffered as a direct result of the defendants' admitted breach of duty. The ordinary measure of compensatory damages will cover all they have suffered as a result of that breach, physically, psychologically and mentally. Full account will be taken of the distress and anxiety which such an event necessarily causes. To the extent that any of these effects was magnified or exacerbated by the defendants' conduct, the ordinary measure of damages will compensate. The question is whether, in addition to that full compensatory measure, the plaintiffs have pleaded a sustainable claim for additional compensation by way of aggravated damages. This is claimed ... on the basis that the plaintiffs' feelings of indignation were aroused by the defendants' high-handed way of dealing with the incident. I know of no precedent for awarding damages for indignation aroused by a defendant's conduct. Defamation cases in which a plaintiff's damages are increased by the defendant's conduct of the litigation (as by aggressive cross-examination of the plaintiff or persistence in a groundless plea of justification) are not in my view a true exception, since injury to the plaintiff's feelings and self-esteem is an important part of the damage for which compensation is awarded. In very many other tort actions (and, for that matter, actions in contract, boundary disputes, partnership actions and other disputes) the plaintiff is indignant at the conduct of the defendant (or his insurers). An award of damages does not follow; nor, in my judgment should it, since this is not damage directly caused by the defendant's tortious conduct and this is not damage which the law has ever recognised.'

American Cyanamid Co v *Ethicon Ltd* [1975] 2 WLR 316 House of Lords (Lord Diplock, Viscount Dilhorne, Lord Cross of Chelsea, Lord Salmon and Lord Edmund-Davies)

Interlocutory injunctions

Facts
The appellants registered a patent in relation to surgical sutures and alleged that the respondents were proposing to introduce a product which would infringe it. The appellants sought an injunction.

Held
The injunction would be granted. There were serious questions to be tried and the balance of convenience favoured it.

Banque Bruxelles Lambert SA v *Eagle Star Insurance Co Ltd* [1995] 2 WLR 607 Court of Appeal (Sir Thomas Bingham MR, Rose and Morritt LJJ)

Damages – measure of damages

Facts
The plaintiff mortgagees claimed damages against the defendants, who had acted as valuers. The

plaintiffs alleged that the property had been negligently over-valued, and that but for that valuation they would not have entered into the transaction with the borrower. Following a general fall in the property market the borrowers defaulted, and so on possession and sale the plaintiffs obtained much less than the figure at which the property had been valued. In their claim for damages the plaintiffs included a sum in respect of the loss due to the market fall between the date of valuation and date of realisation. At first instance the judge refused to award a sum arising from the market fall. The plaintiffs appealed to the Court of Appeal.

Held
Where a lender would not, but for the negligent valuation, have entered into the transaction with the borrower, that negligence was the cause of the plaintiff's loss. A fall in the market was foreseeable and was not to be treated as a new intervening cause breaking the link between the valuer's negligence and the loss sustained. Thus the lenders could recover damages for the loss they had sustained due to the market fall.

BBMB Finance (Hong Kong) Ltd v *Eda Holdings Ltd* (1990) The Times 12 February Privy Council (Lord Bridge of Harwich, Lord Templeman, Lord Griffiths, Lord Goff of Chieveley and Lord Lowry)

Damages – conversion

Facts
Certain shares had been converted and the judge had awarded the value of the shares at the date of conversion less the value of replacement shares at the date of replacement.

Held
His decision had been correct. When property is irreversibly converted, damages are measured by the value of the property at the date of conversion.

Bradburn v *Great Western Rail Co* (1874) LR 10 Ex 1 Exchequer Division (Bramwell, Pigott and Amphlett BB)

Damages – insurance monies

Facts
The plaintiff passenger was injured on the defendants' railway in consequence of the negligence of the defendants' servants. The plaintiff was insured against such accidents and he received compensation of £31 from the insurers in respect of his injuries.

Held
The amount so received should not be deducted from the damages payable by the defendants.

British Transport Commission v *Gourley* [1956] 2 WLR 41 House of Lords (Earl Jowitt, Lord Goddard, Lord Reid, Lord Radcliffe, Lord Tucker, Lord Keith of Avonholm and Lord Somervell of Harrow)

Damages – income tax

Facts

The plaintiff was injured as a result of the defendant's negligence. The trial judge awarded him £37,720 damages in respect of loss of earnings (actual and prospective) paying no regard to the tax and surtax he would have had to pay if he had not been injured. This tax would have reduced the earnings award to £6,695.

Held (Lord Keith of Avonholm dissenting)

The judge ought to have taken the tax position into account. The award in respect of lost earnings should be reduced to £6,695.

Brunsden v Humphrey (1884) 14 QBD 141 Court of Appeal (Lord Coleridge CJ, Sir Baliol Brett MR and Bowen LJ)

Damages – different causes of action

Facts

The plaintiff sued the defendant for damage to his cab and was awarded damages. Afterwards, he sued for damages for personal injury suffered in the same collision.

Held (Lord Coleridge dissenting on the facts)

There were two distinct causes of action and the second proceedings were not barred by the first.

Burton v Winters [1993] 1 WLR 1077 Court of Appeal (Lloyd LJ and Connell J)

Right of self-help

Facts

In an action for trespass and nuisance, the plaintiff sought an injunction requiring the defendants to remove a portion of a garage which encroached on her land. A declaration was granted that part of the garage was on the plaintiff's land, but no injunction was granted. Some time afterwards the defendants were granted an injunction restraining the plaintiff from trespassing onto and from interfering with their property. The plaintiff appealed, and the question arose as to whether she was entitled to exercise the right of self-help.

Held

That the right of self-help for trespass by encroachment was a summary remedy which was justified only in clear and simple cases or in an emergency. In the present case there was no emergency, some difficult issues were raised and the disproportionate consequences of self-help, namely the demolition of the garage, made the case unsuitable for the remedy of self-help.

Cassell & Co Ltd v Broome [1972] 2 WLR 645 House of Lords (Lord Hailsham of St Marylebone LC, Lord Reid, Lord Morris of Borth-y-Gest, Viscount Dilhorne, Lord Wilberforce, Lord Diplock and Lord Kilbrandon)

Libel – damages

Facts

P, a retired sea captain of unblemished reputation, won a libel action against the author and publisher of the book *The Destruction of Convoy PQ17* in which he had been blamed for the loss of a large number of merchant vessels and many lives.

The jury awarded:

a) £1,000 in respect of the publication of 60 copies of the book; and
b) £14,000 'compensation', in respect of the hardback edition; and
c) £25,000 exemplary damages.

The publishers appealed against the £25,000 exemplary damages award.

Held

The appeal would be dismissed. Although the figure was high, it would be wrong for the judiciary to interfere with the function of a jury. An arbitrary limit should *not* be imposed. In any event, this was a case of a particularly bad libel.

Exemplary damages should only be awarded for:

1. Oppressive, arbitrary or unconstitutional action by servants of the government.
2. Where D's conduct has been calculated to make more profit for himself than he might have to pay to the plaintiff in damages. (This head has become popular in America).
3. Where such an award is expressly authorised by statute.

Lord Hailsham discussed terminology:

'Special damage' – actual past losses;
'Aggravated damage' – a 'compensatory' figure which expresses the Court's indignation;
'Exemplary' – an award designed to teach the defendant that 'tort does not pay'; or
'At large' – cases where awards may include, eg damages for loss of reputation, ie which cannot necessarily be quantified.

Commentary

Followed: *Rookes* v *Barnard* [1964] AC 1129.
  Approved: *McCarey* v *Associated Newspapers Ltd* [1965] 2 WLR 45.
  Distinguished: *E Hulton & Co* v *Jones* [1910] AC 20.
  See also *AB* v *South West Water Services Ltd* [1993] 2 WLR 507.

Colledge v *Bass Mitchells & Butlers Ltd* [1988] 1 All ER 536 Court of Appeal (Sir John Donaldson MR, Glidwell LJ and Sir Denys Buckley)

Damages – redundancy payment

Facts

The plaintiff severely injured his back at work and he sued his employers alleging negligence. Before the action was heard he was offered and he accepted voluntary redundancy and he received a payment of £9,000. The trial judge held that the employers were liable, but he refused to deduct the £9,000 from the damages awarded. The employers appealed as to the amount of damages.

Held

The appeal would be allowed as the redundancy payment should have been deducted.

Sir John Donaldson MR:

'In my judgment the starting point is Lord Reid's classic judgment in *Parry* v *Cleaver* [1970] AC 1 at 13. In effect Lord Reid states an equation "a-b=c", where "a" represents the sums which the plaintiff would have received but for the accident, but which by reason of the accident he can no longer get, "b" represents the sums which he did in fact receive as a result of the accident, but which he would not have received if there had been no accident, and "c" represents the compensation to which he is entitled.

On the judge's findings, but for the accident the plaintiff would have been unlikely ever to have been made redundant and would have worked for the defendants until his retirement. Whilst the judge did say that if the plaintiff's employment by the defendants ended prematurely, he would have been able to obtain other employment, he did not suggest that such a change would have benefited the plaintiff by enabling him to take a redundancy payment and immediately obtain other employment without loss of wages. Prima facie, therefore, the £9,000 is part of "b", but no part of "a" and accordingly falls to be deducted.'

Cookson v *Knowles* [1978] 2 WLR 978 House of Lords (Lord Diplock, Viscount Dilhorne, Lord Salmon, Lord Fraser of Tullybelton and Lord Scarman)

Damages – calculation

Facts
In December 1973 plaintiff's husband was killed in a motor accident caused negligently by the defendant. At death, H was 49, in steady employment as machinist. The trial was in May 1976. The trial judge awarded dependency at £2,250 x 11 (the multiplier) = £24,750 and awarded interest at 9 per cent on the whole amount from death to judgment.

Held
1. Because of the current financial climate, the more reliable assessment of a dependant's loss in fatal accidents would be best achieved by splitting the award into two parts: a) the pecuniary loss from death to trial (pre trial loss) and b) the pecuniary loss which it is estimated would be suffered from trial onwards (future loss), for which the proper multiplicand was the figure to which it was estimated the annual dependency would have amounted by the date of trial, and damages should in general be assessed in this way in all such cases.
2. No additional allowance should be made for inflation because this would be taken care of in the higher interest rates. Interest on pre trial loss should be at half the short term rates current during that period. No interest should be awarded on future loss.

Commentary
Applied in *Auty* v *National Coal Board* [1985] 1 WLR 784.

Cresswell v *Eaton* [1991] 1 WLR 1113 High Court (Simon Brown J)

Damages – death of mother

Facts
A mother of three young children was killed while crossing the road as a result of the defendant's negligent driving. She had recently divorced her husband and she was in full-time employment. The children went to live with grandmother and, after grandmother's death, with an aunt (with two children

of her own) who gave up her job to care for them. The children sought damages under the Fatal Accidents Act 1976 for loss of dependency, including compensation for the aunt's loss of salary.

Held

As it had been entirely reasonable for the aunt to give up work and to remain unemployed to care for the children on a full-time basis, damages for loss of services would be calculated by reference to a notional housekeeping wage during the short period of the grandmother's care, discounted by 30 per cent to reflect the part-time nature of the mother's care, and by reference to the aunt's net earnings loss projected over the remaining period of dependency for each child, again discounted by 15 per cent to reflect the mother's part-time care, the discounts also being intended to take into account the children's broadly diminishing need for care and the loss of the special qualitative factor of maternal care.

Darbishire v *Warran* [1963] 1 WLR 1067 Court of Appeal (Harman and Pearson LJJ and Pennycuick J)

Damages – mitigation of loss

Facts

The plaintiff's Lea Francis shooting brake collided with the defendant's car: the accident was entirely the defendant's fault. Although he could have brought a similar Lea Francis for £85-£100, the plaintiff did not attempt to find one: instead, he had his repaired at a cost of £192. The plaintiff sought to recover the difference between the amount received from his insurance company (£80) and the repair costs.

Held

His claim would fail as he had not taken all reasonable steps to mitigate the damage, ie, bought a replacement vehicle.

Dodd Properties (Kent) Ltd v *Canterbury City Council* [1980] 1 WLR 433 Court of Appeal (Megaw, Browne and Donaldson LJJ)

Damages – assessment

Facts

In 1968 the plaintiffs' building was damaged by the defendants' pile-driving operations on an adjoining site. Shortly before the hearing in 1978 the defendants admitted liability and the question arose as to the date at which damages should be assessed.

Held

The cost of repairs was to be assessed at the earliest date when, having regard to all the circumstances, they could reasonably be undertaken. Taking due account of, inter alia, the plaintiffs' financial stringency in 1970 (the earliest date when it would have been physically possible to put the work in hand), the fact that it made commercial sense to postpone the repairs until the outcome of the action and the defendants' wrongful denial of liability, the cost of the repairs should be assessed at the date of the action, ie 1978.

Megaw LJ:

> 'The general principle, referred to in many authorities, ... [is] that "as a general rule in English law damages for tort or for breach of contract are assessed as at the date of the breach". But ... it is stressed that it is not a universal rule. That it is subject to many exceptions and qualifications is clear. ... Indeed,

where, as in the present case, there is serious structural damage to a building, it would be patently absurd, and contrary to the general principle on which damages fall to be assessed, that a plaintiff, in a time of rising prices, should be limited to recovery on the basis of the prices of repair at the time of the wrongdoing, on the facts here, being two years, at least, before the time when, acting with all reasonable speed, he could first have been able to put the repairs in hand. Once that is accepted, as it must be, little of practical reality remains in postulating that, in a tort such as this, the 'general rule' is applicable. The damages are not required by English law to be assessed as at the date of breach. The true rule is that, where there is a material difference between the cost of repair at the date of the wrongful act and the cost of repair when the repairs can, having regard to all the relevant circumstances, first reasonably be undertaken, it is the latter time by reference to which the cost of repairs is to be taken in assessing the damages.'

Commentary
Distinguished: *The Edison* [1933] AC 449.

Doleman v Deakin (1990) The Times 30 January Court of Appeal (Dillon, Ralph Gibson and Stuart-Smith LJJ)
Bereavement damages

Facts
The deceased was unmarried and under 18 years of age when he suffered injuries, from which he died, as a result of the defendant's negligence. However, he did not die until after his 18th birthday: were his parents entitled to bereavement damages under s1(A) of the Fatal Accidents Act 1976?

Held
They were not as the cause of action had accrued at the date of death and on that date their son was not a minor.

Dominion Mosaics and Tile Co Ltd v Trafalgar Trucking Co Ltd [1990] 2 All ER 246 Court of Appeal (Fox, Stocker and Taylor LJJ)
Measure of damages

Facts
The plaintiffs sold part of their freehold premises to the local authority, the second defendants, who engaged the first defendants to demolish the buildings on the part sold. As a result of the first defendants' negligence, the buildings retained by the plaintiffs were severely damaged by fire. The premises' diminution in value was about £60,000, rebuilding would have cost £570,000 and loss of profits during the rebuilding period would have been £300,000 a year. In view of these factors, the plaintiffs purchased the lease of other premises (with 20 per cent more floor space) at Waterden Road for £390,000 and then the freehold for £60,000. On moving again, they resold this freehold for £690,000. Amongst other things, the fire destroyed 11 carpet-holding machines which the plaintiffs had recently purchased at a special sale price of £13,500: replacement new machines would have cost £65,000, but they had not in fact been replaced. The plaintiffs claimed the cost of the lease (£390,000) and the cost of new machines (£65,000).

Held
They were entitled to succeed.

Taylor LJ:

'There was no suggestion that the [plaintiffs] could have availed themselves of premises in which to resume business anywhere else, or any quicker than they did. In as much as they were remiss in failing to resume their retail trade at Waterden Road as soon as they might, they conceded they could claim only a limited period for lost profits. Although the ground area was somewhat greater at Waterden Road than their original premises, I consider that this falls within the sort of betterment for which no reduction should be made. It is not a case, as this court instanced in the *Harbutt's Plasticine Ltd* case, of a rebuilding deliberately incorporating enlargement, improvement or added facilities. Here it was a question of finding some existing premises which most nearly matched the [plaintiffs'] requirements. Against the extra floor space there would have to be considered the saving in lost profits of obtaining Waterden Road quickly, and the need to adapt and modernise premises not purpose-built for the [plaintiffs].

But then counsel for the [defendants] sought to bring later dealings into account. The [defendants], by the comparatively modest expenditure of £60,000 in 1986, acquired the freehold of Waterden Road and were then able to sell it for £690,000 in April 1987. It is argued that, since all of this happened before trial, it should all be brought into account in the [defendants'] favour. There should, up to the trial, be in effect a running account between the parties so that any gain to the [plaintiffs] from whatever cause in regard to their property or its proceeds can be used by the [defendants] to diminish their liability.

The judge rejected this argument on the practical ground that the gains made by the [plaintiffs] were attributable simply to the inflationary rise in the value of real property during the relevant period. I agree with him; but further, as a matter of principle, I do not accept that a defendant is entitled to the benefit of any successful dealing which the plaintiff may have had up to trial ...

[As to the machines,] counsel's arguments ... were based solely on the alternative awards of £13,500 or £65,000. No intermediate figure was canvassed. It was not suggested by the [defendants], either in evidence or by submission, that there was any secondhand source of paternoster machines. The [plaintiffs'] evidence was that no such source existed to their knowledge. Where this is the case and the only way the owner of destroyed chattels can replace them is by buying new ones, the measure of damages is the cost of doing that, unless the result would be absurd ...

Accordingly the proper figure here was prima facie £65,000 ... That figure could not, in regard to such recently new machines, be called absurd ...

Had it been argued that in fairness to the [defendants] some discount from £65,000 should have been allowed to reflect the depreciation of the machines in their few months of service, the point would have merited consideration. But no such submission was made, nor was there any evidence on which to base an assessment of an appropriate discount. In these circumstances I consider that, of the two alternatives contended for, £65,000 was the proper sum.'

Commentary
Applied: *Harbutt's Plasticine Ltd* v *Wayne Tank and Pump Co Ltd* [1970] 2 WLR 198.

Fetter v *Beale* see *Fitter* v *Veal*

Fitter v *Veal* (1701) 12 Mod Rep 542 Court of King's Bench (Holt CJ)

Damages – further surgery

Facts
The plaintiff was assaulted by the defendant and he sued and recovered damages. Long after the award, P discovered that he would require further surgery. As a result, P sought to bring a further action.

Held

Damages are recoverable once only for the same injury. Accordingly, P was not entitled to bring a second action.

Gammell v *Wilson* [1980] 3 WLR 591 House of Lords (Lord Diplock, Lord Edmund-Davies, Lord Fraser of Tullybelton, Lord Russell of Killowen and Lord Scarman)

Damages – lost years

Facts

The plaintiff's 15-year-old son was killed in a road accident. The defendants admitted liability and the damages awarded included a sum in respect of loss of future earnings during the boy's lost years.

Held

The award would not be disturbed.

Lord Edmund-Davies:

' ... the assessment of compensation for the "lost years" rests on no special basis of its own and it proceeds on no peculiar principle. It may present unusual difficulties, but the task itself is the ordinary one of arriving at a fair figure to compensate the estate of the deceased for a loss of a particular kind sustained by him in his lifetime at the hands of the defendant.'

Commentary

Applied: *Pickett* v *British Rail Engineering Ltd* [1978] 3 WLR 955.

Hayden v *Hayden* [1992] 1 WLR 986 Court of Appeal (Parker, McCowan LJJ and Sir David Croom-Johnson)

Damages – death of mother – father caring for child

Facts

The infant plaintiff's mother was killed when a car driven by the defendant father overturned. The father admitted liability and he sought to replace the mother's lost services by giving up his job and caring for the plaintiff himself.

Held (McCowan LJ dissenting)

Section 4 of the Fatal Accidents Act 1976 did not apply (the father's services were not a benefit which had accrued as a result of the death) and the value of the father's services should be taken into account in assessing the plaintiff's damages.

Parker LJ:

'It was long ago established that a dependant child could recover under the Fatal Accidents Act damages for the loss of the gratuitous services of a deceased mother who had been killed due to the negligence of a tortfeasor. In such cases, even without complications, the court is faced with the task of quantifying in money that which cannot in reality be so quantified. This is difficult enough but the facts of this case are such that the difficulties of reaching a just solution are greatly increased.

The essential facts are that the infant plaintiff (Danielle) who was aged four at the time of the accident lost her mother's services, that in order himself to replace such services her father, whose negligence had caused her mother's death, gave up his employment to look after her and that his remuneration from his former employment had been £15,000 pa.

For the defendant it is submitted that the value of his services should be taken into account, ie set against the value of the mother's lost services in arriving at her loss and for the plaintiff that the father's services must be wholly disregarded by reason of the provisions of s4 of the Fatal Accidents Act 1976 as amended by the Administration of Justice Act 1982 ...

With conflicting decisions on the point whether the gratuitous services of a relative do or do not result from the death of the mother I for my part have no hesitation in following *Hay* v *Hughes* [1975] 2 WLR 34 rather than *Stanley* v *Saddique* [1991] 2 WLR 459 and if this is right s4 of the 1976 Act does not apply. This however does not dispose of the matter because in *Hay* v *Hughes* the benefit of such gratuitous services was excluded, quite apart from any relevant statutory exclusion, on the grounds that they did not result from the death. That decision was considered to be the result of s2 of the 1846 Act and the common law.

Section 2 of the 1846 Act has now been replaced by s3 of the Fatal Accidents Act 1976 as substituted by s3(1) of the Administration of Justice Act 1982 ... There is no material difference between this provision and s2 of the 1846 Act. The reference to the jury is dropped but this is immaterial. Damages remain a "jury question", albeit now decided by a judge. This is plain from *Hay* v *Hughes* itself ...

If then it is a jury question, would a jury be likely to say that the tortfeasor who had provided the services and given up his job so to do must nevertheless pay what it would cost to provide the services which he himself has provided? That a jury could conceivably come to the conclusion must I suppose be accepted but if it reached the opposite conclusion it could not in my view be held to have reached an unreasonable verdict. Suppose for example that the deceased mother was hopelessly inadequate, that the tortfeasor was a trained nanny and, appalled by what she had done, gave up her job and provided the child with services infinitely better than those provided by the deceased mother. Can it possibly be the law that she must then pay the cost of employing another nanny? I think not and, if it were, I would regard it as regrettable.

What then has the judge done in this case? He had before him a figure of £48,000 as being the full cost of a nanny until Danielle was 11 and half such cost from 11 to 15. He then, without giving specific reasons concluded that an appropriate figure would be £20,000, apportioned £15,000 to date of trial and £5,000 thereafter. I do not consider that we have before us material to enable us to interfere with this award, which if I am right as to the approach, appears to me to be an entirely reasonable award and to do justice between the parties ...

I would add by way of postscript that, where the provider of the replacement services is the tortfeasor, arguments successfully advanced in earlier cases that it would be unjust if the tortfeasor were to benefit from the generosity of a third party cannot apply.'

Hicks v *Chief Constable of the South Yorkshire Police* [1992] 2 All ER 65 House of Lords (Lord Templeman, Lord Bridge of Harwich, Lord Griffiths, Lord Goff of Chieveley and Lord Browne-Wilkinson)

Damages – fear of impending death

Facts
The plaintiffs, parents of two girls who were crushed to death in the Hillsborough disaster, as joint administrators of the girls' estates claimed damages for the benefit of each estate under s1(1) of the Law Reform (Miscellaneous Provisions) Act 1934 and s1(1)(b) of the Administration of Justice Act 1982. The trial judge dismissed the action on the ground that the plaintiffs had failed to prove that the girls had suffered any recoverable damage for pre-death pain and suffering and the Court of Appeal adopted a similar approach.

Held

The plaintiffs' further appeal would be dismissed as it was impossible to say that the courts below had been clearly wrong to conclude that no physical injury had been suffered by the girls prior to the fatal crushing injuries.

Lord Bridge of Harwich:

'The evidence here showed that both girls died from traumatic asphyxia. They were in the pens at one end of the Hillsborough Stadium to which access was through a tunnel some 23 metres in length. When the pens were already seriously overcrowded a great number of additional spectators, anxious to see the football match which was about to start, were admitted through the turnstiles and surged through the tunnel causing the dreadful crush in the pens in which 95 people died. Medical evidence which the judge accepted was to the effect that in cases of death from traumatic asphyxia caused by crushing the victim would lose consciousness within a matter of seconds from the crushing of the chest which cut off the ability to breathe and would die within five minutes ... Hidden J was not satisfied that any physical injury had been sustained before what he described as the "swift and sudden [death] as shown by the medical evidence". Unless the law were to distinguish between death within seconds of injury and unconsciousness within seconds of injury followed by death within minutes, which I do not understand to be suggested, these findings, as Hidden J himself said "with regret", made it impossible for him to award any damages ... I do not intend myself to embark on a detailed review of the evidence. In the circumstances I think it sufficient to say that, in my opinion, the conclusion of fact reached by Hidden J and the Court of Appeal was fairly open to them and it is impossible to say that they were wrong ...

It is perfectly clear law that fear by itself, of whatever degree, is a normal humane motion for which no damages can be awarded. Those trapped in the crush at Hillsborough who were fortunate enough to escape without injury have no claim in respect of the distress they suffered in what must have been a truly terrifying experience. It follows that fear of impending death felt by the victim of a fatal injury before that injury is inflicted cannot by itself give rise to a cause of action which survives for the benefit of the victim's estate.'

Hodgson v *Trapp* [1988] 3 WLR 1281 House of Lords (Lord Mackay of Clashfern LC, Lord Bridge of Harwich, Lord Brandon of Oakbrook, Lord Oliver of Aylmerton and Lord Goff of Chieveley)

Damages – deduction of allowances

Facts

The plaintiff was almost totally physically and mentally incapacitated as the result of an accident caused by the negligence of the defendant. The trial judge awarded the plaintiff damages of £431,840 and refused to make any deduction in respect of the attendance and mobility allowances payable to the plaintiff under ss35(1) of the Social Security Act 1975 and he also increased the multipliers for future cost and future loss of earnings to take account of the higher rates of tax payable on the interest from the award of damages.

Held

The deduction should have been made but the multiplier should not have been increased.

Lord Bridge of Harwich:

'In the end the issue in these cases is not so much one of statutory construction as of public policy. If we have regard to the realities, awards of damages for personal injuries are met from the insurance premiums payable by motorists, employers, occupiers of property, professional men and others. Statutory benefits payable to those in need by reason of impecuniosity or disability are met by the taxpayer. In this context to ask whether the taxpayer, as the "benevolent donor", intends to benefit "the wrongdoer", as represented by the insurer who meets the claim at the expense of the appropriate class of policy holders, seems to me entirely artificial. There could hardly be a clearer case than that of the attendance allowance payable under s35 of the 1975 Act where the statutory benefit and the special damages claimed for cost of care are designed to meet the identical expenses. To allow double recovery in such a case at the expense of both taxpayers and insurers seems to me incapable of justification on any rational ground. It could only add to the enormous disparity, to which the advocates of a "no-fault" system of compensation constantly draw attention, between the position of those who are able to establish a third party's fault as the cause of their injury and the position of those who are not.

A separate and subordinate point was raised on behalf of the plaintiff in relation to mobility allowance … I see no reason why the whole of the mobility allowance should not be regarded, just as the attendance allowance, as available to meet the cost of her care generally and thus as mitigating the damages recoverable in respect of the cost of that care.'

Lord Oliver of Aylmerton:

'The second ground of appeal raises a quite distinct issue which arises in this way. It was agreed at the trial before Taylor J that the plaintiff had suffered a continuing loss of salary of £3,267.77 per annum and there was, in addition, an assessed loss of £3,000 per annum in respect of freelance work in which the plaintiff had engaged prior to the accident. To these multiplicands Taylor J applied a multiplier of 11, which is not challenged. That figure, however, he increased to 12 in order to take account of the fact that the income likely to be produced from conventional investment of the sums awarded would attract income tax at the higher rate … Similarly in relation to the prospective cost of nursing care and attendance, the judge adopted a multiplicand of £11,000 to which he applied a multiplier of 13, which again is not challenged. To that, however, he again added a further one year in order to take account of the incidence of taxation at the higher rates. The defendants do not challenge the general proposition that the prospective incidence of higher-rate income tax may, in exceptional circumstances, be a factor which can legitimately tip the scales in favour of selecting a multiplier at the higher end of the conventional scale. They do, however, challenge the correctness of an approach which involves, after the calculation of the appropriate multiplier in accordance with the conventional scale, the making of a specific addition to the multiplier in order to take account, as a separate and individual feature, of the higher taxation rates which may be attracted by the income likely to be produced by the investment of a very substantial award …

I am, as I have said, content to deal with the question raised on the footing that the answer is not already subsumed in the answer given by this House in *Lim Poh Choo* v *Camden and Islington Area Health Authority* [1980] AC 174 to the allied question of whether specific allowance should be made for inflation. The principle, however, appears to me to be much the same. That tax will be levied is, no doubt, as Benjamin Franklin observed, one of the two certainties of life, but the extent and manner of its exaction in the future can only be guessed at. It is as much an imponderable as any of the other uncertainties which are embraced in the exercise of making a just assessment of damages for future loss. The system of multipliers and multiplicands conventionally employed in the assessment takes account of a variety of factors, none of which is or, indeed, is capable of being worked out scientifically, but which are catered for by allowing a reasonably generous margin in the assumed rate of interest on which the multiplier is based. There is, in my judgment, no self-evident justification for singling out this particular factor and making for it an allowance which is not to be made for the equally imponderable factor of inflation…

In my opinion, the incidence of taxation in the future should ordinarily be assumed to be satisfactorily taken care of in the assumption of an interest rate applicable to a stable currency and the selection of a multiplier appropriate to that rate.'

Commentary
Followed in *McCamley* v *Cammell Laird Shipbuilders Ltd* [1990] 1 All ER 854.
Overruled: *Thomas* v *Wignall* [1987] 2 WLR 930.

Housecroft v *Burnett* [1986] 1 All ER 332 Court of Appeal (O'Connor, Slade LJJ and Bristow J)

Damages – personal injury

Facts

When she was aged 16, the plaintiff suffered severe injuries resulting in tetraplegia. The defendant admitted liability and the plaintiff appealed against the amount awarded as damages.

Held

In April 1985, the average award in such a case for pain, suffering and loss of amenity should be £75,000. Where the plaintiff is to be looked after under the National Health Service, a nil award should be made in respect of nursing care. Where care is provided by a relative out of love, a capital sum should be included in the award and it should be sufficient to enable the plaintiff to make reasonable recompense to the relative. Where a relative gives up work, the court should award sufficient to ensure that he or she does not lose as a result; the ceiling would be the commercial rate.

Commentary

Applied: *Donnelly* v *Joyce* [1973] 3 WLR 514.

Hunt v *Severs* [1994] 2 All ER 385 House of Lords (Lord Keith, Lord Bridge, Lord Jauncey, Lord Browne-Wilkinson and Lord Nolan)

Plaintiff cared for by the tortfeasor – whether value of these services recoverable

Facts

The plaintiff was seriously injured whilst riding as a pillion passenger on the defendant's motor cycle. She later married the defendant who assisted in her care. Liability was admitted but the defendant disputed, inter alia, claims for the value of the services rendered by him to the plaintiff. Recovery was allowed at first instance and upheld on appeal to the Court of Appeal. The defendant appealed to the House of Lords.

Held

The appeal would be allowed. Where services in the form of care and assistance were gratuitously rendered by a defendant tortfeasor, the plaintiff could not recover the cost of these services via damages. The object of an award for voluntary care received by the plaintiff was compensation for the voluntary carer, and where the tortfeasor had rendered services there was no ground for requiring the tortfeasor to pay to the plaintiff a sum of money which the plaintiff then had to repay to him.

The House also held that an injured plaintiff who recovers damages as recompense for services rendered by a voluntary carer holds them on trust for the voluntary carer, upholding the dictum of Lord Denning in *Cunningham* v *Harrison* [1973] 3 All ER 463. The criticism of *Cunningham* in *Housecroft* v *Burnett* [1986] 1 All ER 332 must now be regarded as invalid.

Lord Bridge:

'The law with respect to the services of a third party who provides voluntary care for a tortiously injured plaintiff has developed somewhat erratically in England. The voluntary carer has no cause of action of his own against the tortfeasor. The justice of allowing the injured plaintiff to recover the value of the services so that he may recompensate the voluntary carer has been generally recognised, but there has been difficulty in articulating a consistent juridical principle to justify this result … But it is nevertheless important to recognise that the underlying rationale of the English law, as all the cases before *Donnelly* v *Joyce* demonstrate, is to enable the voluntary carer to receive proper recompense for his or her services and I would think it appropriate for the House to take the opportunity so far as possible to bring the law of the two countries [England and Scotland] into accord by adopting the view of Lord Denning MR in *Cunningham* v *Harrison* that in England the injured plaintiff who recovers damages under this head should hold them on trust for the voluntary carer.'

Hussain v *New Taplow Paper Mills Ltd* [1988] 2 WLR 266 House of Lords (Lord Bridge of Harwich, Lord Havers, Lord Ackner, Lord Oliver of Aylmerton and Lord Goff of Chieveley)

Damages – deduction of sickness benefit

Facts
The appellant sustained an injury in the course of his employment by the respondents which necessitated the amputation of his left arm below the elbow. Under his contract of employment, he received full pay for 13 weeks and thereafter 50 per cent of his pre-accident earnings by way of long-term sickness benefit payable under an insurance scheme run by the defendants who had covered this liability by means of an insurance policy entirely at their own expense. Under the plaintiff's contract of employment such long-term benefit was a continuation of earnings and taxable: there was no evidence that his wages would have been any higher if the defendants had not operated the insurance scheme.

Held
The benefit should be brought into account and deducted from the damages awarded to the plaintiff for pre-trial and future loss of earnings.

Lord Bridge of Harwich:

'Counsel for the plaintiff seeks to apply by analogy a principle said to be established by *Parry* v *Cleaver* in support of the argument that all payments to an employee enjoying the benefit of the defendants' permanent health insurance scheme are effectively in the nature of the fruits of insurance accruing to the benefit of the employee in consideration of the contributions he has made by his work for the defendants prior to incapacity. Much emphasis was laid on the long-term nature of the scheme payments to which the plaintiff has become entitled and it was submitted that they are strictly comparable to a disability pension. Both these arguments fall to the ground, as it seems to me, in the light of the concession rightly made at an early stage that the nature of payments under the scheme is unaffected by the duration of the incapacity which determines the period for which payments will continue to be made. The question whether the scheme payments are or are not deductible in assessing damages for loss of earnings must be answered in the same way whether, after the first 13 weeks of incapacity, the payments fall to be made for a few weeks or for the rest of an employee's working life. Looking at the payments made under the scheme by the defendants in the first weeks after the expiry of the period of 13 weeks of continuous incapacity, they seem to me indistinguishable in character from the sick pay which the employee receives during the first 13 weeks. They are payable under a term of the employee's contract by the defendants to the employee qua employee as a partial substitute for earnings and are the very antithesis of a pension, which is payable only after employment ceases. The fact that the defendants happen to have insured their liability to meet these contractual commitments as they arise cannot affect the issue in any way.'

Commentary
Distinguished in *McCamley* v *Cammell Laird Shipbuilders Ltd* [1990] 1 All ER 854.

Jefford v *Gee* [1970] 2 WLR 702 Court of Appeal (Lord Denning MR, Davies and Salmon LJJ)

Damages – interest

Facts
The defendant knocked the plaintiff off his motor scooter. P had many broken bones and lost teeth for which he had to stay off work for a long time. Waller J gave £5,631 damages, including £2,131 special damages; he awarded interest under s3 of the Law Reform (Miscellaneous Provisions) Act 1934 at 6.5 per cent of general damages of £3,560 from date of trial. He allowed no interest on the special damages.

D appealed and P cross-appealed on interest. He argued that on the basis of s22(1) of the Administration of Justice Act 1969 (amending s3 of the 1934 Act), obliging the court to award interest on damages, this meant on all damages after 1 January 1970.

Held
Interest should be awarded where P had been 'kept out of his money'. The appropriate rate is that payable on money in court on short investment account taken as an average over the period of the award. In general, interest should be granted on special damages from date of accident until trial at half the appropriate rate. No interest should be awarded on damages in respect of loss of future earnings and interest should be awarded on pain and suffering and loss of amenities from date of writ to trial.

Accordingly, the order was varied to give 3 per cent interest on the special damages from accident to trial; and on the £2,500 – that part of the general damages which related to pain and suffering and loss of amenities at 6 per cent pa from date of accident to date of trial.

Jones v *Jones* [1985] 2 QB 704 Court of Appeal (Stephenson, Dunn and Robert Goff LJJ)

Damages – divorce

Facts
The plaintiff, in an accident, sustained severe personal injuries and suffered permanent brain damage, which in turn caused the breakdown of his marriage. By a court order, the plaintiff was required to make periodical payments to his wife in the sum of £2,445 per annum (less tax) and to his children, payments of £64 per month; he was further ordered to pay a lump sum of £25,000 to enable his wife to buy a house for herself and the children, and claimed damages for his injuries including the payments he had to make to his family.

Held
The plaintiff was entitled to recover damages to compensate him for having to make financial provision for his family.

Commentary
Applied: *McLoughlin* v *O'Brian* [1982] 2 WLR 982.

Not followed in *Pritchard* v *J H Cobden Ltd* [1987] 2 WLR 627.

Lim Poh Choo v *Camden and Islington Area Health Authority* [1979] 3 WLR 44

House of Lords (Lord Diplock, Viscount Dilhorne, Lord Simon of Glaisdale and Lord Scarman)

Personal injury – damages

Facts

The plaintiff was admitted to hospital, aged 36, for minor surgery. She was reasonably healthy and worked as a senior psychiatric registrar. She suffered a cardiac arrest and irreparable brain damage due to the negligence of a member of the defendants' staff. She had no dependants. Her only relatives were an elderly mother in Penang and a sister. Her life expectancy was 37 years. If she had not suffered the injuries, she would have become a consultant by 1978. She would require care permanently for the rest of her life. She had no sensation of what had happened to her. She would eventually have to live in an institution. The trial judge awarded a total sum of £254,765 damages (the breakdown of which appears in the summary below). The defendants appealed on quantum, having admitted liability.

Held

Lord Scarman:

'1. *Pain, suffering and loss of amenity*
The judge awarded £20,000 for this which we uphold on the basis that this award was made on the fact that the plaintiff had lost most of her amenities and the sum should not be varied, on the basis of *Wise* v *Kay* and *H West & Son Ltd* v *Shephard*, where even though the injured person was not aware of the deprivation of amenities, nevertheless they could recover a full award for loss under this head. The reversal of these cases would cause widespread injustice. The sum is certainly not too high nor should it be increased: in the context of current money values, it is still substantial. [Distinguished: *Benham* v *Gambling* [1941] AC 157.]

2. *Loss of earnings*
The plaintiff is entitled to substantial damages for loss of earnings despite the fact that she will never be in a position to enjoy them. However, there should not be any duplication of damages, nor should P receive an award which is above what she could have earned. Accordingly, the expenses which she would have incurred in earning the money must be deducted and so should her future living expenses be. In the case of a plaintiff who was permanently incapacitated but whose life expectancy has not been shortened, any duplication between damages for loss of earnings and damages for cost of care can be remedied by deducting P's future living expenses from the damages awarded for the cost of care. The judge's award of lost future earnings at £92,000 (including pension) was correct. [Applied: *Pickett* v *British Rail Engineering Ltd* [1978] 3 WLR 955.]

3. *Cost of future care*
This should be awarded and on the basis that capital as well as income was to be used to meet the cost and, therefore, any award is to be calculated on an annuity basis. Future living expenses should also be deducted from the award. In all the circumstances, the multiplier should be 12 which will give £76,800 (as opposed to £105,500 at trial).

4. *Effect of future inflation*
In *Cookson* v *Knowles*, Lord Diplock's remark that future inflation is taken care of in a rough way because the multiplier only assumes interest at 4-5%, whereas in reality it is much higher and, therefore, the plaintiff gains approximately 8-13% per annum. No allowance should be made for inflation: (1) because it is pure speculation and (2) it is best left to be dealt with by an investment policy. [Applied: *Taylor* v *O'Connor* [1970] 2 WLR 472.]

5. *The total award*

The total award was not excessive merely because of its size and should not be reduced because of its size. The amended total is, therefore, £229,298.64.'

Commentary

Applied in *Auty* v *National Coal Board* [1985] 1 WLR 784.

McCamley v *Cammell Laird Shipbuilders Ltd* [1990] 1 WLR 963 Court of Appeal (O'Connor, Croom-Johnson and Balcombe LJJ)

Damages – deduction of insurance moneys

Facts

The defendant employers admitted liability for the serious injuries suffered by the plaintiff in the course of his employment and the judge awarded £387,790 by way of damages. The defendants ('the insured') had a personal accident group insurance policy for the benefit of their employees ('the insured persons'). The plaintiff had not contributed to this policy and, before his accident, he had not been aware of it. He received £45,630 under the policy and also attendance and mobility allowances: were these sums, or any of them, to be taken into account in assessing damages?

Held

The allowances were deductible but the payment under the policy would be disregarded.

O'Connor LJ:

' … the payment to the plaintiff was a payment by way of benevolence, even though the mechanics required the use of an insurance policy. The payment was not an ex gratia act where the accident had already happened, but the whole idea of the policy, covering all the many employees … was clearly to make the benefit payable as an act of benevolence whenever a qualifying injury took place. It was a lump sum payable regardless of fault or whether the employers or anyone else were liable, and it was not a method of advancing sick pay covered by a contractual scheme such as existed in *Hussain's* case … That the arrangement was made before the accident is immaterial. The act of benevolence was to happen contingently on an event and was prepared for in advance. To refer to Lord Bridge's speech in *Hussain's* case this payment was one analogous to "one of the two classic exceptions" to the rule that there should be no double recovery.

The point was well made on behalf of the plaintiff that this sum was not to be payable in respect of any particular head of damage suffered by him and was not an advance in respect of anything at all. To say that does not mean that in an appropriate case there may not be a general payment or an advance to cover a number of different heads of damage. The importance in the present case is that the sum was quantified before there had been an accident at all and when it could not have been foreseen what damages might be sustained when one did take place.'

Commentary

Followed: *Hodgson* v *Trapp* [1988] 3 WLR 1281.

Distinguished: *Hussain* v *New Taplow Paper Mills Ltd* [1988] 2 WLR 266.

As to the deduction of social security benefits from tort damages, see now s82 Social Security Administration Act 1992.

McLeish v *Amoo-Gottfried & Co* (1993) The Times 13 October High Court (Scott Baker J)

Facts

The plaintiff was wrongly convicted of a criminal offence due to his solicitor's admitted negligence. The plaintiff claimed damages for distress and mental anxiety and injury to reputation.

Held

The plaintiff could recover damages for distress and mental anxiety. No award for injury to reputation had ever been made in a case of negligence, although it was a possible head of damages in other torts. The court held that damages for loss of reputation could not be recovered in the instant case as a separate head of damage, but that in so far as any loss of reputation was an integral part of the plaintiff's distress it could enhance his award for distress and mental anxiety.

Meah v *McCreamer* [1985] 1 All ER 367 High Court (Woolf J)

Damages – sexual assaults

Facts

The plaintiff sustained serious head injuries and brain damage in a car accident which was caused by the defendant's negligence. He underwent a personality change and attacked and sexually assaulted three women. As a result he was sentenced to life imprisonment.

Held

Although the plaintiff had suffered no financial loss as a result of being sent to prison, his damages would take account of his imprisonment, using, as a guideline, awards for wrongful imprisonment. An overall sum of £60,000 was awarded.

Morris v *Redland Bricks Ltd* see *Redland Bricks Ltd* v *Morris*

Parry v *Cleaver* [1969] 2 WLR 821 House of Lords (Lord Reid, Lord Morris of Borth-y-Gest, Lord Pearce, Lord Wilberforce and Lord Pearson)

Damages – deductions

Facts

The appellant police constable was injured, as a result of the respondent's negligence, whilst he was directing traffic. In the following year he was discharged from the force and granted a police ill-health award for life.

Held (Lord Morris of Borth-y-Gest and Lord Pearson dissenting)

In computing damages, the ill-health award was not deductible in assessing the amount payable for loss of earnings, although it would have to be brought into account in respect of his loss of retirement pension.

Lord Reid:

'It would be revolting to the ordinary man's sense of justice, and therefore contrary to public policy, that the sufferer should have his damages reduced so that he would gain nothing from the benevolence of his friends or relations or of the public at large, and that the only gainer would be the wrongdoer. We do not have to decide in this case whether these considerations also apply to public benevolence in the shape of various unconvenanted benefits from the welfare state, but it may be thought that Parliament did not intend them to be for the benefit of the wrongdoer.

As regards moneys coming to the plaintiff under a contract of insurance, I think that the real and substantial reason for disregarding them is that the plaintiff has bought them and that it would be unjust and unreasonable to hold that the money which he prudently spent on premiums and the benefit from it should enure to the benefit of the tortfeasor. Here again I think that the explanation that this is too remote is artificial and unreal. Why should the plaintiff be left worse off than if he had never insured? In that case he would have got the benefit of the premium money; if he had not spent it he would have had it in his possession at the time of the accident grossed up at compound interest ... Then I ask – why should it make any difference that he insured by arrangement with his employer rather than with an insurance company? In the course of the argument the distinction came down to be as narrow as this: if the employer says nothing or merely advises the man to insure and he does so, then the insurance money will not be deductible; but if the employer makes it a term of the contract of employment that he shall insure himself and he does so, then the insurance money will be deductible. There must be something wrong with an argument which drives us to so unreasonable a conclusion.'

Commentary
See also *Colledge* v *Bass Mitchells & Butlers Ltd* [1988] 1 All ER 536.
Applied in *Smoker* v *London Fire and Civil Defence Authority* [1991] 2 WLR 1052.

Pickett v *British Rail Engineering Ltd* [1978] 3 WLR 955 House of Lords (Lord Wilberforce, Lord Salmon, Lord Edmund-Davies, Lord Russell of Killowen and Lord Scarman)

Damages – loss of future earnings

Facts
The plaintiff, the widow of H, appealed to the House of Lords on quantum. He had been a fit man until he was 53, working for the defendants, but he contracted asbestosis and his life expectancy was reduced to one year instead of the 12 which he could have expected. The Court of Appeal refused to award any sum for earnings during the lost years. The Court of Appeal had increased general damages from £7,000 to £10,000.

Held (Lord Russell of Killowen dissenting)
Where P's life expectancy was diminished as a result of D's negligence, P's future earnings were an asset of value of which he had been deprived and which could be assessed in money terms and were not merely an intangible prospect to be disregarded. He or his wife/widow had been deprived of the money over and above that which he would have spent on himself. Accordingly, this head of loss of earnings for the lost years forms a separate head and should *not* form part of the 'loss of expectation of life' head. The judge's general damages award was restored.

Commentary
Applied in *Lim Poh Choo* v *Camden and Islington Area Health Authority* [1979] 3 WLR 44 and *Gammell* v *Wilson* [1980] 3 WLR 591.
Overruled: *Oliver* v *Ashman* [1961] 3 WLR 669.

Pidduck v *Eastern Scottish Omnibuses Ltd* [1990] 1 WLR 993 Court of Appeal (Purchas, Glidewell LJJ and Sir Roger Ormrod)

Damages – widow's allowance

Facts
The plaintiff received a pension from her late husband's former employers, the Bank of England. The pension fund also made provision for the payment of certain allowances should the pensioner die within five years of retirement. The plaintiff's husband was killed within that period as a result of the defendant's negligence: she was awarded damages under s3(1) of the Fatal Accidents Act 1976: should the amount of her allowance be deducted?

Held
It should not.

Sir Roger Ormrod:

' ... as I understood the argument of counsel for the defendants, he founded primarily on s3(1) of the Fatal Accidents Act 1976 (as amended). By applying, in its simplest form, Lord Reid's test in *Parry* v *Cleaver* [1970] AC 1, ie by comparing the plaintiff's position "before and after", he contends that the widow has suffered no loss and hence no "injury" because, whereas "before" she was supported by the Bank of England Pension's Fund via her husband, "after" she was supported by the same fund via the widow's allowance and there is no significant difference in the amounts involved.

This argument goes too far. If it is right, it would pre-empt the express provisions of s4 of the 1976 Act and emasculate it in many cases because it would apply to all pension fund cases where the deceased was living on a pension and the scheme included a widow's benefit. In my judgment, the "injury" suffered by the widow is the loss of her dependency on her deceased husband. The value of this loss is to be quantified in accordance with the provisions of s4. The widow's allowance is, therefore, to be disregarded in the calculation.'

Pritchard v *J H Cobden Ltd* [1988] Fam 22 Court of Appeal (O'Connor, Croom-Johnson LJJ and Sir Roger Ormrod)

Damages – divorce

Facts
In 1976 the plaintiff was injured in a motor accident caused by the defendant's negligence. The plaintiff as a result suffered a character change and he and his wife divorced in 1984. This cost him £53,000 in settlement to his wife. The trial judge added this sum to the damages that he recovered from the defendant.

Held
Owing to the special nature of matrimonial proceedings, generally it would be very difficult to calculate what the plaintiff would have to pay to his wife. As such the damage would be too remote. Generally it was undesirable to bring family matters into personal injury litigation.

Commentary
Not followed: *Jones* v *Jones* [1984] 3 WLR 862.

Redland Bricks Ltd v *Morris* [1969] 2 WLR 1437 House of Lords (Lord Reid, Lord Morris of Borth-y-Gest, Lord Hodson, Lord Upjohn and Lord Diplock)

Damages – mandatory injunction

Facts

Due to lack of support, some of the respondents' market garden slipped into the appellants' clay quarry. The judge, inter alia, granted a mandatory injunction requiring the appellants to 'take all necessary steps to restore the support to the [respondents'] land within a period of six months'.

Held

Although there was a strong probability of further slippage, the injunction would be discharged as it did not inform the appellants exactly what they had to do.

Lord Upjohn:

'1. A mandatory injunction can only be granted where the plaintiff shows a very strong probability on the facts that grave damage will accrue to him in the future … It is a jurisdiction to be exercised sparingly and with caution but, in the proper case, unhesitatingly.

2. Damages will not be a sufficient or adequate remedy if such damage does happen. This is only the application of a general principle of equity …

3. Unlike the case where a negative injunction is granted to prevent the continuance or recurrence of a wrongful act the question of the cost to the defendant to do works to prevent or lessen the likelihood of a future apprehended wrong must be an element to be taken into account: (a) where the defendant has acted without regard to his neighbour's rights, or has tried to steal a march on him or has tried to evade the jurisdiction of the court or, to sum it up, has acted wantonly and quite unreasonably in relation to his neighbour he may be ordered to repair his wanton and unreasonable acts by doing positive work to restore the status quo even if the expense to him is out of all proportion to the advantage thereby accruing to the plaintiff … (b) but where the defendant has acted reasonably, although in the event wrongly, the cost of remedying by positive action his earlier activities is most important for two reasons. First, because no legal wrong has yet occurred (for which he has not been recompensed at law and in equity) and, in spite of gloomy expert opinion, may never occur or possibly only on a much smaller scale than anticipated. Secondly, because if ultimately heavy damage does occur the plaintiff is in no way prejudiced for he has his action at law and all his consequential remedies in equity.'

Rigby v *Chief Constable of Northamptonshire* [1985] 1 WLR 1242 High Court (Taylor J)

Negligence – police action

Facts

Police officers fired a CS gas canister into the plaintiff's shop during a siege, causing a fire. They knew that there was a risk of fire, but no fire-fighting appliances were present at the time. The plaintiff brought an action in negligence, nuisance, trespass and under the rule in *Rylands* v *Fletcher* alleging the escape of a dangerous thing.

Held

The police officers had been negligent in using the canister without having fire-fighting equipment available and the plaintiff was therefore entitled to succeed. The trespass claim failed because the defence of necessity was available to the defendants. The claim in nuisance added nothing to the trespass action, and that under *Rylands* v *Fletcher* failed on the ground that the gas had been deliberately released by the defendants.

Commentary
Distinguished in *Hughes* v *National Union of Mineworkers* [1991] 4 All ER 278.

Smith v *Marchioness/Bowbelle* [1993] NLJ 813 High Court (Master Topley)

Dependants and dependency

Facts
The plaintiff was the mother of a young woman who was drowned in an accident. Liability was admitted and the plaintiff claimed, inter alia, on behalf of herself and the deceased's maternal and paternal grandparents as dependants under the Fatal Accidents Act 1976.

Held
The court found that the plaintiff had lost a contribution to the household of £25 per week for shopping and £5 per week for chores. The court also found that the deceased gave her grandparents birthday and Christmas presents valued at £300 for each grandmother and received gifts from her grandparents valued at £30, making a net claim of £270 for each grandmother. These amounts, multiplied by the appropriate multiplier, were awarded, inter alia, under the 1976 Act.

Commentary
The definition of dependants, under s1(3) of the Fatal Accidents Act 1976, is wide. This case takes a wide approach to the question of whether a person who comes within s1(3) is financially dependent on the deceased.

Smoker v *London Fire and Civil Defence Authority, Wood* v *British Coal Corp* [1991] 2 WLR 1052 House of Lords (Lord Mackay of Clachfern LC, Lord Bridge of Harwich, Lord Brandon of Oakbrook, Lord Templeman and Lord Lowry)

Damages – pension deductible?

Facts
In the first case, the plaintiff fireman was disabled and his employers were liable in respect of his injuries. In relation to his claim for loss of earnings, the question arose whether there should be deducted from the amount of damages the amount that he had received by way of ill-health and injury pension and gratuity under a compulsory pension scheme to which he had contributed 10.75 per cent of his wages and his employer twice that amount.

The same question as to deductibility from loss of earnings damages arose in the second case where the injured former employee had received an incapacity retirement pension under a scheme to which he had contributed 5.14 per cent of his pay and the employer a like amount.

Held
In neither case were the pensions deductible.

Lord Templeman:

'The [former employers] claim that there has been a change of circumstance in that it can be shown that *Parry* v *Cleaver* [1970] AC 1 introduced uncertainty in the law and that since 1970 there has been a clear trend at common law against double recovery. But *Parry* v *Cleaver* established clearly that pension benefits are not deductible and that double recovery is not involved. The cases on which the appellants rely are mainly those in which the courts have decided that payments which correspond to wages must be taken into account when assessing loss of wages. Thus unemployment benefit (*Nabi* v *British Leyland* [1980] 1 All ER 667), family income supplement (*Gaskill* v *Preston* [1981] 3 All ER 427), supplementary benefit (*Lincoln* v *Hayman* [1982] 2 All ER 819), payments under job release schemes and student maintenance grants are statutory wages which reduce the loss of contractual wages resulting from the tort. In *Hussain* v *New Taplow Paper Mills Ltd* [1988] 1 All ER 541 at 547 the plaintiff was entitled to receive full-scale pay over 13 weeks and thereafter half his pre-accident earnings, and the House held that these payments were deductible because, in the words of Lord Bridge of Harwich:

" ... it has always been assumed as axiomatic that an employee who receives under the terms of his contract of employment either the whole or part of his salary or wages during a period when he is incapacitated for work cannot claim damages for a loss which he has not sustained ..." ...

I can find nothing in the authorities which casts doubt over the effect or logic of this House in *Parry* v *Cleaver*.

The appellants relied on s22 of the Social Security Act 1989 and Sch 4 to that Act. These provisions direct that social security benefits shall not be deducted in the assessment of damages for tort but that the tortfeasor shall repay to the state out of the damages thus assessed the amount of the social security benefits provided by the state for the benefit of the victim. These provisions, far from assisting the appellants, only demonstrate that Parliament is quite capable of legislating in this field but has not legislated to reduce the damages payable to the tortfeasor.'

Commentary
Applied: *Parry* v *Cleaver* [1970] AC 1.

Stanley v *Saddique* [1991] 2 WLR 459 Court of Appeal (Purchas, Ralph Gibson LJJ and Sir David Croom-Johnson)

Benefit should be disregarded?

Facts
A minor's mother had been killed in a road accident as a result of the defendant's negligence. On the hearing of a claim under s4 of the Fatal Accidents Act 1976, as amended by s3(1) of the Administration of Justice Act 1982, it appeared that the minor's father had since married Tracy and the judge found that Tracy was providing excellent motherly services to the minor which were of a higher quality than could foreseeably be expected to have been provided by the minor's mother. In the light of this finding it was contended that as the minor was better off in the home provided by his father and Tracy than he would ever have been with his mother there was no loss of dependency and, therefore, no damages to be awarded under the Act.

Held
This contention had properly been rejected: the benefits accruing to the minor as a result of his absorption into the family unit consisting of his father and stepmother and siblings should be wholly disregarded in assessing damages. However, the deceased mother's shortcomings was a matter which should have been taken into account when calculating the damages for loss of dependency.

Commentary
See also *Hayden* v *Hayden* [1992] 1 WLR 986, above.

Sutcliffe v *Pressdram Ltd* [1990] 2 WLR 271 Court of Appeal (Lord Donaldson of Lymington MR, Nourse and Russell LJJ)

Libel – damages

Facts
The jury found that *Private Eye* had libelled the plaintiff, the wife of 'the Yorkshire Ripper', and awarded her £600,000 by way of damages. The defendant publishers appealed.

Held
The award would be set aside and a new trial ordered.

Nourse LJ:

' ... I come to the particular question which we have to decide. There having been no claim for exemplary damages, is the jury's award of £600,000 by way of compensatory damages one with which this court can and ought to interfere? The various tests which have been stated in the past can be summarised by saying that a jury's award will only be interfered with on appeal if it is so large or so small as to be irrational, that is to say incapable of having been arrived at by a process of reason and necessarily arrived at through emotion, prejudice, caprice or stupidity, or simply on a wrong basis. Among juries trying civil actions in the late 1980s, we ought to be confident that prejudice, caprice and stupidity are possibilities which exist only in theory. But we must recognise that out of the human attributes for which we prize them they may sometimes make an award on a wrong basis, seasoned perhaps with some seasonable emotion.

The basis on which it was open to the jury to make an award of damages to Mrs Sutcliffe was compensation for the injury to her reputation (in such an amount as was appropriate to vindicate her) and for the injury to her feelings, including the aggravation caused by *Private Eye's* misconduct ... I have dwelt on the injury, original and aggravated, to Mrs Sutcliffe's feelings, because it is on that injury that she must principally rely in order to sustain the award of £600,000 as one exclusively of compensatory damages. But I bear in mind also that Mrs Sutcliffe was entitled to proper and vindicative compensation for the injury to her reputation. Taking account of all material considerations and with a disposition to resolve and assume everything in her favour, I nevertheless conclude that the amount of the award was very substantially in excess of any sum which could reasonably have been thought appropriate to compensate Mrs Sutcliffe. It must have been made on a wrong basis. I think that the jury, without realising that they were exceeding their function, have included a very large exemplary element in their award ... However grave the injury to Mrs Sutcliffe's reputation, however pressing the need for its vindication, however profound the injury to her feelings and however disgraceful *Private Eye's* conduct, they could not, these ordinary men and women, think that that enormous sum was appropriate, far less necessary, as compensation for one who in other circumstances might have been numbered among them.'

Watson v *Willmott* [1990] 3 WLR 1103 High Court (Garland J)

Damages – effect of adoption

Facts
The plaintiff's mother was killed in an accident caused by the negligence of the defendant and, some months later, his father committed suicide as a result of the depression caused by the death of his wife. The plaintiff was looked after by his aunt and uncle who later adopted him. The defendants argued that

the effect of the adoption was to preclude the recovery of any loss of dependency after the date of the adoption because from that date the child was treated in law as if he had been born as a child of the adoptive parents. The plaintiff, on the other hand, argued that the adoption had no effect on his claim because his cause of action accrued as at the dates of death of his parents and it could not be abrogated or extinguished by his subsequent adoption.

Held

Both arguments would be rejected and, drawing an analogy with the 'stepfather' cases, the adoption would be taken into account in the *quantification* of the dependency. In the case of the loss of the plaintiff's father, the loss of dependency was to be calculated by comparing the plaintiff in the position he would have been in had his father lived with his position with his adoptive father; therefore the sum to be awarded was the plaintiff's loss of dependency on his father less his dependency on his adoptive father. But, in so far as his dependency on his mother was concerned, the adoption replaced his non-pecuniary dependency on his deceased mother and therefore the non-pecuniary dependency on his mother was to be passed only up to the date of his adoption.

Willson v *Ministry of Defence* [1991] 1 All ER 638 High Court (Scott Baker J)

Provisional damages – 'chance' of 'serious deterioration'

Facts

The plaintiff injured his ankle at work and he was left with continuing disability and pain. In an action against his former employers, he applied for an award of provisional damages under s32A of the Supreme Court Act 1981. Medical reports stated that there would be degeneration of the ankle joint, that he would remain prone to further injuries and that there was a possibility that he would develop arthritis.

Held

The application for an award of provisional damages would fail and damages would be awarded on a lump sum basis.

Scott Baker J:

'A "chance" ... is not defined in s32A ... It seems to me that the legislature has used a wide word here and used it deliberately. I think [counsel for the defendants] is right when he points out that it can cover a wide range between, on the one hand, something that is de minimis and, on the other hand, something that is a probability. In my view, to qualify as a chance it must be measurable rather than fanciful. There is certainly, in my judgment, in this case a chance of osteoarthritis developing and a chance of the plaintiff suffering further traumatic injury. I think that there is a chance that he will develop arthritis to the extent that he requires surgery. I think that there is a chance that he will develop arthritis to the extent that he has to change his employment and I think there is a chance that he will suffer further injury in the nature of further damage to his ankle or elsewhere. However slim those chances may be, I think that they are measurable within the meaning of this section ...

The second question turns on the words "serious deterioration in his physical condition". It is clear that, as drafted, the word "serious" appears to qualify the words "deterioration in his physical condition". There is a question of how "serious" should be interpreted in the light of this section. On one view, "serious" could cover a wide range of circumstances from something not far beyond the trivial at the bottom end of the scale to something approaching the catastrophic at the top end of the scale.

In my judgment, what is envisaged here is something beyond ordinary deterioration. Whether deterioration is serious in any particular case seems to me to be a question of fact depending on the circumstances of that case, including the effect of the deterioration upon the plaintiff. For example, where a plaintiff suffers a hand injury and there is a deterioration it may be a matter of great gravity for a concert pianist but a matter of rather less importance for somebody else ... I am not ... satisfied that it is established that there is a chance of *serious* – and I emphasise that word – deterioration in this case. That is not a matter that I have found entirely easy ...

When the criteria set out in s32A(1) are all met the court then has to exercise a discretion whether or not to make an order for provisional damages. This is clear from the use of the word "may" in RSC Ord 37 r8(1), as opposed to the word "shall".

The question then arises as to which cases are appropriate for a provisional damages award and which are not. I deal with this because, although I formed the view that there was no serious deterioration envisaged, that was not a matter that I found entirely easy and indeed there are some matters that may more properly be dealt with under the heading of "discretion" rather than taking into account the circumstances of the case in looking at whether or not the section was complied with.

The general rule in English law is that damages are assessed on a once-and-for-all basis. Section 32A of the 1981 Act creates a valuable statutory exception. In my judgment, the section envisages a clear and severable risk rather than a continuing deterioration, as is the typical osteoarthritic picture.

In my judgment, many disabilities follow a developing pattern in which the precise results cannot be foreseen. Within a general band this or that may or may not occur. Such are not the cases for provisional damages. The courts have to do their best to make an award in the light of a broad medical prognosis.

In my judgment, there should be some clear-cut event which, if it occurs, triggers an entitlement to further compensation ...

It seems to me that the case falls within the general run of cases where there are uncertainties as to the future. Nobody can look into a crystal ball and see precisely how the plaintiff's ankle will develop, but I think that the uncertainties are such that they can all properly be taken into account in making a once-and-for-all assessment of damages today. My conclusion therefore is that this is not an appropriate case in which to exercise discretion in favour of a provisional damages order.'

Wood v *British Coal Corp*

See *Smoker* v *London Fire and Civil Defence Authority*.

Wright v *British Railways Board* [1983] 3 WLR 211 House of Lords (Lord Diplock, Lord Fraser of Tullybelton, Lord Scarman, Lord Bridge of Harwich and Lord Brandon of Oakbrook)

Damages – interest

Facts
The plaintiff guard was awarded damages, inter alia, for pain, suffering and loss of amenity against his employers, the defendants. The question arose as to the rate of interest to be paid.

Held
It should be 2 per cent from the date of service of the writ to the date of judgment.

Lord Diplock:

'As regards the fixing of the conventional rate of interest to be applied to the conventional figure at which damages for non-economic loss have been assessed, the rate of 2% adopted and recommended as a guideline by the Court of Appeal in *Birkett* v *Hayes* [1982] 1 WLR 816 covered a period during which inflation was proceeding at a very rapid rate ... I see no ground that would justify this House in holding that guideline to have been wrong, or to overrule the trial judge's application of it to the instant case. Although the rate of inflation has slowed, at least temporarily, since the period in respect of which the

2% guideline in *Birkett* v *Hayes* was laid down, no one yet knows what the long-term future of the phenomenon of inflation will be; and the guideline, if it is to serve its purpose in promoting predictability and so facilitating settlements and eliminating the expense of regularly calling expert economic evidence at trials of personal injury actions, should continue to be followed for the time being at any rate, until the long-term trend of future inflation has become predictable with much more confidence. When that state of affairs is reached, and it would be unrealistic to suppose that it will be in the immediate future, it may be that the 2% guideline will call for examination afresh in the light of fresh expert economic evidence, which may show that assumptions that could validly be made at the time of *Birkett* v *Hayes* as to what was the current rate of interest obtainable in the market that was attributable to forgoing the use of money will have ceased to hold good. But there is no material before your Lordships to suggest that the time is yet ripe for this.'

29 Miscellaneous Defences and Limitation

Broadley v *Guy Clapham & Co* [1994] 4 All ER 439 Court of Appeal (Balcombe, Leggatt, Hoffmann LJJ)

Limitation period for personal injury – date of plaintiff's knowledge for s11 and s14 Limitation Act 1980

Facts

In 1980 the plaintiff underwent a knee operation. Her condition did not improve and subsequent examinations revealed that she had left foot drop. In 1983 the plaintiff instructed the defendant solicitors who took few steps to prosecute the action. In August 1990 the plaintiff sued the defendants alleging that they had failed to take any adequate action, and as a result her claim for medical negligence had become time-barred under the Limitation Act 1980.

The question arose for determination as a preliminary issue as to whether the plaintiff's date of knowledge of her cause of action was before or after August 1981. At first instance it was held that the plaintiff knew before this date that her injury was significant, although she did not have knowledge of its cause or pathology, and while such knowledge did not satisfy s14(1) it was sufficient to fix the plaintiff with constructive knowledge under s14(3)(b), namely knowledge that the operation had in some way caused her injury. The plaintiff appealed.

Held

The appeal was dismissed. A person who alleged that medical negligence had occurred during a surgical operation was fixed with a cause of action for the purposes of s14(3) of the 1980 Act when he knew, or could have known with the help of medical advice reasonably obtainable, that his injury had been caused by damage resulting from an act or omission by the surgeon during the operation. Knowledge which was detailed enough to enable the plaintiff's advisers to draft a statement of claim was not required before time began to run.

Dobbie v *Medway Health Authority* [1994] 4 All ER 450 Court of Appeal (Sir Thomas Bingham MR, Beldam and Steyn LJJ

Limitation period for personal injury – date of plaintiff's knowledge

Facts

In 1973 the plaintiff was admitted to hospital for the removal of a lump from her breast. During the operation, the surgeon considered the lump to be cancerous and performed a mastectomy. Subsequent examination showed that the growth was benign. In 1988 the plaintiff heard of a similar case and realised, for the first time, that her breast need not have been removed until the lump had to be examined and found to be malignant. In 1989 she issued proceedings in negligence. The defendant contended that the claim was time-barred under s11(4)(b) and s14(1) of the Limitation Act 1980 as the time limit for actions for personal injuries was three years from the date of knowledge of the person injured which was defined as the date on which the plaintiff first had knowledge (a) that the injury was significant and (b) that it was attributable in whole or part to the act or omission which was alleged to constitute negligence. At first instance it was held that the action was statute-barred. The plaintiff appealed.

Held

The appeal was dismissed. Time started to run against a claimant for the purposes of s14(1) when he knew that the injury on which he founded his claim was capable of being attributed to an act or omission of the defendant, irrespective of whether at that point he knew that the act or omission was actionable or tortious. It thus followed that the plaintiff's cause of action was time-barred since she knew within the limitation period that she had suffered a significant injury which was attributable to the defendant's act or omission, even though she had not been aware until after this period that the conduct might be actionable.

Commentary

It would seem from *Broadley* and *Dobbie* that very little knowledge indeed is necessary to cause time to run under s14 of the Limitation Act 1980.

Donovan v *Gwentoys Ltd* [1990] 1 WLR 472 House of Lords (Lord Bridge of Harwich, Lord Templeman, Lord Griffiths, Lord Oliver of Aylmerton and Lord Lowry)

Limitation period – discretion.

Facts

In 1979 the plaintiff, then aged 16, fell at work: she strained a wrist and aggravated a knee condition. She received industrial injury benefit for the wrist but made no mention of the knee: she left the defendants' employment in 1980. Shortly before any action became statute-barred by virtue of ss11 and 28 of the Limitation Act 1980, the plaintiff consulted solicitors: they applied for legal aid but failed to issue a writ to protect her position. A writ was issued in October 1984 (5 1/2 months after the expiration of the limitation period) but the defendants did not receive full information regarding the plaintiff's claim for injury to her knee, alleging negligence and breach of statutory duty, until June 1987. The defendants contended that the action was statute-barred: the plaintiff sought to rely on s33 of the 1980 Act. The trial judge decided in favour of the plaintiff, confining himself to a consideration of the prejudice to the defendants resulting from the 5 1/2 months' delay: the Court of Appeal upheld this decision: the defendants appealed.

Held

The appeal would be allowed. The judge's discretion under s33(1) of the 1980 Act had been unfettered, especially in relation to s33(3). He should not have confined himself to the 5 1/2 months period, but considered all the circumstances, in particular the fact that it was 5 years before the defendants had been notified of a claim. The balance of prejudice was heavily in favour of the defendants, especially as the plaintiff had a strong claim against her solicitors for failing to issue a protective writ.

K v *P* [1993] 1 All ER 521 High Court (Ferris J)

Extent of the ex turpi causa defence

Facts

The plaintiffs sued various defendants, alleging fraud and conspiracy to defraud. One defendant issued a third party notice against the plaintiffs' accountant under s1(1) of the Civil Liability (Contribution) Act 1978 claiming an indemnity against any damages payable to the plaintiffs on the grounds that the accountant had acted in breach of contract or negligently. The question arose as to whether a party who was held to be merely negligent could be required to contribute to damages payable by a party who had been guilty of fraud, and whether the maxim ex turpi causa non oritur actio afforded a defence under the 1978 Act.

Held

The ex turpi causa defence was not available to a claim for contribution under the 1978 Act, since the specific purpose of that Act was to enable claims to be made between parties who had no claim under the general law. The only necessary ingredient for an action under the Act was that the plaintiffs had a cause of action against a third party as regards the same damage that gave rise to the plaintiffs' cause of action against the defendants. To permit the ex turpi causa defence to be relied on would substantially narrow the deliberately wide wording of s6(1) of the Act. Thus it was irrelevant that the plaintiffs' cause of action against the defendants arose out of fraud while their cause of action against the third party arose from breach of contractual or tortious duty of care. Additionally, under s2(1) and s2(2) of the 1978 Act all of the factors which were relevant to the ex turpi causa defence could be taken into account when assessing the amount of contribution, and could result in a nil contribution.

Moore (DW) & Co Ltd v *Ferrier* [1988] 1 WLR 267 Court of Appeal (Kerr, Neill and Bingham LJJ)

Negligence – limitation of action

Facts

Having agreed in 1971 and 1975 to issue shares in the company to Fenton, an employee and director of the company, subject to his entering into a covenant against setting up as an insurance broker if he left the company, the plaintiff insurance brokers consulted the defendant solicitors who drew up agreements containing a restrictive covenant which would apply if Fenton ceased 'to be a member of the company'. In 1980 Fenton decided to set up business in a way which appeared to breach the covenant: he resigned as an employee and director but remained a shareholder and it was then discovered that the covenant was effective only if he ceased to be a shareholder. In consequence, the plaintiffs were unable to enforce the covenant and in 1985 they sued the defendants alleging negligence in drafting the covenant.

Held

The plaintiffs' cause of action had accrued more than six years before they brought their action and it was therefore time-barred.

Bingham LJ:

'The limitation of tort actions in negligence is, and has for many years been, governed by two main rules: first, that time runs against the claimant from the date when his cause of action accrues; and second, that his cause of action accrues when he suffers damage caused by the negligence complained of.

In the great majority of cases these rules work well, because the claimant knows of his injury or damage at about the time he suffers it, and if he does not take action within the generous time limits provided he has only himself to blame. But difficulty has arisen in the minority of cases where a claimant does not know that he has suffered injury or damage, so that time begins to run, and may even expire, before he is aware of the damage or injury, or of his right to complain against its author ... [The Limitation Acts passed in 1963 and 1975 were] only concerned with personal injuries and the problem was not confined to that field. Architects and engineers designing or supervising the construction of buildings or other structures, barristers and solicitors and accountants giving advice and settling documents, may all make negligent mistakes in circumstances where the mistake may not become apparent for many years. Following the 24th Report of the Law Reform Committee (Latent Damage) (Cmnd 9390) this problem also was the subject of legislative intervention, in the Latent Damage Act 1986. But that Act does not affect this action, which is subject to the law which governed negligence actions not involving personal injury before it was passed. Under that law, in the absence of fraud, concealment or mistake (which are not suggested here), time runs for the date of damage whether the claimant knows of the damage or not.

So the crucial question here is when the plaintiffs suffered damage ... It seems to me clear beyond argument that from the moment of executing each agreement the plaintiffs suffered damage because instead of receiving a potentially valuable chose in action they received one that was valueless.'

Rigby v *Chief Constable of Northamptonshire* [1985] 1 WLR 1242 High Court (Taylor J)

Necessity as a defence to trespass

Facts

The police fired a canister of CS gas into the plaintiff's shop in an effort to flush out a dangerous psychopath who had broken into it. The canister set the shop ablaze and the plaintiff sued the police (inter alia) in trespass.

Held

That the defence of necessity was available in an action for trespass.

Stubbings v *Webb* [1993] 2 WLR 120 House of Lords (Lord Templeman, Lord Bridge of Harwich, Lord Griffiths, Lord Ackner and Lord Slynn of Hadley)

Trespass to the person – limitation period

Facts

In August 1987 the respondent issued a writ claiming damages for personal injuries arising out of alleged sexual and physical abuse by the appellants between December 1959 and January 1971. The alleged abuse was said to have taken place when the respondent was between the ages of 2 and 14.

Held

The claim was within s2 (as opposed to s11) of the Limitation Act 1980 and it was therefore time-barred.

Lord Griffiths:

'I accept that *Letang* v *Cooper* [1964] 3 WLR 573 was correctly decided in so far as it held that negligent driving is a cause of action falling within s2(1) of the Law Reform (Limitation of Actions etc) Act 1954. But I cannot agree that the words "breach of duty" have the effect of including within the scope of the section all actions in which damages for personal injuries are claimed which is the other ground upon which the Court of Appeal decided *Letang* v *Cooper*. If that had been the intention of the draftsman it would have been easy enough to say so in the section. On the contrary the draftsman has used words of limitation; he has limited the section to actions for negligence, nuisance and breach of duty and the reason he did so was to give effect to the recommendation of the Tucker Committee that the three-year period should not apply to a number of causes of action in which damages for personal injury might be claimed, namely damages for trespass to the person, false imprisonment, malicious prosecution or defamation. There can be no doubt that rape and indecent assault fell within the category of trespass to the person.

Lord Denning MR in *Letang* v *Cooper* was not prepared to assume that Parliament did intend to give effect to the Tucker Committee's recommendations, but we can now look at Hansard and can see that it was the express intention of Parliament to do so. The proposer of the Bill ... in moving the second reading said:

> "In its main provisions the Bill follows precisely the recommendations of the committee which sat under the chairmanship of the then Lord Justice Tucker. There is only one comparatively minor point upon which the provisions vary from the recommendations of the Tucker committee."

The minor point I have already identified: it was to substitute a fixed period of three years for a two-year period which might be extended to six years ...

Even without reference to Hansard I should not myself have construed "breach of duty" as including a deliberate assault. The phrase lying in juxtaposition with "negligence" and "nuisance" carries with it the implication of a breach of duty of care not to cause personal injury, rather than an obligation not to infringe any legal right of another person. If I invite a lady to my house one would naturally think of a duty to take care that the house is safe but would one really be thinking of a duty not to rape her. But, however this may be, the terms in which this Bill was introduced to my mind make it clear beyond peradventure that the intention was to give effect to the Tucker recommendation that the limitation period in respect of trespass to the person was not to be reduced to three years but should remain at six years. The language of s2(1) of the 1954 Act is in my view apt to give effect to that intention, and cases of deliberate assault such as we are concerned with in this case are not actions for breach of duty within the meaning of s11(1) of the 1980 Act.

The language of s2(1) of the 1954 Act was carried without alteration into the 1975 Act and then into s11(1) of the 1980 Act where it must bear the same meaning as it had in the 1954 Act.

It thus follows that the respondent's causes of action against both appellants were subject to a six-year limitation period. This period was suspended during her infancy but commenced to run when she attained her majority: see s28 of the 1980 Act. This period expired many years before she issued her writ in these proceedings. There are no provisions for extending this period and her actions are therefore statute-barred and cannot proceed.'

Tinsley v *Milligan* [1993] 3 WLR 126 House of Lords (Lord Keith, Lord Goff, Lord Jauncey, Lord Lowry and Lord Browne-Wilkinson)

Extent of ex turpi causa defence

Facts

The plaintiff and defendant formed a joint business venture to run lodging houses. Using funds generated by the business they purchased a house in which they lived together and which was vested in the sole name of the plaintiff, on the understanding that they were the joint beneficial owners of the property. The purpose of this arrangement was to perpetrate a fraud on the Department of Social Security, and over a number of years both the plaintiff and the defendant made false benefit claims on the Department. The plaintiff brought proceedings against the defendant claiming sole ownership of the property and the defendant counterclaimed for a declaration that the property was held by the plaintiff on trust for the parties in equal shares. The judge dismissed the plaintiff's claim and allowed the counterclaim. The plaintiff appealed to the Court of Appeal who dismissed the appeal, and thence to the House of Lords.

Held

The appeal was dismissed on the grounds that a claimant to an interest in property, whether based on a legal or equitable title, was entitled to recover if he was not forced to plead or rely on illegality, even though the title on which he relied was acquired via an illegal transaction. In the circumstances, by showing that she had contributed to the purchase price of the property and that there was a common understanding between the parties that they owned the property equally, the defendant had established a resulting trust. There was no necessity to prove the reason for the conveyance into the plaintiff's sole name, which was irrelevant to the defendant's claim, and since there was no evidence to rebut the presumption of a resulting trust the defendant's counterclaim succeeded.

Note that the House rejected the 'public conscience' test used by the Court of Appeal.

Lord Goff:

'Finally, I wish to revert to the public conscience test favoured by Nicholls LJ in the Court of Appeal. Despite the fact that I have concluded that on the authorities it was not open to the Court of Appeal to apply the public conscience test to a case such as the present, I have considered whether it is open to your Lordships' House to do so and, if so, whether it would be desirable to take this course. Among the authorities cited to your Lordships, there was no decision of this House; technically, therefore, it may be said that this House is free to depart from the line of authority to which I have referred. But the fact remains that the principle invoked by the appellant has been consistently applied for about two centuries. Furthermore the adoption of the public conscience test, as stated by Nicholls LJ, would constitute a revolution in this branch of the law, under which what is in effect a discretion would become vested in the court to deal with the matter by the process of a balancing operation, in place of a system of rules, ultimately derived from the principle of public policy enunciated by Lord Mansfield CJ in *Holman* v *Johnson*, 1 Cowp 341, which lies at the root of the law relating to claims which are, in one way or another, tainted by illegality. Furthermore, the principle of public policy so stated by Lord Mansfield cannot be disregarded as having no basis in principle. In his dissenting judgment in the present case Ralph Gibson LJ pointed out [1992] Ch 310, 334:

"In so far as the basis of the ex turpi causa defence, as founded on public policy, is directed at deterrence it seems to me that the force of the deterrent effect is in the existence of the known rule and in its stern application. Lawyers have long known of the rule and must have advised many people of its existence. It does not stop people making arrangements to defraud creditors, or the revenue, or the DSS. Such arrangements as are under consideration in this case are usually made between married couples as in *Tinker* v *Tinker*, or between unmarried lovers as in this case or in *Cantor* v *Cox*, 239 EG 121. If they do not fall out, no one will know. If they do fall out, one side may reveal the fraud. It is an ugly situation when that is done. I think that the law has upheld the principle on the simple ground that, ugly though its working may be, it is better than permitting the fraudulent an avenue of escape if the fraud is revealed."

I recognise, of course, the hardship which the application of the present law imposes upon the respondent in this case; and I do not disguise my own unhappiness at the result. But, bearing in mind the passage from the judgment of Ralph Gibson LJ which I have just quoted, I have to say that it is by no means self-evident that the public conscience text is preferable to the present strict rules. Certainly, I do not feel able to say that it would be appropriate for your Lordships' House, in the face of a long line of unbroken authority stretching back over 200 years, now by judicial decision to replace the principles established in those authorities by a wholly different discretionary system.'

30 Torts to Chattels

Armory v *Delamirie* (1722) 1 Stra 505 Court of Kings Bench (Sir John Pratt CJ)

Boy finds jewel – was he entitled to it?

Facts
A chimney sweeper's boy found a jewel set in a socket and took it to a goldsmith 'to know what it was'. The goldsmith returned the socket but retained the jewel so the boy sued for its recovery.

Held
His action would be successful

Sir John Pratt CJ:

> 'the finder of a jewel, though he does not by such finding acquire an absolute property or ownership, yet he has such a property as will enable him to keep it against all but the rightful owner, and consequently may maintain trover ...' As to the value of the jewel, several of the trade were examined to prove what a jewel of the finest water that would fit the socket would be worth; and Sir John Pratt CJ, directed the jury that, unless the defendant did produce the jewel and show it not to be of the finest water, they should presume the strongest against him and make the value of the best jewels the measure of their damages, which they accordingly did.

Commentary
Applied in *Bridges* v *Hawkesworth* (1851) 21 LJQB 75 and *Parker* v *British Airways Board* [1982] 1 All ER 834.

Bridges v *Hawkesworth* (1851) LJ QB 75 Court of Queen's Bench (Pattison and Wightman JJ)

Parcel found in shop – who should have it?

Facts
The plaintiff traveller, having visited the defendant's shop on business, noticed a parcel on the floor: the parcel contained bank-notes. The plaintiff asked the defendant to keep the notes until they were claimed by their owner. After three years, the notes having not been claimed, the plaintiff asked the defendant to return them to him; he refused. In an action in the county court it was found that when the plaintiff passed the notes to the defendant he (the plaintiff) had not intended to give up any title to them that he might possess.

Held
The plaintiff was entitled to the notes as against the defendant.

Pattison J:

'The notes which are the subject of this action were dropped by mere accident in the defendant's shop by the owner of them. The facts do not warrant the supposition that they had been deposited there intentionally, nor has the case been put at all upon that ground. The plaintiff found them on the floor, they being manifestly lost by someone. The general right of the finder to any article which has been lost as against all the world except the true owner, was established in *Armory* v *Delamirie* (1722) 1 Stra 505, which has never been disputed. This right would clearly have accrued to the plaintiff had the notes been picked up by him outside the shop of the defendant; and if he once had the right, the case finds that he did not intend by delivering the notes to the defendant, to waive the title (if any) which he had to them, but they were handed to the defendant merely for the purpose of delivering them to the owner, should he appear.

Nothing that was done afterwards has altered the state of things ... The case, therefore, resolves itself to the single point on which it appears that the judge decided it, namely, whether the circumstance of the notes being found in the defendant's shop gives him, the defendant, authority in our law to be found directly in point... The notes never were in the custody of the defendant, nor within the protection of his house, before they were found, as they would have been had they been intentionally deposited there ... We find, therefore, no circumstances to take this case out of the general rule of law that the finder of a lost article is entitled to it as against all persons, except the real owner; and we think that that rule must prevail, and that the judge was mistaken in holding that the place in which they were found makes any legal difference.'

Commentary

Followed in *Hannah* v *Peel* [1945] KB 509 and *Parker* v *British Airways Board* [1982] 1 All ER 834.
  Distinguished in *South Staffordshire Water Co* v *Sharman* [1896] 2 QB 44.

Bute (Marquess) v *Barclays Bank Ltd* [1955] 1 QB 202 High Court (McNair J)

Crossed warrants – conversion?

Facts

A Mr McGaw managed the plaintiff's sheep farms. Under the terms of his contract of employment, all sums received by him in respect of the farms had to be taken to the estate office for payment into the plaintiff's farm account. In January, in accordance with his duty, he applied for sheep subsidy; he resigned in April and left the plaintiff's service in May. Later that year, McGaw received three crossed warrants in satisfaction of the January claim: they were drawn in his favour '(for Marquess of Bute)'. McGaw opened an account with the defendant bank and paid in the warrants which were specially crossed by a rubber stamp bearing the defendants' name and forwarded by them for payment. The plaintiff sued for the amount of the warrants, inter alia, as damages for conversion.

Held

His action would be successful as he had been entitled to immediate possession of the property converted.

McNair J:

'In substance, three grounds of defence were taken by the bank. First, it was said that McGaw was at all material times the true owner of the warrants and their proceeds, though he was accountable to the plaintiff, that the plaintiff was not the true owner and that, accordingly, the plaintiff is not entitled to sue either in conversion ...

As to the first ground, the short answer, in my judgment, is that, in order to claim in conversion, it is not necessary for the plaintiff to establish that he is the true owner of the property alleged to have been converted. It is sufficient if he can prove that at the time of the alleged conversion he was entitled to immediate possession. McGaw's employment was terminated not later than May 9, 1949, and thereafter the plaintiff was clearly entitled, if he so wished, to require McGaw to deliver the warrants to him when they were received, since McGaw's only title to receive them stemmed from his appointment as manager; and thus, I think, it is clear that at the date of the alleged conversion in September 1949, the plaintiff was entitled to immediate possession and, accordingly, was entitled to sue in conversion. I have no doubt that, if the plaintiff had known the true facts in September 1949, before McGaw approached the bank, he could successfully have applied for an injunction to restrain McGaw from dealing with the warrants otherwise than by handing them over to him...

Counsel for the defendants, rightly as I consider, submitted that the test in this case was to be found in the intention of the drawer as expressed in the document. Though it was argued that, as a matter of construction, the words "for Marquess of Bute" were merely inserted for the information of McGaw, I consider that these words, particularly having regard to their position on the warrants, form an essential part of the description of the drawee. On this view the warrants contain a promise to pay A for B ... Having regard ... to the fact that the warrants on their face purported to be payments in respect of hill sheep subsidy, which, to the knowledge of the drawers, was due to the plaintiff and not to McGaw, it seems to me to be plain that the intention of the drawers, as evidenced by the warrants, must be taken to have been that the plaintiff should be the true owner of the warrants and their proceeds and not that the true owner should be McGaw, and McGaw should be merely accountable to the plaintiff ... Accordingly, quite apart from the fact that at the material time McGaw's authority had been terminated, I consider that at all times, including the date of the conversion, the plaintiff was the true owner and not McGaw.'

Greenwood v *Bennett* [1973] QB 195 Court of Appeal (Lord Denning MR, Phillimore and Cairns LJJ)

Stolen car – cost of repair

Facts

A Mr Searle stole a Jaguar car from a garage of which Mr Bennett was manager. Searle involved the car in a collision with another vehicle and, in its damaged state, sold it to a Mr Harper who bought it in good faith for £75. Harper repaired the car at a cost of £226 and then sold it to a finance company which let it on hire purchase to a Mr Prattle for £450. The police recovered the vehicle and Mr Greenwood, the chief constable, asked the court to whom they should return it. Harper accepted the county court judge's ruling that Bennett was entitled to possession, but appealed against his decision that Bennett was not obliged to reimburse the amount that he (Harper) had expended on repairs.

Held

The appeal would be allowed.

Lord Denning MR:

'To decide this case, I think it helpful to consider the legal position as if the police had not taken possession of the car, but it had remained in Mr Prattle's possession. In the first place, if Mr Bennett's company had brought an action against Mr Harper for conversion of the car (relying on his purchase of it from Mr Searle for £75 as the act of conversion) then the damages would be £75 as its value at that time; whereas, if they had brought an action for conversion (relying on his sale of it to the finance company as the act of conversion) the damages would be its improved value at the time of sale, but Mr Bennett's company would have to give credit for the work which Mr Harper had done on it: see *Munro* v *Willmott* [1949] 1 KB 295 ... if Mr Bennett's company had brought an action against Mr Prattle for specific delivery of the car, it is very unlikely that an order for specific delivery of the car would be made. But if it had been, no court would order its delivery unless compensation was made for the improvements ... I should have thought that the county court judge here should have imposed a condition on Mr Bennett's company. He should have required them to pay Mr Harper the £226 as a condition of being given delivery of the car. But the judge did not impose such a condition. They have regained the car, and sold it. What then is to be done? It seems to me that we must order them to pay Mr Harper the £226 for that is the only way of putting the position right.

On what principle is this to be done? Counsel for Mr Bennett has referred us to the familiar cases which say that a man is not entitled to compensation for work done on the goods or property of another unless there is a contract express or implied to pay for it... That is undoubtedly the law when the person who does the work knows, or ought to know, that the property does not belong to him. He takes the risk of not being paid for his work on it. But it is very different when he honestly believes himself to be the owner of the property and does the work in that belief ... Here we have an innocent purchaser who bought the car in good faith and without notice of any defect in the title to it. He did work on it to the value of £226. The law is hard enough to him when it makes him give up the car itself. It would be most unjust if Mr Bennett's company could not only take the car from him, but also the value of the improvements he has done to it – without paying for them. There is a principle at hand to meet the case. It derives from the law of restitution. Mr Bennett's company should not be allowed unjustly to enrich themselves at his expense. The court will order them, if they recover the car, or its improved value, to recompense the innocent purchaser for the work he had done on it. No matter whether they recover it with the aid of the courts, or without it, the innocent purchaser will recover the value of the improvements he has done to it.'

Hannah v *Peel* [1945] KB 509 High Court (Birkett J)

Brooch found in house owner had never occupied

Facts
A house was conveyed to the defendant in 1938 but he had never actually occupied it. War broke out, the house was requisitioned and the plaintiff soldier found a brooch there. The real owner of the brooch not having been traced, the plaintiff claimed it as the finder.

Held
His action would be successful.

Birkett J:

'I think it is fairly clear from the authorities that this proposition would not be doubted, *viz*, that a man possesses everything which is attached to or under his land. Secondly, it would appear to be the law from the authorities I have cited, and particularly *Bridges* v *Hawkesworth* (1851) 21 LJ QB 75 that a man does not necessarily possess a thing which is lying unattached on the surface of his land even though the thing is not possessed by someone else. But the difficulty arises because the rule which governs things an occupier possesses as against those which he does not has never been very clearly formulated in our law. He may possess everything upon the land from which he intends to exclude others ... or, he may possess those things over which he has a *de facto* control ... These things are not clearly laid down in cases. That is all that I think I can usefully say about the authorities. Neither do I think that a discussion of the merits helps at all.

There is no doubt that the brooch was lost in the ordinary connotation of that term, and from the appearance of the brooch when found, *ie*, the dirt and cobwebs, it had apparently been lost for a very considerable time ...

It is clear that the defendant, as I gather from the agreed statement of facts, was never physically in possession of these premises at any time. It is clear the brooch was never his in the ordinary acceptation of the term, in that he had the prior possession. He had no knowledge of it until it was brought to his knowledge by the finder. As I say, a discussion of the merits does not seem to help a great deal, but it is clear on the facts (i) that the brooch was lost in the ordinary meaning of words, (ii) it appears to me clear that the brooch was found by the plaintiff in the ordinary meaning of words, and (iii) it is clear that the true owner of the brooch has never been found. The defendant was the owner of the premises and had his notice drawn to this matter by the plaintiff who found the brooch. In all those circumstances I asked for a little time in order that I might consider these authorities which are very difficult to reconcile. The conclusion to which I have come is that I propose to follow the decision in *Bridges* v *Hawkesworth* and I propose to give judgment in this case for the plaintiff.'

International Factors Ltd v *Rodriguez* [1979] 1 QB 351 Court of Appeal (Buckley, Bridge LJJ and Sir David Cairns)

Factoring agreement – right to possession of cheques

Facts
The plaintiffs entered into a factoring agreement with a company: the company's book debts were assigned to the plaintiffs for 98.5 per cent of their full value. Four cheques were sent to the company and, knowing that it was in breach of the factoring agreement, the defendant director paid them into the company' account. The plaintiffs sued for conversion.

Held
They were entitled to succeed as the agreement gave them a right to immediate possession of the cheques.

Sir David Cairns (Bridge LJ agreeing):

'It is clear law that a contractual right to have goods handed to him by another person is not in itself sufficient to clothe the person who has that right with power to sue in conversion ...

In my view, however, there was here something more than a contractual right ... the agreement provided both that the supplier was to hold any debt paid direct to the supplier in trust for the factor, that is, the company was to hold in trust for the plaintiffs, and immediately after receipt of a cheque, in the case of payment by cheque, to hand over that cheque to the company. Taking together the trust which was thereby set up and the obligation immediately on receipt to hand over the cheque to the plaintiffs, I am satisfied that the plaintiffs had here a sufficient proprietary right to sue in conversion.'

Buckley LJ:

'...whether or not an enforceable trust would attach immediately on the payment of any debt direct to the company by cheque, whether or not an immediate trust would attach to such a cheque, I think that there is a contractual right here for the plaintiffs to demand immediate delivery of the cheque to them, and that that is a sufficient right to possession to give them a status to sue in conversion. On the findings of the learned judge the defendant was personally responsible for the payment of each of the four cheques to which this case relates into the company's account, and in those circumstances the right conclusion appears to me to be that it was the defendant who misapplied the cheque and who is liable for conversion. Counsel for the defendant has suggested that he could only be made liable in conversion if the company itself was guilty of conversion and so he, as an officer of the company, could be made vicariously responsible for conversion. In my view that is the wrong approach; the cheque was physically in the possession or under the control of the defendant, it was he who applied it wrongly in a manner in conflict with the right of the plaintiffs, and in my judgment it was he who was guilty of conversion as a primary participant and not merely as a secondary participant in the transaction.'

Jerome v Bentley & Co [1952] 2 All ER 114 High Court (Donovan J)

Conversion – sale to third party

Facts

Believing that he would try to sell a diamond ring for him, the plaintiff dealer allowed Major Tatham to take the ring. It was arranged that, if he sold the ring, Tatham would give the plaintiff £550 and keep any surplus; if the ring was not sold within seven days, it was to be returned to the plaintiff. After the seven days had expired Tatham, representing that he was the owner of the ring, sold it for £175 to the defendants who bought it in good faith and re-sold it. The plaintiff claimed damages for wrongful conversion.

Held

He was entitled to succeed.

Donovan J:

'That brings me to the circumstances in which Major Tatham sold the ring ... his sole duty was to hand the ring back to the plaintiff, and he had no authority to deal with it in any way except for the purpose of its safe custody. He has admitted that he stole the ring as a bailee. In other words, when he entered the shop he intended fraudulently to convert the ring to his own use, and he accomplished that purpose. He then became a thief of the ring ... No one represented Major Tatham to the defendants as the plaintiff's agent with authority to sell the ring. The defendants knew nothing of the plaintiff. In fact, they made Major Tatham show his identity card and sign a declaration that the ring was his. So they dealt with him on the footing of a principal selling his own property...

The plaintiff here did nothing which misled the defendants. Is the circumstances I hold that no property in this ring passed to the defendants and there is nothing to prevent the plaintiff from setting up his title as against them. Therefore, I decide in his favour. On the evidence before me I value the ring at £250, and I give judgment for the plaintiff in that amount.'

Kowal v Ellis (1977) 76 DLR (3d) 546 Manitoba Court of Appeal

Abandoned pump – finder could keep it?

Facts

Driving across the defendant's land, with the defendant's permission, the plaintiff saw an abandoned pump.

Held

The plaintiff's claim to the pump prevailed over that of the defendant.

O'Sullivan JA:

'One can imagine cases where a chattel is abandoned by its true owner and may then become the property of someone else, perhaps a land-owner who exercises control and dominion over it. In such a case, the land-owner would assert a claim against the finder, not by virtue of his right as owner of land, but by virtue of his right as owner of the chattel. In the case before us, however, the defendant asserts no such right of ownership. The pump in question appears to have been cached rather than abandoned. So this is a case where the defendant does not even assert that he is the owner of the chattel in question; that being so, the defendant can succeed only by showing that he himself was in possession of the pump at the time of the finding in such a way that he, the defendant, had already constituted himself a bailee for the true owner. I know there have been weighty opinions expressed in favour of the proposition that the possessor of land possesses all that is on the land, and there is a sense in which that may be so, but to oust the claim of a bailee by finding it is not enough to establish some kind of metaphysical possession. What must be shown is that the land-owner claimant, who has not acquired ownership of a chattel, is a prior bailee of the chattel with all the rights, but also with all the obligations, of a bailee. I am sure that no one would be more surprised that the defendant if, prior to the finding by the plaintiff, the true owner had come along and asserted that the defendant land-owner owed him any duty either to take care of the pump or to seek out the owner of it. The reality is that the defendant, not even being aware of the existence of the pump, owed no duty with respect to it to its true owner. He was not a bailee of the pump and consequently has no claim to possession which can prevail over the special property which the plaintiff has by virtue of his having become a bailee by finding.'

Commentary

Applied in *Parker* v *British Airways Board* [1982] 1 All ER 834.

Manders v *Williams* (1849) 4 Ex 339 Court of Exchequer (Parke, Alderson and Platt BB)

Empty casks – customer bailee

Facts

The plaintiffs were merchants in Dublin and they sent porter in casks to John David, a customer in Wales. Empty casks were to be returned to them within six months at David's expense or paid for by him. The defendant sheriff seized and sold, under a writ of execution against David, 300 of the casks which were lying empty in his cellar. The plaintiffs sued for trover in respect of these casks: did they have sufficient possession of the casks to maintain this action?

Held

They did and they would be awarded the price of the casks.

Parke B:

'The true construction of the contract is to give David an interest only until the casks were empty. I agree … that, in this contract, every stipulation is for the benefit of the vendors, not the vendee. The latter is to incur all risk; he is under the obligation of sending the empty casks to Dublin at his own expense and before the end of six months from the date of the contract; if not, there is an option for the benefit of the vendors of calling on him to purchase the casks at a fixed price. Those stipulations show that the interest of the vendee was never meant to extend beyond the right to keep the casks until the porter was consumed. Possibly, he might within the six months have transferred the porter in the casks to a sub-vendee, but as soon as the casks were emptied the right to them reverted to the vendors. According to the true construction of this contract, I am satisfied that it was never intended that David should have the casks for any other purpose than keeping the porter. Indeed, I do not see what advantage there could be in his right of possession continuing after the casks were empty; for, during the residue of the six months, he could neither let them to anyone else nor make any further use of himself without being a wrongdoer and, at the end of the six months, he was bound to return them.

So soon as the casks were empty, the right of property and the right of possession reverted to the plaintiffs, and David was in the situation of a mere bailee during pleasure. No proposition can be more clear than that either the bailor or the bailee of a chattel may maintain an action in respect of it against a wrongdoer; the latter by virtue of his possession, the former by reason of his property.'

Moffatt v *Kazana* [1969] 2 WLR 71 High Court (Wrangham J)

Hidden bank-notes – who owns them?

Facts

A man (Mr Russell) hid some bank-notes in a tin box which he placed in the roof of his house. The house was sold to the defendant, one of whose employees found the money. Meanwhile, Mr Russell had died; his executors sued to recover the cash.

Held

Their action would be successful.

Wrangham J:

'It is clear therefore that in the existing authorities there is an implication at least from the language in which the judgments are expressed that the true owner of a chattel found on land has a title superior to that of anybody else. Accordingly, having disposed of the authorities in that way, counsel on behalf of the plaintiffs was able to say that the plaintiffs are, as representatives of Mr Russell, the true owners of this money and they must be held to remain the true owners of the money unless they or Mr Russell had divested himself or themselves of the ownership by one of the recognised methods, abandonment, gift or sale. Abandonment is not suggested. One does not abandon property merely because one has forgotten where one put it. Gift is not suggested. There remains only sale …

I am content to ground my judgment on this, that the conveyance itself, in view of the language of s62 [of the Law of Property Act 1925], cannot be said to have transferred the ownership of these £1 notes from Mr Russell to the defendant and that there is no other way in which it is even suggested that the ownership of these notes could have been transferred from Mr Russell to the defendant. If Mr Russell never got rid of the notes, that is to say, never got rid of the ownership of the notes, he continued to be the owner of them and, if he continued to be the owner of them, he had a title to those notes which nobody else, whether the owner of the land on which they were found, or the finders, or anybody else would have.'

Parker v *British Airways Board* [1982] 1 QB 1004 Court of Appeal (Eveleigh, Donaldson LJJ and Sir David Cairns)

Finders keepers?

Facts

A passenger found a gold bracelet in the British Airways executive lounge at Heathrow. He handed it to an employee, asking that it should be returned to him if it was not claimed. The owner never claimed the bracelet; the airline sold it and kept the proceeds; the passenger sued for its value.

Held

He was entitled to succeed.

Donaldson LJ:

'Mr Parker was not a trespasser in the executive lounge and, in taking the bracelet into his care and control, he was acting with obvious honesty. Prima facie, therefore, he had a full finder's right and obligations. He in fact discharged those obligations by handing the bracelet to an official of British Airways, although he could equally have done so by handing the bracelet to the police or in other ways such as informing the police of the find and himself caring for the bracelet.

Mr Parker's prima facie entitlement to a finder's rights was not displaced in favour of an employer or principal. There is no evidence that he was in the executive lounge in the course of any employment or agency and, if he was, the finding of the bracelet was quite clearly collateral thereto. The position would have been otherwise in the case of most or perhaps all of British Airways' employees.

British Airways, for their part, cannot assert any title to the bracelet based on the rights of an occupier over chattels attached to a building. The bracelet was lying loose on the floor. Their claim must, on my view of the law, be based on a manifest intention to exercise control over the lounge and all things which might be in it. The evidence is that they claimed the right to decide who should and who should not be permitted to enter and use the lounge, but their control was in general exercised on the basis of classes or categories of user and the availability of the lounge in the light of the need to clean and maintain it. I do not doubt that they also claimed the right to exclude individual undesirables, such as drunks, and specific types of chattels such as guns and bombs. But this control has no real relevance to a manifest intention to assert custody and control over lost articles. There was no evidence that they searched for such articles regularly or at all.

Evidence was given of staff instructions which govern the action to be taken by employees of British Airways if they found lost articles or lost chattels were handed to them. But these instructions were not published to users of the lounge and in any event I think that they were intended to do no more than instruct the staff on how they were to act in the course of their employment.

It was suggested in argument that in some circumstances the intention of the occupier to assert control over articles lost on his premises speaks for itself. I think that this is right. If a bank manager saw fit to show me round a vault containing safe deposit boxes and I found a gold bracelet on the floor, I should have no doubt that the bank had a better title than I, and the reason is the manifest intention to exercise a very high degree of control. At the other extreme is the park to which the public has unrestricted access during daylight hours. During those hours there is no manifest intention to exercise any such control. In between these extremes are the forecourts of petrol filling stations, unfenced front gardens of private houses, the public parts of shops and supermarkets as part of an almost infinite variety of land, premises and circumstances.

This lounge is in the middle band and in my judgment, on the evidence available, there was no sufficient manifestation of any intention to exercise control over lost property before it was found such as would give British Airways a right superior to that of Mr Parker or indeed any right over the bracelet. As the true owner has never come forward, it is a case of "finders keepers".'

Commentary
Applied: *Armory* v *Delamine* (1722) 5 Stra 505, *Bridges* v *Hawkesworth* (1851) 21 LJQB 75 and *Kowal* v *Ellis* (1977) 76 DLR (3d) 546.

Perry (Howard E) & Co Ltd v *British Railways Board* [1980] 1 WLR 1375 High Court (Sir Robert Megarry V-C)

Strike – wrongful interference with goods

Facts
Steelworkers were on strike; to assist them, the National Union of Railwaymen refused to transport steel. Fearing escalation of the dispute, the defendants refused to deliver the plaintiff stockholders' steel or to allow the plaintiffs to collect it from their (the defendants') depots. The plaintiffs sought an order under the Torts (Interference with Goods) Act 1977 that they be allowed to collect the steel.

Held
They were entitled to succeed.

Sir Robert Megarry V-C:

'What I have to consider here is a case in which the defendants are in effect saying to the plaintiffs: "We admit that the steel is yours and that you are entitled to possession of it. Yet because we fear that industrial action may be taken against us if we permit you to remove it, we have refused to allow you to collect it for some weeks now, despite your demands, and we will continue to refuse to allow you to collect it until our fears have been removed." Looking at the matter as one of principle, I would conclude that this is a clear case of conversion. The defendants are denying the plaintiffs most of the rights of ownership, including the right to possession, for a period which plainly is indefinite. It may be short, or it may be long; but it is clearly uncertain. I do not think that a period which will not end until the defendants reach the conclusion that their fears no longer justify the withholding of the steel can very well be called "definite". There is a detention of the steel which is consciously adverse to the plaintiffs' rights, and this seems to me to be of the essence of at least one form of conversion. A denial of possession to the plaintiffs does not cease to be a denial by being accompanied by a statement that the plaintiffs are entitled to the possession that is being denied to them ... For the defendants to withhold the steel from the plaintiffs is a wrongful interference with goods within the 1977 Act unless the reason for the withholding provides a justification. I cannot see that it does. This is no brief withholding made merely in order that the defendants may verify the plaintiffs' title to the steel, or for some other purpose to confirm that the delivery of the steel would be proper. This is a withholding despite the plain right of the plaintiff's to the ownership and possession of the steel, on the ground that the defendants fear unpleasant consequences if they do not deny the plaintiffs what they are entitled to.'

South Staffordshire Water Co v *Sharman* [1896] 2 QB 44 High Court (Lord Russell of Killowen CJ and Wills J)

Rings found in pool

Facts

The plaintiff freeholders of a pool employed the defendant, amongst others, to clean it out. In the course of this work the defendant found two gold rings: the plaintiffs sued to recover them.

Held

They were entitled to succeed.

Lord Russell of Killowen CJ:

'*Bridges* v *Hawkesworth* (1851) 21 LJQB 75 really stands by itself and on its own special grounds, and, standing on its own grounds, I think the decision was perfectly right. There a person had dropped a bundle of bank notes in a public shop, public, that is to say, in the sense that it was open to the public. A customer came in and picked up the bundle of notes and showed it to the shopman, and afterwards gave it to the shopkeeper in order that he might advertise it. The owner was not found, and the shopkeeper afterwards refused to give up the notes to the customer who had found them. The customer then brought an action against the shopkeeper for the notes, and it was held that he was justified in demanding the notes, and the true ground of that decision is stated by PATTESON J, where he says:

"The notes never were in the custody of the defendant, nor within the protection of his house before they were found."

The general principle within which the case falls seems to me to be that where there is possession of a house or land, with a manifest intention to exercise control over it, and the things in or upon it, and with control over that particular locus in quo, then if something is found on it by a person who is either a stranger or a servant, the presumption is that the possession of the thing so found is in the owner of that locus in quo. For these reasons I think judgment must be for the plaintiffs.'

Union Transport Finance Ltd v *British Car Auctions Ltd* [1978] 2 All ER 385 Court of Appeal (Cairns, Roskill and Bridge LJJ)

Termination of bailment – right to sue

Facts

The plaintiffs bought an Audi motor car and let it on hire purchase to a Mr Smith (or Smithers). In breach of the agreement, Smith altered the car's registration number and, without disclosing the agreement, instructed the defendant auctioneers to sell it, later receiving the net proceeds of sale. Unaware of any of this, when instalments were overdue the plaintiffs served notice to terminate the agreement. When they discovered what had happened, they sued for conversion and the defendants argued it, inter alia, that the plaintiffs had not been entitled to immediate possession at the time of the sale.

Held

This was not the case and the plaintiffs were entitled to judgment.

Roskill LJ:

'It seems to me that there is no room for doubt that the position at common law is this: if the bailee acts in a way which, to use the phrase used in argument, destroys the basis of the contract of bailment, the bailor becomes entitled at once to bring that contract to an end, and thus at once acquires the right to immediate possession of the article bailed ...

In those circumstances, it seems to me that the only question that remains for consideration is whether the provisions of the present contract affect the basic common law position. Counsel for the defendants strenuously argued that they do. He contends that because there is this express contractual right to bring this contract to an end only after notice of termination, there is no room for the survival as between the plaintiffs and Mr Smith of the basic common law rule ... I think, with respect, that this argument is misconceived for a number of reasons. When one looks at these clauses one can see why they are there. They give a modicum of protection to the hirer but they also give certain specific contractual rights to the bailor in the happening of certain events. They give him the right to bring the contract to an end and to re-take possession in the event of certain things happening. But they do not expressly deprive the bailor of any other rights that he may have at common law; and still less, in my view, do these clauses, either expressly or impliedly, confer any right, possessory or otherwise, on the bailee which would lead to a conclusion different from that which would follow at common law if the bailee deliberately, as happened here, tears up the contract of bailment by fraudulently selling the car through an auctioneer, to an innocent third party. Therefore, it seems to me, following the reasoning in *North Central Wagon and Finance Co Ltd* v *Graham* [1950] 1 All ER 780, that even if there be room in principle for the existence of a contract which may contract out of the basic common law rule, it would require very clear language to deprive the bailor, of his common law rights in circumstances such as these. In the case of the present contract the language used is nothing like strong enough to achieve that result.'

Waverley Borough Council v *Fletcher* [1995] 3 WLR 772 Court of Appeal (Sir Thomas Bingham MR, Auld and Ward LJJ)

Ownership of chattels found on land

Facts

The plaintiff council were owners of a park and the defendant, whilst in the park, used a metal detector to locate a mediaeval gold brooch buried in the ground. He excavated the soil to a depth of nine inches and recovered the brooch, and the question arose as to whether the plaintiff or the defendant had the better title to the brooch.

Held

Where an object is found in or attached to land, the owner or lawful possessor of the land had a better title to the object than the finder; where the object was unattached on land the owner or lawful possessor only had a better title than the finder where he had exercised such manifest control over the land as to indicate an intention to control it and anything found on it.

Wilson v *Lombank Ltd* [1963] 1 WLR 1294 High Court (Hinchcliffe J)

Trespass to goods – car taken from garage

Facts

The plaintiff motor car dealer bought a car from a man who had no title to sell. As the car needed repair, the plaintiff took it to his regular garage; after completion of the work the car was placed on the garage forecourt. Believing – mistakenly – that they had a legal right to do so, the defendants took the car away. On discovering that the true owner was a finance company, the defendants returned the car to them. The plaintiff claimed damages for alleged trespass.

Held

He was entitled to succeed and to recover the value of the car and the full cost of the repair.

Hinchcliffe J:

'... in my judgment the plaintiff was in possession of the car; not only did he have the right to immediate possession, but I do not think that, in the circumstances of this case, the plaintiff ever lost possession of the car. In my view, the plaintiff at all times could have demanded the return of the car ... I do not think that there was a lien on the motor car, having regard to the course of dealing between the plaintiff and the Haven Garage over a period of eight years, during which time there existed this monthly credit. On the view which I have formed, that the plaintiff never lost possession of the motor car, it seems to me that the defendants wrongfully took the car and that the plaintiff is entitled to recover damages.'

31 Malicious Prosecution

Abbot v *Refuge Assurance Co Ltd* [1962] 1 QB 432 Court of Appeal (Omerod, Upjohn and Davies LJJ)

Malicious prosecution – reasonable and probable cause

Facts

On the advice of experienced counsel, to whom the facts were put fully and fairly, the defendants preferred charges against the plaintiff and he was convicted of, inter alia, forgery arising out of the payment of certain insurance moneys. The Court of Criminal Appeal ruled that the case should not have been allowed to go to the jury; the plaintiff was discharged; he sought damages for malicious prosecution.

Held

His action would fail.

Ormerod LJ:

'Taking all … matters into account, in my judgment the defendants had reasonable and probable cause to initiate the prosecution of the plaintiff. I regard the opinion of counsel as a factor, in this case a potent one … It is not, however, conclusive.'

Malz v *Rosen* [1966] 1 WLR 1008 High Court (Diplock LJ)

Private citizen a prosecutor?

Facts

An altercation having occurred over the parking of cars, the defendant gave a police sergeant an honest and accurate account of the incident. The sergeant said that the plaintiff had committed an offence and the defendant agreed to prefer a charge against the plaintiff and give evidence. After giving a written statement, the defendant signed a charge of using insulting behaviour. Although it had been intended that the prosecution would be conducted by a police officer, the plaintiff having instructed a solicitor the police instructed a solicitor and counsel. The plaintiff was acquitted and he sued for malicious prosecution.

Held

Although the defendant had been the prosecutor, he had had reasonable and probable cause for the prosecution and the plaintiff's action therefore failed.

Diplock LJ:

'It was needless to say, never intended or thought by anyone that the defendant would conduct or have the actual conduct of the prosecution at the magistrates' court. The original intention of the police was that one of the police officers would conduct it, but on … the day fixed for the hearing, the plaintiff appeared by his solicitor and the matter was adjourned. In the result at the adjourned hearing the prosecution was represented by a solicitor and counsel who were instructed by the Metropolitan Police.

... I accept that the defendant was in the position of prosecutor and that, therefore, if it can be shown that he brought the accusation without reasonable or probable cause and with malice, an action for malicious prosecution will lie against him. I am, however, quite clear ... that, if an ordinary private citizen such as the defendant goes to the police and having given them an accurate and honest account of circumstances which have occurred, is told by a responsible police officer that according to those facts, an offence has been committed, and is asked by the police officer whether he is prepared to prefer a charge, then, if the ordinary citizen accepts that advice, there is no doubt that in law he has reasonable and probable cause for the prosecution. In saying that, I am adopting what Viscount Simonds said in *Glinski* v *McIver* [1962] 2 WLR 832 in relation to a charge brought on the advice of counsel or of a competent legal adviser.'

Martin v *Watson* [1995] 3 WLR 318 House of Lords (Lords Keith, Slynn, Lloyd, Nicholls and Steyn)

Malicious prosecution – who can be a defendant

Facts
The defendant made a complaint of indecent exposure against the plaintiff to the police. The police arrested the plaintiff and he was prosecuted under s4 Vagrancy Act 1824. At the hearing the prosecution offered no evidence and the charge was dismissed. The plaintiff sued the defendant for malicious prosecution and succeeded in the county court. On appeal, the Court of Appeal allowed the appeal on the grounds that an essential element of the tort of malicious prosecution was proof by the plaintiff that the defendant had prosecuted him by setting the law in motion, and that where the plaintiff had been prosecuted on the basis of a deliberate false allegation to the police, but the defendant had not taken part in the decision to prosecute, that the defendant was not liable in malicious prosecution. The plaintiff appealed.

Held
Where a complainant had falsely and maliciously supplied information to the police relating to an offence, and those facts were solely within the complainant's knowledge so that the prosecuting officer could not have exercised any independent discretion, and the false information caused the prosecution, then the complainant could properly be said to have been responsible for the prosecution and so could be sued for malicious prosecution. The prosecutor could not be sued in these circumstances.